Katy Cable's

Party With Your Pup

TASTY RECIPES, TRICKS AND TIPS
FOR DOG INCLUSIVE ENTERTAINING

DISCLAIMER

This publication contains the ideas and opinions of the authors and is designed to provide useful and interesting information on the subject matter covered.

The authors, editors and publisher specifically disclaim any responsibility, if any, for any liability, loss or risk, personal or otherwise which is incurred as a consequence, directly or indirectly, by the use and/or application of any contents of this book.

The information in this book is not intended to diagnose, treat, cure, or prevent disease. This book is for information purposes only and does not replace the expert care and advice provided by your veterinarian. Dietary and other healthcare changes should be made under guidance and supervision of your vet, particularly when underlying health conditions exist.

Nutrition is just one part of a total, holistic approach to health. Many medical conditions also require other forms of treatment, either conventional or complementary. If you are interested in finding a holistic veterinarian who approaches nutrition as a cornerstone of total health, and is familiar with the benefits of fresh, minimally processed and home-prepared foods, please visit the American Holistic Veterinary Medical Association online at: wwwahma.org/

This book is dedicated to my late mother who insisted our family get a dog in the first place.

CONTENTS

INTRODUCTION

I wasn't always a dog person, -quite the contrary! I would go so far as to say I was the antithesis of a dog person in every regard. As you probably guessed, like many formerly reluctant dog parents, that all changed the minute a darling, curly-tailed pug trotted in and turned our lives right side up! Dogs have a way of changing everything we thought we knew.

It all began with those dreaded words, "Let's get her a dog!" My husband's idea of a perfect birthday present for our daughter was my worst nightmare. From my passion for all things designer, my love of a tidy house, and my persistent allergies, everything in me resisted. Still, the loving mom in me wanted to make my daughter happy, so I lost this battle.

The day we adopted our pug, Raisin, our family felt whole in a way that's difficult to describe. And, as for me, just like that, I would never be the same again. Raisin filled all our lives with a new joy I never imagined a dog could provide. Raisin completed our family. Not only did I understand why there are "dog people," but I was now a proud, card-carrying member of the club. My designer wardrobe now included shirts, jackets, and hats with slogans like "Dog Mom," and "Don't Shop, Adopt!"

Raisin was a typical, fun-loving, food-obsessed, cuddly, co-dependant, pug! He had the sweetest temperament and everywhere he went people fell in love with him. He was adventurous and up for whatever we happened to be doing. He had an extensive wardrobe and put up with wearing all the crazy outfits I dressed him in. But, in true pug form, he struggled with the multiple health issues inherent to his breed. From the start, he was plagued with skin rashes, lumps, bumps, missing teeth, poor eyesight, chronic bladder infections, ear infections, and hip dysplasia. At the time, prescription foods and traditional veterinary medicine were the only things I knew of that seemed to manage his ailments. I would later learn the power of holistic medicine to prevent rather than mask the symptoms of chronic health conditions. Sadly, at the age of 13, Raisin passed and left all of us absolutely heartbroken.

The same month he died, my daughter moved across the country to attend college. An empty-nester in every sense of the word, I became severely depressed. In an effort to keep busy and get out of the house, I took a part-time job representing a new pet food company called Nulo. Gone were my days of wearing high heels and enjoying fancy corporate lunches. My new uniform was sneakers and a lanyard and my managers were half my age. I doubted I would last through the first pay period.

Much to my surprise, I realized I was having the time of my life. Working with pet parents fulfilled me in a very special way no other career ever had. I had found my calling. The only drawback was my new position made it impossible for me to live without a dog of my own. I began obsessively searching every shelter and rescue for another pug. After several months I was losing hope of ever finding another dog when, out of the blue, I received a call from an animal shelter way out in the Coachella desert. They had found a young Pug puppy on the side of the road who had just given birth to a litter of pups. She was likely a breeder dog who had never been out of a crate. She needed quite a bit of attention and care, and they asked if I would be interested. And that's how I found my Olive. A sick and neglected pug who would heal my heart as much as I healed hers.

Olive was in serious need of a health overhaul. -Serendipitously, Nulo was an innovative new pet food company founded on the power of food to heal and prevent dis-ease. Who better to try out Nulo than my new little pug?

AF
AF
nulo

When I started Olive on Nulo dog food, I began documenting how a low-carb, minimally processed diet was miraculously transforming her. I started brushing her teeth nightly, giving her CBD oil, and adding fresh foods to her diet. The results I saw were amazing! They inspired me to start my ongoing blog and show, The Weekly Runt. The Weekly Runt features simple health tips, dog-inclusive events, and must-have products, all gathered from my experience rehabilitating Olive and other pets. In five years it has grown significantly and now reaches over 2 million pet enthusiasts each week. **www.weeklyrunt.com.**

But good nutrition wasn't just a pet project. The correlation between high-quality pet food and excellent health transformed not only the way I keep my pet thriving but also how I improved my personal health.

My diet was another story altogether! A chronic dieter plagued with eating disorders since I was a teen, I was going downhill faster than a snowball in an avalanche. I was a vegetarian who lived on bread, pasta, rice, legumes, and veggies. I chased that down with a stiff dose of caffeine and a "serving spoonful" of sugar. I was a "sugarholic" addicted to processed junk food and candy. I loathed cooking and rationalized that I didn't have time to do it. My idea of meal prep was microwaving frozen pizzas. I never in a million years would have thought my "plant-based" diet was the culprit behind so many of my ailments. I managed fairly well until I began perimenopause. Initially, I resigned myself to the hair loss, fatigue, brain fog, puffiness, and weight gain as just a part of getting older. But the answer wasn't nearly that simple.

In 2018, I was diagnosed with an autoimmune disease called Hashimoto's Thyroiditis. What sounds like a fancy Teppan restaurant is actually a serious condition in which my immune system attacks my thyroid as if it were a foreign invader. I consulted with countless physicians and was given a laundry list of medications to take, but nothing seemed to help. And then it hit me. -An epiphany! I realized that the food I was eating was exacerbating my illness! What I needed to do was apply what I had done for Olive and so many other dogs' health, to my own. So I read everything I could find written by holistic and functional doctors, offering suggestions on how to heal my condition. Utilizing their recommendations and protocols, I found my condition improved dramatically. A major part of my healing was healing my gut by removing gluten, sugar, dairy, soy, caffeine, and processed foods from my diet. So, in a sense, I now eat the way a dog should eat: fresh, whole foods, high protein, and low-glycemic carbs.

There is a famous quote by Hippocrates, "Let Food Be Thy Medicine And Medicine Be Thy Food." What you put in your mouth has the power to heal you. It also has the power to make you sick. You truly are what you eat! And I learned this firsthand. Even so, although I felt much better eating healthier foods, living with huge dietary restrictions was extremely difficult. Especially when my job includes hosting and attending so many dog-inclusive parties and events. Desperate to indulge in my favorite foods without a flare-up, I learned to modify popular dishes with whole foods and easy swaps. And that's when I found lightning in a bottle.

I realized many of my "adjusted" meals were a safe, healthy addition to Olive's regular diet. Since she doesn't have a very discerning palate, I asked my friends and family, and their dogs, to sample my creations. When they were met with rave reviews I was completely blown away. The only thing more rewarding was revealing all the health benefits in these recipes.

And that is how this book came about. It comprises some of my favorite, most well-received recipes, tips, and tricks. You will learn how to whip up everything from a delicious brunch to cocktails, plus decadent desserts the entire family will love...including the dog. I'll show you how to modify recipes to make them both dog-friendly, and healthier. Plus, they will work for people with common food sensitivities.

All these recipes can be made with simple ingredients you probably already have in your cupboard. Everything is relatively easy to make. Many recipes are easy enough for young children to prepare. Best of all, these dishes are far healthier and typically less expensive than buying meals packaged or prepared. The money you spend on fresh foods at the market will save you much more on fewer visits to the doctor and veterinarian, or buying pricey medications.

But that's not all, over the years, my career as a dog health and lifestyle coach has introduced me to a huge, loving, dog community. Our fur babies are important, celebrated, members of our families, and treated as such. Birthdays, "gotcha" days, "adopt-iversaries" and holiday gatherings fill our calendars. Gone are the days when our family dogs are thrown into a back bedroom during a party. This book goes far beyond recipes, it also includes everything you need to throw a fabulous, unforgettable, "PAWty!"

I've divided the book into four sections: winter, spring, summer, and fall, with a fun, creative, dog-inclusive "PAWty" theme for each month of the year. Not only will you find an appealing menu with cocktails, "yappitizers," main dishes, and desserts, for both humans AND your pups, but you'll find tips and ideas for invites, decorations, activities, and "sWAG."

Lastly, this book features my most popular and requested health tips such as preventing and treating ear infections, healing allergies, dealing with sensitive tummies, and "The A, B, C's of CBD." Plus, important suggestions for the brand new pet parent.

So, whether you're inviting all your friends with dogs over for a "tail-gating" party, or simply watching your favorite movie with your family at home, you can make food into a fun and healthy "dog-inclusive" celebration.

SHOULD DOGS EAT HUMAN FOODS?

Not a day goes by when I don't come across a pet parent who is adamant about not ever feeding their dog human food. Funny enough, I used to be that pet parent. If my pug's food didn't come out of a bag or can that featured a picture of a healthy pug on the front, I felt it was sub-par. It certainly could not be ideal food. If it was an expensive brand I'd seen on TV and in all the stores, I would feel even better about my dog food purchase.

WOW! Have I done a complete turn-around! Sadly, I too had fallen for the same marketing spin as nearly all other pet owners. A hype that was created by large food corporations in an effort to sell highly-profitable pet foods. Nearly all major pet foods, (as well as many veterinary hospitals, and large pet retailers) are owned by the same huge companies that make candy, cereal, and possessed snacks. These foods are the main culprit for skyrocketing cases of obesity, heart disease, cancer, diabetes, and other chronic illnesses in the USA. Literally, Americans are eating far too much processed junk, and not getting enough nutrients from our meals. We have a SAD diet (Standard-American-Diet.) We are overeating AND starving to death at the same time! And now, a majority of these popular pet foods are making our pets sick as well! Giant food companies have brainwashed us into thinking, cooked brown balls of highly processed ingredients are far better than fresh human foods.

Unfortunately, I learned this lesson too late to save my pug Raisin from many of the chronic conditions he suffered from. I am positive a change in his diet would've drastically improved most of his ailments and extended his life.

When we know better we can do better. Since incorporating healthier food choices, I have seen a huge difference in my pug Olive. In the seven years I've had her, she has needed only one course of antibiotics. She has healthy gums and white teeth without ever needing professional dental cleanings. She has avoided many health issues such as ear infections, skin conditions, digestive problems, and allergies inherent to her breed. My veterinarian is always astounded by how healthy Olive looks after seeing sick animals every day.

The good news is, by using this book, you can do the same thing for your dog! Offering your pup some fresh foods will vastly improve their health and ward off many common ailments. According to a published study in the Journal of the American Veterinary Medical Association, simply adding green leafy vegetables to a dog's diet three times a week, can drastically lower the incidence of many cancers by 90%. No! That's not a typo! Fresh foods are also ideal in order for your dog to maintain a healthy weight, have a shinier coat, and have healthier stools. Best of all, dogs fed a diet including fresh, whole foods, lived 30% longer than those fed entirely processed dog foods.

That being said, as wonderful as it would be to prepare homemade food for our dogs each and every day, I realize that is going to be impossible for most busy pet owners. -Myself included! The good news is, this book is filled with simple, delicious recipes you can make for your family and share with your dog. Use them on occasion or every day as additions to your pet's main diet. I personally use NULO, a high-quality, minimally-processed, dog food as the main staple of Olive's diet. Then I add many of my creations in this book as treats, toppers, or a special occasion meal. This way, I expose her to a variety of healthy, fresh, new foods without overwhelming her sensitive digestive system. She also gets a complete and balanced diet from her regular pet food. Plus, I save money by stretching out how much pet food she needs, by mixing in fresh foods each day. Olive loves the variety and doesn't get bored with meals. In typical pug fashion, she always looks forward to getting some small bites of what we're having for dinner!

When I was diagnosed with Hashimoto's, the first thing my doctor told me was, if I wanted to feel better and put my disease in remission, I needed to eliminate inflammation in my body. It was imperative that I slow down, de-stress, remove toxins, and stick to a diet of clean, whole foods. I cut out highly inflammatory foods such as gluten, dairy, soy, sugar, alcohol, grains, legumes, and most processed foods. In exchange, I added more protein and eliminated high-glycemic carbs. I laughed because it sounded just like the diet Olive followed to stay healthy. In a sense, my dog had been eating far healthier than I ever did.

Changing my diet was very difficult at first, but the results were astounding. In a matter of days, I was looking and feeling much better. The dark circles and puffy bags under my eyes (that made me look like a Basset Hound) were gone. My skin was glowing, and my puffiness and bloating were gone. For months my joints were so stiff and sore that I couldn't make a tight fist or use the stairs without pain. Now I could do cartwheels again! After 12 weeks, continuing on this path to regain my health, my blood work proved that there is a huge correlation between diet and disease. -And not just for our dogs! I now live by the motto: What you put in your mouth is either healing you or making you sick.

If you are suffering from a chronic condition, or just want to feel better, this book will be perfect for you as well! These aren't just your typical "dog food recipes." Instead, I have modified my favorite human meals, drinks, appetizers, snacks, and desserts. I made them "DOG FUR-ENDLY" and healthier. Therefore, you don't need to have a dog to take advantage of these delicious, healthy, and simple recipes. They will make feeling your best a lot more fun and easy! But, even better if you can throw a memorable party and share them with your B-F-F's! -Best Furry Friends! *BONE APPETITE!*

TOO MUCH OF A GOOD THING IS NOT A GOOD THING!! RECOMMENDED PORTION SIZES:

This is a biggie! When I say, "too much of a good thing..." I mean that literally and figuratively! When it comes to feeding our dogs, most people run into problems, myself included, by not adhering to some simple pointers:

⚠ **START SMALL.**

⚠ **START SLOW.**

⚠ **ONE NEW THING AT A TIME.**

While fresh, home-cooked foods can definitely be ideal for a dog, they need time to transition to new diets. Giving your pet too many new foods too quickly (and giving them treats the size of Smart Cars) can cause serious digestive issues. While most healthy dogs can tolerate trying a new treat or meal addition very well, changing their entire diet or going overboard on new foods can spell disaster. Even "healthy delicacies" can go through Fido like a laser beam. To avoid this problem, you will notice the dog portions I serve are "nibbles" and not large portions. These new creations are meant to accompany your dog's regular diet, not to replace it. Over time, you can possibly add more fresh items or incorporate fresh meals more frequently, but always start slowly.

The best indicator on how much and how fast will be your dog's stool. If things start looking soft and runny, you've fed too much and need to scale back on new foods.

Keep in mind a dog's digestive system is much different than a humans. A dog has a higher, more acidic PH, designed to digest raw animal meats. Their digestive tract is also much shorter than a humans. For that reason, it's important to purée fruits and veggies.

Most people and pets do very well and enjoy having a variety in their diets. However, for sensitive pets, senior pets, and/or pets with underlying health issues, I highly recommend discussing any food modifications with your veterinarian. Many conditions require specific nutritional ratios that are not ideal for healthy pets. It's always better to play it safe.

SUPERFOODS FOR YOU AND YOUR DOG

WHAT EXACTLY ARE SUPERFOODS?

As with most things, this buzzword came about in the early 1900s when the United Fruit Company launched a marketing campaign to sell their most popular import, bananas. Doctors published research showing the effectiveness of bananas in treating diabetes and celiac disease and the term took off. Now it is a common term used to sell everything from foods to supplements.

According to the dictionary, a superfood is one that is rich in compounds (such as essential fatty acids, antioxidants, vitamins, minerals, and fiber) considered beneficial to a person's health. Superfoods are nutrient-dense and typically provide a huge nutritional bang for your buck.

When it comes to your dog, many foods are indeed "SUPER" and safe for them to eat. However, there are a few that are not! For example, dark chocolate is a popular human superfood, but it is highly toxic for dogs. As are macadamia nuts. Please read the section on toxic foods for dogs so you are familiar. In addition, I have highlighted toxic ingredients to be mindful of in all the recipes in this book.

The following is a list of my favorite 15 superfoods for you and your dog. All the recipes in this book contain at least one superfood, many include two or three. By reading the list below and learning about the health benefits they offer, you can get creative and incorporate them into more of your own recipes and meals.

1. ANCHOVIES/SARDINES: I would have to be starving to death to eat these myself, but dogs LOVE THEM! And it's a good thing because these little fishies are one of the best sources of vitamin B 12 of all seafood. They are rich in protein, helping to maintain strong and healthy bones. In addition, they are one of the best sources of omega 3 essential fatty acids for glowing coats and flexible joints. But that's not all, anchovies and sardines contain DHA which is essential to puppies and supports vision, heart, and brain function. They contain calcium, as well as a range of minerals and trace minerals including zinc, vitamin D, E, and K. Unlike other fish, these tiny guys are so low on the food chain they feed on plankton and not other fish. Therefore, they don't contain the high levels of mercury and toxins often found in many kinds of seafood.

2. BLUEBERRIES/BLACKBERRIES/RASPBERRIES: These are considered the crown jewels of the berry family. They contain very high levels of antioxidants, which go to work slowing damage to cells. The rich blue color in blueberries and blackberries comes from flavonoid pigment which has both anti-inflammatory and antioxidant properties. These berries are higher in fiber and lower in sugar than most other fruits. Having just a few berries a day has been proven to help digestion, brain function and prevent many cancers. They also give a boost to the immune system. They taste amazing and are so easy to add to things.

3. BONE BROTH: Don't let the name fool you. As a former vegetarian, this word made my stomach turn. Now, bone broth is a staple in my diet as well as my dog's. Bone broth is made by simmering animal bones for 24 hours or more. The result is a nutrient-dense stock. The collagen in cartilage and bone produces gelatin, a protein that supports both the gut microbiome and joint health. Bone broth also contains glucosamine and chondroitin, which have been shown to slow or halt the progression of degenerative joint diseases like hip dysplasia and arthritis. In addition to being a simple source of protein, bone broth contains an array of anti-inflammatory amino acids, vitamins, and minerals such as calcium, magnesium, and phosphorus. This can be made yourself or bought in stores and it's a great substitute for anything using regular soup stock.

4. CARROTS: Beta-carotene is what gives carrots their bright orange color. It boosts immune health and benefits your dog's skin and coat. Carrots are also loaded with fiber which is great for their digestive tract. Crunching on a raw carrot can help remove tartar and plaque from your dog's teeth and gums.

5. CHIA SEEDS: These tiny seeds are a nutritional powerhouse, loaded with protein, fiber, antioxidants, calcium, iron, magnesium, B vitamins, and omega-3 fatty acids. Just a few can give a big boost to your dog's immune system, help improve their skin and coat, support their joints, and improve digestive function. Chia seeds are a great addition to meals, especially for dogs that need to lose a bit of weight. The seeds soak up water, slow down digestion and keep dogs feeling fuller longer. They also support insulin function and regulate blood sugar. Best of all, it's so easy to add them to foods.

6. COCONUT OIL: This powerhouse is a Medium Chain Fatty Acid that offers loads of benefits both as a food and topically. For starters, it can be great for help with metabolism and weight loss. It gives an immediate boost of energy and increased stamina. It helps improve brain function and is great for allergies and gut health. There are so many uses for coconut oil, I encourage you to read my blog on the subject.

7. EGGS: Packed with high-quality protein, amino acids, essential fatty acids, vitamins, and minerals, the health benefits of eggs are abundant. They are terrific for improving your dog's skin and coat. Eggs are easy for dogs to digest so they are a perfect food to offer if your pup is recovering from stomach issues.

8. FERMENTED FOODS: Adding fermented foods to your dog's diet (and yours) is the best way to maintain healthy gut flora. Fermented foods provide lots of beneficial bacteria which over-run harmful bacteria. It's this bad bacteria that can lead to infections, diseases, and parasites. I was astounded to learn how much gut health contributes to overall health. In fact, around 70% of your immune cells are located in your gut. Your gut microbiome is responsible for everything from preventing sickness and disease to warding off depression and anxiety. Yogurt, kefir, cider, sauerkraut, and pickled veggies are excellent sources of fermented foods that are safe for dogs.

9. GINGER: The ginger root is a relative of turmeric. Just like turmeric, (also a superfood) it has amazing anti-inflammatory properties. Ginger is one of the best things to use to soothe digestive issues such as nausea and bloat. Ginger may help lower blood sugar and blood pressure.

10. OLIVE OIL: Loaded with Omega 3 and Omega 6 fatty acids, it's known for helping reduce the risk of cancers, heart disease, and diabetes. Olive oil also contains antioxidants that prevent free radical damage. Unlike other oils, it has anti-inflammatory properties and is wonderful for improving skin and coat issues.

11. PUMPKIN: This is such a popular superfood and I have included an entire section on its benefits. You can read all about it in the month of September.

12. SPINACH, KALE AND DARK, LEAFY GREENS: We all know how good greens are for us humans, but science is showing us they are AMAZING for our dogs too! Several research studies have concluded that feeding dogs green veggies as little as two times a week, reduced their risk of developing cancer by 90%! That's HUGE! Leafy green vegetables like kale and spinach are rich in phytonutrients, which give them antioxidant and anti-inflammatory properties. They are also high in calcium, iron, potassium, vitamins A, C, and K as well as fiber.

13. TURMERIC: This powerful spice makes a healthy addition to most foods and snacks. The health-boosting compound of turmeric is called curcumin which has a myriad of health benefits. Curcumin contains antioxidant, anti-inflammatory, antiviral, antibacterial, and antifungal properties. It helps cleanse the blood and is used to help fight cancer, relieve arthritis, support the liver, and improve gastrointestinal function. I literally sprinkle this on everything including all my dog's meals.

14. PLAIN GREEK YOGURT: Yogurt is best known for its beneficial probiotic effects which foster gut health. I have included an entire blog on probiotics since it is so crucial to both you and your dog's overall health. In a nutshell, good gut health can lead to a stronger immune system. Plain, Greek-style yogurt is an excellent source of protein and isn't loaded with sugar the way many yogurts are. Be advised, dogs and humans can be sensitive to dairy, so try this in small amounts.

15. WATERMELON: Just like the name says, watermelon contains a lot of water so it is particularly helpful for cleansing the kidneys and liver. It is a great source of fiber and contains lycopene, an antioxidant that helps prevent cancer. Watermelon is loaded with amino acids, vitamins A, B, and C plus potassium and magnesium. Just be careful to remove the seeds before offering watermelon to your dog.

CAUTION: TOXIC FOODS FOR DOGS

Most of the recipes contained in this book have been adapted to suit a dog's needs and preferences. Several of the recipes are twists on classic favorites. Although the recipes have been modified for your dog, the following list includes **ingredients that should NOT be included in your dog's diet.** These dangers will be also noted throughout the book in recipes where they may be warranted. Typically, if a toxic ingredient is usually used in that recipe, (ie: nutmeg in pumpkin desserts and drinks) I will highlight it again as a reminder NOT to use that ingredient.

TOXIC FOODS FOR DOGS:

UNDER NO CIRCUMSTANCES SHOULD THESE FOODS BE GIVEN TO A DOG:

- ☠ CHOCOLATE (The darker the more toxic)
- ☠ CANDY (Especially any sugar-free varieties using XYLITOL)
- ☠ SUGAR-FREE PRODUCTS (Including peanut butter, which contain XYLITOL or ARTIFICIAL SWEETENERS)
- ☠ GRAPES, RAISINS, CURRANTS
- ☠ MACADAMIA NUTS/WALNUTS/PECANS
- ☠ ONIONS/GARLIC *A small amount is ok based on a dog's weight.
- ☠ FATTY MEATS/FATTY MEAT TRIMMINGS
- ☠ POULTRY AND FISH BONES
- ☠ COOKED BONES
- ☠ AVOCADO PITS & SKIN
- ☠ PEACH AND OTHER FRUIT PITS OR SEEDS
- ☠ ALCOHOL
- ☠ COFFEE/COFFEE BEANS/CAFFEINE/ENERGY DRINKS
- ☠ YEAST AND DOUGH
- ☠ POPCORN KERNELS (choking hazard)
- ☠ NUTMEG / PUMPKIN SPICE

For a complete list of substances that are toxic to pets visit the ASPCA Animal Poison Control Center online.

IF YOU SUSPECT YOUR PET HAS INGESTED A TOXIC SUBSTANCE, CALL YOUR 24hr. EMERGENCY VETERINARY CLINIC IMMEDIATELY

BUYING YOUR INGREDIENTS

When using this book, you'll notice most of the ingredients call for ORGANIC. You may be wondering, "why should I pay more money for organic?" "Is it really any better?" Actually, - quite a bit! Organic produce and products have been farmed without the use of synthetic, (human-made) herbicides, fertilizers, and pesticides. Many of these chemicals have been linked to cancers and other diseases. Organic produce is grown in more nutrient-rich soil. That means it contains more vitamins and minerals. So, no harmful stuff and more good stuff! You really do end up getting much more bang by spending a few more bucks.

I also recommend using fresh, local, seasonal, produce from smaller grocers, farmer's markets, or direct from the farm if possible. I shop at small, regional grocery chains that offer organic produce from local farms. They also carry many wonderful locally-made products. Not only does this support local economies, but the foods will be much tastier and fresher since they don't need to travel great distances before arriving in your kitchen. You can also try growing some of your own fruits and vegetables. You will notice how delicious home-grown, in-season produce tastes. Even a small window sill can offer enough space to grow herbs and many small veggies. However, if the only thing you can successfully grow is weeds and this type of shopping is too prohibitive for your schedule, don't worry! Everything you need to make the recipes in this book can be found at most supermarkets or purchased online.

HEALTHIER SWAPS:

Now that my Hashimoto's is in remission, I don't want to go back to what it was like before! Not only do I eat differently, but I also shop differently. Instead of buying fast, processed food for snacks and meals, I make healthier swaps. Yes, it's a bit of a taste adjustment at first, but it's well worth it! My husband, on the other hand, hasn't noticed a difference. In fact, he feels better and says my swaps taste better too! Not only has my health improved dramatically, but my husband has also never been in better health. I would recommend trying out a recipe or two and try swapping one or two ingredients for the healthier options. Over time, you may enjoy your new recipe even more and you will certainly feel better. Try them out on family and friends and see if anyone notices a difference. Chances are, if they do, they will like the new recipe better. They will certainly like the health benefits!

ANTI-INFLAMMATORY RECIPES:

The ingredients listed below are staples in my kitchen as well as what is used in most of the recipes in this book. These items tend to be much healthier options than ultra-processed, enriched, white flour and sugar. They also don't trigger inflammation in the body which is the leading cause of allergies and DIS-EASE! That being said, gluten-free, sugar-free, and dairy-free products often have a different consistency and may not taste exactly the same as your standard favorites. I have spent a lot of time experimenting with a variety of products to find the tastiest substitutes needed to make things gluten-free and/or dairy-free if desired. I highly recommend these healthier swaps for your dog. Just like us, our dogs can have the same, if not more adverse reactions to processed grains, gluten, and sugars. Plus, it's highly unlikely your dog will notice the difference if you make a healthier swap! Actually, my pug Olive is over-the-moon with these creations.

MOST RECIPES IN THIS BOOK USE ONE OR MORE OF THESE INGREDIENTS:

- ORGANIC GLUTEN-FREE FLOUR: I have a variety of coconut, brown rice, quinoa, and all-purpose baking flours. I have experimented with many to get the taste and consistency as close to regular flour as possible.
- ORGANIC EXTRA VIRGIN OLIVE OIL- EXTRA-VIRGIN OLIVE OIL COOKING SPRAY
- ORGANIC, UNFILTERED COCONUT OIL-ORGANIC COCONUT OIL COOKING SPRAY
- ORGANIC AVOCADO OIL-AVOCADO OIL COOKING SPRAY
- ORGANIC COCONUT MILK/ COCONUT WATER/SPARKLING WATER
- COCONUT WHIP CREAM
- ORGANIC ALMOND MILK/ ALMOND MILK WHIPPED CREME
- PLAIN GOAT'S MILK KEFIR
- GOAT'S MILK CHEESE
- ORGANIC PLAIN GREEK YOGURT
- ORGANIC PLAIN KEFIR
- EXTRA-LEAN GROUND TURKEY (ORGANIC AND PASTURE-RAISED)
- EXTRA-LEAN GROUND BEEF (HORMONE-ANTIBIOTIC FREE/ PASTURE-RAISED/GRASS FED)
- EXTRA-LEAN GROUND LAMB
- PASTURE-RAISED, FREE-RANGE CHICKEN, EGGS (NO HORMONES OR ANTIBIOTICS)
- ORGANIC PUMPKIN PUREE
- FRESH, ORGANIC, FRUITS AND VEGGIES IN SEASON
- ORGANIC GROUND CINNAMON/TURMERIC/PINK HIMALAYAN SEA SALT/BLACK PEPPER/ CHIA SEEDS/HEMP SEEDS/FLAX SEEDS
- A GOOD GLUTEN-FREE/ UNSWEETENED PEA PROTEIN POWDER
- DEHYDRATED RAW DOG FOOD

New Beginnings

HAPPY NEW YEAR!

AHHHHH WINTER! The temperatures are dropping, the days are shorter and the holiday season kicks into high gear! It takes the dedication and strength of a Navy Seal to stay sane and healthy during the trifecta of juggernaut holidays. I'm referring to Thanksgiving, Christmas, and New Year's. It's crazy busy. So much so that I feel as though I'm racing everywhere without a minute to stop and smell the gingerbread. Or enjoy much merriment!

I know what you're thinking, "Umm, Katy,...isn't this a book about throwing parties and entertaining?!?!?!" Yes. It absolutely is! I love parties, and I love to celebrate, but what I don't like is feeling obligated to host, cook, decorate, gorge or buy loads of gifts. I get very overwhelmed with so much happening at once and such high expectations.

You see, for a long time, I had a bad case of what I call, "the disease to please." As I talked about in the introduction of this book, my drive to learn more about food as medicine came out of my own diagnosis of Hashimoto's Thyroiditis. This often serious autoimmune disease was essentially brought on not just by my food choices, but by me running my body into the ground over and over again. The holiday season was always a huge trigger and aggravated my condition. Year after year, I went to extreme lengths to attend every party, buy perfect gifts for everyone, and end the year with a bang during the busiest season at work. All season long you could find me racing from work to events to parties then falling into bed exhausted after a 16-hour-day. Free time was spent standing in endless holiday lines to buy groceries or gifts, jacked up on triple gingerbread lattes. The holidays seemed more like an Olympic event and not something enjoyable. I spent the entire season fantasizing about a day spent in my PJs cuddling with my sweet pug, Olive.

Typically, just after New Year's, I would get really sick. I would vow to do it differently and scale back the next year, but it never happened. By the time the holidays rolled around again, I had forgotten to pace myself and believed I had superpowers to "do it all!"

One holiday season, my Hashimoto's flared up with a vengeance and stopped me in my tracks faster than a sneeze. I had pushed myself too hard for too long, and my body completely rebelled. I had no choice but to slow down and focus on my health. I scaled way back. I didn't go off the deep-end eating holiday goodies and I got my rest. Because I had to turn down a lot of invitations, I planned my own festive gatherings. I experimented with making my favorite holiday dishes and treats using healthier ingredients. It turned out to be the best holiday season ever! My parties were so easy and such a hit, I wanted to share my ideas with you. If your hectic holiday schedule prohibits throwing a party, these easy menu items are simple and delicious. They are just what you need to help get you through a busy season.

January

January is typically seen as the beginning of the year, but in my opinion, January is about endings as well. To me, January means the end of weekends jammed with holiday get-togethers; the end of late nights walking my dog because she wasn't allowed to come to any of the holiday festivities; the end of being buried up to my armpits in wrapping paper; the end of hemorrhaging money; and the end of the non-stop, go-go-go.

Just when we have hit our limit, spent our last dollar, and can't listen to Mariah Carey sing that damned Christmas song one more time, the new year is upon us! We are ready to relax. We want to cleanse our bodies, slow down, and give ourselves some major TLC! If that isn't something to look forward to and celebrate, what is? So here is my, "re-set and re-charge," holiday hangover-relief party. Now, If you're simply too wiped out to even think of another party, I get it! This menu is simple and can be enjoyed while lounging in bed with your dog and binge-watching your favorite series on Netflix! And the foods (and drinks) are loaded with healthy ingredients to have you feeling refreshed and energized faster than you can say, "HAPPY NEW YEAR!"

Let's get this party started!

HAIR OF THE DOG NEW YEAR'S HANGOVER BRUNCH

The anticipation of my Hair of the Dog Hangover Party is how I make it through the hectic holiday season. In some ways, this is an anti-party. The goal is to have a relaxing, low-key get-together with your closest friends and their pooches! Chances are everyone has been so busy over the holiday season, you are all way overdue for a time to casually hang out and chill out. We all know that January is famous for health-related resets, goal-setting, and re-prioritizing. This event encourages just that. It is a party for daydreaming, relaxing, and enjoying healthy, healing foods for your friends and their "plus-one" pups! Now, if the idea of hosting one more party is as appealing as a rash, no worries...I encourage you to keep this really simple. Ask your friends to help by bringing, not just their dog but their favorite dish, some magazines, or craft supplies to make vision boards, and possibly a re-gift for the white elephant gift exchange. Encourage guests to come dressed in PJs, sweats, or robes. Then get everyone involved by asking for help with setting up, making the food and drinks, and cleaning up. I think you will have so much fun it may become your new tradition.

MENU

Bloodhound Bloody Mary's ⸺ Green Eggs and Ham ⸺ Blueberry Mini Muffins

INVITES: Keep it simple. Call/text friends or send out free e-vites. Chances are everyone is "party-pooped" and doesn't want the stress of attending another formal soiree.

DÉCOR: Nothing!--Feel free to NOT decorate! Maybe you still have your tree and holiday decor out, but the important thing is that you and your guests feel comfortable.

ACTIVITIES: This is your choice. See what your guests are up for. You can simply put on a movie and chat or try one of these no stress options:

Re-Gift Exchange - Hey, it's January. If you are like me, you received a gift and...well, it's not your thing. Invite your friends to bring over their less-then-favorite holiday gift and have yourselves a fun (and potentially very funny) gift exchange. Those that wish to participate bring a gift they received that isn't their cup of tea. Everyone who brings a gift gets a number. Number 1 chooses from the pile of gifts. Number 2 can either steal another opened gift or choose one from the pile. Once the gift has been stolen twice, it stays with that person.

Vision Boarding - Invite everyone to design vision boards for the year ahead. Arts and crafts like this can be cathartic! I purchase small canvases for party guests and bring fabric swatches, glitter, crafting items, and magazines, then let everyone create whatever they want to manifest in the New Year. Looking back on my vision boards, it's surreal how they have a strange way of manifesting. SO DREAM BIG!

Spa Day: As a belated holiday gift, buy some inexpensive facial masks and everyone can do a facial. You can also trade off giving simple mani/pedi's or massages. Maybe you can all pitch in and have someone come over and do a sound bath or give massages.

PARTY FAVORS: Although this is highly unnecessary if you love handing out favors, these items fit the theme, are inexpensive, and are things most people will use and enjoy. *Epsom salts to relieve aching muscles. (Infuse by adding lavender or essential oils.) *Snuggy Socks *All-natural soaps *Eye masks *Lotions *Crystals *Small dog bowls you can customize with paints. These party favors could also serve as great belated holiday gifts for your friends.

BLOODHOUND BLOODY MARY'S

Prep Time: 10 minutes
Serves 6 adults & 6 dogs

My twist on this classic cocktail is very nutritious! Tomatoes are high in vitamins, minerals, and rich in lycopene. This powerful antioxidant has impressive health benefits, including keeping toxins out of the cells while allowing nutrients in. As a result, lycopene is great for the immune system and brain health. It can help prevent diabetes, strokes, cancer, macular degeneration, and osteoporosis. It is perfect to get you feeling your best after a busy holiday season.

INGREDIENTS FOR PUPS:

- ½ can tomato juice*
- ½ cup dill pickle juice
- 1 tsp apple cider vinegar
- chia, hemp, flax seeds (optional-for rim of glass)
- Garnish options: thick pickle slice, celery slice/leaf, or a small shrimp or bacon bit, sprinkle with seed mixture

***IMPORTANT**: For dogs, look for an organic, low-sodium tomato juice without added salts or sugars.

INGREDIENTS FOR PEOPLE:

- 1 ½ cans tomato juice
- 1 jar of olive juice
- Worcestershire sauce (to taste)
- ½ tsp horseradish
- Hot sauce (to taste)
- One shake cayenne pepper
- Vodka (optional)
- Kosher salt and/or celery salt (for rim of glass)

DIRECTIONS FOR PUPS:

1. Mix ingredients in a small pitcher.
2. Dip rim of shot glass in vinegar and stamp in a plate covered with chia, hemp or flax seeds (or a mix of all.)
3. Garnish to your pup's liking!

☠ **CAUTION**: Toothpicks can be a hazard for dogs. Instead, float a leaf of a celery stalk, or a small piece of bacon or shrimp on the top.

DIRECTIONS FOR PEOPLE:

1. Mix ingredients in a large pitcher.
2. Salt rims by rubbing a slice of lemon along the rim of glass and then dabbing on a plate with sea salt and/or celery salt to replace electrolytes.

GREEN EGGS AND HAM

Prep Time: 15 minutes
Serves 6 adults & 6 dogs

What's a brunch without an egg dish? This fun twist on the Dr. Seuss classic is simple and a perfect, healthy, comfort food.

INGREDIENTS FOR PUPS AND PEOPLE:

- 1 dozen organic, free-range eggs
- 1 cup extra finely chopped fresh, organic broccoli
- 1 cup of shredded cheese (I use vegan or goat's milk crumbles)

DIRECTIONS FOR PUPS AND PEOPLE:

1. Scramble eggs and broccoli together over medium heat.
2. Once eggs are firm, take eggs off heat sprinkle cheese on top.
3. Set aside ¼ of the mixture to serve to dogs.

FOR PEOPLE:

1. Sprinkle salt and pepper to taste

CAUTION: ALWAYS MAKE SURE FOOD ISN'T TOO HOT BEFORE SERVING DOGS!

POOCH-FRIENDLY MINI BLUEBERRY MUFFINS

Prep Time: 45 minutes (including baking time.)
Serves 12 mini muffins / 6 regular sized

This is an easy gluten-free recipe made with anti-inflamatory swaps perfect for those who need a re-charge. Blueberries are a superfood packed with essential nutrients and powerful antioxidants. Having just a few blueberries a day has been proven to help digestion and prevent many cancers. They also give a boost to the immune system which everyone needs after a hectic holiday season. They taste delicious and smell better than any scented candle or air freshener!

INGREDIENTS FOR PUPS AND PEOPLE:

- You will need small and regular size muffin pans and muffin/candy paper cups.
- ¼ cup flax meal
- ½ cup fresh blueberries
- ½ cup coconut powder
- 1 Tbsp kelp powder
- 1 tsp vitamin C powder (optional)
- 2 large free-range eggs
- ¼ cup plain Greek yogurt (may use coconut or oat for dairy intolerance)
- 1 Tbsp olive oil

DIRECTIONS FOR PUPS AND PEOPLE:

1. Preheat oven to 350°F.
2. Combine all dry ingredients.
3. Fold in blueberries.
4. Add remaining 3 moist ingredients and stir to form a thick batter.
5. Pour batter into muffin pans lined with paper muffin cups or greased. Fill ½ way.
6. Bake for 25 min. regular-sized muffins, 10-15 min. dog-sized small muffins. Muffins should be firm on outside and cooked through when inserting a toothpick in the center.
7. Cool and serve (may be refrigerated for one week and also frozen.)

February

...And then suddenly it's February! It's still cold outside but the calendar year is just warming up. Aside from celebrating Presidents Day (boring!) February brings us the first really festive day of the year...Valentine's Day!

It has brought me a lot of joy in the last few years the way that people have been broadening who and what we celebrate on Valentine's Day. In the past, couples went out on the exact same date, bought the same red roses, and had the same steak dinner while all the single people stayed home feeling worthless! But these days people are mixing it up! They are celebrating love in all its forms. I bet if you asked any pet parent, they would tell you the love they get from their pooch is the foundation of one of the purest and most enduring relationships they have! Why not celebrate our love for our furry family members the way we celebrate our pals, spouses, and family? Here are some recipes and party ideas to help you do just that.

Let's get this party started!

PUPPY LOVE PUP-ENTINE'S DAY CELEBRATION!

Here's another thing I love about how Valentine's Day is celebrated now: Instead of stuffy, exclusive, one-on-one events, people are making their own party. Don't get me wrong, romance is important, but I guess I never understood what was so "romantic" about stressing out over dinner reservations--especially when Valentine's Day lands on a random Tuesday or something! Anyway, I think a party like this takes the pressure off everyone and keeps it fun! So I had "no reservations" about putting together a little menu for a sweet Pup-entine's Day celebration that will leave everyone's tail wagging!

MENU

Dog Rosé 🥄 Pups-ghetti 🥄 Hot "Coco" 🥄 No-Bake Carob Bark 🥄 Un-Chocolate Cake 🥄 Carob-Covered Strawberries

DÉCOR: Decorate a pretty table to serve as your "sweetheart buffet." A few strings of pink and white lights and some glitter hearts will really showcase all the delicious dishes. Since the menu is dog friendly you simply need to supply small bite-sized dishes for the dogs and larger ones for human guests. Get in the mood by making a great playlist of favorite love songs!

Hearts - I realize you don't need my help reminding you that hearts are kind of a "thing" on Valentine's Day but if I didn't put it here you'd think I was nuts! Remember, there really isn't a way to go "over-the-top" on Valentine's Day...so decorate your heart out!-- Pun intended!

ACTIVITIES:

Valentine-Making Station - Offer a craft table where guests can get creative and make Valentine's Day cards and a "doggy bag" of one of the fun recipes below. The carob bark is easy to make and guests can take home a sweet treat as a party favor! Offer little heart-decorated cellophane bags for each guest and their dog.

Sweethearts Station - Set up a pretty heart-themed backdrop with heart-shaped balloons and all the Valentine decor you can fit out the door of the Dollar Tree. Ask guests to dress festively and have this Instagram/TikTok station perfect for capturing all the love.

LOVE POTIONS: The standard human drinks for Valentine's Day are pretty obvious: red wine, rosé and pink champagne. Those are nice...but, to be honest, I don't tolerate alcohol well. I rarely drink it, and when I do I feel awful. It's a bummer because every time I go to a party there are a dozen booze selections for everyone else, and then bottled water or cranberry juice (or whatever juice they are adding to the signature cocktail for the night) for me. If I am lucky the host finds a diet Coke hidden at the back of their fridge!

When I host parties, I like to have a lot of non-alcoholic options. One of my favorite "mocktails" is a tall glass of sparkling coconut water with a splash of cranberry juice, muddled raspberries, and mint. It's delicious! I also like to make sure all my doggy guests have something fun to drink as well! Obviously, alcohol is horrible for dogs, but what you may not know is that several companies offer pet-friendly variations on spirits such as Char-DOG-nay, Zinfan-TAIL, and bark brews. Check my website to find these brands and order. Since not everyone has the desire or budget for high-end doggy cocktails, here is a fun recipe to create your own.

DOG ROSÉ

Prep time: 5 minutes
Serves 12 dogs

Not only is this drink refreshing and delicious, but it is also loaded with health benefits. February is all about love and cranberry juice contains polyphenols that boost heart health. Plus they contain antioxidants and phytochemicals which fight oxidative damage. That makes cranberries a great choice for their anti-aging properties. So go ahead and drink up!

INGREDIENTS FOR PUPS:

- 2 cups coconut water
- ¼ cup unsweetened 100% cranberry juice
- Fresh cranberries (for garnish)

DIRECTIONS PUPS:

1. Combine ingredients in large pitcher.
2. Serve in small shot glasses or ramekins.
3. Garnish with a small cranberry.

PUPS-ghetti

Prep time: 30 minutes
Yields 22 cups

Who isn't a fan of pasta! This recipe always has me thinking about the dogs sharing a bowl of spaghetti in the movie Lady and the Tramp. This real-life version is dog-friendly and amazing. Plus, for very sensitive dogs, you can add all the seasonings to the sauce for humans at the very end and save some plain sauce for the pups. The recipe can also be modified for vegetarians and those on gluten-free diets.

INGREDIENTS FOR PUPS AND PEOPLE:

- 2 lb. lean ground chuck or beef
- 1 lb. ground pork
- 3 Tbsp light olive oil
- 2 large green peppers
- 2 (14.5 oz.) cans organic diced tomatoes
- 1 (2.5 oz.) can black olives
- 2 Tbsp parsley
- 1 tsp basil
- 1 tsp garlic powder
- ½ tsp rosemary
- ¼ tsp turmeric
- ¼ tsp sea salt
- 1 ½ tsp finely ground eggshell (sprinkle this over dog servings only)
- 2 (6 oz.) cans organic, tomato paste
- 4 cups water
- 1 (16 oz.) package spaghetti, rotini, or other pasta. May use gluten-free or zucchini spirals as well

DIRECTIONS FOR PUPS AND PEOPLE:

1. Brown meat in the olive oil in a large Dutch Oven or stockpot.
2. Finely chop olives and green peppers. Mix with the diced tomatos and add to the pot.
3. Stir in the seasonings. (except eggshell - this will be sprinkled over dog servings only.)
4. Combine the tomato paste and water. Stir into the pot.
5. Simmer covered until the green peppers are soft, giving the flavors time to meld.
6. Cook the spaghetti just past the al dente point. Strain and rinse. Set aside.
7. Remove from heat and mix in the cooked spaghetti.

*For a vegetarian option, cook meat separately. Set aside the plain pasta sauce after cooking for your vegetarian guests and add meat to the remaining sauce.

SWEETS AND TREATS

It just wouldn't be Valentine's Day without chocolate! Heck, the entire holiday revolves around it. Just look at the line that goes clear down the block at See's candy leading up to the big day. But dog parents know chocolate is toxic for our fur babies. Therefore, I have swapped carob for regular chocolate in my Valentine's recipes.

These simple goodies are perfectly edible for humans and safe for dogs. Personally, I would suggest staying away from having any chocolate at your party. Dogs have been known to jump up on tables and eat whatever they can get their paws on! If you are going to include chocolate desserts at your party, I recommend having a separate food table for the dogs and use labels to separate dog treats from human sweets. Also, be mindful that the chocolate treats are out of harm's way for the dogs. Nothing breaks hearts (and wallets) faster than rushing a party guest to the emergency vet because they got into a toxic treat.

HOT "COCO" FOR PUPS

Prep Time: 15 minutes
Serves 10 dogs

Who doesn't love a delicious mug of hot cocoa? This non-chocolate version is perfectly safe for your pup to enjoy. It tastes like a liquid Almond Joy candybar due to the coconut milk. Not only is it yummy for dogs, it can be a great option for those with allergies or dairy intolerance.

INGREDIENTS FOR PUPS:

- 1 13 oz can of coconut milk (can also use 1 liter of plain kefir)
- 2 Tbsp carob powder
- Coconut whip cream (for garnish)

DIRECTIONS PUPS:

1. In a medium saucepan bring coconut milk to a simmer.
2. Stir in carob powder and simmer until absorbed (not boiling.)
3. Take saucepan off heat and allow to cool until luke-warm (test before serving.)
4. Pour small servings (2-3 Tbsp) into a small mug or paper cup.
5. Top with coconut whip cream and sprinkle with carob powder.

WHAT IS CAROB: Extracted from the carob bean which grows on carob trees, these flowering shrubs are from the pea (FABACEAE) family. Boasting a naturally sweet flavor similar to chocolate, carob beans can be ground into powder or made into chips. Carob packs a nutritional punch containing vitamins A, B, and D as well as calcium, magnesium, iron, potassium, and protein. It's a great source of both fiber and pectin which help flush toxins from the body. SO DIG IN!

WHY CAROB INSTEAD OF CHOCOLATE?: Chocolate contains several dangerous substances including caffeine, formamide, and the highly toxic theobromine. Humans can metabolize these but a dog's digestive system is so much slower that it builds up in your dog's body. Depending on how much is ingested and how dark the chocolate is (the darker the chocolate the more the theobromine.) a dog's reaction may range from suffering a horrible stomach ache, to having a seizure. In extreme cases, dogs may have a heart attack which may be fatal. Carob, on the other hand, doesn't contain any of these harmful ingredients.

NO-BAKE CAROB "BARK"

Prep time: 5 minutes. Freeze time: 30-40 minutes
Makes 6 small bags

This delicious treat will have guests and their pets begging for more. It's so easy to make, you can put out the ingredients and let guests make a bag to take home. Once they've made their bark, pop it in the freezer so it is ready to break, bag, and take home at the end of the party.

*Note: Because coconut oil is so rich, limit servings to one quarter-sized piece per day or they will go through your dog like a laser beam. Any more can cause some tummy upset.

INGREDIENTS FOR PUPS AND PEOPLE:

- ¾ cup organic coconut oil
- ¼ cup carob powder
- 1 tsp vanilla extract
- ¼ cup chopped unsalted almonds or peanuts (humans) ☠ **No Macadamia nuts**
- ¼ cup dried blueberries/cranberries or both

DIRECTIONS FOR PUPS AND PEOPLE:

1. Fill a large bowl half-way with hot water and then place a medium bowl in the hot water.
2. Add the coconut oil to melt.
3. Once melted, stir in carob powder and vanilla extract. Blend thoroughly.
4. Remove from the hot water and let the mixture sit while it thickens.
5. Stir again. Add chopped nuts (human batch) and berries to the mixture and stir.
6. Spread mixture on a greased cookie sheet and place in the freezer until hardened.
7. Break into pieces and place and serve, or place in small valentine bags for your guests to take home as party favors.

CARROB CAKE

Prep Time: 90 minutes (including baking time)
Serves 6 Adults & 6 dogs

It just wouldn't be a cook book without a recipe for a delicious, chocolate cake! After too many trips to the ER vet for my dog accidentally getting into chocolate, I've now banned it from my home. Plus, chocolate cake sends my autoimmune condition into a tailspin. But not "having my cake and eating it too" wasn't an option, so here it is! My my recipe substitutes chocolate with carob. It uses healthy ingredients making it gluten-free, low glycemic, and anti-inflammatory. But don't let that scare you off, this cake tastes amazing and won't leave you feeling horrible after you, and your dog, indulge. Get creative and try garnishing it with other favorite fruits like coconut flakes, or bananas with peanut butter drizzled on top to switch it up! -Remember to first check the list of toxic foods for dogs.

INGREDIENTS FOR PUPS AND PEOPLE:

INGREDIENTS: (CAKE)

- ½ cup organic coconut flour
- ½ cup organic brown rice flour
- ½ tsp baking soda
- ½ tsp baking powder
- ¼ cup + 2 Tbsp carob powder
- ¼ cup + 2 Tbsp water
- ¼ cup + 2 Tbsp almond milk or coconut milk
- 1 Tbsp vinegar
- ¼ cup + 2 Tbsp olive oil
- 1 egg
- ½ tsp vanilla extract

INGREDIENTS: (ICING)

- ¼ cup organic maple sugar **(make sure it doesn't contain Xylitol)**
- ¼ cup carob powder
- ½ cup organic coconut oil
- ½ cup almond butter
- Strawberry slices (optional for decorating)

DIRECTIONS FOR PUPS AND PEOPLE:

DIRECTIONS: (CAKE)

1. Preheat oven to 350°F.
2. Spray cake pan with non-stick coconut oil.
3. Combine all the ingredients in a large mixing bowl and mix on low speed for 30 seconds. Scrape the sides of bowl to get all ingredients mixed into the batter.
4. Fill cake pan ½ way from the top.
5. Bake for about 30 minutes until the center is cooked. You should be able to poke the center with a toothpick and have it come out clean.
6. Cool for 15 minutes and remove from the pan. Put on a cake plate.

DIRECTIONS: (ICING)

1. In a medium bowl, mix together all the ingredients and stir well until smooth and creamy.
2. Place in refrigerator and chill for 30 minutes.
3. If needed, add more maple syrup until the consistency is perfect.
4. Cover the cake with frosting and add strawberry slices.

CAROB-COVERED STRAWBERRIES

Prep time: 1 hour

Yields around 20 medium berries

Although it's perfectly fine to make these on their own, ideally, you can just use any frosting leftovers from the carob cake and add this to the strawberries. You can also drizzle the frosting over other berries as well. For dogs, I cut the berries into smaller pieces.

INGREDIENTS FOR PUPS AND PEOPLE:

- See the above icing recipe for carob cake
- 20 organic medium-sized strawberries or berries of choice
- OPTIONAL IDEAS to sprinkle over berries: crumbled kibble (DOGS), granola, coconut, flax, hemp, or chia seeds

DIRECTIONS FOR PUPS AND PEOPLE:

1. Add icing to pastry bag (or plastic sandwich bag with a small hole cut in the corner.)
2. Cut strawberries into tiny bite-sized pieces.
3. Pop one or two into a small ramekin and drizzle with frosting mixture by pushing it out the hole in the corner of the bag.
4. OPTIONAL IDEAS: May add crumbled kibble (DOGS), granola, coconut, flax, hemp, or chia seeds, and sprinkle it over the berries.
5. Refrigerate until ready to eat.

STRAIGHT OUTTA RESCUE...

How to give your new shelter dog a proper housewarming.

So you're rescuing a new dog! Congrats! As a volunteer with several shelter and rescue groups, there's nothing more exciting than sharing the joy of a dog going off to their new forever home. **When a dog is surrendered to a shelter, it brings a tremendous amount of stress to the animal. Here are tips to help them make the transition from rescue dog to family pet much smoother!** A rescued or adopted dog may react fearfully when first introduced to a new home. Common behaviors can include:

- Fearful body language and facial expressions (Tail hung low, droopy head, not making eye contact, shaking their head, panting, excessive licking.
- Finding places to hide
- Wariness and general inhibited behavior
- Lack of appetite

Keep in mind your new pet's personality and temperament may not emerge on his first day home, or even during the first week or two. Heck, I feel like it took me 2 years to get Olive out from under the table after I first rescued her.

Before bringing your dog home, be sure you've puppy-proofed it for safety. Even an older or seemingly well-trained dog will be curious about their new surroundings and needs to be kept safe from harm.

Some dogs will be very uncomfortable with too much affection. Hugging and snuggling may be a ways off. Start slowly and let your dog lead the way as they get to know you better. As difficult as it is, lavishing too much attention on your new pup can result in major separation anxiety behaviors when you must leave.

In the beginning, less is more. Aim to have a slightly bored pup. The worst thing is to over-stimulate them from the get-go! Try and get them on a regular routine that works for you. Perhaps start with a few short walks and tossing around some new toys. This fun interaction will help their physical and mental state.

Mealtimes may also be a challenge. While some dogs live for food, others might not have much appetite in the first few days at home. Try to keep their diet as familiar as possible, slowly adding more nutritious, fresh foods. Feed them in a calm, quiet setting. After an appropriate amount of time, pick up their food dish and get them on a regular feeding schedule. Don't hesitate to call the vet if their appetite has not improved after a day or so of adjustment. -Or if anything seems off!

Remember, this is an adjustment for everyone. By practicing these skills you and your pet can have a much smoother start. Please visit my website **www.weeklyrunt.com** for many more resources to help.

March

I must confess, one of my favorite months of the year is March. It's not because of spring temperatures or any holiday, but because March is awards season baby! You see, while I am crazy about dogs, I am also a huge fan of pop culture, TV, movies, and FASHION!! March is a month studded with glitz, glamour, and fun! My ideal Sunday is cozying up to my dog and watching hours and hours of red carpet interviews. I love them! I can't get enough! I thrive on picking apart what celebrities are wearing and Googling all the gossip about so-and-so while Ryan Seacrest throws them softball questions until someone inevitably says, "Oh, Ryan, it's an honor just to be nominated!" And then they glide away down the red carpet. -Heaven! It's silly! It's meaningless! It's the best!

While it's great to enjoy the awards shows at home with my dog, it's much more fun to host a red-carpet party and make the dogs the stars of the show!

If there is one thing I have learned since becoming part of the pet-parent community, it's that parents of pets are just as proud of their fur babies as parents of humans are of their kiddos. I know! I am the parent of both a pet and a human! But while human parents have recitals, awards banquets, graduations, and many opportunities for bragging rights about their kids, pet parents really don't get many chances to give their dogs a moment in the spotlight!

So in the month of March, I am combining my love of high fashion and encouraging pet parents to grab their friends, roll out the red carpet, whip up an award-winning spread, and have a star-studded soirée, - just because!

Let's get this party started!

THE MUTT GALA

Are you ready to party like a celebrity? You'd better be! Let's celebrate with a play on fashion's MET GALA with a MUTT GALA! In the spirit of the glam season, invite your friends to an over-the-top, fully-costumed viewing party for any one of the awards shows this spring! Or you can simply screen a famous pet movie like 101 Dalmatians and make it a premiere!

I know what you might be thinking, "Will people want to go through all this trouble?" Short answer: Yes, they will. Especially if you allow them to get their pets in on the act. In my experience, people are usually dying for a chance to dress up and be over-the-top, so treat your friends and furry pals to a night of excess glitz and fun! Encourage people to wear formal attire, or select a theme like "Famous Couples," "Silver Screen Heroes," or "Met Gala's Most Memorable." I'm sure you'll be surprised by the creativity and enthusiasm your friends will bring to the party!

And then there's the menu! I've created star-studded drinks and dishes such as Canine Champagne and Caviar to delicious Red-Velvet Pupcakes and made them healthier and dog-friendly. Your guests will truly feel like celebrities.

MENU

Canine Champagne 🥄 "Star" Cuterie 🥄 Canine Caviar Waffle Bites 🥄 Red Velvet Pupcakes

ACTIVITIES & DÉCOR:

Red Carpet Star Experience: For reasons I should not have to explain, you'll want to make sure you set up some kind of photo opp for this event! Line up a red carpet runner with a backdrop listing all your favorite dog haunts. If you are feeling really creative, you can even make an awards-show backdrop. A simpler version is to run to a fabric store and get some glittery fabric to hang in the corner. Boom! You're done! The PAW-parrazi can be out in full swing, shooting cute pics for social media. Prior to entering the party, guests can sign in by dipping their paw in pet-friendly, vegan, ink and stamping the pawtograph book.

Awards: Create categories based on your theme, hand out ballots, and vote on the costumes. Be sure to have little awards ready for humans and dogs alike!

Dog Walk Of Fame: Create your own "walk of fame" by cutting out large squares of paper and having your guests and dogs leave their mark! It also makes a fun party favor guests can take home!

CANINE CHAMPAGNE

Prep Time: 5 minutes
Serves 6 adults & 6 dogs

It wouldn't be a red carpet event without champagne flowing. In addition to the bubbly, this cocktail is perfect for the pups and non-drinkers alike. Simply add sparkling water/lemon-lime soda or champagne to cranberry juice and you can modify this for humans.

INGREDIENTS FOR PUPS AND PEOPLE:

- ¼ cup organic unsweetened cranberry juice
- ¾ cup coconut water
- 3 cups sparkling water or lemon-lime flavor soda (for humans)
- 1 bottle of champagne (for humans- optional)

DIRECTIONS FOR PUPS AND PEOPLE:

1. In a glass or decorative pitcher, combine juice and coconut water.

FOR PUPS:

1. Pour into small shot glasses, dog champagne glasses, or ramekins.
2. Garnish with a fresh cranberry.

FOR PEOPLE:

1. Fill champagne glasses ¾ full with champagne/soda or sparkling water.
2. Add a splash of the juice mixture. Garnish with cranberries and serve.

"STAR" CUTERIE

Prep Time: 20 minutes
Serves 6 -10 adults & dogs

For this over-the-top Mutt Gala, I want to give you tips for creating a great "Star" Cuterie spread that is simple but decadent. There are many ways to do this and if you check out Instagram and Pinterest you'll see that you can really get creative. I recommend using a pretty gold, shimmering tablecloth. Bright red also works. Then fill the table, placing food elements from the suggestions below. Once the food is placed, add some stars, tinsel, no-burn candles, and food labels to make it look star-studded.

Using small, wooden cheese boards, or inexpensive appetizer-sized plates, let each pet parent select food for themselves and also make a dish for their fabulous pups. Prior to the party, decorate boards or plates with each pet's name using paint pens and add star stickers! Send them home, along with their red carpet photos as souvenirs for your guests. While many food items are pet-friendly, it's nice to set up one side for humans and one end for dogs. I like to use premium meats for humans and chopped organ meats for dogs.

An important word of caution, this spread can sometimes bring out the BEAST in even the most docile of dogs. Have pet parents closely supervise their dogs at all times around the food.

INGREDIENT IDEAS:

- Meats: shredded chicken, turkey, thin slices of salmon
- **Chopped organs**
- Anchovies/Sardines
- Shrimp
- Small sliced pickles
- Pitted, sliced olives
- Vegetables including small bites of sweet potatoes, bell pepper, carrots, broccoli
- Small cubes of cheese
- Apple slices
- Small Melon balls
- Avocado slices
- **Variety of dog kibble in small bowls**
- **Variety of dog pates**
- Avoid grapes, raisins, currants, garlic, onions, and any cooked bones in meats

DIRECTIONS:

1. Arrange items in a visually-pleasing way.
2. Set our tongs and forks for guests to select foods.
3. Offer small paper plates or cheese boards to make individual servings.

☠ AVOID TOOTHPICKS

Ingredients in bold are for the pups only.

CANINE CAVIAR WAFFLE BITES

Prep Time: 15 minutes
Makes 2 dozen appetizers

Impress your human and canine guests alike with this simple and lavish caviar dish. Caviar is the ultimate in luxe hors d'oeuvres, but it can be extremely pricey and too high in salt for dogs. This recipe works without those issues. If you're sharing with canines, try a low-salt variety or trout caviar. And, as usual, keep the portions small, bite-sized pieces.

INGREDIENTS FOR PUPS AND PEOPLE:

- 1 (1.1 oz jar) Caviar (Try trout or low-salt for dogs)
- Chopped fresh chives (for garnish)
- 3 Tbsp crème fraîche, plain Greek yogurt, or cream cheese
- 4 Frozen toaster waffles (I use Van's or Trader Joe's Gluten-Free Belgian Waffle varieties)

DIRECTIONS FOR PUPS AND PEOPLE:

1. Following the waffle grid marks as a guide, cut each waffle into small rectangles with 2x3 squares. Square waffles work best but round ones can be used and the edges discarded.

2. Spoon creme fraiche, softened cream cheese, or Greek yogurt into a small ziplock plastic bag: snip off the tip of a corner of the bag to form a ¼" opening. Fill one square with creme fraiche. Fill another square with caviar.

3. Garnish creme fraiche square with chives and serve.

Another option for dogs is to fill 1 square with ½ creme fraiche and ½ caviar. Making a portion out of 1 square for dogs and 2 squares for humans.

RED CARPET-RED VELVET PUPCAKES

Prep Time: 15 minutes . Cook Time: 20 minutes
Serves 32 mini pupcakes

This delicious dessert needs no explanation. Although it's been modified to be safe and healthy as a dog treat, it's perfect for those that want a treat without all the added sugar and gluten.

INGREDIENTS FOR PUPS:

PUPCAKES

- 1 beet (¾ cup worth)
- ¼ cup strawberries (about 3 large)
- ½ cup applesauce
- ⅓ cup plain Greek yogurt
- 2 eggs
- 2 cups oat flour (or put rolled oats in a food processor and make your own)
- ¼ cup carob powder
- 1 tsp baking powder

ICING

- 3 tbsp plain, Greek yogurt
- 1 Tbsp cornstarch
- 1 block cream cheese
- ¼ cup strawberries/blueberries for color and taste
- 1 tsp vanilla extract

DIRECTIONS FOR PUPS:

PUPCAKES

1. Preheat oven to 350°F.
2. Dice beet and place in a blender or food processor.
3. Add applesauce and yogurt.
4. Blend until smooth.
5. Add eggs and dry ingredients and stir together in a mixing bowl.
6. Spoon batter into small candy cups inside a small muffin tin. Fill ¾.
7. Bake for 20 min. or until a toothpick can be poked in the center and comes out clean.
8. Cool before frosting.

Or, make larger size cupcakes for humans and bake for 25-30 min.

ICING

1. Place the softened cream cheese and yogurt in the bowl and mix until fluffy.
2. Add cornstarch and vanilla.
3. Add frosting to a piping bag or fill a plastic bag and cut out the corner.
4. Swirl or spread to your heart's content.
5. Decorate with a strawberry or small dog treat.

Spring Fever

HAPPY SPRING!

Happy spring! It's such a wonderful time of year. After the cold, dark, days of winter, life is once again in bloom! In honor of the floppy-eared Easter bunny, I thought this was a perfect time to discuss one of the most common problems I "hear" from Pug parents...**EAR** infections.

My first pug Raisin was plagued with ear infections throughout most of his life. Ironically they began coming on about a year after I switched him from homemade organic dog food to a crappy, expensive "prescription" food I used to treat his urinary issues. As time went on, and I kept filling him with processed corn, wheat, grains, gluten, and poultry by-product meals, the infections got much worse.

After a few years of misery and living on pricey antibiotics, Raisin underwent extensive surgery where a small hole was drilled under his jaw and a tiny tube was inserted deep in the canal of his inner ear allowing it to drain and heal. It was a traumatic, painful ordeal for the poor little guy but it was successful. However, not too long after, he began having problems in his other ear, and eventually, the infections returned with a vengeance.

At age 13 he got another painful infection, deep in his inner ear. Antibiotics were no longer effective and he was not in any condition to undergo another exhaustive surgery. We made the heartbreaking yet humane decision to let him go. I wish I had known then what I knew now because I truly feel I could've avoided most if not all his chronic ear issues.

If your dog is experiencing persistent ear problems or is a breed predisposed to them, -read on. These simple tips should save you a lot of expense, hassle, and heartache.

NOW HEAR THIS!

Tips for Healing and Preventing Ear Infections in Your Dog.

Ear problems in dogs are the result of inflammation and/or infection. Any untreated inflammation can lead to infection. If your dog's ears are warm to the touch, red, swollen, and/or itchy, but there's little to no discharge, chances are the problem is inflammation. However, if one or more of those symptoms is present along with a brown, green, or bloody discharge, that can be anywhere from thin and runny to a thick sludge, chances are it's an infection.

The most common reason for ear inflammation in dogs is allergies. An allergic response to food or something in the environment can cause inflammation anywhere throughout your pet's body, including the ears. A dog with allergy-related ear inflammation will shake their head a lot and also scratch incessantly at their ears. It is also common for them to butt their head along your legs or furniture in an attempt to relieve their discomfort. If you notice your dog doing any of these things be sure to check their ears for any signs of irritation, redness, and/or swelling.

Another cause of ear inflammation is moisture. This is commonly known as "swimmer's ear." Although it is very common during the warmer months when dogs are playing in the water more, if you live here in So Cal, where we enjoy outdoor beach weather year-round, or you live in a rainy or humid area, your dog can be at higher risk. Wetness and moisture in the ear canals coupled with a warm body temperature can create an infection faster than a sneeze. It's extremely crucial to thoroughly dry your dog's ears each time they come out of the water or are groomed - particularly if you have a high-risk breed!

The third major reason for ear problems is wax buildup. The presence of some earwax is healthy and normal, and, just like humans, different dogs have varying amounts. Some dogs, like my sweet Raisin, needed his ears cleaned 2x's daily and little Olive has rarely needed a cleaning. Certain breeds, such as English & French Bulldogs, Pugs, Cocker Spaniels, Basset Hounds, Poodles, Labradors, and Retrievers, in general, produce more earwax. If you have one of these breeds, you should get your dog accustomed to having their ears cleaned regularly from the time they're a puppy.

Ear infections typically involve the outer canal, which is actually very deep. The medical term used for these infections is "otitis externa." An infection that frequently recurs or never really clears is termed, "chronic otitis." There are a number of things that can cause these infections including:

- Moisture in the ear creates a warm breeding ground for infection.
- Heavy ear wax production. Excess glands in the ears that produce wax and sebum and clog up.
- Narrowing of the ear canal.
- Heavy, hanging ears such as a Cocker Spaniels & Bassett's.
- Foreign material in the ear, such as from a plant like a foxtail.

If your dog has an ear infection, it's very important to identify whether it's a bacterial or fungal infection, (or both), in order to treat the problem.

Bacterial infections of the ear are the most common. They can either be pathogenic, which is a bacterial picked up from a source outside the body, such as contaminated ocean water, or non-pathogenic which is a bacteria that are normal inhabitants of your dog's body, such as staph. Any bacteria can become overgrown and quickly cause an infection.

Fungal ear infections in dogs are most commonly caused by yeast. This is the type of ear infection that constantly plagued Raisin. Some yeast is always present on the bodies of animals, but when the immune system isn't in prime condition, (or they are eating a diet high in starchy carbs, as was also the case with Raisin), the fungus can grow out of control and cause an infection.

Most dogs prone to yeast infections need to have their ears cleaned and dried frequently. I would also recommend a grain-free,-low-carb diet, using fresh or moist food. I could always detect a yeast infection since Raisin's ears would either smell very sweet or horribly rancid. In any case, there was a distinct odor.

HOW TO PREVENT EAR INFECTIONS IN YOUR DOG

Unfortunately, pugs are much more prone to ear infections than many other breeds. If you're a pug parent (or have another susceptible breed) *YOU MUST BE DILIGENT* and check their ears daily. Any dirt, wax, or whatnot, left in the ear canal can bring on a raging infection quicker than norovirus spreads on a cruise ship.

If your dog's ears aren't squeaky clean, *CLEAN THEM.* An ounce of prevention is definitely worth a TON of cure! There are many ear solutions available in pet stores and your vet may recommend an anti-fungal rinse but this is an all-natural, inexpensive one you can easily make at home for far less money and can be used regularly:

DO IT YOURSELF ALL-NATURAL EAR CLEANING SOLUTION:

- Mix equal parts distilled or alkaline water with organic apple cider vinegar (Great for frequent yeast infections)
- Add one drop of tea tree oil (NEVER for cats!)
- 1 Tbsp organic coconut oil.

You can also dab a cotton ball, cotton round, or sterile gauze with witch hazel, cooled green tea, or hydrogen peroxide, add a dash of coconut oil, and begin cleaning.

☠ **NEVER** use rubbing alcohol or wipes containing alcohol to clean your dog's ears. It is much too abrasive and can cause extremely painful burning especially if there's inflammation.

HOW TO PROPERLY CLEAN YOUR DOG'S EARS:

1. Apply a generous amount of solution on a cotton ball, round, or sterile gauze. (Never use a Q-tip inside the ear canal as it can damage or rupture the eardrum)
2. Gently wipe the ears clean. You may need to repeat and use several cotton balls to adequately clean the ears. Once the cotton is clear of any dirt and wax, you are finished.
3. This should do the trick for most dogs, but if you have a dog with heavy wax buildup, like my Raisin, I would do the following ear cleansing routine and I would ask your vet for a stronger medicated rinse until it's under control.
4. Put your dog on your lap or for large dogs, lay their head in your lap with one ear facing up so the solution can roll down their ear canal.
5. Squirt a small amount of solution directly into the dog's ear filing up the canal.
6. Gently massage the jawline under the ear as the solution dissipates.
7. Repeat on the other side. At this point your dog should begin shaking their head like crazy, spraying you with ear cleaning solution!
8. Now, grab that cotton and clean all the loosened wax and debris out of your dog's ears as directed above.
9. Follow with lots of praise and a treat. (A HEALTHY TREAT -not a big Milk-Bone made of junk!)

HOW TO TREAT AN EAR INFECTION IN YOUR DOG

If you suspect your pug might possibly have an ear infection, make an appointment with your veterinarian immediately! - DON'T WAIT!

Should your sweetie be suffering from an infection they may require antibiotics and/or special medicated cleaning solutions. Letting an infection go untreated can lead to rupture of the eardrum and further complications.

If your dog is being treated for an ear infection it's even more important to keep their ears clean. Adding topical medication to dirty, waxy ears filled with gunk will just be adding fuel to the fire. Extra moisture and warmth will allow the bacteria to grow like wildfire. Also, the medication will not easily reach and penetrate the infected tissue.

If your vet diagnoses your dog with a bacterial ear infection, make sure they determine the EXACT STRAIN and course of treatment. This will be extremely helpful if your dog has re-current infections and/or develops a resistance to certain antibiotics. And, just like with humans, it is extremely important to finish any medication your veterinarian prescribes. Don't try and save a few bucks by stopping the course of treatment early and stashing the medication if your dog's infection clears. This can lead to the regrowth of resistant organisms and eventually make them completely ineffective. Currently, there are many strains of bacteria causing ear infections which are resistant to many (if not all) conventional medications.

I also recommend adding some probiotics to replace the healthy bacteria being destroyed by antibiotics. A few tablespoons of plain Kefir is ideal and can be found where milk and yogurt drinks are sold. Many of the recipes in this book, contain probiotics and other powerful ingredients which help build up your dog's immune system.

If your dogs ear issues are driving you nuts, I HEAR YOU! These tips should be a game changer. If you'd like recommendations on products I use, please visit my website: **www.weeklyrunt.com**

April

I vividly remember the day I brought my new Pug, Olive, home. As I wrote in the introduction to this book, I had given so much of myself to the process of raising my daughter that when she left for school I felt lost and depressed. I had become so good at loving and caring for others that I didn't know who "I" was. Finding Olive and making her a part of my life transformed me in ways I could have never imagined. If I could go back in time, knowing now what that dog was going to bring to my life, I would have made a much bigger deal around her arrival.

April is all about showers! Rain showers, baby showers, engagement showers, and now, puppy showers. This is a perfect time of year to celebrate the welcome of a new furry family member. And why not? We acknowledge other new additions to our families. A Sip-and-See is a perfect way to introduce a new pet to your close circle of friends and their dogs.

Let's get this party started!

SIP-AND-SEE PAWTY

If you have never been to a Sip-and-See for a new pup, then let me tell you, you've been missing out! A Sip-and-See is everything you love about a baby shower and happy hour, rolled into one fun, sweet, party. Guests are invited to come and meet a new four-legged friend while enjoying delicious drinks and snacks. This is not a get-together where the host needs to feel pressure to feed anyone (human or dog) an entire meal. It's just a fun and breezy opportunity for friends and family to get some cuddles with a new furry member of their social constellation.

A Sip-and-See should be held after a new puppy reaches about 3-4 months old and has gotten all their puppy shots. For older pups, wait until they have acclimated to their new home and it's not too overwhelming. Plan this event like an open house where guests can come and go within a 3-4 hour window. Encourage guests to bring their own (well-behaved) dogs and kids. You may wish to schedule time slots for each guest so the puppy or new pet can be socialized without being overstimulated.

MENU

Puppy Punch ⸱ Tooty-Fruity Chicken Salad ⸱ Canine Quiche ⸱ Mini Pavlovas

This party is best held outside so the dogs can run and play.

DÉCOR:: Stick large paw prints down on the ground leading the way to the party outside. Offer plenty of puppy bowls with water around the outside area. In addition to offering water, you can provide flavored bone broths in small bowls for the dogs to enjoy. Decorate a large table with food. Offer plenty of cushions, chairs, and blankets for outdoor seating. I like to decorate a special chair and dog bed for the guests of honor. Don't forget to create a cute backdrop/photo station so each guest can get a picture with the new pup!

INVITES: "COME, SIT, STAY and JOIN US at a SIP & SEE PAWTY" Ask everyone to RSVP so you can coordinate timing. Make sure everyone knows their dog must be on a leash and supervised at all times. Please leave anxious, aggressive, dogs at home.

PARTY FAVORS: "Doggy Bags" can include a decorative paw print cookie or small frame guests can use to hold a picture from the party.

SIPS: PUPPY PUNCH

Prep Time: 10 minutes
Serves 12 Adults & 12 dogs

This tasty and refreshing beverage can be modified perfectly for pups and those who prefer their drinks "unleaded!" Experiment with flavors. For instance, I enjoy using strawberry soda or sparkling water for a sweeter twist. Another option is using pink champagne.

INGREDIENTS FOR PUPS AND PEOPLE:

- 1-liter sparkling water, 7 Up, or Sprite (humans
- 1 bottle champagne (humans)
- 1-quart coconut water (may use flavored)
- 1 14 oz can coconut milk
- 9 large strawberries (6 for recipe / 3 to garnish drinks)
- Small paper cups, shot glasses, or ramekins for serving dogs
- Paper straws in primary colors
- 3 cups of ice cubes

DIRECTIONS FOR PUPS AND PEOPLE:

1. In a large pitcher add ice cubes.
2. Wash and cut tops off strawberries.
3. Slice berries lengthwise and mash with the back of the spoon into the ice.
4. Add coconut water and coconut milk.
5. Stir well. Pour ⅓ pitcher into a new pitcher.

DIRECTIONS FOR PUPS:

1. Take the new pitcher with ⅓ mixture and serve small, 2-4 Tbsp amounts to pups in small paper ramekins or shot glasses.
2. Garnish with strawberry slices.

DIRECTIONS PEOPLE:

1. Add one liter of soda, sparkling water or champagne, to pitcher (LABEL IT!) or fill individual guest's glasses with 2-3 Tbsp mixture then top with seltzer, soda or champagne.
2. Garnish with strawberry slice.

TOOTIE FRUITY CHICKEN SALAD

Prep time: 20 minutes
Serves 8 humans & 8 dogs

This recipe is always a favorite and one that is often requested by friends. It's simple to make, and it's a perfect meal for a spring day. It also makes a lovely side dish or snack. FUN FACT: Did you know plain Greek yogurt offers live probiotics which can restore gut health? This is especially important if puppies have just had shots or if you or your dog have recently been on a course of antibiotics. Apple cider vinegar is a natural flea repellent when ingested and it's also amazing for gut health.

INGREDIENTS FOR PUPS AND PEOPLE:

- 4 cups chicken (cooked and cut into cubes)
- ½ cup celery very thinly sliced or diced)
- ½ cup cantaloupe melon cut into small cubes
- ½ cup fresh mango, peeled and cut into cubes
- 1 cup plain Greek yogurt (or kefir/ goat's/oat or coconut milk yogurt)
- 2 Tbsp apple cider vinegar
- 2 Tbsp pineapple juice
- Chia seeds, and coconut flakes to garnish

DIRECTIONS FOR PUPS AND PEOPLE:

1. In a large mixing bowl, toss chicken, celery, melon, and mango together.
2. Mix yogurt, and liquids together and pour over salad.
3. Dust with Chia seeds, coconut flakes and serve immediately or refrigerate until ready to serve.

Serving size: ½ Tbsp for dogs.
¼ cup scoop for humans.

This dish also be used as a topper to your dog's meals.

☠ DO NOT BE TEMPTED TO ADD GRAPES, RAISINS OR CURRANTS TO THIS DISH! These have the potential to cause kidney failure in dogs.

CANINE QUICHE

Prep Time: 1 hr. /Yields 1 pie

Here's a delicious way to get your dog to eat more healthy veggies, throw them into a yummy pie crust with eggs and cheese. Humans might want to add more sea salt, pepper or salsa to their individual servings. I recommend small, bite-sized servings for dogs even though they will be begging for more!

INGREDIENTS FOR PUPS AND PEOPLE:

- 1 frozen, gluten-free pie crust
- 3 cups plain kefir (may substitute for light cream for humans only)
- 1 Tbsp fresh basil
- ½ cup fresh spinach leaves
- ¼ cup chopped mushrooms
- 1 Tbsp extra virgin olive oil
- 4 free-range eggs lightly beaten
- ¼ tsp pink sea salt
- A few grinds black pepper
- ⅓ cup parmesan cheese
- ¼ cup cooked ground beef or diced chicken

DIRECTIONS FOR PUPS AND PEOPLE:

1. Preheat oven to 400°F.
2. Warm basil, kefir, and mushrooms in small saucepan over low heat for 10 minutes.
3. Set aside. Add oil to medium skillet, add spinach and cook gently until wilted.
4. Mix kefir, basil, mushrooms, eggs, salt, pepper, and cheese.
5. Add to spinach, stirring gently until all is combined.
6. Sprinkle meat into pie crust and cover with mixture.
7. Bake on the bottom rack for 15 minutes. Move to the middle rack of the oven.
8. Turn heat down to 350°F and bake for another 30 minutes or until the quiche feels firm on the top.
9. Cut small portions (2" square) for dogs **allowing quiche to cool thoroughly before serving.**

MINI PAVLOVA'S DESSERTS

Prep time: 10 minutes
Serves 12 adults & 12 dogs

One of my most favorite desserts is an Australian delicacy named after the famous Russian ballerina Anna Pavlova. Unfortunately, it's loaded with sugar and not something I can eat if I want to avoid a Hashimoto's flare-up. Luckily, I found a way to modify this dessert and make it HEALTHY and "dog-inclusive!" In addition, by adding a bit of turmeric you can help reduce inflammation and pain associated with arthritis. It tastes so good, nobody will notice they got an extra "boost!'

INGREDIENTS FOR PUPS AND PEOPLE:

- 1 package or box of meringues. (I use Trader Joe's)
- 1 16oz container Greek yogurt* (or two 4oz plain for pets and 2 flavored for humans.) You may also use oat or coconut yogurt for a non-dairy option.
- 1 package organic frozen berry mix or one box of fresh organic strawberries & blueberries
- Whip cream (or coconut whip cream)
- Cinnamon
- Turmeric

DIRECTIONS FOR PUPS:

1. Crumble one meringue in a small ramekin.
2. Add one dollop of plain yogurt. 1 tsp of mashed strawberries, blueberries and/or raspberries and their juices.
3. Top with a dash of whip cream and sprinkle with cinnamon and turmeric.

DIRECTIONS FOR PEOPLE:

1. Use 3-4 meringues and 1-2 Tbsp. yogurt/fruit. (I like vanilla bean flavored yogurt or coconut yogurt for non-dairy option.)
2. Top with a dash of whip cream and sprinkle with cinnamon and turmeric.

May

IT'S PROM SEASON! Okay...I know what you may be thinking: "It's not prom season for ME, I graduated high school...ahem, a while ago!" Regardless of when you graduated, I would bet that prom was either completely overrated, or it was so magical it might be fun to re-live! After all, why should teenagers have all the fun!

Think about it, even if you were prom King or Queen and you had the perfect date, the first time you went to prom you were a kid. Bless your heart, you were in the midst of a teenage wasteland and probably nervous as hell about the whole thing. There was so much pressure! This time around you won't have to kill yourself trying to find just the right dress, or come up with an ingenious way to ask the person you fancy if they will be your date! You already have the perfect partner right by your side...

let's get this party started!

THE PUPPY PROM

So what the heck is a "Puppy Prom" you ask? It's a night where you and your dog-loving friends can dress up, put on music, and dance (or trot) the night away. Personally, I love any chance to dress up with my pup, and what could be a better party than recreating the prom of my dreams!

MENU

Spiked Prom Punch · Mac & Cheese Balls · Meatballs · "Edibles" Bow-Wow Brownies

This party is best held outside so the dogs can run and play.

INVITES: You can always do online evites, but it may be fun to send out invitations on old 45 records, or glue the invites on pages out of an old yearbook. Even better if you can get guest's pictures copied from their yearbooks. Make sure everyone knows to dress their dog for the occasion. But advise guests to leave anxious, skittish, highly-spirited and aggressive dogs at home. The music, lights, and craziness may simply be too much for some dogs.

DÉCOR: Nothing says prom like disco and dayglo! Set up your party area with lots of colored streamers, balloons, large cut-out paw prints and music notes. Change light bulbs to black light bulbs and watch the decor glow in the dark. Thrift stores and dollar stores have lots of fun, inexpensive décor for your theme. Add old yearbooks and memorabilia from high school such as letterman jackets, megaphones, trophies, and cheer uniforms. Ask your guests to bring old memorabilia that might fit this theme.

ACTIVITIES: Have each guest vote on the Prom King and Queen and plan a crowning dance. Dance contests are also fun and you can award funny socks or trophies to winners.

PARTY FAVORS: When guests arrive give each couple (dog and date) a matching glow necklace. Personalize it with a charm and their name. Another nice touch is to make small corsages for guests and their dogs. These can be easily made by attaching small flowers to scrunchie hair ties or hot gluing plastic flowers onto 1" wide satin ribbons. Don't forget to grab crowns for your Prom King & Queen.

SPIKED PROM PUNCH

Prep Time: 10 minutes
Serves 12 Adults & 12 dogs

It just wouldn't be prom without somebody spiking the punch. And while this punch is absolutely delish without alcohol, it can easily be spiked for some grownup fun!

INGREDIENTS FOR PUPS AND PEOPLE:

- 1 pint vanilla ice cream (may substitute for non-dairy coconut, almond, oat milk ice cream too)
- 1 14oz can chilled coconut milk
- 4 medium strawberries (for garnish)
- Small paper cups, ramekins, or shot glasses for dogs
- Paper straws themed colors

INGREDIENTS FOR PUPS:

- 12oz beef or chicken bone broth

INGREDIENTS FOR PEOPLE:

- 1 liter chilled cola or root beer
- 1 bottle rum (My favorite is Malibu)

DIRECTIONS FOR PUPS AND PEOPLE:

1. In a large pitcher add coconut milk, and ice cream rolled into small spoon-sized scoops.
2. Pour ⅓ pitcher into a new pitcher for dogs.

DIRECTIONS FOR PUPS:

1. Take the new pitcher with ⅓ mixture, add bone broth and serve small, 2-4 Tbsp amounts to pups in small paper ramekins or shot glasses.
2. Garnish with strawberry slices.

DIRECTIONS PEOPLE:

1. Take the new original pitcher and add 1 liter of soda. Mix well.
2. Have shot glasses and a bottle of rum at the bar for spiking.

MAC & CHEESE BALLS (GLUTEN FREE)

Prep time: 30 minutes
Yields 32-36 bites

These meatball recipes are some of my favorites. Not only are they easy enough for your kids to help you make, they are always a crowd-pleaser. I've included two recipes since some folks (and their pups) are more sensitive to cheese and pasta. I recommend making a few extra to put in "doggy bags" and sending them home with guests.

INGREDIENTS FOR PUPS AND PEOPLE:

- 1 ½ cups dry (gluten free) macaroni noodles
- 2 Tbsp butter
- 3 Tbsp coconut flour
- 1 ½ cups milk, or goat's milk kefir 2 cups shredded cheddar cheese
- 2 oz cream cheese
- ½ tsp sea salt *Not in dog only recipe
- 4 grinds black pepper *Not in dog only recipe
- 2 eggs beaten
- ½ cup bacon crumbles
- ¼ cup dry gluten-free bread crumbs
- May use freeze-dried raw food if using strictly for dogs

DIRECTIONS FOR PUPS AND PEOPLE:

1. Preheat oven to 400°F.
2. Cook macaroni according to the package. Drain and set aside.
3. Spray mini muffin tin with cooking oil and coat each cup with breadcrumbs or raw food that is crumbled into a powder.
4. Melt butter, adding flour and stirring until smooth. Slowly add milk and simmer.
5. Add shredded cheese (reserving ½ cup), cream cheese, salt and pepper. Mix until smooth and melted. Remove from heat.
6. Add pasta, eggs and bacon. Mix thoroughly.
7. Spoon mixture into muffin tin. Sprinkle with remaining cheese.

TIP: I would make a batch for dogs and send extras home with guests. Or you can freeze extras for future dog treats. I think all the human ones will be eaten!

MEATBALL APPETIZERS (GLUTEN FREE)

Prep time: 1 hour
Yields 20 bites

INGREDIENTS FOR PUPS AND PEOPLE:

- 1 pound ground turkey/lamb or beef
- ¾ cup cooked quinoa/brown rice or oats
- ¾ cup finely chopped broccoli or carrots
- ½ tsp oregano
- 1 egg

DIRECTIONS FOR PUPS AND PEOPLE:

1. Preheat oven to 375°F.
2. In a bowl, combine all ingredients.
3. Form small, bite-sized balls with mixture and place on a greased baking sheet.
4. Bake for 20 minutes. Let cool for 10 minutes.

"Edible" BOW-WOW BROWNIES

Prep Time: 1 hour
Yields 36 small 2" brownies

Finally, a brownie that's delicious and safe for dogs to enjoy. We've all heard about those "edible" brownies that sometimes make their way to prom; well by adding a few drops of CBD, you can make this "edible" treat into a safe, functional, dessert for your pup.

INGREDIENTS FOR PUPS AND PEOPLE:

- ¼ cup coconut/olive oil
- 2 Tbsp honey
- 1 cup gluten-free coconut flour
- 4 eggs
- 1 tsp vanilla
- ½ cup carob chips
- ¼ cup carob powder
- 1 tsp baking powder
-

FROSTING INGREDIENTS:

- 12 oz cream cheese (softened)
- 1 tsp honey
- 1 tsp vanilla

DIRECTIONS FOR PUPS AND PEOPLE:

1. Preheat oven to 350°F.
2. In a medium sized bowl, blend oil and honey.
3. Add remaining ingredients and mix well.
4. Pour onto a greased 15x10 baking sheet.
5. Bake 30-35 minutes.
6. Cool and frost (if desired.)
7. FOR EDIBLES top with 1-2 drops CBD oil.

ICING DIRECTIONS:

1. Blend with a mixer.
2. Spread with spatula over pan of cooled brownies. Cut into 2' bites.

PUGS 101... A few crazy facts about this amazing breed.

PUG-ALICIOUS PUGS! Diamonds may be a girl's best friend, but for me, I'll take PUGS! As you can see, I'm OBSESSED! They are darling. They are hysterical. They tug at your heartstrings and just like that you're hooked and have to have one.

For those of you who are interested in adding a Pug to your family, I want to educate you on some important facts that should come with the buyer's manual on this special breed. While no two pugs are alike. there are some generalizations that tend to be SPOT ON:

Pugs have a variety of unique quirks that drive some people bonkers. They can be nosy, inquisitive, and often right underfoot. Most are tremendously and **dangerously food-driven** and will consume things that you don't consider edible. -I'm not kidding! They will eat poop, grass, rocks, coins, packaging, and basically anything they can get in their jaws around.

It is your most important job to pug-proof your home in order to avoid tragedy! I never trust a pug around any food source, garbage can, or even cabinets that they can reach. In my home, trash cans sit up high on cupboards, gates are installed, cabinets are locked, and chairs are pushed away from tabletops. If there's a possibility they can get where the food is, even a sedentary pug will muster up the energy to "table surf!" I have many ER vet bills to prove it. And it's not just tables. I've had contents of entire trash cans devoured. Things I never knew lived under the bed and old food left in a jacket pocket or a backpack have been devoured in a NY minute.

Pugs can easily get fat! No matter how much you feed them they will tilt their heads and act like they haven't eaten in a week. As cute as they look with their broad shoulders, thick necks, round faces, and barreled chests, it is really easy to let them get dangerously obese! Pugs in particular need the right amount of food for their activity level. You significantly shorten their lifespan and quality of life by letting them get obese. (See my blog "Dog Pounds" available on my website.)

Pugs are very sensitive. They have a lot of allergies with food sensitivities topping the list. Pugs must be fed a high-quality diet. Grocery store kibble won't cut it! You can avoid a host of future problems if you feed your pug wholesome, premium, food. Good nutrition is the number #1 way to promote health, lower vet bills, and give your pug a longer life.

Pugs are referred to as "multim in parvo" meaning "A lot of dog in a small space." Pugs are tough and pack a lot of punch in their compact bodies. They are confident and have no clue how small they are. While many people perceive pugs as goofy, dumb dogs. They aren't. In fact, most are extremely smart. Their outrageous food drive usually makes them fairly easy to train. They make amazing therapy and service dogs. You also won't find better sports about dawning costumes for photos and videos.

A high-maintenance breed. Don't get me wrong. I adore pugs, but they are, without a doubt, a high-maintenance breed. To say they need and want a lot of attention is an understatement! Pugs are and were bred for the sole purpose of being companion animals. They need people. If you're going to be gone for long periods of time and/or be too tired to engage with your pug when you get home from work, then a pug likely isn't the dog for you. Pugs are often referred to as a "VELCRO DOG" so if you don't want a pet that is going to be wherever you are all the time (including in the bathroom), then rethink getting a pug.

Pugs are one of the most affectionate, funny, and overtly loving breeds you can ever own. For me, and many others, they are simply the best dogs EVER! They're worth every bit of effort, expense, and time they require. But, I don't want anyone blindsided. I promise you these little clowns will provide hours of entertainment and completely melt your heart!

June

If you haven't figured it out by now, I am a very, VERY, proud dog mom. I never hold back when it comes to expressing my love for my pug. Between the events, parties, outfits, special meals, and pug memorabilia,my obsession is off the charts. That being said, believe it or not many people find pugs ugly. I have had more than one person comment on how pugs, with their flat, wrinkly faces, don't look like dogs. I've also had people shame me for dressing my pug. The worst was when a man screamed at me for not putting my first little pug, Raisin to sleep. He thought Raisin was too old once he was past his prime and needed wheels to get around.

That's the wonderful thing about dogs: there's a breed, mixed breed, size and shape for everyone. While some find pugs ugly, I'm obsessed with their wrinkly faces and funny personalities.

In my community, June is pride month. It's all about celebrating love and acceptance for all. That translates right over to our dogs. Anyone who has had a deep, meaningful relationship with their pet will completely understand. They bring so much joy to our daily lives. For many people all over the world, including veterans, abuse survivors, and those born with disabilities, dogs are sometimes the only thing that gives them the courage and motivation to move through their daily lives. To me, this unique and powerful bond is one that deserves to be celebrated.

Let's get this party started!

DOGGY PRIDE SUMMER SOIRÉE

I live in Long Beach, California. It's a port town between Los Angeles and San Diego. We are known for lots of fun places to eat, Long Beach State University, The Queen Mary Ocean Liner, and of course Long Beach Pride! One thing I love about Long Beach is what a dog friendly place it is. Another thing I love about the LBC is the diversity. The entire month of June, the city embraces Pride Month. Streets are decorated with colorful flags and it's full of happy energy. There's weekend-long, back-to-back celebrations including parades, concerts, street fairs, and other pride events. Dogs are out in full force as well. They're dressed to the 9's and 10's in the colors of the rainbow and these hounds are ready to party. This month, wherever you live, grab your friends, family, and DOGS and get your pride on!

MENU

Watermelon Barkaritas 🥄 **Avocado Toast** 🥄 **Chicken Lollipops** 🥄 **Rainbow Pupsicles**

TIPS: Plan your party around the peak heat of the day which may be too hot for pups. I like to do a late afternoon or early evening event to keep dogs from overheating. If you are including pools with water make sure someone is assigned to supervise because dogs can drown in very shallow bodies of water.

INVITES: "COME SHOW YOUR PRIDE AND TRUE COLORS" Send colorful, glittery rainbow invitations to all your friends. Invite them to come show their pride and chill on a hot summer day. The more rainbows and colors they wear the better.

DÉCOR: Go crazy with rainbows. Grab a few plastic kiddie pools and fill them with beach balls and ball-pit plastic balls and water for the dogs. If your yard is large enough, have a sprinkler section to cool off. Set up your yard with beach towels, lounge chairs, beach balls, umbrellas and outdoor games. Offer plenty of puppy bowls with water around the outside area. I recommend setting up your food table indoors unless you have a large yard and it won't get in the way of the outdoor fun.-Don't forget trash cans with secure lids and plenty of poop bags. Set up a photo station with a RAINBOW PRIDE banner and snap a picture of each guest with their pup! Even better, try and capture a group photo of everyone.

PARTY FAVORS: Have rainbow pride bandanas for all your guests and their dogs to wear at the party and take home. Send dogs home with small packets of bone broth or dog treats in cellophane bags with rainbows.

WATERMELON BARKARITAS

Prep Time: 15 minutes
Serves 24 dogs

Yummmm! Who doesn't love a cold margarita on a hot summer day? You will love this refreshing twist on an old favorite. Watermelon is a superfood. It is 92% water and a great way to rehydrate. Their pretty red color comes from the powerful antioxidant lycopene. In fact it contains more than any other fruit or vegetable including tomatoes. Lycopene is great for eye health as well as reducing inflammation, and cutting the risk of cancer and diabetes. Watermelon is also a great source of vitamins B-6, and C, potassium and fiber. Just remember to remove all the seeds which may cause an intestinal blockage if swallowed.

INGREDIENTS FOR PUPS AND PEOPLE:

- 1 14oz box chicken/turkey or beef bone broth (DOGS)
- 1 ½ cups cubed watermelon
- 1 quart coconut water
- 8 small watermelon wedges for garnish
- Small plastic margarita cups for dogs
- Paper straws in rainbow primary colors
- Hemp & chia seeds (for rim)
- ½ tsp Himalayan salt (humans)
- 1 lime sliced for garnish (humans)
- ½ cup fresh lime juice (humans)
- 1-2 Tbsp confectioners' sugar (humans)
- 1 cup tequila (humans)
- ½ cup orange liqueur (humans)
- 3 cups ice cubes

DIRECTIONS FOR PUPS:

Tip: Bone broth can be frozen into cubes ahead of time to speed the drink making process the day of.

1. Pour bone broth into 2 ice cube trays. Fill ½ way and freeze.
2. When bone broth has frozen, pop cubes, ½ cup cubed watermelon, coconut water in a blender and blend.
3. Sprinkle a plate with chia & hemp seeds.
4. Dip each small glass in frozen mixture then tap into seeds.
5. Fill each glass, add a bite-sized spear of watermelon and serve.

DIRECTIONS FOR PEOPLE:

1. Rinse blender, combine the cubed watermelon, tequila, lime juice, orange liqueur, sugar, salt, and ice cubes in a blender. Blend until smooth.
2. Divide among glasses, garnish each with lime & melon spear.

AVOCADO TOAST

Prep Time: 10-15 minutes
Yields 12 human pieces/8 dog bites

This simple recipe makes a perfect snack that dogs can enjoy too! Avocado is delicious healthy fat that is wonderful for your skin and hair. It's also great for your dog's coat.

INGREDIENTS FOR PUPS AND PEOPLE:

- 4 large organic avocados (should yield a bit to a gentle squeeze)
- Juice from ½ lemon (remove any seeds)
- Juice from 1 lime (remove seeds)
- 1 Tbsp salsa
- ¼ tsp salt and pepper
- 4 slices gluten free or bread of choice or
- 8 small plain rice cake rounds
- 1 cup organic mixed greens (washed thoroughly and thinly sliced)
- ¼ cup balsamic vinegar
- 8 small organic cherry tomatoes sliced
- Chia seeds to garnish

DIRECTIONS FOR PUPS:

1. Take one large avocado, peel, remove the pit and cut out any brown spots.
2. Cut in cubes and place in a bowl. Mash against the bowl with a fork.
3. When creamy and smooth, spread on rice cake round or gluten-free toast.
4. Top with thinly sliced mixed greens and drizzle with vinegar.
5. Top with small cherry tomato slice and chia seeds.

DIRECTIONS FOR PEOPLE:

1. Toast bread until golden brown and crunchy.
2. Peel and remove the pit from avocados. Cut out any brown spots.
3. Cut in small cubes and place in a bowl.
4. Add lemon and lime juice, salsa, salt and pepper.
5. Spread mixture onto bread and slice into 4 triangles or 3 slices.
6. Top with thinly sliced mixed greens & tomato slices.
7. Drizzle with vinegar and seeds.

CHICKEN LOLLIPOPS FOR DOGS

Prep Time: 10 min. Cook time 20 minutes
Yields 12-15 lollipops

Here's an easy and super healthy snack for your pup. Don't be surprised if they are begging like crazy to get their paws on these. Feel free to use another variety of cheese such as cottage cheese and reduce the bone broth slightly for consistency. These lollipops may be stored in an airtight container in the fridge for up to a week. They can also be frozen and reheated.

INGREDIENTS FOR PUPS:

- 1 cup dehydrated raw dog food broken into fine powder (I like Nulo chicken)
- ¼ cup diced chicken
- 3 tbsp sharp cheddar cheese
- 1 large free-range egg beaten
- 1 cup unsalted bone broth
- 5 paper straws to use as sticks

DIRECTIONS FOR PUPS:

1. Preheat oven to 350°F.
2. Hydrate dog food by adding bone broth and stir.
3. Mix all remaining ingredients into a batter.
4. Spoon the mixture into cherry sized balls and place on a greased baking sheet. Flatten slightly with back of a spoon.
5. Bake at 350°F for 20 minutes.
6. Cut straws into 3rds and place one straw on the end of each piece to make a lollipop.
7. Cool & serve.

*In addition to labeling, make dog lollipops slightly smaller or use different colored straws to avoid guests being confused which ones are for dogs and which ones are for people.

CHICKEN LOLLIPOPS FOR HUMANS

Prep Time: 40 min
Yields 28-30 lollipops

Here is a safer version of the traditional chicken lollipops. The last thing you need is a dog swallowing a chicken bone after they accidentally grab the wrong lollipop at the party. These are very easy to make and a big crowd pleaser - without sending anyone to the vet with their dog.

INGREDIENTS FOR PEOPLE:

- 1 lb ground chicken
- 3 cloves minced garlic
- 1 egg whisked
- 3 Tbsp gluten free breadcrumbs
- 2 tsp Worcestershire sauce
- 1 tsp hot paprika
- 1 tsp onion powder
- 1 tsp chopped fresh oregano (about 1 sprig)
- 5 sprigs chopped fresh thyme
- 1 tsp brown sugar
- 1 lemon zested
- Kosher salt and ground black pepper
- 1 Tbsp unsalted butter
- 1 Tbsp extra virgin olive oil
- 10 paper straws cut into 3rds for lollipop sticks

DIRECTIONS FOR PEOPLE:

1. In a large bowl, gently mix chicken, garlic, onion powder, oregano, thyme, brown sugar, lemon zest, 2 healthy pinches of salt and 4 grinds of pepper.
2. Form into mini meatballs slightly smaller than a golf ball.
3. Add seasoned lollipops to egg mixture. Lightly coat each one then roll in breadcrumbs. Flatten with the back of a spoon.
4. In a large pan, warm butter and oil over medium heat. Transfer lollipops to pan and let them brown for 3 minutes without disturbing.
5. Keep cooking until golden brown and crispy on the outside but still juicy and plump with a spring to the touch.
6. Transfer to a paper towel and blot. Poke each lollipop with straw for the lollipop stick.

*Once prepared, separate dog lollipops from human lollipops by using different colored straws and labeling the serving plates.

RAINBOW PUPSICLES

Prep Time: 5 minutes plus 2 hours to freeze
Serves 6 large popsicles & 12 dog pops

WOW! Not only are these beautiful to look at, this healthy dessert is low on sugar and big on taste. Use fruits in season to make a rainbow of fun. Other than the freezing time, these take a quick 5 minutes to make and are loaded with vitamin C, potassium and magnesium. Great for staying hydrated and reducing muscle aches from all that dancing. And they almost look too pretty to eat.

INGREDIENTS FOR PUPS AND PEOPLE:

Choose fruits from the ideas below to make a rainbow of color.

- RED: Strawberries/raspberries/watermelon
- ORANGE: mandarin oranges/mango
- YELLOW: banana/pineapple
- GREEN: Kiwi (**Do not use grapes for dogs**)
- BLUE: Blueberries/blackberries
- Popsicle molds/Ice cube trays for Pups
- 1 Quart coconut water (you may use a flavored variety but choose one without added sugar)

DIRECTIONS FOR PEOPLE:

1. Chop fruit by color into small, popsicle sized chunks.
2. Place fruit into mold, stacking in the colors of the rainbow.
3. Pour coconut water into mold and tap lightly on the counter to release any air bubbles.
4. Insert popsicle mold sticks and place in the freezer until frozen.

DIRECTIONS FOR PUPS:

1. Fill small candy molds or ice cube trays with each color of the rainbow. If the molds are too small for all of the colors, do 2 fruits. Or make a tray of each fruit.
2. Add a splash of coconut water and freeze.

Just five minutes to make and are loaded with vitamin C, potassium and magnesium!

Dog Days of Summer

IT'S THE DOG DAYS OF SUMMER!

I live at the beach in Southern California and we have beautiful beach weather year-round. In the summer, my quaint seaside community turns into a noisy, busy, popular destination that attracts families like a fruit platter attracts flies. I like living here in the summer as much as I like a parking ticket and prefer to leave and return in the fall when I have it all to myself again.

And then there's the big 4th of July holiday. Here at the beach, we have fireworks exploding nightly from Memorial Day through Labor Day. It's A LOT for the poor dogs that live here.

Several years ago, before it was even a "thing," I wrote a blog about the astounding results I was seeing in dogs using CBD oil to keep them calm during the 4th of July fireworks. And that was just the tip of the iceberg. Arthritic pets, pets with seizures, anxiety, psychosis, depression, end-of-life issues, trauma, even cancer, and metabolic diseases were all seeing unbelievable results from CBD oil.

In a very short amount of time, CBD and hemp products have gone from underground to the hot new thing! What was once only a handful of established companies selling CBD pet products, is now a booming market with everyone including Martha Stewart and Snoop Dog in the CBD business.

If all this "buzz" (-pun intended) about CBD has you confused and apprehensive, let me clarify all the important things you need to know.

When I first heard the words "HEMP", "CBD" & "CANNABIS", the thing that came to mind was getting "high" and I got scared. I would never want to turn my little pugs into "pot-heads" and have CBD cause more excessive sleeping and binge snacking. I was extremely reluctant and apprehensive about using them.

Once I turned to my trusted, holistic/integrated vets for some clarification, I realized I was way off base. These vets have been using CBD successfully for some time and straightened out my misconceptions.

WEEDING THROUGH THE HYPE!

In a very short amount of time, CBD and hemp products have gone from underground to the hot new thing! What was once only a handful of established companies selling CBD pet products, is now a booming market with everyone including Martha Stewart and Snoop Dog in the CBD business.

What is CBD anyway? All mammals have an endocannabinoid system which is located in the brain and central nervous system. It's crucial for establishing and maintaining health. Among its many functions are regulating memory, metabolism, immunity, sleep, mood, appetite, and pain sensation. CBD (short for cannabinoids) act on any imbalance in these various receptors in the body. They create balance and provide the support needed for relaxing, repairing, or restoring any deficiencies in the body.

There are many varieties of cannabis plants with hemp and marijuana being two popular ones. These plants contain, THC (tetrahydrocannabinol) which is a "psychoactive" cannabinoid that produces the "high." Dogs naturally have an abundance of receptors in their brains and are therefore extremely sensitive to THC. So much so that should your pet get into your stash of edibles it could make them gravely ill.

That put the fear of God into me about ever giving my pet CBD until I was informed pet CBD is NON-PSYCHOACTIVE, meaning it contains NO THC. They are 100% non-toxic and safe. So, you get all the relaxation without intoxication. And now they've become mainstream health-boosting, miracle workers.

HOW CBD CAN HELP YOU & YOUR DOG! - THE ABC's

A's-

ANXIETY: CBD has been extensively studied for its amazing effect on stress, anxiety, and noise phobias. I couldn't believe how great it worked on dogs who would typically go off the charts ballistic on the 4th of July. With CBD they were calm and content. It also worked miracles on Olive. Although she has no issues with the 4th of July, car rides and nail trims were a whole different story. These caused such extreme stress and anxiety she would vomit, drool, and shake even after trying nearly every anti-anxiety drug and natural supplement. Now after taking CBD, she relaxes and has no problem.

I have also witnessed amazing results with frantic barking dogs in animal shelters or suffering from separation anxiety. It's the perfect remedy for anxious dogs visiting the vet, having nail trims, or dental procedures! And it's not just for your pets. CBD can be a tremendous help for those suffering from panic disorders, PTSD, and anxiety. Best of all there are NO SIDE EFFECTS.

APPETITE: I know many cancer patients taking medical marijuana to increase appetite, and now CBD is found to also work wonderfully. Not only with cancer but for many illnesses and aging. So if you're having trouble getting your pet to eat, try some CBD to help stimulate their appetite.

ANTIOXIDANT: With natural antibiotic properties, CBD protects the brain from cell death caused by free radicals and toxins. It's a great anti-aging supplement.

AUTOIMMUNE DISEASES: CBD has been shown to decrease the production and release of inflammatory cytokines that can cause allergies and a wide range of autoimmune conditions.

B's-

BRAIN HEALTH:

CBD can help with neurodegenerative diseases: For dogs suffering from spine and nerve issues, CBD shows a lot of promise. CBD fights free radicals that cause aging and helps repair dying brain cells.

CBD can treat seizures and epilepsy: I know so many pugs (and other breeds of dogs) suffering from seizures. Most dogs are put on strong drugs such as phenobarbital and potassium bromide. While they may help control the seizures, they can be extremely harmful to your dog's liver and other organs. And the drugs don't work in all cases. CBD has been working well in about 15 dogs I personally know. Dogs went from such frequent seizures they were considering having them euthanized until CBD cut the frequency from hourly to monthly! I am SO excited about this and hope more people will look into this option for their pets suffering from seizures.

C's-

CHRONIC INFLAMMATION/PAIN RELIEVER: CBD inhibits the production of inflammatory macrophages and decreases chronic inflammation. I've seen over 20 dogs, unable to walk without assistance or limping, bounce back quickly after using CBD. It works so well for pain that scientists are considering them a new class of drugs for the treatment of chronic pain.

CANCER: With its anti-tumor effect, CBD has even been shown to stop cancer cells from growing and increased tumor cell death. This is HUGE! Cancer is the #1 threat facing our pets with 2 out of 3 dogs getting cancer in their lifetime. How exciting to have this promising new option that is affordable and doesn't have the horrible side effects of most conventional treatments.

CBD is legal, safe & non-toxic: Because CBD oil for pets contains no THC, all 50 states have now approved the use of hemp-based CBD for human and animal products. With so many studies showing the health benefits of CBD, the most encouraging result is that CBD is completely safe, even when taken in high doses and over extended periods of time. CBD is non-toxic and animals don't appear to build up a tolerance.

Choosing A High Quality CBD Oil

I'm sure you're excited to race out and purchase some of this magic CBD oil but I urge you to do your research first! With any product that has this kind of results and interest, you must be very mindful. Not all CBD oils are the same and with minimal regulation, you must be extremely careful. Here are a few things to look for:

1. Check the sourcing: Only use companies that farm without the use of pesticides, fungicides, or solvents.

2. Get the analysis: Ask the manufacturer for a lab analysis of the amount of CBD in the product as well a certificate of analysis. Many CBD products contain only small amounts of poor-quality CBD. You'll also want to make sure there is no THC in the product.

3. Don't shop based only on the price: This isn't a product where you want to be pinching pennies. Don't bargain hunt with CBD. It's plain and simple, the higher the quality and purity, the more expensive it usually is. Make sure the quality is human grade, organically grown, and has good ratios of CBD. Make sure the results are verified by an outside analysis.

4. For serious/chronic conditions use CBD in a tincher. You can buy CBD in treats, but I recommend you use a dropper bottle first. This way, you can adjust your dog's dose drop by drop to make sure they get the most benefit. Then you can supplement with treats or use treats sparingly and adjust your pet's dosage. You also will have the advantage of using the drops topically which is great for sore joints, abrasions, and injuries. CBD is absorbed far more quickly when given this way.

While there are several excellent CBD companies, my favorite is BAILEY'S CBD. Not only do I use their amazing dog CBD products, like the CBD shampoo, paw & nose balm, and soft chew treats, I use many of their products daily to manage my own autoimmune disease. All products use only the highest quality, human-grade, ingredients. CBD is grown and hand farmed by Moon Farms of Colorado. They actually do reiki and bless their CBD crops. Every product is put through extensive testing for purity and potency by a 3rd party medical lab. The analysis can be pulled up by a QR code on each product label. Bailey's is formulated by a veterinarian and each product is gluten-free. Products are also vegan, non-GMO, and certified organic. When you use Bailey's CBD, you can be sure you're getting a premium product. I love supporting this wonderful family-owned business. Best of all, they are PUG OWNERS!

I enjoy CBD myself when flying (no anxiety and no hangover!) and I give CBD treats to Olive as a healthy snack. I also give them to friends who are trying to use more natural pain relief methods for everything from chronic pain management to mensural cramps. And it's perfect for relaxing and dozing off to sleep at night.

BAILEY'S
VETERINARIAN FORMULATED
FULL SPECTRUM
HEMP CBD
600MG PER BOTTLE
10MG PER ML
PLANT-BASED CANNABINOIDS
NET WT. 2OZ (60ML)
WE SET THE STANDARD
PETS OVER PROFITS
SAFE & NON-INTOXICATING
ARTISANAL QUALITY
SMALL FARM SOURCED
HAND HARVESTED HEMP
RESCUE AWARENESS

July

No other holiday sends chills up the spines of dog owners like the 4th of July. For many, it may very well be the worst day of the year. I must admit, when it comes to Independence Day, I'm right up there with most dogs. I like this holiday as much as I like a parking ticket. Huge crowds of drunk, disorderly people invade my little beach community, and it becomes a loud, crazy, war zone. Ironically, my little Pug Olive, who's frightened of her own shadow, has no problem with fireworks. I'm typically the one who is under the bed eating CBD treats, wearing my noise-canceling headphones chilling out. Good news! Here are my SURE-FIRE, "tried & true" "red, white & blue" tips for surviving the 4th! I've utilized these tips to show you how to create your own fun, dog-friendly 4th of July party as well.

PLAN AHEAD:

Let's start with your dog. If they have exhibited "off-the-chart" anxiety that would be more than even Cesar Millan could conquer -PLAN AHEAD! I recommend if you can't stay with your dog, you consider making a reservation to board your dog overnight in a sound-proof facility. I know most facilities book quickly for this holiday (many are reserved a year in advance!) so call NOW!!! Hopefully you'll get lucky and find availability.

If boarding isn't going to work, look into hiring a pet-sitter to stay with your anxious dog. Be safe, and either take your dog to their home (preferably somewhere that has minimal firework activity), or find someone to dog-sit at your place.

Don't delay, stock up now! Whether you're staying with your dog, boarding them, or getting a pet-sitter, I recommend looking in stores or online for the following items that help with anxiety:

- **CBD:** The very best defense I have found for firework anxiety is CBD. These treats, oils, and capsules have been a game-changer for fearful dogs. Not all CBD products are as potent or sourced as stringently so you must do your research. CBD works MIRACLES on a variety of issues including firework anxiety and has ZERO side effects.
- **New Toys & Treats:** Grab an arsenal of brand new toys and treats. I like to fill a Kong with some canned and dry turkey dog food. If it's a hot day, I pop the filled Kong in the freezer for 30 minutes. I give the dog this yummy treat right when the fireworks are beginning. The tryptophan in the turkey acts as a natural sleep inducer and will help relax your anxious dog. Often the dog is so focused on their stress-relieving chew, they forget about the fireworks. Other great options are rope toys made of hemp, or toys containing pheromones, and other calming herbs. Most pet stores have a great selection of "calming toys" to choose from.

Check their microchip/ ID tag: Did you know more pets go missing or end up in shelters during the 4th of July holiday than at any other time during the year? It's crucial to check your dog's ID tag and micro-chipping (your vet can scan and confirm your contact information is up-to-date and it's working.) If your dog's collar is loose, getting worn out, or the contact number is hard to read, get a new one! That way, God-forbid your dog goes missing, your chances of being reunited are much more likely.

ON THE 4th:

Begin the day by getting plenty of exercise. It will no doubt be crowded, but try and get out early before the heat and craziness kicks into high gear. Even an older dog can go for a nice, long, albeit slow, walk. Or, for less mobile dogs, a long stroll in a wagon is perfect! Taking them out in the fresh air and sunshine will get their adrenaline going, get their heart rate up, and best of all, tire them out. Hopefully, they will sleep like a baby later on.

When fireworks begin, distract your pet from the "bombs bursting in air" noise by engaging them with interactive play. Many people baby and pamper their frightened pets. This only encourages fearful behavior. Instead, snap them out of this state by grabbing a toy and playing chase, or tossing a toy and telling them to go fetch.

Set up a "calming zone" in a quiet place with your dog's bed, a covered crate, a diffuser containing lavender oil, pheromones (hormones found to reduce stress and anxiety.) Add a few new toys. Don't let your dog have access to this area until the evening gets going. Toys will be a new and exciting distraction from fireworks. Try to drown out firework noise with the TV or music. If it's still too loud, maybe move this spot to the bathroom and run a warm bubble bath. (Never leave a pet unattended around a tub of water!)

THE LAST RESORT:

If you must leave your dog, and can't hire anyone to pet-sit, put your pet in their calming area and put on classical music which has shown to reduce stress in dogs. There are several great stress-relieving music sources for canines if you search online. I love doing Houndbath/ Soundbaths. Try and stay with your pet until they are relaxed and calm. Follow the tips above, remembering to exercise them and give them CBD before you leave.

Make sure pets are left in a secure place and can't escape. Before leaving: always double and triple-check all windows, doors, and gates. (When in a state of panic, dogs can scale walls and achieve other miraculous feats.) If possible, use a camera to check on your dog while you're away. It's not an ideal time to leave them alone, and depending on the stress level, I would only do this as a last resort for a very short amount of time.

Whether you choose to throw a party or just try and get through the holiday, these suggestions will hopefully allow YOU AND YOUR PUP to enjoy a stress-free "Safe & Sane" Fourth of July.

let's get this party started!

DOG BLESS AMERICA 4th of JULY PAWTY

MENU

Red, White & Blueberry Mojitos 🥄 CBD Infused Patriotic Toast 🥄 Turkey Burgers 🥄 Watermelon Stars

TIPS: Your friends with dogs will be thrilled to have a dog-inclusive way to spend this holiday. Perhaps you can start some new "dog-friendly" traditions. Gather all your dog friends over for a mid-day celebration. Wear out the pups and send them home to hopefully relax and not be disturbed by all the fireworks. For an evening party, bring everyone inside and create a ZEN ROOM for a calming experience instead of the typical fireworks.

RED, WHITE and BOOM PAWTY: See if a trainer or friend can come assist with doing agility or a calming sound bath for your guests and their dogs. Instead of spending top dollar sending your dog to a sound-proof shelter, being around other dogs in a safe, calm, fun environment may be just what they need to get through the night.

DÉCOR & ACTIVITIES: For starters, go crazy decorating with all the traditional red, white, and blue decor. Dollar Tree and discount stores have lots to choose from. Add a playlist of patriotic music. If you have enough outdoor space, set up an obstacle course where dogs can practice drills. Use your imagination. A few simple things dogs can jump over, crawl under and walk along should do fine. Have a trainer teach skills to the dogs to tire them out. Older dogs can go on a sniffari. Hide a few odds and ends in your yard and see what dogs can track them. For an evening experience, set up a ZEN ROOM by closing blinds, turning on soft lights, (salt lamps are perfect) and throwing cozy pillows, blankets and dog beds around for everyone to get comfy. Drown out firework noise with classical music or better yet, hire someone to do a calming sound bath. If that's not an option, check out some free meditations on YouTube or another meditation app. Spritz dogs and humans with calming essential oils such as lavender and CBD. Another great touch is to borrow or purchase a small fountain for tranquil, relaxing water sounds. With everyone together in a calm and relaxed state, even normally high strung dogs should get through the holiday with ease. It may be the best 4th of July yet.

PARTY FAVORS: Have plenty of CBD handy and offer it generously. Make small favors with CBD treats. For brands I use that offer small sample-size packages, check my website **www.weeklyrunt.com**.

RED, WHITE & BLUEBERRY MOJITOS

Prep Time: 10 minutes
Makes 1 pitcher (about 5 drinks) / 6 dog sized drinks

This is a favorite drink of mine and at just 130 calories per drink, it has a lot less sugar than most other fancy cocktails. Not only is it very patriotic looking, the best part is that all the berries are filled with antioxidants. Coconut water is a healthy mixer loaded with nutrients and four times as much potassium as a banana. Just wait until you have a sip of these delicious drinks! They're sure to set off fireworks!

INGREDIENTS FOR PUPS AND PEOPLE:

- 2 large limes cut into 8 slices each (humans)
- 40 fresh mint leaves
- 4 Tbsp fresh blueberries
- 5 large strawberries sliced
- 6 oz Malibu Rum (humans - optional)
- 2 cups coconut water
- 1 can sparkling water or Sprite (humans)
- crushed ice

DIRECTIONS FOR PUPS AND PEOPLE:

1. Put lime slices and 30 mint leaves into a pitcher. Muddle together until limes have released their juices and mint is broken down.
2. Add 3 Tbsp blueberries & 3 strawberries.
3. Muddle again until fruit is broken down but still slightly chunky.
4. Put remaining berries in another pitcher for dog drinks and muddle with 10 remaining mint leaves.
5. Fill pitchers with crushed ice. Add ½ cup coconut water to the dog pitcher, 1½ cups of coconut water to the pitcher for the humans.

Follow steps below:

DIRECTIONS FOR PUPS:

1. Take the dog pitcher with ⅓ mixture and serve small, 2-4 tbsp amounts to pups in small paper ramekins or shot glasses.

DIRECTIONS FOR PEOPLE:

1. Add rum (optional), and a can of sparkling water or soda.
2. Top each drink with a mint sprig and berries.

CBD INFUSED PATRIOTIC TOAST

Prep Time: 10 minutes
Makes 8 slices / 12 dog sized snacks

For a simple recipe even the kids can prepare, look no further. This healthy snack is a tasty favorite. It's so creative and patriotic too! I would make these just before the party begins so the bananas don't turn brown from sitting out.

INGREDIENTS FOR PUPS AND PEOPLE:

- 12 slices bread of choice
- 4 large bananas
- 1 container fresh blueberries
- 1 container soft cream cheese
- I jar strawberry jam or jelly
- CBD oil for dogs

DIRECTIONS FOR PEOPLE:

1. Lightly toast bread. While bread is toasting, slice bananas lengthwise into small circles then cut each circle in half. Divide blueberries into groups of 9 (for small bread slices) or 12.
2. Spread toast with a thin layer of cream cheese. In the upper left corner of toast, make a small square with rows of 3 or 4 blueberries across and 3 or 4 blueberries down.
3. Spread a thin layer of jam onto the toast not covered with the blueberry square.
4. Using the banana slices, make a small stripe lining the flat edge of the slice on the bottom of the toast. Leave a bit of space and make another row with banana slices running just under the blueberry square. Add approx. 2 banana slices next to blueberry square. This should resemble an American flag. Slice in an "X" to make 4 small sections for the dogs. Top each with 2 drops of CBD oil.

TURKEY BURGERS

Prep Time: 40 minutes
Makes 6-8 burgers plus 6-8 dog sized sliders

While most people prefer a beef burger, on this holiday there are several reasons I prefer to use turkey. Not only is this a leaner form of protein, but it also contains the amino acid tryptophan. Your body needs this essential mineral to make serotonin, which plays an important role in mood, sleep, learning, and appetite control. Did you know that the tryptophan in turkey is what causes everyone to feel sleepy after eating it? What you may not know is that tryptophan is also found in tomatoes. By using the sun dried version in this recipe, you will have a healthier and tastier twist on ketchup which is loaded with sugar. I encourage you to pile on healthy greens to bulk up the nutrition in your burger. This meal should help keep you and the dogs extra calm and relaxed during this often stressful holiday. The small amount of garlic is safe for dogs and can help ward off pesky summer fleas and mosquitos.

INGREDIENTS FOR PUPS AND PEOPLE:

- 2 lbs lean ground turkey
- 1 cup sun dried tomatoes in oil, chopped.
- 4 cloves of garlic, chopped
- 2 cups grated mature cheddar cheese
- 2 Tbsp dried Italian seasoning
- ¼ tsp turmeric
- Freshly ground pepper to taste
- For humans, add ½ tsp dried chili flakes
- 6-8 gluten-free ciabatta rolls

DIRECTIONS FOR PUPS AND PEOPLE:

(These can also be BBQ'd if you prefer.)

1. Preheat oven to 400°F.
2. Add all ingredients besides the ciabatta in a large bowl and mix well.
3. Divide mixture into 6-8 burgers and 6-8 smaller/slider-sized patties for dogs.
4. Place on a lightly greased cookie sheet with a slight lip around the edge to catch any juice from burgers.
5. Cook for approx. 30 minutes until burgers are cooked through and no longer pink in the middle.

- Burgers for humans may be served in gluten-free ciabatta rolls with pickles, mayonnaise, and all your favorite trimmings.
- For sensitive dogs, prepare ground turkey on it's own w/out seasonings, cheese, tomatoes, and garlic.

WATERMELON STARS

Prep Time: 10 minutes

Makes 16-20 stars depending on cookie cutter size

This refreshing light treat is fun and easy to make. It's always a favorite with dogs on hot summer days. Loaded with essential vitamins and minerals, it's been shown to improve eye health, lower blood pressure, and the magnesium can help relieve muscle soreness. After an exciting day with lots of running around, this treat will be a perfect remedy.

INGREDIENTS FOR PUPS AND PEOPLE:

- Star-shaped cookie cutter (may want to use a large one for humans and small one for the dogs)
- 1 large seedless watermelon
- 24 large blueberries
- 1 can coconut whipped cream (or regular)

DIRECTIONS FOR PUPS AND PEOPLE:

1. Cut watermelon into 2" width slices. Lay flat and use a cookie cutter to punch out star shapes with the meat.
2. Top with a circle of whip cream in the center of the star and add a single blueberry to the middle of each star on the whip cream. Serve on a white platter.

August

AHHHHHH! It's the most wonderful time of the year! Back to school. Most parents are thrilled when it's time to wrap up the summer fun and send the kids back to the classroom. A new school year is a big and exciting milestone for kids. Dogs, however, do not get the fanfare they deserve for their educational milestones. Neither do their humans. Training is a big deal and so important to having a healthy and well-balanced relationship with your dog. That's why I think a Bark-to-School Party is just what pet parents need to stay motivated and feel supported when it comes to training their pups.

This Bark-to-School Party format can be used for celebrating the kids heading back to the classroom as well as for pups beginning training or graduating with new obedience skills. Additionally, if your child has a special bond with their doggy like my daughter did, throwing a pet-inclusive back to school event for kids is a really fun way to spend a summer afternoon. Enjoy!

Let's get this party started!

BARK TO SCHOOL PAWTY

It's time to get back to school. Why not throw a last hurrah of summer and welcome in the fall. The weather is likely to still be warm so these simple spreads should work well. Ideally, this is a party held outdoors on a mild summer day. It's the perfect setting for lots of fun, active play for the dogs and guests. If you don't have a large yard (or any) and your outdoor space is limited, no worries! I've roped off driveways and made this work with very little outdoor space. I simply limit the number of dogs and guests. If you can't get a trainer to come out and teach some tricks to the dogs, you can provide a large jar of tennis balls and a basket of frisbee's for party favors that guests can use to play with their dogs at their leisure during or after the party.

MENU

Iced Chunky Monkey Puppaccinos • Assorted Finger Sandwiches • Apple Dippers

INVITES: *BEST IN CLASS.* I like to make a written invitation on brown butcher paper. I place it in a brown lunch bag (sometimes I add confetti.) I decorate the bag and seal it with apples, gold stars, and other school-themed stickers. Write addresses as if it were an over-sized envelope and deliver or pop in the mail. There's also lots of Evites you can use if that's easier. I think it's always fun for people to get a little something in their mailbox.

DÉCOR: Offer plenty of puppy bowls filled with water around the outside area. Put tennis balls and frisbees in a variety of colors, into a large bucket or basket. These can be used during the party and also make a great party favor for your four-legged guests. Set up a large table and use brown butcher paper as a tablecloth. Put out your spread of food and add small lunch-sized bags of chips, dog kibble sample bags, and decorative school supplies. Set up a photo station so you can capture a "bark-to-school" picture of each guest. Better yet, a group picture of everyone.

PARTY ACTIVITIES: Invite a dog trainer to give some tips and pointers to the party guests' dogs. Have prizes for dogs that master the skills the best. It's a great time to do fun games outdoors if you have the space. Try a corn-hole contest. Set up a ping-pong table if there's room. Or set up a large craft table and let each guest decorate a reusable lunch bag or lunch box. Fill it with school or office supplies like tape, post-its, pens, paperclips, and fun stickers.

PARTY FAVORS: Send pawty guests home with their decorated "doggy bags" or lunch boxes. These provide a perfect way to take home extra treats and party favors.

ICED CHUNKY MONKEY PUPPUCCINOS

Prep Time: 15 minutes 30 min. to chill
Serves 6 small drinks / 12 dog servings

This cookbook was nearly complete when my husband insisted this recipe be added. It's a drink he always orders from our favorite coffee house, and I figured out a way to make it into a healthier drink that I can also enjoy. My husband now prefers my drink. Not only is it much less expensive, it's a super healthy treat, loaded with protein. I recommend using the Coconut Cult Gelato, which is a coconut-based frozen dessert that 's loaded with billions of powerful gut-healthy probiotics. And just wait until you taste this! It's delicious! If you're making this to share with your dog, just swap the chocolate ingredients for peanut butter. I hope this will be your new fav iced drink.

INGREDIENTS FOR PUPS:

- ½ cup almond or coconut milk
- 1 Tbsp organic peanut butter (Make sure it doesn't contain Xylitol)
- ½ small banana sliced into rounds and frozen
- 1 Tbsp raw coconut flakes
- dash of turmeric
- dash of cinnamon
- 4 ice cubes or ¼ cup crushed ice
- Whipped cream (I use coconut whipped cream)

INGREDIENTS FOR PEOPLE:

- 6-8 shots espresso (humans)
- 1 cup milk (I use almond or coconut milk and would use this for dogs)
- 2 Tbsp organic protein powder (I use Vanilla Orgain or Trader Joes Vanilla Pea Protein)
- 1 Tbsp raw coconut flakes
- ½ small banana sliced into rounds and frozen
- 2 Tbsp Coconut Cult FudgesicleTriple Choco Honey Mama's Fudgesicle Coconut Gelato
- You can also use any chocolate ice cream you like.
- dash of turmeric
- dash of cinnamon
- 1 tsp vanilla extract
- 4 ice cubes or ¼ cup crushed ice
- Whipped cream (I use coconut whipped cream)

DIRECTIONS FOR PUPS:

1. Put milk, peanut butter, banana rounds, coconut flakes, and ice cubes into a blender and blend on high until creamy.
2. Pour 2-3 Tbsp servings into small cups or ice cube tray and freeze.
3. Top drinks with whipped cream and a dash of turmeric and cinnamon.

DIRECTIONS FOR PEOPLE:

1. Prepare espresso and put in freezer for 20-30 minutes to chill.
2. Put milk, protein powder, coconut flakes, frozen banana rounds, gelato, vanilla and ice into a blender and blend on high until mixed and creamy.
3. Pour mixture into small glasses. Top drinks with whipped cream and a dash of cinnamon and turmeric.

SANDWICH ASSORTMENT

Prep time: 30 minutes
Makes 32 assorted finger sandwiches

Nothing says "Back-to-School" like lunches packed with a favorite sandwich. These are some of the most popular varieties, with options for vegans and vegetarians. Feel free to improvise on any meat/cheese combo you like, and there is always PB&J! Or, depending on your guest's preferences, you may modify the number of sandwiches you make of each variety.

INGREDIENTS FOR PUPS AND PEOPLE:

- 16 slices of bread (Use a variety, including gluten-free)
- 8 mini rice cakes (plain)
- Mayonnaise and mustard as condiments
- Jar of dill pickles
- Assortment of lunch sized bags of chips
- Small can of Pate dog food (Dog's)
- Sardines/Anchovies (Dog's)

Ham & Cheese

- 6 Ham or other cold-cut meat slices
- 4 slices Swiss or other cheese varieties

Tuna Salad

- 1 can all white meat tuna
- 2 Tbsp mayonnaise
- 1 Tbsp sweet relish
- 1 Tbsp finely chopped apple bits

Combine all ingredients in a bowl, mix well.

Cucumber & Cream Cheese (A British Fav!)

- 1 large cucumber sliced thin in circles
- 1 package soft spreadable cream cheese

Cut crusts off bread and spread a thin layer of cream cheese on bread. Top with cucumber slices.

Cut sandwich in four small triangles by making and "X" in the full sandwich.

Hi-Roller Turkey, Avocado, Veggie Wrap

- 4 large wraps or tortillas
- 4 thin slices turkey breast
- 2 thin slices of cheddar cheese
- 1 package soft, spreadable cream cheese
- (may use from cucumber sandwich)
- 1 large avocado, peeled, pitted, and sliced
- 1 large carrot shredded

1. Spread cream cheese over wraps.
2. Cover with turkey slices.
3. Layer cheese slices over turkey.
4. Drizzle carrot shavings down the middle.
5. Place avocado slices down the middle.
6. Starting with one side of the wrap, tightly roll until it looks like an open ended burrito.
7. Slice into four sections.

FOR PUPS:

Use mini rice cakes or gluten-free bread and make open-faced sandwiches. I like to spread a canned pate dog food on small rice cakes, top with a sardine or anchovy and serve.

Dogs can also enjoy the human sandwiches.

FOR PEOPLE:

Cut sandwiches "X" diagonally to make 4 small triangles of each variety.

NO-BAKE APPLE DIPPERS DESSERT

Prep Time: 15 minutes
Serves 24 dippers / 12 dog servings

These delicious snacks are much easier to make and much healthier than candy apples. Another plus, this treat is loaded with fiber which helps digestion and keeps you feeling full longer. The nut butters are healthy fats, which are amazing for glowing skin and heart health. The best part is you can share these treats with your dog.

INGREDIENTS FOR PUPS AND PEOPLE:

- 6 small, red apples (I love organic honeycrisp)
- 1 jar organic, all natural peanut butter (double check it doesn't contain xylitol)
- 1 jar organic almond butter
- 1 bag gluten-free granola (Use a variety WITHOUT RAISINS) I like Kind peanut butter flavor
- cinnamon
- turmeric

DIRECTIONS FOR PUPS AND PEOPLE:

1. Wash and slice apples into 8 slices (Use an apple cutter to remove centers.)
2. Slightly warm butters in microwave or double boiler.
3. Dip half of each slice of apple in nut butter.
4. Dip buttered side into granola mix.
5. Dust with cinnamon & turmeric.
6. Chill in fridge until ready to serve.

Bark 2 School
IT'S GONNA BE OKAY

September

Let's face it, September is the last month of the year where our lives are not consumed by some kind of holiday madness. Everyone can enjoy the kickoff of football season and the kiddos going back to school! It's also an ideal time to get a good footing (or paw) in a solid health and wellness routine before we find ourselves surrounded by seasonal temptations. Speaking of temptations..."Pumpkin Spice" will be making its annual debut. This usually happens before I've packed away my summer whites or lost my glorious tan. Although here in Southern California the temperatures are still soaring and it seems a bit early, it doesn't matter once you learn what a nutritional powerhouse pumpkin is. And not just for you, but your fur babies as well. These amazing tidbits about Pumpkin are guaranteed to make you feel all lit up and warm inside.

I learned about the amazing superfood pumpkin when I was a new pug mom many years ago. I vividly remember coming home from a quick trip to the market. The second I walked in the door, I found my pug, Raisin, on top of my dining room table, devouring the contents of a gift basket like a ravenous grizzly bear. A dozen gourmet marshmallows were long gone, and he was halfway through a tin of Almond Roca (gold foil wrappers and all.)

I raced him to the vet, and after a thorough examination, they gave him the OK to return home. The vet advised me to add a few spoonfuls of pumpkin to his diet. Well, genius that I am, I raced into the nearest market and grabbed pumpkin pie filling! But it still worked like magic. Since that incident, canned pumpkin is now my secret weapon for tummy troubles. I recommend every pet parent stock up this time of year while it's readily available (and likely on sale.) I also recommend keeping a can or two in their cupboard year-round to be safe.

Canned pumpkin, along with pumpkin seeds, are incredible "superfoods!" These can be a healthy addition to your dog's regular diet as well as a perfect ingredient to use in treats. Just look at all the health benefits pumpkin can provide for you and your dog.

Urinary Tract Support: Veterinarians believe that the oils in the seeds and flesh of pumpkins support urinary health in dogs and cats. Anyone whose pet has had kidney or bladder stones (or the horror of both) can attest to how much suffering they cause. Regularly adding pumpkin to your pet's diet can help avoid this painful condition.

Digestion: Our furry friends need fiber to stay regular just like we do, and pumpkin is a great source. The benefits go both ways—diarrhea, as well as constipation, can be eliminated with just one or two tablespoons of plain pumpkin (not sweetened or spiced), fed to your pet daily until the condition has cleared.

Skin and Coat: The antioxidants and essential fatty acids in pumpkin seeds help moisturize your pet's skin and fur from the inside out. Although they may enjoy slurping down the fresh, slimy version, to be on the safe side, I toast and grind them down: Spread seeds evenly onto a baking sheet, lightly spray with coconut oil, roast in a 375°F oven for 5 or 10 minutes, and cool. Pop seeds into a coffee grinder and sprinkle ½ tsp over food or homemade treats.

Parasites: Tapeworms and other intestinal parasites become paralyzed by cucurbitacin, an amino acid in pumpkin seeds that acts as a natural de-worming agent. The most effective way to prepare seeds for this purpose is by grinding up fresh or properly preserved pumpkin seeds into a powder. Check with your vet on dosing, but I give a 20lb dog roughly 1/2 teaspoon twice a day.

Nutrition: Pumpkin flesh and seeds are loaded with beta-carotene, vitamin A, iron, potassium, magnesium, manganese, copper, and zinc. They also contain antioxidants, which may prevent some cancers from forming and help your pet stay healthy and young. Just don't overdo the portion sizes since minerals like iron and fat-soluble vitamins such as vitamin A can accumulate to unhealthy, even toxic, levels. Check with your vet, but a teaspoon per day is normally plenty for a 20lb dog..

Weight Loss: Obesity is a common issue that is even more dangerous for dogs than for humans. If your pooch can stand to drop a few pounds, mix their food with a tablespoon of canned pumpkin. The pumpkin fiber helps their tummy feel full, and they'll enjoy the new taste treat.

ALWAYS CONSULT with your veterinarian beforehand. Although pumpkin is quite safe and healthy for MOST dogs and cats, your vet will be able to recommend safe usage for your specific pet. Each animal is different and "one-size-does-NOT-fit-all."

Before you race out the door with your pooch to grab a few cans (and a Starbuck's Pumpkin Carmel Spiced Latte), consider this: the typical 13oz can of pumpkin contains around 29 tablespoons and lasts about a week in the refrigerator. Unless you're catering for a small shelter or pack of canines, this is too much pumpkin for one or two dogs to consume in a week.

To keep this bounty out of your garbage can, I suggest freezing extra in ice cube trays and pop out the cubes into a freezer bag. Thaw one out when you need it, mix with a spoon to blend any separation of water, and refrigerate the leftover pumpkin cubes to serve at your pet's next meal.

This month's delicious, seasonal recipes will not only keep everyone's belly happy and healthy, but should also be met with cheers!

What do you get when you drop a pumpkin?

Squash!

California
dmv.ca.gov

let's get this party started!

FALL "TAIL"-GATING PAWTY

Gather all your friends and their pups for a "tail-gating" pawty! Schedule the festivities during a favorite football game on TV! Try and mix your guests so you have a few people supporting each team. Encourage them to dress in their team's colors. Ask ahead for pizza topping ideas and maybe have a contest to see who can build the best new, original pizza. This menu features crowd-pleasing favorites. Using fresh, seasonal ingredients and "superfoods," dishes will not only taste amazing but will help ward off the colds and flus that always seems to come on with the change of seasons during the early fall.

MENU

Apple Cider 🥄 Make-Your-Own Pizza Bar 🥄 Healing Fall Stew 🥄 Pumpkin Mudd Pie

DÉCOR: Grab banners, pom-poms, and spirit items in the team colors. With butcher paper, line your buffet table and draw a football field on the paper. Buy some roll-up synthetic turf and place pizza toppings, food, and drinks on it! It might be fun to do a football pool or have prizes for those that predict the score and other highlights of the game. Do a team photo before everyone leaves.

ACTIVITIES: Start a football pool and have guests vote on a favorite team and/or point spread. Also, invite people to create unique pizzas and award prizes for the fan favorites.

PARTY FAVORS: I like to make up bandanas in my team's colors and give them to the party guests. You can add iron-on decals or paint them with markers to personalize them for your guests. Instead of handing out favors as the guests leave the party, give out bandanas when they arrive and have everyone wear them during the party.

APPLE CIDER

Prep Time: 10 minutes/4-6 hrs. to cook
Servings: 1 gallon of cider

It just wouldn't be fall without some apple cider. This beverage works well either heated up or chilled depending on what you're in the mood for. This recipe is unsweetened so it has far less sugar and carbs. You can add some honey or maple syrup if you want more sweetness. Apples are loaded with fiber, copper, potassium and vitamin C, so this is a very healthy, hydrating beverage for you and your dog. If you really want to go all-out, cut the tops off medium sized apples, scoop out the centers leaving about ¼" of apple and skin. Then fill them with cider and use them as cups.

INGREDIENTS FOR PUPS AND PEOPLE:

- 10 fresh apples (I use organic honeycrisp & pink lady)
- You may add honey or sweetener to more sour varieties of apples.
- 1 gallon filtered water
- 1 orange
- 2 cinnamon sticks
- A dash of ground cloves or 4-6 whole cloves

DIRECTIONS FOR PUPS AND PEOPLE:

1. Wash apples well and peel if they aren't organic.
2. Cut into thin slices and place in a slow cooker.
3. Wash orange and cut into 8 slices. Add to slow cooker.
4. Add spices.
5. Pour water into the slow cooker and turn on for 4-6 hrs. You can also simmer this on very low heat on the stove. This will make your house smell heavenly for the party.
6. Strain the apples, oranges and spices with mesh cloth or a thin strainer.
7. I like to place the cider in the fridge and serve it cold or mix it 50/50 with iced tea. On cooler days, you can enjoy as a warm drink.

MAKE-YOUR-OWN PIZZA BAR

Prep time: 30 minutes/Cook: 35 min.
Yields 4 small pies

Sure, you can always order in pizzas or grab frozen ones from the store, but why not let everyone have fun and get creative by making their own! This amazing crust will have everyone begging for the recipe. I bet nobody will notice the gluten is gone.

INGREDIENTS FOR PUPS AND PEOPLE:

- 1 cup warm water, about 110°F
- 1 Tbsp honey
- 1 ½ tsp instant yeast
- 1 ¼ cups gluten free 1:1 Baking Flour (I like King Arthur)
- ¼ cup almond flour
- 1 tsp baking powder
- ¼ tsp salt
- 1 Tbsp psyllium husk powder (don't skip this! It gives pizza a delicious crunch and texture.)
- 2 Tbsp olive oil

DIRECTIONS FOR PUPS AND PEOPLE:

1. Whisk to combine warm water, honey, and yeast in a glass measuring cup.
2. While the yeast is proofing for 3-4 minutes, combine the flour, baking powder, salt and psyllium husk powder in the bowl. Mix on low, slowly adding the yeast mixture and oil. Increase the speed to medium-high and beat for 3-4 minutes.
3. Using an oiled spatula, scrape the dough off the sides of bowl and form into a ball. Cover and let rise for 30 min.
4. Preheat the oven to 425°F. Oil a 12" cookie sheet press the dough into the pan making 4 small, round pizzas. The dough will shrink slightly as it bakes, so press it thin. Let dough rise for another 10 min.
5. Bake for 15-20 minutes. Remove from the oven. Set crusts out for guests to add their desired toppings. Bake for another 10 minutes and serve.

☠ **Dispose of yeast after use!**

This can be deadly if a dog gets into it!

TIPS: To keep things simple, I purchase pizza sauces at the store or from my favorite local Italian deli. Put a variety of sauces out on the table and label them. Offer a selection of cheeses and possibly a vegan option. Place bowls with toppings out on your spread and let guests build their own pizzas as well as one for their dog. **Most toppings are dog-friendly except the onions & garlic.** See who has the best new pizza creation. After guests have designed their pizzas, pop them back in the oven for 10 minutes.

PIZZA TOPPING IDEAS:

You may already have your own favorite pizza toppings, but for your dog, you may like to cut pies into quarters and consider swapping pizza sauce for a canned pate dog food to spread on the crust. I like Nulo duck pate.

For the topping, my dog Olive likes goat cheese crumbles and anchovies, You could also add crumbled dog kibble and/or Raw Toppers (Nulo is the best with amazing probiotics). Pizza is a perfect way to introduce new superfoods and flavors to your dog's diet.

Make sure pies have cooled before offering them to dogs. **BONE-APPETITE!**

HEALING FALL STEW

Prep Time: 3 hours total including cook time
Serves 6 adults & 12 dogs

This is my miracle, go-to, cure-all! I eat it regularly to maintain good health. The bone broth is loaded with collagen, protein, and amino acids. It's a superfood for your immune system. This recipe also incorporates the fall root vegetables that are in season. And wait until you smell it cooking! This can be mixed into your dog's regular food or as a stand-alone meal. I recommend serving it in small cups in your team's colors with spoons for guests and small ramekin cups for dogs.

INGREDIENTS FOR PUPS AND PEOPLE:

- 1 cup beef (or chicken) bone broth (buy extra to add and make a soup)
- 4 cups lean beef stew meat
- 2 Tbsp olive oil
- 2 slices bacon, chopped
- 1 butternut or seasonal squash diced into 1" cubes
- 2 carrots cut into bite-sized pieces
- 1 turnip quartered
- 2 organic tomatoes quartered
- 3 garlic cloves, crushed and chopped (optional)
- 1 bay leaf (optional)
- Pinch of tumeric

*Garlic can be toxic to dogs but only in large amounts. According to the Whole Dog Journal, a healthy dog can consume and tolerate 1 medium clove per day for every 20 lbs of body weight. It can be very beneficial for preventing fleas and ticks.

DIRECTIONS FOR PUPS AND PEOPLE:

1. Preheat oven to 350°F.
2. Cut the meat into large cubes or ask your butcher to prepare it for you.
3. In a large frying pan, heat the olive oil and add the bacon and meat until lightly browned.
4. Add remaining vegetables and any spices you're using.
5. Transfer to a glass casserole dish. Cover ingredients with bone broth.
6. Cook at 350°F for 2 hours.

I also make this into a soup by adding more bone broth to thin it out to a soup consistency.

PUMPKIN MUDD PIE

Prep time: 10 minutes/Freezing time: 2 ½ hours
Yields 1 pie

Here's a canine-friendly version of pumpkin pie. This can be modified and made for cats and humans as well. Best of all, it is super healthy and a great treat to offer if your dog has digestive issues. I can't have dairy so I use a non-dairy coconut or almond milk ice cream and top the dessert with coconut whip cream.

INGREDIENTS FOR PUPS AND PEOPLE:

- 2 cups Nulo (or another brand) dried dog food (any flavor) crumbled finely
- Put kibble in firm plastic bag and hammer it until crumbled
- 1 cup canned pumpkin puree
- 1 cup plain Greek yogurt, kefir, goat's milk or non-dairy yogurt
- 1 store-bought graham cracker pie crust (IF Making for humans)
- 2 pints pumpkin ice cream (if making for humans)
- cinnamon (PUMPKIN PIE SPICE AND NUTMEG ARE TOXIC TO DOGS)
- Caramel sauce (humans)
- Whipped cream

DIRECTIONS FOR PUPS:

1. Spread 1 cup crumbled dog kibble in a greased 9 x 13 glass casserole dish or add kibble to the bottom of greased mini muffin cups.
2. In a mixing bowl, combine pumpkin and yogurt and mix thoroughly.
3. Pour mixture on top of kibble in either casserole dish or muffin cups.
4. Freeze for 2 hours (1 hour for small muffin cups.)
5. Drizzle with remaining kibble, a dollop of whip cream and dust with cinnamon.

DIRECTIONS FOR PEOPLE:

1. Let ice cream soften at room temperature.
2. Scoop into pie crust and smooth mixture evenly.
3. Drizzle with caramel.
4. Place in freezer for 2 hours.
5. Top with a dusting of spices and whip cream.
6. Wait about 10 minutes before cutting pieces with a hot knife.

Festivities

FALL FESTIVITIES

OHHHHHHH HOW I LOVE THE FALL! It's the most magical time of year. The leaves are turning, and everything has a beautiful, picturesque, golden tone. The summer is winding down, the kiddos are heading back to school and I have my local beach back to myself. The fall literally brings many dogs and their owners to tears. -It's not only tears of joy however, this time of year, the great outdoors can be anything but for allergy sufferers.

The fall brings weepy-eyed, runny-nosed pet parents coming to me in desperation. Not only are they suffering but their poor dogs are relentlessly itching, chewing their paws, and covered in rashes and hot spots. If the allergies weren't bad enough, the vet bills, medications, and products they've bought for relief have likely set them back hundreds of dollars.

Good news! As someone who has suffered from severe allergies all my life and also worked with highly sensitive dogs, these tried and true remedies will get both you and your dog feeling better faster than butter melts on a hot potato.

ALLERGIES...
SCRATCHING THE SURFACE FOR RELIEF
... Tips for preventing and healing your dog's seasonal allergies.

Did you know your dog can suffer from seasonal allergies just as you do? Most humans who experience seasonal allergies suffer from dry, red, itchy, puffy, weeping eyes. In addition, they likely have frequent sneezing and a dry persistent cough. Dog allergies more commonly take the form of skin irritation or inflammation — a condition called allergic dermatitis. This causes a dog's coat to become very itchy. You'll notice them scratching excessively, and they will most likely bite or chew their paws or other areas of their body. If your pup is rubbing up against you (especially if you don't have food in your hands) most likely they are desperately trying to relieve uncomfortable itchiness as best they can.

Another tell-tale sign of an allergy is redness. Allergic pets often have puffy red eyes, red gums, a red, possibly bumpy, blemished chin, red paws, and even a red anus. Many dog breeds can also suffer from ear problems as a result of allergies. Respiratory symptoms, especially in "brachy" (flat-faced) dogs can also occur. A running nose, watery eyes, coughing, sneezing and that scary "back-breathing" can also attack seasonal allergy sufferers.

Helping a pet suffering from environmental allergies. We all need to enjoy the great outdoors but limit exposure during peak readings for pollen, ragweed, etc. During a rough season, it's important to shower both at night and in the morning to remove allergens. I recommend you do the same for your dog if they are symptomatic. Also, use an air purifier and close windows during windy days and the peak pollen hours. Check the allergens and air quality with a phone app so you're prepared.

- Frequent baths give complete, immediate relief to an itchy pet and wash away the allergens on the coat and skin. Make sure to use a grain-free, fragrance-free shampoo. I like Bailey's CBD shampoo. This pure, gentle cleaning agent won't strip or harm your pet's natural oils but will do the trick to remove allergens. Plus it has CBD to heal and soothe.

- Foot soaks are also a great way to reduce the number of allergens your pet tracks into the house and spreads all over their indoor environment. Plus, when they lick their paws they ingest allergens. You can also wipe their paws with a damp cloth and a gentle soap or shampoo (mentioned above) after coming in the door. Or use hypoallergenic pet wipes. You may wish to use booties or socks on your pet during allergy season.

- Keep the areas of your home where your pet spends most of their time as allergen-free as possible. Vacuum and clean floors, toys, and pet bedding frequently using simple, non-toxic, hypoallergenic cleaning agents that don't contain dyes and fragrances. Close up those windows during peak pollen hours and on high pollen count days. Get a good home air purifier as well.

- Vaccines stimulate the immune system, which is the last thing your pet with seasonal environmental allergies needs. Talk to your vet about "titers" as an alternative to automatically vaccinating. Or, wait until they're not symptomatic.

- Switch your pet to a human-grade, species-appropriate, anti-inflammatory food. Foods that create or worsen inflammation are high in carbohydrates, grains, and gluten. (Most dry kibble is 40-60% carbs.) This is a good time to try a canned, raw, or fresh food diet.

- Add those Omega-3 fatty acids which help decrease inflammation throughout the body. Adding them into the diet of all pets — particularly pets struggling with seasonal environmental allergies — is very beneficial. The best sources of omega 3s are anchovies and sardines packed in spring water. They make an inexpensive easy treat or meal topper and are too small a fish to worry about contamination.

- Coconut oil contains lauric acid, which helps decrease the production of yeast. I have seen amazing results with dogs suffering from horrific skin/yeast problems by simply adding a dollop of organic coconut oil to their diet. You can also use this topically on their coat, paws, tear-stains, nose, teeth, and hot spots for relief.

- Get out during non-peak pollen hours to exercise or play with your pooch and wear them out. If they are tired they may sleep better and not be sitting around itching and uncomfortable. Upon returning home, wash your dog's coat to remove any environmental allergens. At the very least, use the shampoo on a wet cloth and wash their paws, around their bottoms, face, ears, and any wounds. These cleansers are gentle enough to use daily without drying your pet's coat.

TREATING HOTSPOTS

Allergic dermatitis can include patches of hair loss, open sores on the skin, and scabbing. If left untreated, hot spots can develop. A hot spot is raw, red, inflamed, infected skin that occurs when your dog's natural bacteria overwhelms an area. Typically the skin will be very red, and often there is weeping, bleeding, and hair loss.

When a dog constantly licks and chews certain spots on their body, they eventually become red, raw, inflamed, and ITCHY! The area never gets a chance to heal because the dog won't leave it alone. At this point, it's easy to develop a bacterial or fungal infection which are also extremely itchy. The secondary condition then makes the itch much worse exacerbating the itch-lick cycle.

If your dog is suffering from any sort of skin infection, they should be evaluated immediately by your vet. Typically it's an allergy to a flea bite, food, or something in the environment. But, it's quite possible they have skin mites or have developed a fungal or bacterial infection that requires prompt attention. It may also be the result of compulsively licking and biting their skin to relieve stress and anxiety.

GET RID OF HOT SPOTS...

Regardless of the cause, start building up your dog's immune system with a nutritious diet. GET RID OF THOSE BAD CARBS! I would switch to a wet/moist food since kibble by nature is nearly twice as high in carbs. Wet food is much easier to digest due to the higher water content.

Stick to a limited ingredient diet using one single meat, fish, fowl, or poultry protein source. Typically, turkey and lamb cause the least amount of issues. Feeding foods that contain chicken, beef, or a variety of different proteins, can be too taxing on your dog's already weakened immune system right now. I personally use canned Nulo Turkey.

READ THOSE LABELS! Look for high-quality meat proteins as the first 3 ingredients! Stay away from corn, wheat, potatoes, rice, and oats. All are very high in sugar. I'm astounded at how many vets put allergy-suffering dogs on popular brands of dry, RX foods. Basically, it's the same as serving yourself a heaping bowl of sugar chunks cereal to cure your yeasty rash! While you're at it, cut out all fruit and treats. It's not forever, just while your dog is healing.

Grab a hypoallergenic, gentle, fragrance/color-free, puppy shampoo and read the label. Don't use any products containing OATMEAL. While oatmeal can be a gentle exfoliating ingredient, many dogs are highly sensitive to grains, and applying it directly to their coats can further aggravate things. Your vet may prescribe a medicated wash as well.

CARING FOR THE WOUNDS...

It's critical to keep your dog's mouth away from the wound while it heals. The sooner the licking stops, the faster the healing. Many dogs will chew right through bandages which adds another problem to your growing list, so pick up an Elizabethan (E-collar) or soft collar. If your dog's obsessive licking is caused by a behavior issue, this collar will also do the trick by breaking the cycle.

Keeping the wound clean is imperative. I recommend disinfecting with Betadine twice a day. After disinfecting the wound, apply a topical remedy to speed healing. No one remedy works for every dog, so my advice is to try different topicals until the wound is healed. A few options to consider:

CBD OIL: Apply a few drops to the wound 2x's daily. Your dog may be very uncomfortable so I use CBD oil both topically and on the wounds to calm dogs down and bring relief.

MANUKA HONEY: (This is a special type of anti-bacterial honey found in New Zealand & Australia. NOT the honey found in the plastic bears at the supermarket!) applied to the wound twice a day

RAW ALOE: Break open a fresh filet of aloe leaf and place it, gooey side down, on the wound. Hold in place with a bandana, t-shirt, or dressing and replace every four hours.

PAVIA NATURAL WOUND CARE CREAM applied twice daily.

Your vet may prescribe antibiotic creams or medications but these will hopefully work to keep things from developing or getting worse. You can also give these home remedies a try immediately while waiting to see your vet.

Another great way to promote healing is through physical activity. If dogs get a lot of exercise they'll be preoccupied and also sleep better at night. If the outdoors is too high on the allergy index, jump into some indoor agility, nose work, or training classes.

This is the time to keep stress levels under control. A bored dog left home alone all day or a dog who's been sent to a kennel while you're away on vacation can begin obsessively licking or bring wound healing to a screeching halt.

Get in the habit of running your hands over your dog and inspecting their coat and paws daily checking for fleas, ticks, bumps or damp fur. Some hot spots can pop up within a matter of hours, while others take longer to appear. Don't wait until there's a nasty irritation before seeking advice from your veterinarian. And as the saying goes, "An ounce of prevention is worth a pound of cure!" Trying these suggestions will certainly reduce a lot of problems AND COST!

Be sure to follow me on social and visit my website: **www.weeklyrunt.com** or lots of fun, pet-friendly activities going on in your area and healthy tips.

October

It's Halloween time, and nobody loves this holiday more than ME! I mean, what's more fun than dressing up as whoever or whatever you want and going door-to-door scoring free candy! I will never outgrow that!

But all my excitement isn't shared when it comes to my pug Olive. And she isn't alone when it comes to dogs "getting spooked" by Halloween! Think about it, a pup witnesses a barrage of boisterous costumed strangers pounding on the door. Their usually safe environment is now dark or billowing with fog, candles, and flashing lights. Their highly sensitive ears pick up sounds of dogs barking, cats hissing, chains clanking, footsteps, plus deafening screams and moans. If you're not careful, pets can literally be "scared to death!" Many pet owners, myself included, get so caught up in the fun they can easily forget how frightening things can be for Fluffy and Fido!

Halloween is one of the busiest holidays for pet emergencies, so whether you throw a party, attend one, or stay home, here are a few "TRICKS AND TREATS" to have a great time AND keep your pet safe!

1. KEEP YOUR PETS CALM: A frightened pet can react by barking incessantly, losing bladder control, racing out the door, or escaping. They can act out with aggression and biting. Keep your dog happy and calm with natural CBD*. These natural treats contain none of the harmful THC and will do wonders for calming a frantic pet.

2. KEEP YOUR PETS SAFE INSIDE: Not everyone has good intentions, and there are always several awful stories about killed, tormented, injured, or stolen pets on Halloween. Don't allow your dog to be the helpless victim of an evil prankster.

3. KEEP YOUR PETS AWAY FROM THE FRONT DOOR: The constant knocking or ringing of the doorbell and excited trick-or-treaters can send dogs into protective mode. Don't risk your doggie bolting out the door and running away or getting hit by a vehicle. Also, you don't want your terrified dog biting a costumed visitor.

4. BE CAREFUL WITH DECORATIONS: I've seen wagging dog tails knock over candles and nearly burn down a house. I've witnessed many excited pets jumping up on tables, knocking over glass decorations, eating harmful foods, and causing total mayhem! Make sure all decorations are secured and not in reach of pets, -that goes for electrical cords too! Check that pets cannot get trapped or entangled in large spider web decorations. Also, they may think the decor is a chew-toy and eat something hazardous if it's within their reach.

5. NO CANDY FOR DOGS! It should go without saying not to give your dog candy. Chocolate contains theobromine, which can be lethal if ingested. Lollipop sticks can be a choking hazard or cause damage to internal organs if swallowed—ditto for caramel apples and their wooden sticks. Foil wrappers can be as sharp as razors if swallowed. The very worst are the sugar-free treats which contain toxic xylitol. Dogs love the smell and bright colors of sugary candy, and it just takes a few minutes of distractions to realize your dog has consumed an entire bowl of Halloween goodies. Even dog treats can cause major GI problems if too many are consumed. Remember, ONE dog treat or a few healthy nibbles is PERFECT!

6. STAY HOME ON HALLOWEEN! Think twice before you take your dog in the car or out with the kids trick-or-treating. All the crowds and excitement might turn your normally chill dog into a terrified, aggressive, or protective bully. It may be way too distracting to manage both costumed kids AND a dog that gets freaked!

👻 If you do venture out with your pet for Halloween festivities, here are a few tips:

1. **Give costumes a trial run to let your dog get used to them.** Make sure their costume is not too binding or restrictive and that your pet can walk normally. Be very careful of masks. Dogs need to be able to see and breathe with ease. Nothing should go over their nose. Be extremely careful about dogs overheating, especially Pugs, Bulldogs, and other flat-nosed (brachy) breeds. Make sure dogs can freely drink water in their costume. Some dogs (like my Olive) simply don't do well with costumes. Perhaps a lighted collar, decorative harness, or bandana would be a better option.

2. **Make sure your dog is microchipped and wearing a collar or harness with your contact number on the tag.** If you will be out after dark, add reflective strips to your pet's costume and grab a small light to attach to their collar so they remain visible.

3. **BE AWARE!** While you are admiring those amazing costumes, your dog could be devouring chocolate bars someone tossed on the sidewalk.

4. **If you plan to host a Halloween bash that's NOT dog-inclusive, consider keeping your dog safe at a boarding facility.** With guests coming in and out, even if your dog is secluded in a quiet bedroom, it just takes one person to open a door and BOOM! Your dog escapes. Loud guests in strange costumes can scare and overwhelm even a normally easy-going dog. Some guests aren't familiar with pets and don't know alcohol, sweets, and many human foods can be deadly. A well-intentioned guest wanting to indulge your dog may bring them undue harm. Even if they aren't offered, a cup left on a table or half-eaten plates of food and desserts lying around can be far too tempting and could make your dog very sick. It isn't easy to keep your eyes on pets while hosting a party.

Don't take the risk. Many boarding facilities have special packages and fun activities planned. This way, you won't end up with a real Halloween horror of a sick or injured dog on your hands.

let's get this party started!

HOWL-O-WEEN COSTUME PAWTY!

EAT DRINK AND BE SCARY! Yes, it's a spooky time of year for pets, but Halloween can also be one of the most fun holidays to share with them! Some dogs, pugs, in particular, are such great sports about costumes and fanfare, that this is a perfect opportunity to have some fun and laughs getting dressed up. Therefore, I recommend throwing your own "pet-friendly" bash. If you choose to have the party on Halloween that's great, but you may also consider hosting your event on another day and staying in on Halloween. With all the tricks and treats being offered this month, this menu is not only delicious but NUTRITIOUS. It will keep you and your dog feeling your best even if you over-indulge in sweets. Using fresh, seasonal ingredients, meals will taste amazing and the best part is they're perfect for those with tummy troubles. Happy Halloween!

MENU

Pumpkin Spice Puppuccinos 🥄 Tummy-Mending Turkey Tacos
🥄 Miracle Mushroom Soup 🥄 Oatmeal Recovery Bars

DÉCOR: This should be fairly easy. You can go crazy at any Halloween Superstore or Dollar Tree. Keep in mind that many dogs don't know the difference between decorations and the real thing and they can get SPOOKED. Be mindful of candles and other hazardous Halloween decor.

ACTIVITIES: This is a perfect time to have everyone participate in a costume contest. Pick someone as a judge or have a celebrity judge. You can even boost your social media presence by doing a live feed and having followers vote on their favorites. If you know a pet psychic, reading Tarot cards or communicating with pets that have passed on, can be a fun activity that isn't too stressful for anxious dogs. Don't know any psychics, schedule an online session with one from my website directory.

PARTY FAVORS: Make up small trick-or-treat bags for your guest pups and pop in the recipes to the above items. These recipes will be a huge help if their pet is under the weather. I also like to add some CBD treats to the favor bags to help keep pets calm over the entire spooktacular month.

PUMPKIN SPICE PUPPUCCINOS

Prep Time: 10 minutes
Servings 10 human beverages/10 dog-sized sips

This is a perfect beverage for any fall party as well as a healthy option for your dog. Pumpkin is not only high in dietary fiber but it is loaded with vitamins and minerals. For dog versions, I like to use dairy-free options or kefir/goat's milk which offers lots of probiotics without any of the problems cow's milk can incite. Be mindful of spices. Nutmeg is toxic to dogs so I substitute it with turmeric which is loaded with healthy properties.

INGREDIENTS FOR PUPS AND PEOPLE:

- 10 shots espresso (or cups of coffee)
- ¼ cup canned pumpkin puree
- 1-quart milk of choice (almond/oat/regular)
- 1 cup plain kefir or goat's milk (or goat's milk kefir)
- A dollop of whip cream or coconut whip cream
- Dash of cinnamon
- Dash of turmeric

DIRECTIONS FOR PUPS:

1. Place 3 Tbsp pumpkin puree in a blender.
2. Add 1 cup of preferred milk and blend.
3. Pour into small paper ramekins and top with a dollop of whip creme, a dash of turmeric & cinnamon.

DIRECTIONS PEOPLE:

1. Blend remaining pumpkin and 1 cup of preferred milk.
2. Add to a milk frother or warm in a saucepan over medium heat.
3. Add mixture to espresso shots/coffee
4. Top with a dollop of whip creme, a dash of turmeric & cinnamon.

MIRACLE MUSHROOM SOUP

Prep Time: 30 minutes
Yields 12 bowls/10 dog-sized servings

This recipe is a favorite go-to all year long. I make it when I'm under the weather or just to stay healthy during flu season. It's loaded with collagen, immunity-building antioxidants, amino acids, and vitamins. Feel free to be creative and add other favorite veggies or meats. I add an additional serving of protein powder which makes the soup very thick, so I save some bone broth to add for the desired consistency. See how great you feel after a bowl of this! ENJOY!

INGREDIENTS FOR PUPS AND PEOPLE:

- 2 quarts beef or chicken bone broth
- 1 14oz can or box of coconut milk
- 1 cup frozen riced cauliflower
- 3 cups mushrooms, chopped
- 1 cup cut green beans
- 1 cup sweet potato diced in small cubes
- ¼ cup olive oil
- 2 cloves garlic finely chopped
- Protein powder (For humans -optional)
- Salt and pepper to taste

DIRECTIONS FOR PUPS AND PEOPLE:

1. In a large pot combine bone broth, coconut milk, cauliflower, green beans, and sweet potatoes.
2. In a small saucepan sauté garlic and mushrooms in olive oil. When lightly browned add to the pot of soup.

FOR PUPS:

Serve 4-6 Tbsp or use as a topper for kibble.

FOR PEOPLE:

Add a scoop of protein powder to bolster up nutrition. Salt & pepper to taste.

TUMMY MENDING TURKEY TACOS

Prep Time: 30 minutes
Yields 36 street tacos

Here's a twist on yummy tacos that are also amazing for restoring a pup's upset stomach. When a dog has tummy issues, most people give them chicken and rice, but this is a far healthier recipe. Turkey is a very mild protein that doesn't cause the sensitivities chicken often does. Rice is very high in carbs and sugar. It doesn't digest easily. Sweet potatoes, on the other hand, offer tons of gentle fiber and a plethora of vitamins and minerals. Plus pets love the taste. Just skip the tortillas until they're feeling better. These tacos taste so good, everyone will be surprised at how super healthy they are!

INGREDIENTS FOR PUPS AND PEOPLE:

- 36 small street taco-sized organic corn tortillas or 3 large bags of tortilla chips
- 3 cups lean fresh ground turkey
- 3 cups raw sweet potatoes sliced into small cubes
- Coconut oil
- Fresh chopped parsley
- ¼ cup kefir (optional)
- Guacamole/salsa (optional)

INGREDIENTS FOR PUPS AND PEOPLE:

1. Lightly sauté the turkey in a medium saucepan until browned. Set aside.
2. Add coconut oil to saucepan and sauté the sweet potatoes until soft.
3. In a lightly oiled saucepan, warm tortilla for 20 seconds on each side.

DIRECTIONS FOR PUPS:

1. Spoon 1-2 Tbsp ground turkey and sweet potatoes onto a warm tortilla.
2. Top with a drizzle of kefir and a parsley sprig.

DIRECTIONS PEOPLE:

1. Add guacamole, spices, and salsa to taste.

OATMEAL RECOVERY BARS

Prep Time: 10 minutes / Cook Time: 45 minutes
Yields 24 small bars

This vegan, gluten-free, recipe is a favorite among several Ironman World Champions. These bars are delicious and deliver the nutrients to help replenish lost electrolytes. They also offer low-glycemic carbs and protein to fuel recovery. This will provide long-lasting energy without a crash. These make a delicious, healthy dessert for the natural athlete in your dog.

INGREDIENTS FOR PUPS AND PEOPLE:

- 2 cups gluten-free, steel-cut oats
- 1 cup unsweetened shredded coconut
- ½ cup finely chopped roasted pumpkin seeds
- ½ cup carob chips (never use chocolate for dogs)
- Choice of nuts (FOR HUMANS ONLY)
- ½ cup dried figs
- ½ tsp sea salt
- 1 tsp cinnamon
- ¼ cup honey
- ¼ cup coconut oil
- 2 Tbsp almond butter
- ½ cup ripe banana mashed (approx. 1½ bananas)
- ½ cup mashed purple sweet potatoes
- Coconut whip cream (optional)
- Pumpkin ice cream (optional)

DIRECTIONS FOR PUPS AND PEOPLE:

1. Preheat oven to 375°F.
2. Grease a 9x13" casserole dish with a little bit of coconut oil. Then, line with parchment paper.
3. Combine oats, seeds, (nuts if just for humans), and figs in a bowl. In a separate bowl, mix spices, honey, oil, and almond butter.
4. Mix mashed banana and sweet potatoes into liquid, then pour over dry ingredients and mix well.
5. Pour entire mixture into the prepared dish and spread evenly. Bake for 25 minutes or until golden brown.
6. Remove from oven and allow bars to fully cool in pan for 20 minutes before cutting into small squares.
7. Serve alone or with your favorite toppings.
8.

FOR PUPS:

1. Top with a small dollop of coconut whip cream.

FOR PEOPLE:

1. Add a small scoop of pumpkin ice cream to the top and serve!

November

Keep your dog from becoming a stuffed animal this Thanksgiving! This is one of my favorite days of the year. Not for turkey and stuffing but because it centers around family and gratitude. What I love most about the pet parent community is the way we celebrate and embrace a more inclusive form of "family." Not to get too serious, (this is a party book after all) but I am always aware of two things at the kickoff of the holiday season: 1) For some people, the holidays are hard. 2) Our pets often stand-in for relationships, places, and things that had hard outcomes. I think all of us dog owners can agree that we're very thankful for our dogs and the deep bonds we share with these furry pals.

This month I'm including some recipes and ideas for you to host a dog-friendly, PUPSGIVING! That's right! Why not try something completely different and invite your closest friends, and their dogs, to come over and try out some delicious new recipes? Possibly start a new tradition?

Thanksgiving revolves around turkey! Luckily, it's one of the most popular protein varieties for dogs (and people!) You could throw a stick in a pet store and hit 50 different pet foods that include turkey. There's a good reason for its popularity. It's plentiful, economical, and very gentle on the digestive system. Best of all, it doesn't typically cause the same sensitivities for dogs as chicken or beef. This is one celebratory meal that, with caution, dogs can safely enjoy!

If you have a dog and are hosting a thanksgiving soiree, please be advised of the following tips. Nothing sours a holiday faster than an unplanned trip to the emergency vet with your dog. These helpful reminders should keep the occasion safe and memorable for everyone.

KEEP THE DOGS OUTSIDE, in a bedroom, or in a safe place. It's impossible to keep an eye on your dog while you're cooking, cleaning, and preparing for a party. Especially with delicious-smelling food on counters. Once you have gotten your food prepared and safely stored, bring the dog out but possibly gate the kitchen so they cannot run in.

DON'T LEAVE FOOD UNATTENDED! Whether you're doing a dog-inclusive event or tucking your dog in a bedroom while you enjoy your feast, unattended food on the kitchen counter can be way too big a temptation for a dog. Cooked turkey bones can choke a dog. Or they can splinter/break while being eaten. Broken bones can get stuck in any part of your dog's gastrointestinal tract as they work their way through the system.

CLEAR AWAY ALL WRAPPINGS. Tinfoil, cellophane wrap, plastic bags, string, and meat skewers are all potential hazards for your dog. I also recommend putting someone in charge of clearing all the plates, food, and drinks that guests may have left laying around prior to the meal. Clear trash immediately and if you put it in a bin, make sure the lid is securely closed, out of reach from persistent scavengers.

A TIRED DOG IS A GOOD DOG. Do your own "turkey-trot" by getting out and giving your dog a good energetic walk, trot, jog or run in the morning. If you have an older dog, perhaps take them on a stroller ride in the fresh air. This way they will be more relaxed and possibly even sleep a bit during the festivities. If things get too crazy after all the guests have arrived, have everyone grab their dogs, put them on leashes or in strollers, and go on a nice pack walk together.

GIVE DOGS CBD 2 hours before the party. CBD can have a drastic calming effect on anxious dogs. Make sure you use a good brand that has been verified for purity and potency. Check my website for brands I use and discount codes.

STOCK UP ON TOYS FOR DOGS TO PLAY WITH. While you're cooking or if you have to contain your dog, offer them a new toy. I like to present a Kong stuffed with canned turkey and some kibble bits mixed in. Or I use a treat puzzle. If your dog is happily playing they won't be getting into mischief in the kitchen.

JUST TO BE SAFE:

Know the phone number/location of the closest 24-hour emergency animal hospital. Most veterinary offices will be closed for the holiday.

Dogs and cats can get anxious with commotion and unfamiliar crowds of people. Make sure they are wearing their ID collars should they get out.

Remind guests not to indulge the dogs and to be cautious. Those who don't own pets may not completely understand their ability to get into food, or the complete lack of willpower many pets have when it comes to food items. As a reminder, **dogs and alcohol don't mix** either.

While turkey meat and organs can be a wonderful, healthy meal or treat for dogs, rich, fatty foods, such as turkey skin and dark turkey meat, are difficult to digest and can cause vomiting, diarrhea, and in extreme cases, bloat or pancreatitis.*

If you suspect your dog has helped himself to a turkey dinner and is showing any of these symptoms, I suggest you take them to your vet as soon as possible.

***PANCREATITIS** is an inflammation of the pancreas which can be lethal for dogs. The pancreas produces digestive enzymes, and when inflamed, the natural production and release of these enzymes is disrupted. When the digestive enzymes are produced and there's no food to digest, these enzymes will start digesting body tissue instead. This causes further inflammation of the pancreas. The severity of pancreatitis and your dog's prognosis will depend on how he reacts to this inflammation.

Symptoms of pancreatitis include loss of appetite, lethargy, vomiting, abdominal pain, diarrhea, and fever.

laya Picnics

let's get this party started!

A DOG INCLUSIVE "PUPSGIVING"

Our dogs show up at the tippy-top of most of our gratitude lists. They warm our hearts and do so much for us each and every day! Here's a way to honor them with a special Thanksgiving meal of their very own. For a dog-inclusive "Pupsgiving," I'm featuring a menu with items that make a perfect Thanksgiving dinner ENTIRELY for your dog. Gather your friends around the table and offer up a special meal of tasty holiday yapp-itizers and desserts all for the dogs. Ideally, guests can each bring various Thanksgiving staples to round out the feast for humans.

MENU

Cranberry Fizz Cocktails 🥄 Turkey & Cranberry Savories 🥄 Pilgrim Patties 🥄 No-bake Pumpkin Mousse Pie

***TIPS:** I like to set a traditional sit-down Thanksgiving meal. If the weather permits, an outdoor picnic setting can be wonderful. Dogs can be seated on doggie beds next to their humans who can be seated on comfy pillows. Ask guests to bring a dog bed for their dog as well as their favorite Thanksgiving dish for humans. In this chapter, you will get the tools to provide everything for the dogs. Coordinate with guests so each person isn't bringing the same dish. Set up a small buffet area for the food. It's important to put items in a spot where hungry dogs can't get access. Guests can make themselves a plate and then prepare one for their dogs. Food can be taken back to the table and eaten alongside their pets. While you enjoy your meal, your dogs can be feasting on theirs. Having a meal this way should curb any food aggression among the dogs. Be mindful to give each dog their space. Enjoying Thanksgiving outside is ideal for dogs who can get some also get plenty of playtime in during the gathering.

DÉCOR: If you're doing an outdoor picnic, you can pick up one or two wood pallets for next to nothing at a big box store. Place a flattened large cardboard box on top so you have a flat table surface. Then cover with a pretty fall table cloth. A vinyl one might be best just in case there are any spills. You can also decorate some pretty fall leaves from a craft store by adding some glitter and fall-colored ribbon. Write each guest's name in a glitter pen and set one at their place. You can also tie a napkin in it. I like putting a small pumpkin at each guest's seat. Gather pretty decorative paper or plastic plates for both humans and their pets. I prefer to use a separate table as a food buffet to avoid the chaos of food dishes being passed. This may be too much for anxious, food-driven dogs.

PARTY FAVORS: Thanksgiving is a time to express our gratitude. I like to send each guest home with a handwritten card telling why I'm grateful for them. I also make small, gratitude journals out of pretty linen paper stock. You can also press fall leaves in wax paper, place them under a fabric napkin and lightly iron them. Once they cool, cut excess paper from around the leaves and send them home with your guests. There should be plenty of extra savories, so pack up decorative "doggie-bags," label with each pet's name, and let them take those home. Your guests will all be very grateful if you offer them some small CBD samples to take home so their pets can better manage stressful holiday times.

CRANBERRY FIZZ

Prep time: 10 minutes
Servings 10 humans & 10 dogs

Cranberries aren't just a staple at Thanksgiving, they are also loaded with so many health benefits, I should have included them in my list of superfoods. Cranberries are legendary for bladder health and preventing UTIs, but you might be surprised to learn they contain a substance called nondialyzable material (NDM) that prevents the influenza virus from sticking to the cells and causing inflammation. This is a perfect time to indulge in this tasty cocktail and protect yourself during flu season and large get-togethers. It's not just humans who greatly benefit from cranberries. Our dogs can also reap numerous health benefits from them. Since cranberry juice by itself can be extremely tart and many dogs won't enjoy it, or it's loaded with extra sugar which cancels out the health benefits, I've added some bone broth and coconut water to make it heavenly (and keep it healthy) for dogs!

INGREDIENTS FOR PUPS AND PEOPLE:

- 4 cups chilled unsweetened 100% cranberry juice
- 1 cup grapefruit juice chilled (for humans)
- 1 cup orange juice chilled (for humans)
- 2 cups chilled ginger ale (for humans)
- Frozen cranberries
- 1 cup coconut water
- 1 cup bone broth (for dogs)

OPTIONAL: For those guests that want their drinks HARD!

- Rum (optional)
- Triple Sec (optional)
- Vodka (optional but makes a great addition if guests want their drinks LEADED!)

DIRECTIONS FOR PUPS:

1. Fill small shot glass or paper ramekin with a frozen cranberry cube.
2. Add a splash of bone broth and serve in a small shot glass or paper ramekin with a frozen ice cube.

DIRECTIONS FOR PEOPLE:

1. Pour coconut water into ice cube trays and make sure each slot has several berries. Place in freezer until frozen.
2. In a large pitcher or punch bowl combine juices and mix well.
3. Just before serving add in ginger ale and several ice cubes.
4. Add in shots of alcohol for those who desire.

TURKEY AND CRANBERRY SAVORIES FOR YOUR DOG

Prep time: 30 minutes/Cook: 2 ½ hours
Yields 24-30 bite-sized yappitzers

Here's an entire thanksgiving meal for your pet in one savory snack. Your house will smell great, and all the dogs will be so thrilled with their feast that you can enjoy yours without them begging. Send extras home with guests since these can be refrigerated and eaten for up to a week.

INGREDIENTS FOR PUPS:

- 2 cups Nulo freeze-dried raw turkey (may use another brand or protein)
- 2 cups warm, filtered water
- 1 cup raw, lean ground turkey
- ½ cup grated cheddar cheese
- ½ cup cooked, mashed sweet potatoes
- ½ cup finely chopped green beans
- ¼ cup dried cranberries
- 2 free-range eggs

DIRECTIONS FOR PUPS:

1. Heat oven to 350°F.
2. Mix the dehydrated turkey dog food with hot water and stir thoroughly. Set mixture aside to hydrate.
3. In a separate bowl, combine all the remaining ingredients with a wooden spoon then add the hydrated mixture.
4. Using a spoon or your hands, make marble-sized dollops and place them on a greased baking sheet.
5. Bake for 20 minutes until the treats are slightly crispy on the outside.
6. Turn off the oven leaving the treats inside for around 2 hours. This will allow them to dry out and become crispier. Serve once they have cooled.

PILGRIM PATTIES

Prep time: 30 minutes/Cook: 2 ½ hours
Yields 24 small patties

Enjoy all the benefits of a thanksgiving meal in one, dog-sized patty. These are so easy to make and your dog will BOW-WOW for more! Although it features all the traditional flavors of Thanksgiving, this is a year-round favorite recipe, especially if I have am caring for a sensitive pet or one that has tummy issues. Although they're quick and easy to make, I try and keep a few extra in my freezer so I can thaw them out and have them in a pinch.

INGREDIENTS FOR PUPS:

- ½ cup Nulo (or another brand) freeze-dried raw turkey
- ½ cup lean, ground turkey
- ½ cup canned pumpkin puree
- ¼ cup dried cranberries
- 2 free-range eggs
- 2 Tbsp coconut oil
- 2 Tbsp fresh parsley
- ½ cup warm, filtered water

DIRECTIONS FOR PUPS:

1. Preheat oven to 370°F.
2. In a mixing bowl, break chunks of dehydrated turkey dog food into a powder.
3. Mix with the hot water and stir thoroughly. Allow to rehydrate for 5 minutes.
4. Gently fold in the pumpkin, cranberries, oil, and parsley.
5. Beat the eggs in a separate cup and mix in.
6. Stir everything together to form a stiff batter.
7. Using a spoon or your hands, form golf-ball-sized portions and place on a large, greased baking sheet about 2 inches apart. Using spoon or your palm flatten balls into thick patties and bake for about 45 minutes.
8. Serve once patties have cooled.

These may be stored in a sealed container and eaten for up to a week.

NO-BAKE PUMPKIN MOUSSE PIE

Pre-Prep Time: Soak cashews overnight / Prep Time: 15 minutes / Chill for 1 hour
Yields 1 Pie

This paleo pumpkin mousse pie is an amazing fall dessert. Your guests will be so blown away that something this tasty is vegan, dairy, and gluten-free! The best part is you can whip this up in a matter of minutes. Since Pumpkin is such a wonderful superfood, I wanted to modify this recipe and make it safe to share with your dog. **Pecans, macadamia nuts, and walnuts are toxic to dogs**, so just to be on the safe side, I have made this using almonds and peanuts in the crust. Ideally, you make a separate pie that's modified for the canines and everyone can enjoy the treat AND the health benefits.

INGREDIENTS FOR PUPS:

Crust:

- ½ cup dehydrated raw food (I like Nulo turkey)
- ¾ cup dry dog food (I use Nulo turkey)
- 3 pitted dates
- ¼ cup coconut oil

Pumpkin Mousse:

- ⅓ cup coconut milk (shake can well)
- ⅓ cup organic canned pumpkin (not pie filling)
- 1 tsp cinnamon
- ¼ cup melted coconut oil
- drizzle of honey
- 1 tsp tumeric
- 1 tsp cinnamon
- ¼ tsp ginger

DIRECTIONS FOR PUPS:

1. Combine all the crust ingredients into a blender or food processor. Blend or pulse until the mixture is finely ground and sticks together when pressed.

2. Press mixture into a 9" no-stick springform pan, 9x13 greased glass casserole dish, or greased muffin tin. Press a thin layer of mixture on the bottom.

3. Next, add all the mousse ingredients to the blender or food processor and blend until smooth and creamy. You may need to stop and push down the sides of the blender with a spatula to get everything mixed together.

4. Once it's smooth, pour over crust and smooth mixture with a spatula or spoon. Place in the freezer for an hour to set. You can decorate the top with crunched kibble pieces.

5. If making pie in advance, remove it from freezer 30 minutes before serving to soften.

6. Top with a dollop of whip cream and a drizzle of honey.

INGREDIENTS FOR PEOPLE:

Crust:

- ½ cup almond flour
- ¾ cup raw pecans (I use almonds/peanuts)
- 4 pitted dates
- 2 Tbsp coconut oil
- 1 tsp cinnamon
- ¼ tsp salt

Pumpkin Mousse:

- 2 cups raw cashews (soaked overnight in 1 cup cold water then drained.)
- ⅓ cup coconut milk (shake can well)
- ⅓ cup organic canned pumpkin (not pie filling)
- ¼ cup melted coconut oil
- ¼ cup maple syrup
- ¼ cup honey
- 2 tsp vanilla
- 1 tsp cinnamon
- ¼ tsp ginger
- Non-dairy whip cream (optional)

DIRECTIONS FOR PEOPLE:

1. Combine all the crust ingredients into a blender or food processor. Blend or pulse until the mixture is finely ground and sticks together when pressed.
2. Press mixture into a 7" or 9" no-stick springform pan. The 7" will make a thicker mousse but both sizes taste great. Or use a greased pie tin. Form an even layer on bottom of tin or pan.
3. Next, add all the mousse ingredients to the blender or food processor and blend until smooth and creamy. You may need to stop and push down the sides of the blender with a spatula to get everything mixed together.
4. Once it's smooth, pour over crust and smooth mixture with a spatula or spoon. Place in the freezer for an hour to set. You can decorate the top with pecans or nuts. I drizzle more maple syrup on the top.
5. If making pie in advance, remove it from freezer 30 minutes before serving to soften.
6. Top with whip cream and a drizzle of maple syrup and a dusting of cinnamon.

December

Happy Pawlidays, pet people! It's the most wonderful time of the year! December is the one month I don't have to go out of my way to pick a theme for a pup party. Now, you can always go back through this book and put together a fancy, austere pet-inclusive holiday soirée. In fact, my dream for this book is that people pick and choose recipes and party ideas and come up with their own, custom get-together concepts. But for my first "December" in my cookbook series, I wanted to lean into an idea that always pays off: People are dying to be goofy and ridiculous with their dogs.

For the month of December, I have put together tips on throwing an Ugly Holiday Sweater Soirée with a relaxed, potluck feel. These sweater parties are always fun--and easy. Basically, your guests end up being the decorations! It is amazing the lengths people will go to track down the most heinous sweaters known to man, and man's best friend! The effort is always worth its weight in gold with the photos! When you add pups to the mix, things get kicked up to a whole new level of fun. Let's be honest, there are few things more hilarious than a dog in a silly outfit, and with December typically being a back-to-back marathon of "grown-up" cocktail and work parties, people are usually dying for a chance to be comfortable, relaxed, and silly.

Let's get this party started!

UGLY HOLIDAY SWEATER SOIRÉE

There are so many fun things to do this season. My favorite is to keep it fun and light with an Ugly Holiday Sweater Soirée Play classic holiday movie favorites like The Grinch and set up a photo booth to capture great social media posts of everyone. Award prizes for the best ugly holiday attire!

MENU

Eggless Dog Nog 🥄 Holiday Noshers 🥄 Feliz Naughty-Dog Enchiladas 🥄 Gingerbread Cookies

***TIPS:** With things getting expensive and everyone stretched so thin this time of year, offer to host a party for a rescue or shelter and ask each guest to bring a donation for a pet in need.

PARTY IDEAS: There are lots of fun ways to celebrate and get in the spirit without maxing out your credit cards. If your friends are interested, have a small gift exchange and ask everyone to bring a gift under a certain dollar limit. You can see if there's interest and do one for humans and one for dogs. If you're not familiar with a white elephant gift exchange, it works like this; Everyone participating draws a number and puts the gift they brought in the center of a circle. The person with the number 1 goes first and selects a gift. The person with number 2 can either steal that gift or select a new one. Once a gift has been stolen twice, it stays with that person. Another fun idea is awarding prizes for the best "Ugly Holiday Sweater" or who gets the most votes for their gingerbread house or decorated cookie. Fun prizes are Lotto scratcher tickets, funny holiday socks, mugs, bottles of wine, gift cards, and t-shirts.

PARTY FAVORS: Depending on the number of guests, set up a station to decorate gingerbread cookies or houses which will be fun and festive during the party. Guests can take them home afterward. Make a small photo ornament for each of your guests to hang on their tree. Print favorite pics from the party and put them in pretty inexpensive photo ornaments you can buy from a craft store.

EGGLESS DOG NOG

Prep Time: 10 minutes
Serves 5 humans/10 dogs

This tasty holiday eggnog is perfectly safe for dogs. It's also a yummy way to serve eggnog for those that can't have eggs or dairy.

INGREDIENTS FOR PUPS AND PEOPLE:

- 1 small banana soft and ripe
- 2 cups unsweetened almond milk
- 8 Medjoubi dates that have been pitted and chopped
- 1 cup coconut milk
- Dusting of cinnamon (NEVER USE NUTMEG WITH DOGS! IT'S TOXIC)
- Espresso (for humans that wish)
- Brandy, bourbon or dark rum (for humans)

DIRECTIONS FOR PUPS AND PEOPLE:

1. Put banana, almond milk, dates and coconut milk into a blender and blend on high until frothy.
2. Add a sprinkle of cinnamon and blend for 20 seconds.
3. Pour into small shot glasses or ramekins that hold about 2-4 Tbsp and serve.

ADDITIONAL OPTIONS FOR PEOPLE:

This is just as tasty as your standard eggnog but made without eggs or dairy. Make the recipe as instructed above and add a shot of brandy, bourbon, or dark rum. You can also add this mixture to espresso and make an eggnog latte with or without alcohol.

HOLIDAY NOSHERS

Prep time: 10 minutes/Cook: 45 min
Yields 24-30 yappitzers

Here's a yummy, fruity treat that can be easily modified as a healthy snack for your dog. I would make two batches and send some home with your guests in cute holiday "doggie bags."

INGREDIENTS FOR PUPS:

- ½ cup unsweetened applesauce
- 1 free-range egg
- ½ cup almond butter
- 1 tsp vanilla extract
- 1 cup oat flour
- ¼ cup dried blueberries
- ¼ cup gluten-free oats
- ½ cup dehydrated raw food (I like Nulo turkey or lamb)
- ½ cup well-ripened mashed bananas (humans)
- 1 cup warm, filtered water

DIRECTIONS FOR PUPS:

1. Heat oven to 350°F.
2. In a large mixing bowl combine the applesauce, egg, almond butter, vanilla, and water.
3. In a second bowl, combine flour, oats, blueberries, and dehydrated food.
4. Combine all the ingredients of both bowls.
5. Place the dough onto a floured surface and knead until mixed thoroughly.
6. Roll out the dough to ¼ inch thickness and cut with small holiday cookie cutters.
7. Place onto a greased baking sheet and cook for 45 minutes.
8. Cool on rack before serving.

DIRECTIONS PEOPLE:

1. Swap out the dehydrated dog food and add ½ cup ripened mashed bananas.

FELIZ NAUGHTY-DOG ENCHILADAS

Prep time: 30 minutes/Cook: I hour
Yields 24-30 yappitzers

This delicious party favorite is made with a delicious pumpkin sauce. Not only does it have an unbelievable taste but it's packed with nutrition. By leaving out the hot peppers and chili powder, dogs can safely enjoy this yummy dish too.

INGREDIENTS FOR PUPS AND PEOPLE:

- 1 14 oz can pumpkin puree
- 1 Tbsp ground cinnamon
- Kosher salt and black pepper
- Chili powder (humans)
- Extra virgin olive oil
- 2 ½ lbs sliced mushrooms
- 1 Tbsp ground cumin
- 1 Tbsp ground coriander
- 1 red bell pepper finely diced
- 1 jalapeno pepper finely diced (humans)
- 3 cloves garlic, grated
- 1 14 oz can black beans
- 1 cup cooked, shredded chicken.
- 1 14 oz can mild enchilada sauce
- 12 corn tortillas halved
- 1 lb shredded cheddar cheese
- 1 avocado diced (topping)
- Sour Cream or plain kefir (topping)
- Cilantro to garnish

DIRECTIONS FOR PUPS:

1. Heat oven to 375°F
2. In a small saucepan combine pumpkin, cinnamon, a pinch of salt and pepper, and ½ cup water
3. Cook over medium heat, stirring occasionally, to meld the flavors
4. In a large skillet over medium heat, add olive oil, salt, pepper, cumin, coriander, and sauté mushrooms until browned. Move cooked mushrooms to a separate plate. Set aside.
5. In the same pan, add a drizzle of more olive oil and add bell peppers, beans, garlic, and chicken. When sautéed, add in mushrooms and a few spoonfuls of enchilada sauce.
6. Coat a 9x13 baking dish with cooking spray. Spread a thin layer of enchilada sauce on ¾ dish leaving ¼ dish unseasoned for the dog portions.
7. Arrange 8 tortilla halves over top of the dish leaving no gaps. Spoon pumpkin mixture over the tortilla layer and spread evenly with a rubber spatula. Spoon ½ mushroom/chicken/bean mixture over the top of the pumpkin sauce. Spread evenly to cover entire dish. Sprinkle ½ of the cheese on top of the mushroom mixture. Repeat the layers twice more. Spoon a line of enchilada sauce separating the dog portion of casserole from the humans.
8. Cover casserole with foil and bake for 45 minutes. Remove the foil and bake another 10-15 minutes until cheese has melted and is golden brown. Let the casserole rest 15 minutes before serving.
9. Garnish with diced avocado and a dollop of sour cream/kefir and cilantro.

DIRECTIONS FOR PEOPLE:

1. Offer small cups of diced jalapeños and extra enchilada sauce to spoon over. This may be a tad bland for people who like things spicy but we are offering it mild for the sake of sharing it with our dogs. For a vegetarian version, divide the casserole up into thirds and offer a row without meat.

GINGERBREAD COOKIES

Prep time: 10 minutes/Cook: 45 minutes
Yields 24 medium-sized cookies

Nothing says Christmas like gingerbread cookies, but typically these are loaded with sugar and other spices that can be harmful to your dog. This variety is super tasty and in small amounts will be perfectly fine as a special treat. See below for dog-decorating options so guests can get creative with their dog's cookie.

INGREDIENTS FOR PUPS AND PEOPLE:

- Cookie cutters in gingerbread man or holiday shapes
- ½ cup oat flour
- ¼ cup rice flour
- 3 Tbsp potato starch
- 1 free-range egg
- ¼ tsp cinnamon
- ¼ tsp ginger
- ½ Tbsp applesauce
- 4 oz water
- 3 Tbsp honey
- 3 Tbsp coconut oil
- Frosting and candy to decorate (humans)

DIRECTIONS FOR PUPS AND PEOPLE:

1. Heat oven to 325°C.
2. In a large mixing bowl combine all ingredients and fold well until dough is well mixed and firm.
3. Roll dough onto lightly floured surface to ¼ inch thickness. Use holiday or gingerbread man-shaped cookie cutters. Use smaller shapes for dog-sized treats.
4. Place onto a parchment-lined baking sheet about 2" apart.
5. Bake for 20 minutes.
6. Let cool and decorate.

FROSTING/DECORATIONS IDEAS FOR PUPS:

- Almond or peanut butter (Double-check it doesn't contain XYLITOL)
- Chia or hemp seeds
- Dried blueberries, cranberries,
- Drizzle of kefir or plain Greek yogurt
- A pop of whip cream

DECORATING IDEAS FOR PUPS:

Ice each cookie with peanut butter or almond butter. You can add a dried cranberry or blueberry and sprinkle it with chia and hemp seeds. Add a drizzle of plain Greek yogurt or a pop of whip cream.

ACKNOWLEDGEMENTS

This book never would have happened without the excitement and passion of my dear friend, Caitlin Rose Cutt Lemaire. It's pure kismet! Many lifetimes ago, I was starring in the television series, SAFE AT HOME. Caitlin's dad played my older brother. Behind the scenes, I would bounce a then-infant Caitlin on my knee and carry her around every chance I got. The first second I laid eyes on her I fell in love and I truly felt like her auntie. Twenty years later and our paths serendipitously crossed again. I found her on Facebook and she became my then 10-year-old daughter's babysitter. Ironically, they share the same birthday. In 2018, I started an Artist's Way book club, and in walked Caitlin. We reconnected and began working on some television projects. Caitlin insisted I put my recipes and tips into a book. We got together every week for wine, dessert, and brainstorming, and less than a year (and 5 pounds) later, here we are. Many times when I just wasn't in the mood to write or was having my doubts anybody would want to read this book, Caitlin kept me going. I realized working on this project was so much fun, that was all that mattered. In addition to helping make this book happen, Caitlin was holding down the fort as a busy wife to her husband Miles, and mom to their preschooler Jack. Caitlin is a multi-talented podcaster, comedian, writer, and television producer and I feel so blessed she is in my life and on this journey with me.

Once the book was written, I needed someone to bring the vision to life. I lucked out and got the help of my dear friend, and fellow obsessed pug owner, Catherine "Cat" Large. Cat is an extremely talented artist, graphic designer, author, and photographer. Plus, her darling little rescue pug, Jewels is one of Olive's best friends. Likely because Jewels shares all her toys and is a very picky eater so Olive gets all the food samples. Cat not only shot and styled most of the gorgeous photos in this book, but she also did the beautiful graphic design and book layout. Plus, her wonderful husband Dave generously allowed me to invade their home (and take nearly every second of their free time) on many occasions while putting this book together. I had the time of my life, playing dress-up with the pugs, shooting pictures, and eating all the delicious food they made when I was around. It's always fun hanging out with Cat and Dave! They are quite popular and have a lot going on in their busy lives. I am eternally grateful for all their time and help with this project. This book is above and beyond what I ever imagined thanks to you.

I wish to thank my team of brilliant proofreaders and editors: Clara McCarthy, Marissa Mulhouse, Martin Kildare Robinson, and Elizabeth Weiner. I've read through this manuscript so many times I can't see even the most glaring typos. Your corrections, tips, edits, and suggestions were invaluable. You are all so busy juggling so many different things and your help means the world to me.

My daughter, Karley Cable is amazing! She has such a keen eye, amazing taste, and fierce style. Her buy-in means I'm on the right track. And if something is not to her taste, she's extremely kind in her feedback. She is a very busy PR manager but she always took the time to help me when I needed something. And usually, that was some help with figuring out my new computer. I'm so incredibly proud of you Karley and I appreciate your help more than you will ever know! This all happened because you wanted a dog for your 7th birthday. I love you.

My step-daughter Kristin Cable Johnson, is a rock-star lawyer. She is also the wonderful doting mother of an active preschooler Max, AND toddler twins Quintan and Tatum. Thanks for all the help with all my legal questions and for having my back.

For over 23 years, my very best friend, Alex Wood has been my ride-or-die. Thank you for your friendship and support over the years and mostly for always encouraging me and all my crazy ideas. Thank you for being my sounding board. You have always listened patiently and supported me whether it was dealing with the same drama in my life, or complaining about one thing or another. You are truly a one-in-a-million friend.

My dear friend Ed Gutierrez has impeccable taste and a sharp business mind. You make life so much fun! I appreciate all your help getting so many of my endeavors off the ground. -And being my favorite movie date for those arty films nobody else wants to see.

A big thank you to Playa Picnics in Long Beach, California, for the beautiful picnic set-ups featured in the photos. -And their darling dogs that were on hand as party guests. Thank you to Michelle Perez for loaning me her adorable daughter, Sophia, and their precious pug puppy, 2Pug, for our photoshoot. A big thank you to my neighbor Ed for loaning me his Golden, Rusty. I think of him as my dog who lives at another address.

Thank you to long-time friends Susan Madson and Rich Rosensweig for the use of their beautiful backyard and pool for our summer pride photoshoot.

Many thanks to my Nulo family: Founder/CEO Michael Landa, Head of Product Development, Heather Acuff, my awesome manager and Director of National Accounts, Natalie St. Peter, and my fellow-pug lover, Regional Sales Manager, James Torres. This book would not exist without the education on pet food and the opportunities you've provided me. Most of all thanks for offering innovative, healthy, and delicious foods for our pets. I hope this book is a perfect companion to your incredible line of pet foods.

Long before this book came about there was a loving community of pug peeps that have become a family to me. Kristin Andrews, DVM, and co-founder of the OG Las Vegas Pug Party started the ball rolling. It was there I met some of my closest friends: Alicia Nelson, and Fiona who are Surf Gidget the Pug's owners, Lori and Andy of OC PUG SATURDAY, Ronnie & Crystal, pug parents to The Dotty, IQ Pugs, and Divine Canine Treats, Zee & Jimmy pug parents to Chai and Abagail, and owners of Chai Coffee house and Chai's Mountain Retreat, Melissa Simock of Love Pug Circus, Steve Gonzales, Niki Star, of Saint Rue, What The Frenchie, and mom to Fira and Weston, Ninja Nate, Wendy, Briana, Ariana, and JJ the Pug, Wendy Silva, Jay O'keefe, Aaron Argueta, Bailey & Bubba of Bailey's CBD and everyone who embraces dog-inclusive entertaining (and travel) This book is for you.

Thank you to Izabella St. James -- AKA, The Pug Queen, Gwenn Valone, Director at Pug Nation Rescue LA, Sherry Stankowitz at Sparky and the Gang, and the SPCA Coachella, where I rescued my little Olive. You work tirelessly for animals in need and are true saints.

Huge thank you's to Olive's vet team. First and foremost, Dr. Gail Renehen at VCA Airport Irvine Animal Hospital and also my friend, Kristin Andrews, DVM. In addition, I wish to thank Dr. Karen Becker and Rodney Habib for their groundbreaking work. I have learned so much from their blogs, books, videos, and social media. In turn, I have been able to educate others. Your efforts have kept our pets thriving and healthy! You are all a Godsend to so many pet owners.

To my functional medicine doctor, Jennifer Kim Loomis, DO, and my certified nutritionist and health coach, Laura Hannifin. Not only have you restored my health but my will to live. I am so thankful I found you! You have given me my life back. -And a full head of hair! I hope this book can help your other patients who are on the road to healing but have a weakness for desserts.

Justin Rudd has been a friend and beacon in my community. Not only did he open Rosie's Dog Beach right down the street from my home, but he sponsors world-famous fun dog events such as the Howl'oween Costume Parade, the Bulldog Beauty Contest, the Blessing of the Animals, and so many more. Justin makes dog ownership fun! There is no better community to own a dog than right here in the LBC! Thank you!

And last, but certainly not least, there is no way this book could have happened without the unwavering support of my husband Rick. Putting this project together took a lot of time, money, and energy. I'm sure there were many times he would have preferred to put them into his golf game or something other than his wife's cookbook. Rick has a very demanding career and limited free time. He sacrificed so much in order for this book to happen and I will never forget it. Not only that, Rick always jumped in when I needed help. And usually, it was at the most inconvenient times. Whether it was a computer glitch, proofreading, brainstorming, recipe sampling, or needing him to do an entire photoshoot, he stopped what he was doing, and got the job done.

Long before there was even a book, I was a severely depressed wife that insisted we get another dog shortly after our first pug passed away. With a grief-stricken broken heart, and mountains of vet bills still to pay, my husband wanted another dog as much as I want to catch a bad covid variant. However, seeing how thrilled I was to find Olive, he agreed this little shelter pug could stay. Not only that, Rick stepped up to the plate and is an amazing dog dad!

During our 25 years of marriage, we have enjoyed many wonderful times but also big challenges. One of them was my battle with Hashimoto's. In a matter of months, I went from happy and energetic to deeply depressed. I was either sleeping all the time or too stiff and sore to do anything except cry as my hair fell out. This was a hardship for him too. But he stuck with me and helped me in every way possible. I am so thankful I have been able to put my condition into remission and feel happy and healthy again. Rick, this is your book as much as it is mine! I am so appreciative of your love and encouragement every step of the way. I love you.

BIOGRAPHIES

Katy Cable

Katy Cable is the creator of the pug health & lifestyle site, blog, and show, THE WEEKLY RUNT. A frequent guest on many TV shows discussing pet topics, Cable has also appeared in movies including BACK TO THE FUTURE, and starred in the TV series SAFE AT HOME and FIRED UP! In addition to working with pug rescue groups, Cable hosts meetups, and dog-friendly events. She is also a contributing writer to numerous publications including, The Huffington Post, Thrive Global, and Pet Talks. Cable lives at the beach in Southern California with her husband, Rick, and her rescue dog, little black Olive the Pug. For more information visit **www.weeklyrunt.com.**

Catherine Large

Catherine Large is a British artist who lives in Los Angeles. Having enjoyed a thrilling career spanning many areas of media production, including stop frame animation, SFX and VFX in the UK, she moved to Los Angeles and worked for several years growing a digital media technology company. Combining her passion for pugs, photography, design and storytelling, Catherine has created a line of gifts and books featuring her beloved little rescue pug Jewels. Catherine has turned some of their wonderful capers into a collection of fully illustrated fairy tales in her book 'The Pug, The Pumpkin & Other Curiously Curly Tails'. Take a peep at **www.jewelslapug.com.** Catherine is based in LA, but loves to travel and explore with Jewels and her husband Dave.

OFFICIAL MODELS AND TASTE TESTERS

Little Black Olive The Pug

Olive was found roaming the sweltering streets of Coachella. She was a skinny, scared little pug who had just had a litter of puppies. Olive had been a breeder dog living in an airline crate. On November 14, 2015, Katy rescued her from the SPCA in the desert. Olive was no more than a year old. Now she is living her best life down at the beach as Katy and her husband Rick's pampered pug. She loves food and devoured every recipe in this book. She gives then all TWO PAWS UP! Follow Olive's adventures on social media **@katycable.**

Jewels LA Pug

At the age of 2, Jewels found herself in the care of Pug Nation Rescue of Los Angeles. When Catherine walked through their door, Jewels knew she was the human she wanted to go home with. Catherine had little say in this matter, but neither of them have looked back. Jewels enjoys partying and dressing up and just loves to pose for the camera. Jewels has developed a discriminating palate and is very excited to be an official taste tester for this book. Follow Jewels' antics on social media **@jewelslapug.com.**

Made in the USA
Middletown, DE
28 August 2022

72497220R00075

U.S. Army Intelligence and Interrogation Handbook

DEPARTMENT OF THE ARMY

THE LYONS PRESS
GUILFORD, CONNECTICUT
AN IMPRINT OF THE GLOBE PEQUOT PRESS

The Lyons Press is an imprint of The Globe Pequot Press.

Printed in the United States of America

ISBN 0-7394-5505-2

Intelligence Interrogation
TABLE OF CONTENTS

PREFACE

This manual provides doctrinal guidance, techniques, and procedures governing employment of interrogators as human intelligence (HUMINT) collection assets in support of the commander's intelligence needs. It outlines the interrogator's role within the intelligence collection effort and the supported unit's day-to-day operations. Details are presented on how interrogation assets accomplish their assigned collection mission.

Material in this manual applies to operations in low-, mid-, and high-intensity conflicts. Principles outlined are valid under conditions involving use of electronic warfare (EW) or nuclear, biological, or chemical (NBC) weapons.

This manual is intended for use by interrogators as well as commanders, staff officers, and military intelligence (MI) personnel charged with the responsibility of the interrogation collection effort. Unless otherwise stated, descriptions pertaining to duties, functions, and responsibilities of the G1, G2, G3, G4, and G5 apply to equivalent positions at other organizational echelons.

Interrogation is the HUMINT subdiscipline responsible for MI exploitation of enemy personnel and documents to answer the supported specific information requirements (SIR). These SIR responses, along with those of other MI disciplines, are correlated to satisfy the force commander's priority intelligence requirements (PIR) and intelligence requirements (IR).

During previous armed conflicts, interrogators contributed significantly to the overall intelligence collection effort. They revalidated and established keystone interrogation doctrine (for example, theater interrogation facility [TIF] operations) and documented valuable lessons learned. This knowledge became the genesis for evolving interrogation doctrine.

During Southwest Asia operations, interrogators organized and operated a massive document exploitation (DOCEX) effort. Interrogation units screened, interrogated, or debriefed 49, 350 enemy prisoners of war (EPWs), and gathered enough captured enemy documents (CEDs) for DOCEX to fill 18 trailer trucks.

MI interrogation units are a proven and valued collection asset. This manual incorporates the operational experiences and lessons learned. It builds upon existing doctrine and moves interrogation into the 21st century.

These principles and techniques of interrogation are to be used within the constraints established by the following:

- The Uniform Code of Military Justice (UCMJ).
- Geneva Convention for the Amelioration of the Wounded and Sick in Armed Forces in the Field of August 12, 1949, hereinafter referred to as GWS.
- Geneva Convention Relative to the Treatment of Prisoners of War of August 12, 1949, hereinafter referred to as GPW.

- Geneva Convention Relative to the Protection of Civilian Persons in Time of War of August 12, 1949, hereinafter referred to as GC.

Doctrine in this publication conforms with and supports principles contained in FM 34-1.
This publication implements the following Standardization Agreements (STANAGs):

- STANAG 2033, Interrogation of Prisoners of War, Edition 6.
- STANAG 2044, Procedures for Dealing with Prisoners of War, Edition 5.
- STANAG 2084, Handling and Reporting of Captured Enemy Equipment and Documents, Edition 5.

This publication also complies with STANAG 1059 and Quadripartite Standardization Agreements (QSTAGs) 170, 523, and 528.

The use of the terms EPW, detainee, and source are interchangeable during interrogation process.

Unless this publication states otherwise, masculine nouns or pronouns do not refer exclusively to men.

CHAPTER 1
MILITARY INTELLIGENCE MISSIONS AND INTELLIGENCE PREPARATION OF THE BATTLEFIELD

This manual is about interrogation operations. The purpose of this chapter is to define the interrogation mission and its critical elements; describe battlefield operations, IEW operations, and the intelligence processes, disciplines, and the mission, enemy, troops, terrain, and time available (METT-T) factors that shape and drive the interrogation process.

It also addresses the personal qualities and special areas of knowledge of the interrogator and the capabilities and limitations of interrogation. It includes information on the various levels of conflict, interrogation missions, intelligence preparation of the battlefield (IPB), and the intelligence cycle. The level of detail is structured to assist you in understanding the interrogation tactics, techniques, and procedures described in the remainder of the manual.

WARFIGHTING DOCTRINE

Battlefield operations demand seizing and maintaining the initiative. When operations are properly designed and executed, initiative accrues significant benefits from the outset of an operation to final victory. It permits attacking where, when, and what; while forcing the enemy to react and try to adapt to our operations.

To gain the initiative, the commander must—

- See the enemy early and determine the capabilities and intentions of the enemy.
- Find and track enemy follow-on echelons.
- Identify enemy high-value targets (HVTs), which, if successfully attacked, will contribute to the degradation of important enemy battlefield functions.
- Identify, locate, and develop the required targeting data for the attack of high-payoff targets (HPTs), which, if successfully attacked, will contribute to the success of friendly plans.
- Detect enemy weaknesses and develop the necessary data to support the exploitation of these weaknesses.
- Effectively use electronic warfare (EW) assets to support battlefield operations while protecting friendly use of the electromagnetic spectrum.
- Determine the enemy's capability and guard against that capability.
- Protect friendly forces and operations from enemy intelligence collection operations.
- Ensure the enemy is defeated.
- Use the weather and terrain to friendly advantage.

The commander uses defensive and offensive operations to destroy enemy first-echelon forces and deep-attack to simultaneously delay, disrupt, and manipulate enemy follow-on forces. The commander anticipates, creates, and exploits windows of opportunity, using flexible battle planning, to gain the initiative through offensive operations.

By effectively employing maneuver and fire support assets, manipulating the enemy, and expertly using the weather and the terrain, the friendly commander can successfully defeat a superior enemy force. Operation Desert Storm is an example of the successful application of this doctrine.

IEW support is vital to the successful planning and execution of battlefield operations at all echelons. Intelligence support at brigade and battalion levels focuses primarily on close operations, while at division it focuses on close and deep operations. Corps is the focal point for intelligence operations that support rear and deep operations.

THE INTELLIGENCE CYCLE

Intelligence operations follow a four-phase process known as the intelligence cycle, which is shown at Figure 1.1. The intelligence cycle is oriented to the commander's mission. Supervising and planning are inherent in all phases of the cycle.

The intelligence cycle is continuous. Although the four phases are conducted in sequence, all are conducted concurrently. While available information is processed and additional information is collected, the intelligence staff is planning and directing the collection effort to meet new demands. Previously collected and processed information (intelligence) is disseminated as soon as it is available or needed.

INTELLIGENCE DISCIPLINES

The IEW system includes three MI disciplines: signals intelligence (SIGINT), imagery intelligence (IMINT), and HUMINT. Intelligence interrogation falls within the realm of HUMINT.

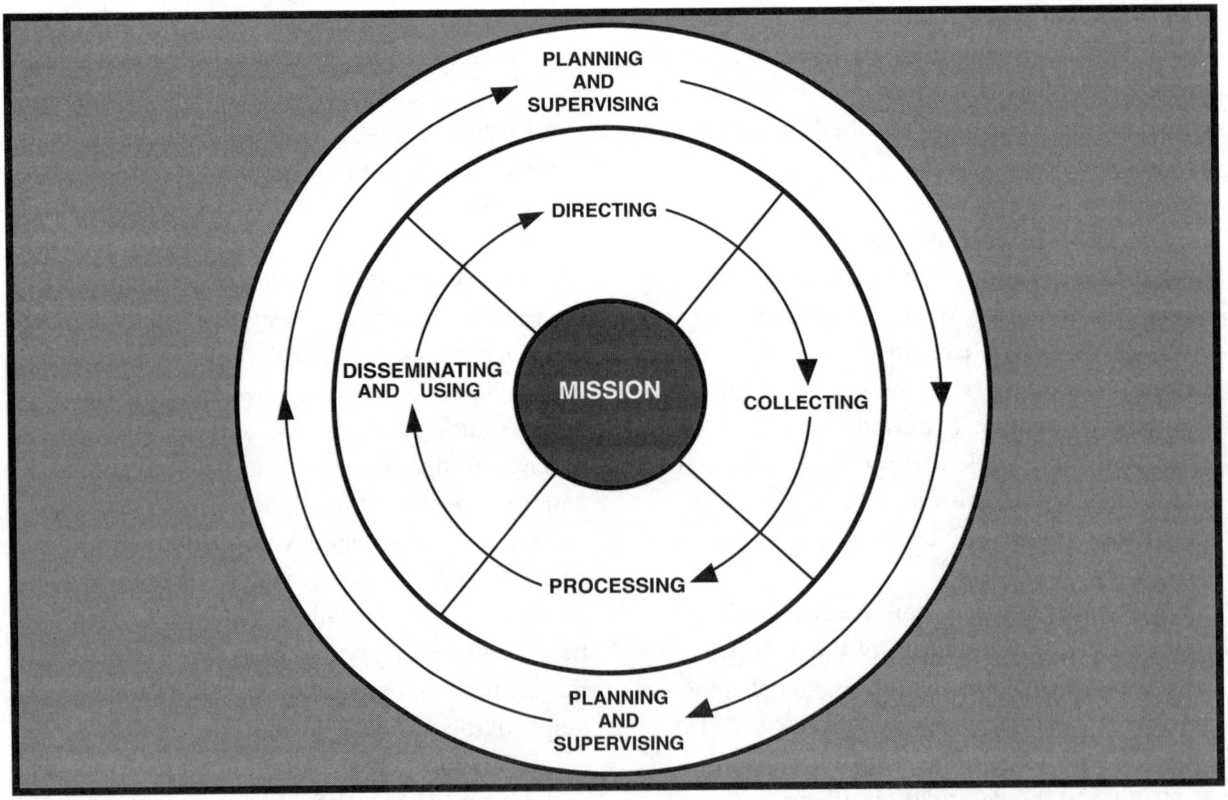

Figure 1-1. The Intelligence cycle.

SIGINT

SIGINT is derived from the intercept, analysis, and exploitation of threat communications and noncommunications radio-electronic emissions.

IMINT

IMINT is obtained from the analysis of radar, photographic, infrared, and electro-optical imagery.

HUMINT

HUMINT is obtained from information collected from human sources and consists of the following intelligence collection operations:

- Interrogation of EPWs, civilian detainees, insurgents, defectors, refugees, displaced persons, and agents or suspected agents.
- Long-range surveillance (LRS) patrols.
- Strategic debriefing.
- Controlled collection operations.
- Open-source exploitation, to include publications and broadcasts.
- Reports of contact from forward units.
- Observation and listening posts.
- Low-level source operations (LLSO).
- HUMINT liaison contacts.

After World War II, the US General Board on Intelligence surveyed 54 division G2s, 18 corps G2s, and 7 Army G2s. It concluded that 43 percent of all intelligence produced in the European theater of operations was from HUMINT, and 84 percent of the HUMINT was from interrogation. The majority of those surveyed agreed that interrogation was the most valuable of all collection operations.

HUMINT is vital in all combat operations, regardless of echelon or intensity of conflict. By nature, HUMINT lends itself to the collection of information about the enemy's thought processes and intentions. HUMINT can provide information on almost any topic of intelligence interest, including order of battle (OB) factors, as well as scientific and technical (S&T) intelligence subjects. During Operation Desert Storm, interrogators collected information which helped to—

- Develop a plan to breach Iraqi defensive belts.
- Confirm Iraqi supply-line interdiction by coalition air strikes.
- Identify diminishing Iraqi troop morale.
- Identify a US PW captured during the battle of Kafji.

INTELLIGENCE AND ELECTRONIC WARFARE OPERATIONS

The intelligence cycle supports six tasks which are common to all echelons and which must be worked, at least in part, concurrently to satisfy the needs of the commander. The commander may have to prioritize these functions when resource and time constraints dictate.

INDICATIONS AND WARNING (I&W)

I&W identifies major shifts in enemy tactics, operations, and strategy which will set or change the terms of battle. They protect the commander from surprise and identify areas or times of risk by detecting enemy actions that are counter to planning assumptions.

- At the operational level, they identify potential enemy action and determine the need for a military response and the probability of hostilities.
- At the tactical level, they focus on the timing of hostilities rather than on their probability.

I&W prevent surprise and minimize risk through the early identification of enemy activities and capabilities.

INTELLIGENCE PREPARATION OF THE BATTLEFIELD

IPB integrates the environment with the enemy's fighting doctrine and actions. It reveals his capabilities and vulnerabilities and allows the commander to systematically predict his actions. It also allows him to understand the battlefield and how to synchronize all of his battlefield operating systems for maximum effect.

The results of IPB and staff wargaming are used to coordinate and synchronize the intelligence system regardless of the echelon at which it is performed or the intensity of conflict. IPB is more than preparation of the field of battle during hostilities. IPB considers the entire environment of conflict, supporting contingency as well as planning operations.

- At the strategic level, IPB focuses on all factors that contribute to military potential and includes political, economic, sociological, and S&T aspects of the enemy's ability and intent to conduct military operations.
- At the operational level, IPB identifies the enemy's political, economic, or military center of gravity, the lines of operation, and the points in time and geography where the decisive engagements of a campaign will occur. It also predicts the courses of action (COAs) the enemy is likely to follow. This is done by incorporating political, economic, social, and geographical factors, as well as military factors (such as his military potential and ability to apply air, ground, and naval power).
- At the tactical level, IPB focuses on the details of the terrain, weather, and enemy. It predicts and prioritizes the enemy's COAs and synchronizes the application of combat power on identified decisive points.

In mid-intensity conflict (MIC) to high-intensity conflict (HIC), IPB focuses on the traditional aspects of terrain, weather, and enemy. Many of the factors evaluated in IPB at the strategic level are used during IPB for low-intensity conflict (LIC) at the operational and tactical levels.

Social, economic, and political factors that affect the environment of conflict are considered in IPB. The population must be examined in as much detail as the enemy and the terrain to understand what an enemy can or cannot do. Figure 1-2 shows the intelligence cycle using IPB.

SITUATION DEVELOPMENT

Situation development confirms or denies the enemy COAs predicted in IPB. It confirms predicted centers of gravity and decisive points and identifies enemy strengths and vulnerabilities. This enables the commander to make timely decisions and effectively apply his combat power.

TARGET DEVELOPMENT AND TARGET ACQUISITION

Target development and target acquisition provide targets and targeting data for attacks by fire, maneuver, and electronic means. They identify and locate those targets that will have the greatest impact on the campaign's decisive engagements. These include deep operational reserves, strategic and operational level command, control, and communications (C^3) nodes, key lines of communication, and air and naval staging facilities

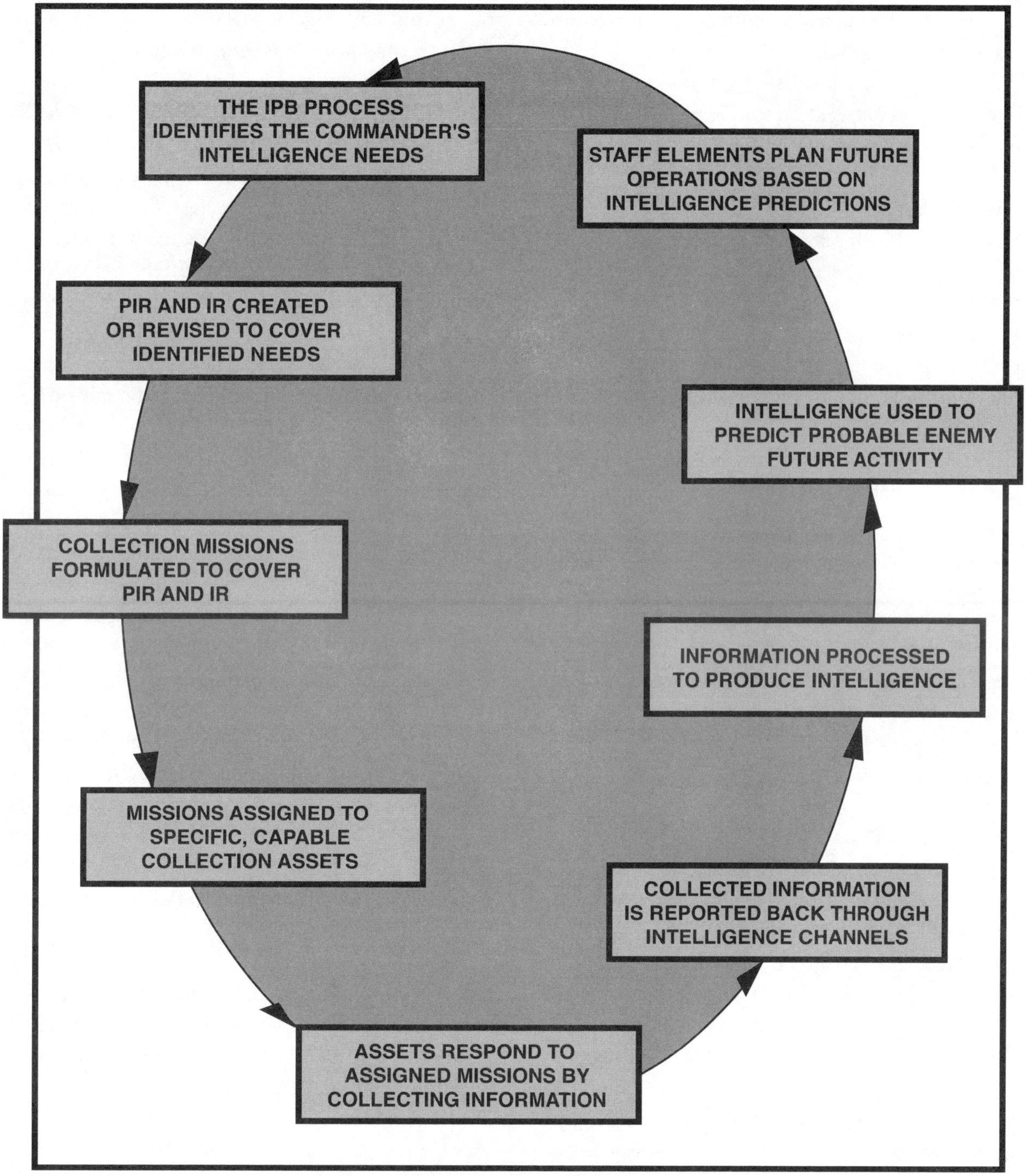

Figure 1-2. Intelligence cycle using IPB.

throughout the enemy's depth that contribute to his combat potential.

At the tactical level, they address those HVTs that directly contribute to the application of combat power at decisive points on the battlefield.

BATTLE DAMAGE ASSESSMENT (BDA)

BDA provides the commander with the effect of friendly operations on the enemy. It focuses on the enemy's remaining military capabilities and potential. At the operational level, it also considers the campaign's effects on the enemy's economy and operational infrastructure as well as his military force structure.

BDA is focused on providing effects of particular strikes and attacks, or a series of them. BDA is performed by the same collection assets used to satisfy the commander's intelligence and targeting priorities; therefore, BDA cannot be performed continuously without degradation of other capabilities, such as situation development and targeting. The commander must prioritize the BDA effort, identifying what he must know and when he must know it, just as he does for his PIR and targeting priorities.

FORCE PROTECTION

Force protection identifies friendly vulnerabilities and the enemy's efforts to exploit them. At the operational level, it includes the early identification of significant improvements in weapon lethality, the introduction of weapons of mass destruction into the conflict, or the commitment of terrorist or other unconventional forces into friendly rear areas.

Force protection goes beyond countering enemy intelligence and includes the protection of all forces that contribute to our combat power. At the tactical level, it emphasizes measures to counter the enemy's intelligence collection capabilities and to protect the force from enemy action.

MISSION, ENEMY, TROOPS, TERRAIN, AND TIME AVAILABLE FACTORS

The METT-T factors are important to the commander when planning interrogation operations. METT-T determines how the commander will use interrogation assets. The effect of METT-T on interrogation missions is discussed below.

MISSION SUPPORT

The supported force's mission bears directly on how the interrogation element will be employed. In cordon and search operations, commanders may determine interrogators are best suited to screen the populace in order to identify insurgents and their supporters. In counter-drug operations, commanders may use interrogators to exploit documents and to train US and foreign agents in interrogation techniques. In all conflicts, the focus will be on EPW interrogation and CED exploitation.

The mission influences interrogation operations in other ways. For example, if the force's mission is offensive, interrogation elements must be highly mobile, with secure communications to the supported G2 or S2. They must be constantly prepared to move forward with the element they are supporting. This limits time available for exploitation and dissemination.

On the other hand, if the mission is defensive, interrogation elements have more time to exploit individual sources. They may also have more flexibility to exploit EPWs or detainees and CEDs, to fulfill the commander's intent to construct operational graphics.

Collection requirements vary according to echelon. Strategic echelon requirements reflect the wide scope of interest of the theater and national command authority (NCA); whereas, tactical PIR and IR—and resultant SIR—reflect the immediate, more narrowly focused intelligence interest of the maneuver commander.

ENEMY

The enemy, and our knowledge of the enemy, can influence interrogator assignments and the complexity of the exploitation process. One factor which affects interrogation operations is the type of opposing enemy force. The techniques and procedures used to collect from insurgents in a LIC may differ from those used to collect from regular enemy forces in a MIC to HIC.

For example, an EPW from a regular forces unit may have undergone political indoctrination, but his commitment to his unit may not be as strong as that of the insurgent who is passionately committed to an ideal. Thus, interrogators may have more difficulty persuading the insurgent to talk.

Another factor affecting interrogation operations is our current intelligence holdings on the enemy force and the interrogator's understanding of the threat. Our intelligence holdings on the composition of a newly formed insurgent organization usually will not be as complete as holdings on the composition of a regular enemy force. Thus, the focus of interrogation efforts in the early stages of a LIC may be on enemy force composition; whereas, the focus in a MIC or HIC may be on enemy force missions or intentions.

Cultural aspects also affect interrogation missions. The employment of some basic interrogation techniques will differ based on the ethnic and cultural background of the enemy, and our failure to understand and adapt to this could hamper the collection effort.

TROOPS

The number, experience level, and language proficiency of interrogators affect the tactical employment of interrogation elements. Due to the limited number of interrogators at any echelon, interrogation element commanders have to pick from available interrogators. They must manage personnel to ensure the most experienced are used to the best advantage (for example, to exploit complex enemy documents) and select EPWs most likely to answer SIR.

Interrogation element commanders often have to contend with a mismatch between language-qualified personnel assigned to the unit and languages needed to perform the mission. They overcome the mismatch by acquiring local national (LN) interpreter support through the Assistant Chief of Staff, G1 (Personnel). They can also augment their interrogators by requesting other available linguists within the supported command to serve as interpreters.

Another troop-related factor which affects interrogation operations is the training of all soldiers on EPW handling and evacuation. EPW treatment during the early stages of capture is critical to the success of subsequent interrogations. The availability of military police (MP) support at brigade and above can enhance interrogation activities. Interrogation operations are more effective in a controlled environment where EPWs are adequately guarded.

TERRAIN

Terrain and weather are relevant to interrogator operations and affect site deployments, communications, and mobility. MP must ensure proper shelter and security for the EPW facility if it is collocated or immediately adjacent to the EPW collecting point or internment facility.

TIME AVAILABLE

Information collected through interrogation operations is valuable only if it is reported in a timely manner. Exploitation procedures may need to be adjusted to make the most use of time available. At the tactical level, interrogations will be brief, PIR driven, and reported in concise formats such as size, activity, location, unit, time, equipment (SALUTE).

At the operational and strategic levels, time will generally allow for a more expanded interrogation effort and flexible reporting format, such as the intelligence information report (IIR).

The challenge is for interrogators to be proficient linguists and skilled members of a highly organized collection activity. This ensures the acquisition of the maximum amount of pertinent information regardless of time available.

Like other intelligence assets, interrogators must serve the commander. Interrogation operations are of no value unless they contribute to the accomplishment of the supported commander's mission. To understand the interrogator's role in mission accomplishment, one must understand the interrogation process.

DEFINITION OF INTERROGATION

Interrogation is the process of questioning a source to obtain the maximum amount of usable information. The goal of any interrogation is to obtain reliable information in a lawful manner, in a minimum amount of time, and to satisfy intelligence requirements of any echelon of command. Sources may be—

- Civilian internees.
- Insurgents.
- EPWs.
- Defectors.
- Refugees.
- Displaced persons.
- Agents or suspected agents.
- Other non-US personnel.

A good interrogation produces needed information which is timely, complete, clear, and accurate. An interrogation involves the interaction of two personalities—the source and the interrogator. Each contact between these two may differ because of individual characteristics and capabilities of the participants. Furthermore, the circumstances of each contact and physical environment vary.

Other forms of intelligence interrogations include interviews, debriefings and elicitations. There are certain principles which generally apply to all types of interrogations; namely, the objective, the prohibition against use of force, and security.

OBJECTIVE

Each interrogation must be conducted for a definite purpose. The interrogator must keep this purpose firmly in mind as he proceeds to obtain usable information to satisfy the assigned requirement, and thus contribute to the success of the unit's mission.

The objective may be specific—Establish the exact location of an ammunition storage facility. Or it may be general—Seek to obtain OB information about a specific echelon of the enemy forces.

In either case, the interrogator must use the objective as a basis for planning and conducting the interrogation. He should attempt to prevent the source from becoming aware of the true objective of the interrogation. The interrogator should not concentrate on the objective to the extent he overlooks or fails to recognize and exploit other valuable information extracted from the source.

For example, during an interrogation, the interrogator learns of the presence of a heretofore unknown, highly destructive weapon. Although this information may not be in line with his specific objective, the interrogator must develop this important lead to obtain all possible information concerning this weapon. It becomes obvious an interrogation objective can be changed as necessary or desired.

PROHIBITION AGAINST USE OF FORCE

The Intelligence Staff Officer (J2, G2, or S2) has responsibility for all command intelligence functions. He assists the commander by—

- Supervising the collection, evaluation, and interpretation of all intelligence information.
- Disseminating intelligence to appropriate higher, lower, and adjacent units.
- Assuming primary responsibility to ensure that all command intelligence functions are conducted in accordance with international, US, and other applicable law and policy. Specifically, the J2, G2, or S2 is responsible to ensure the GWS, GPW, and GC are not violated by intelligence personnel.

One of the significant means used by the intelligence staff is the interrogation of the following:

- EPWs.
- Captured insurgents.
- Civilian internees.
- Other captured, detained, or retained persons.
- Foreign deserters or other persons of intelligence interest.

These persons are protected by the Geneva Conventions for the Protection of War Victims of August 12, 1949, as they relate to captured wounded and sick enemy personnel (GWS), retained enemy medical personnel and chaplains (GWS), enemy prisoners of war (GPW), and civilian internees (GC). Captured insurgents and other detained personnel whose status is not clear, such as suspected terrorists, are entitled to PW protection until their precise status has been determined by competent authority.

In conducting intelligence interrogations, the J2, G2, or S2 has primary staff responsibility to ensure these activities are performed in accordance with the GWS, GPW, and GC, as well as US policies, regarding the treatment and handling of the above-mentioned persons.

The GWS, GPW, GC, and US policy expressly prohibit acts of violence or intimidation, including physical or mental torture, threats, insults, or exposure to inhumane treatment as a means of or aid to interrogation.

Such illegal acts are not authorized and will not be condoned by the US Army. Acts in violation of these prohibitions are criminal acts punishable under the UCMJ. If there is doubt as to the legality of a proposed form of interrogation not specifically authorized in this manual, the advice of the command judge advocate should be sought before using the method in question.

Experience indicates that the use of prohibited techniques is not necessary to gain the cooperation of interrogation sources. Use of torture and other illegal methods is a poor technique that yields unreliable results, may damage subsequent collection efforts, and can induce the source to say what he thinks the interrogator wants to hear.

Revelation of use of torture by US personnel will bring discredit upon the US and its armed forces while undermining domestic and international support for the war effort. It also may place US and allied personnel in enemy hands at a greater risk of abuse by their captors. Conversely, knowing the enemy has abused US and allied PWs does not justify using methods of interrogation specifically prohibited by the GWS, GPW, or GC, and US policy.

Limitations on the use of methods identified herein as expressly prohibited should not be confused with psychological ploys, verbal trickery, or other nonviolent or noncoercive ruses used by the interrogator in the successful interrogation of hesitant or uncooperative sources.

The psychological techniques and principles in this manual should neither be confused with, nor construed to be synonymous with, unauthorized techniques such as brainwashing, physical or mental torture, or any other form of mental coercion to include drugs that may induce lasting and permanent mental alteration and damage.

Physical or mental torture and coercion revolve around eliminating the source's free will, and are expressly prohibited by GWS, Article 13; GPW, Articles 13 and 17; and GC, Articles 31 and 32. Torture is defined as the infliction of intense pain to body or mind to extract a confession or information, or for sadistic pleasure.

Examples of physical torture include—

- Electric shock.
- Infliction of pain through chemicals or bondage (other than legitimate use of restraints to prevent escape).
- Forcing an individual to stand, sit, or kneel in abnormal positions for prolonged periods of time.
- Food deprivation.
- Any form of beating.

Examples of mental torture include—

- Mock executions.
- Abnormal sleep deprivation.
- Chemically induced psychosis.

Coercion is defined as actions designed to unlawfully induce another to compel an act against one's will. Examples of coercion include—

- Threatening or implying physical or mental torture to the subject, his family, or others to whom he owes loyalty.
- Intentionally denying medical assistance or care in exchange for the information sought or other cooperation.
- Threatening or implying that other rights guaranteed by the GWS, GPW, or GC will not be provided unless cooperation is forthcoming.

Specific acts committed by US Army personnel may subject them to prosecution under one or more of the following punitive articles of the UCMJ:

- Article 78 - Accessory after the fact.
- Article 80 - Attempts (to commit one of the following offenses).
- Article 81 - Conspiracy (to commit one of the following offenses).
- Article 93 - Cruelty and maltreatment.

- Article 118 - Murder.
- Article 119 - Manslaughter.
- Article 124 - Maiming.
- Article 127 - Extortion.
- Article 128 - Assault (consummated by battery; with a dangerous weapon; or intentionally inflicting grievous bodily harm).
- Article 134 - Homicide, negligent:
    - Misprision of a serious offense (taking some positive act to conceal a serious crime committed by another).
    - Soliciting another to commit an offense.
    - Threat, communicating.

See Appendix A for the text of these offenses.

While using legitimate interrogation techniques, certain applications of approaches and techniques may approach the line between lawful actions and unlawful actions. It may often be difficult to determine where lawful actions end and unlawful actions begin. In attempting to determine if a contemplated approach or technique would be considered unlawful, consider these two tests:

- Given all the surrounding facts and circumstances, would a reasonable person in the place of the person being interrogated believe that his rights, as guaranteed under both international and US law, are being violated or withheld, or will be violated or withheld if he fails to cooperate.
- If your contemplated actions were perpetrated by the enemy against US PWs, you would believe such actions violate international or US law.

If you answer yes to either of these tests, do not engage in the contemplated action. If a doubt still remains as to the legality of a proposed action, seek a legal opinion from your servicing judge advocate.

The approaches, psychological techniques, and other principles presented in this manual must be read in light of the requirements of international and US law as discussed above.

Authority for conducting interrogations of personnel detained by military forces rests primarily upon the traditional concept that the commander may use all available resources and lawful means to accomplish his mission and to protect and secure his unit.

It is the stated policy of the US Army that military operations will be conducted in accordance with the law of war obligations of the US. The GWS, GPW, and GC establish specific standards for humane care and treatment of enemy personnel captured, retained, or detained by US military forces and its allies. Suspected or alleged violations of these standards will be reported, investigated and, if appropriate, referred to competent authority for trial or other disposition. Violations of the GWS, GPW, or GC committed by US personnel normally constitute violations of the UCMJ.

The commander is responsible for ensuring that the forces under his command comply with the GWS, GPW, and GC. Should violations occur in the conduct of warfare, the commander bears primary responsibility for investigating and prosecuting violations.

SECURITY

The interrogator, by virtue of his position, possesses a great deal of classified information. He is aware his job is to obtain information, not impart it to the source. He safeguards military information as well as the source of that information.

This becomes very clear when one considers that among those persons with whom the interrogator has contact, there are those attempting to collect information for the enemy. The interrogator is alert to detect any attempt made by the source to elicit information.

DEFINITION OF PRISONER OF WAR AND ENEMY PRISONER OF WAR

A PW is a US or allied person detained by an enemy power. An EPW is a person detained by US or allied powers. The first issue interrogators must deal with is who must be afforded PW treatment. Figure 1-3 paraphrases Article 4 of the GPW. In addition, the following personnel shall be treated as PWs: Persons belonging, or having belonged, to the armed forces of the occupied country, if—

- The occupying power considers it necessary by reason of such allegiance to intern them; in particular, if—
- Such persons have made an unsuccessful attempt to rejoin the armed forces to which they belong and which are engaged in combat; or
- Where they fail to comply with a summons made to them with a view to internment.

Obviously, there are many personnel who qualify for and require treatment as PWs. If there is any question whether a person should be treated as a PW, treat the individual as such. The determination whether an individual qualifies as a PW is a Staff Judge Advocate (SJA) function, but has a direct impact on the interrogation effort due to GPW requirements. It is especially important in LICs to distinguish between PWs and criminals.

PERTINENT ARTICLES OF GENEVA CONVENTIONS

Several articles of the GPW apply to interrogators and interrogation operations. The articles most commonly used by interrogators are shown in Figure 1-4.

TYPES OF SOURCES

The interrogator encounters many sources who vary greatly in personality, social class, civilian occupation, military speccialty, and political and religious beliefs. Their physical conditions may range from near death to perfect health; intelligence levels may range from well below average to well above average; and security consciousness may range from the lowest to the highest.

Sources may be civilian internees, insurgents, EPWs, defectors, refugees, displaced persons, and agents or suspected agents. Because of these variations, the interrogator makes a careful study of every source to evaluate his mental, emotional, and physical state, and uses it as a basis for interrogation. He deals mainly with three categories of sources: cooperative and friendly, neutral and nonpartisan, and hostile and antagonistic.

COOPERATIVE AND FRIENDLY

A cooperative and friendly source offers little resistance to interrogation, and normally speaks freely on almost any topic introduced, other than those which tend to incriminate or degrade him personally. To obtain the maximum amount of information from cooperative and friendly sources, the interrogator takes care to establish and pre-

PWs are persons who have fallen into the power of the enemy and who are—

- Members of the armed forces of a party to the conflict, militias, or volunteer corps forming part of such armed forces.
- Members of other militias and volunteer corps, including those of organized resistance movements, belonging to a part of the conflict, and operating in or outside their territory, even if this territory is occupied, provided such militias or volunteer corps, including such organized resistance movements, fulfill the following conditions, by—
  - Being commanded by a person responsible for their subordinates.
  - Having a fixed distinctive sign recognizable at a distance.
  - Carrying arms openly.
  - Conducting their operations by the laws and customs of war.
- Members of regular armed forces who profess allegiance to a government or an authority not recognized by the Detaining Power.
- Persons who accompany the armed forces without being members of it, such as civilian members of military aircraft crews, war correspondents, supply contractors, members of labor units or services responsible for the welfare of the armed forces, if they have received authorization from the armed forces they accompany, who shall provide them for that purpose with an identity card as described in the Geneva Conventions.
- Members of the crews of merchant marine, and crews of civil aircraft of the parties to the conflict, who do not benefit by more favorable treatment under any other provisions of international law.
- Inhabitants of an unoccupied territory, who on the approach of the enemy, spontaneously take up arms to resist the invading forces, without having had time to form themselves into regular armed units provided they carry arms openly and respect the laws and customs of war.

Figure 1-3. Definition of prisoner of war (GPW).

serve a friendly and cooperative atmosphere by not inquiring into those private affairs which are beyond the scope of the interrogation. At the same time, he must avoid becoming overly friendly and losing control of the interrogation.

NEUTRAL AND NONPARTISAN

A neutral and nonpartisan source is cooperative to a limited degree. He normally takes the position of answering questions asked directly, but seldom volunteers information. In some cases, he may be afraid to answer for fear of reprisals by the enemy. This often is the case in LIC where the people may be fearful of insurgent reprisals. With the neutral and nonpartisan source, the interrogator may have to ask many specific questions to obtain the information required.

Article 13—PWs must be humanely treated. Any unlawful act or omission by the Detaining Power causing death or seriously endangering the health of a PW in its custody is prohibited. PWs must always be protected, particularly against acts of violence or intimidation and against insults and public curiosity.

Article 14—PWs are entitled, in all circumstances, to respect for their persons and honor. Women shall be treated with all regard due their sex, and shall always benefit by treatment as favorable that granted men.

Article 15—The Power detaining PWs shall provide, free of charge, for the maintenance and medical attention required by their state of health.

Article 17—This article covers several requirements with direct impact on interrogation.

- Every PW, when questioned on the subject, is bound to give only his surname, first names and rank, date of birth, and army, regimental, personal or (SIC) serial number, or failing this, equivalent information. If he willfully infringes this rule, he may render himself liable to a restriction of the privileges (emphasis added) accorded to his rank or status.
- For example, this does not mean if a prisoner fails to give this information he loses status as a prisoner, only special privileges. An example might be an officer who fails to identify himself as such. An officer cannot be compelled to work (Article 49). An officer who fails to identify himself as such could lose this privilege.
- The questioning of PWs shall be carried out in a language they understand.
- No physical or mental torture nor any other form of coercion may be inflicted on EPWs to secure from them information of any kind whatsoever. EPWs who refuse to answer may not be threatened, insulted, or exposed to unpleasant or disadvantageous treatment of any kind.

Article 18—All effects and articles of personal use, except arms, horses, military equipment and documents, shall remain in the possession of PWs. They will also retain their metal helmets, gas masks, and like articles issued for personal protection. Effects and articles used for their clothing or feeding shall also remain in their possession, even if such effects and articles belong to their regulation military equipment.

- Badges of rank and nationality, decorations and articles having above all a personal or sentimental value may not be taken from PWs.
- Sums of money carried by PWs may not be taken away from them except by order of an officer, and after the amount and particulars of the owner have been recorded in a special register and an itemized receipt has been given, legibly inscribed with the name, rank, and unit of the person issuing said receipt.

Article 19—PWs shall be evacuated, as soon as possible after their capture, to camps situated in an area far enough from the combat zone for them to be out of danger. Only those PWs, who, owing to wounds and sickness, would run greater risks by being evacuated than by remaining where they are, may be temporarily kept back in a danger zone.

Article 33—Medical personnel and chaplains, while retained by the Detaining Power with a view to assisting PWs, shall not be considered as PWs. They shall, however, receive as a minimum, the benefits and protection of the Geneva Convention. They shall continue to exercise their medical and spiritual functions for the benefits of PWs.

Figure 1-4. Pertinent articles of the GPW.

HOSTILE AND ANTAGONISTIC

A hostile and antagonistic source is most difficult to interrogate. In many cases, he refuses to talk at all, and offers a real challenge to the interrogator. An interrogator must have self-control, patience, and tact when dealing with him.

At lower tactical echelons, there is generally insufficient time available to effectively interrogate a hostile or antagonistic source. When time is available, and the source appears to be an excellent target for exploitation, the source should be segregated and approached in an effort to obtain his cooperation. Because of possible high stress and frustration levels that such a source may invoke in you, great care must be taken to maintain you self-control. No matter what the source says or does, you must abide by the provisions of the law of war as previously discussed.

The absence of the use of threats in interrogation is intentional, as threats in and of themselves constitute a form of coercion. Any attempt at enforcement of a threat would constitute an act prohibited by the GWS, GPW, or GC and is punishable under the UCMJ.

A hostile or antagonistic source may be best exploited at echelons where sufficient time and resources will generally be available.

The successful interrogator is a skilled professional who is able to rapidly evaluate sources of information and adapt his approaches and techniques accordingly. The interrogator extracts intelligence from two primary sources: human sources and material sources (primarily CEDs). The senior interrogator determines which of these sources may be most effectively exploited to meet the supported commander's PIR and IR.

CEDs (see Chapter 4) include any piece of recorded information which has been in the possession of a foreign nation and comes into US possession. This includes US documents which the foreign nation may have possessed. There are many ways to acquire a document; some are found in the possession of human sources, on enemy dead, or on the battlefield. There are three types of documents:

- Official (government or military) documents such as overlays, field orders, maps, and codes.
- Personal (private or commercial) documents such as letters, diaries, newspapers, and books.
- Identity (government or military) documents such as cards and books.

PERSONAL QUALITIES

An interrogator should possess an interest in human nature and have a personality which will enable him to gain the cooperation of a source. Ideally, these and other personal qualities would be inherent in an interrogator; however, in most cases, an interrogator can cultivate these qualities if he has the desire and is willing to devote time to study and practice. Some desirable personal qualities is an interrogator are discussed below.

MOTIVATION

Motivation is the most significant factor to achieve success. Without motivation, other qualities lose their significance. The stronger the motivation, the more successful the interrogator. An interrogator may be motivated by several factors; for example:

- An interest in human relations.
- A desire to react to the challenge of personal interplay.
- An enthusiasm for the collection of information.
- A profound interest in foreign languages and cultures.

ALERTNESS

The interrogator must be constantly aware of the shifting attitudes which normally characterize a source's reaction to interrogation. The interrogator—

- Notes the source's every gesture, word, and voice inflection.
- Determines why the source is in a certain mood or why his mood suddenly changed. It is from the source's mood and actions the interrogator determines how to best proceed with the interrogation.
- Watches for any indication the source is withholding information.
- Watches for a tendency to resist further questioning, diminishing resistance, contradictions, or other tendencies, to include susceptibility.

PATIENCE AND TACT

The interrogator must have patience and tact in creating and maintaining rapport between himself and the source, thereby enhancing the success of the interrogation. The validity of the source's statements and motives behind these statements may be obtainable only through exercise of tact and patience. Displaying impatience may—

- Encourage the difficult source to think if he remains unresponsive for a little longer, the interrogator will stop questioning.
- Cause the source to lose respect for the interrogator, thereby reducing his effectiveness.

An interrogator, with patience and tact, is able to terminate an interrogation and later continue it without arousing apprehension or resentment.

CREDIBILITY

The interrogator must maintain credibility with the source and friendly forces. Failure to produce material rewards when promised may adversely affect future interrogations. The importance of accurate reporting cannot be overstressed, since interrogation reports are often the basis for tactical decisions and operations.

OBJECTIVITY

The interrogator must maintain an objective and dispassionate attitude, regardless of the emotional reactions he may actually experience or simulate during the interrogation. Without objectivity, he may unconsciously distort the information acquired. He may also be unable to vary his interrogation techniques effectively.

SELF-CONTROL

The interrogator must have exceptional self-control to avoid displays of genuine anger, irritation, sympathy, or weariness which may cause him to lose the initiative during the interrogation. Self-control is especially important when employing interrogation techniques which require the display of simulated emotions or attitudes.

ADAPTABILITY

An interrogator must adapt to the many and varied personalities which he will encounter. He should try to imagine himself in the source's position. By being adaptable, he can smoothly shift his techniques and approaches during interrogations according to the operational environment. In many cases, he has to conduct interrogations under unfavorable physical conditions.

PERSEVERANCE

A tenacity of purpose can be the difference between an interrogator who is merely good and one who is superior. An interrogator who becomes easily discouraged by opposition, noncooperation, or other difficulties will neither aggressively pursue the objective to a successful conclusion nor seek leads to other valuable information.

APPEARANCE AND DEMEANOR

The interrogator's personal appearance may greatly influence the conduct of the interrogation and attitude of the source toward the interrogator. Usually a neat, organized, and professional appearance will favorably influence the source. A firm, deliberate, and businesslike manner of speech and attitude may create a proper environment for a successful interrogation. If the interrogator's manner reflects fairness, strength, and efficiency, the source may prove cooperative and more receptive to questioning.

However, depending on the approach techniques (see Chapter 3), the interrogator can deliberately portray a different (for example, casual or sloven) appearance and demeanor to obtain the cooperation of the source.

INITIATIVE

Achieving and maintaining the initiative are essential to a successful interrogation just as the offense is the key to success in combat operations. The interrogator must grasp the initiative and maintain it throughout the interrogation.

The source, especially if detained by military forces during tactical operations, normally has undergone a traumatic experience and fears for his life. This anxiety is usually intensified by the source's lack of knowledge and understanding of what is about to occur (fear of the unknown), or by the unfounded fear he will be tortured or executed.

The interrogator has a position of authority over the source. The source realizes this fact, and, in some cases, believes his future might depend upon his association with the interrogator.

SPECIAL AREAS OF KNOWLEDGE

The interrogator must be knowledgeable on a variety of subjects in order to be effective in exploiting sources. Some of these areas are—

- Proficiency in the target language.
- Knowledge of the target country.
- International agreements.
- Enemy materiel and equipment.
- Armed forces uniforms.
- OB information.

In addition to these subjects, the interrogator should have a knowledge of basic psychology and neurolinguistics.

PROFICIENCY IN THE TARGET LANGUAGE

The interrogator must be proficient in one or more foreign languages to exploit both human sources and CEDs. According to the GPW, a prisoner must be questioned in a language he understands.

The more proficient an interrogator is with the target language, the better he will be able to develop rapport with his source, understand the nuances of the source's speech, and follow up on source leads to additional information.

The skilled linguist will be able to translate CEDs quicker and more accurately than the interrogator who is merely familiar with the target language.

KNOWLEDGE OF THE TARGET COUNTRY

The interrogator should be familiar with the social, political, and economic institutions; geography; history; language; and culture of the target country. Since many sources will readily discuss nonmilitary topics, the interrogator—

- May induce reluctant prisoners to talk by discussing the geography, economics, or politics of the target country.
- May gradually introduce significant topics into the discussion to gain insight about the conditions and attitudes in the target country.
- Should keep abreast of major and current events as they occur in the target country to better understand the general situation, as well as causes and repercussions.

LAW OF WAR

The interrogator should understand US law of war obligations contained in the GWS, GPW, and GC regarding the treatment of EPWs, retained personnel, and civilian internees (see Figure 1-4).

ENEMY MATERIEL AND EQUIPMENT

The interrogator should be familiar with the capabilities, limitations, and employment of standard weapons and equipment so he may recognize and identify changes, revisions, and innovations. Some of the more common subjects of interest to the interrogator include the following:

- Small arms.
- Infantry support weapons.
- Artillery.
- Aircraft.
- Vehicles.
- Communications equipment.
- NBC defense.

ARMED FORCES UNIFORMS AND INSIGNIA

Through his knowledge of uniforms, insignia, decorations, and other distinctive devices, the interrogator may be able to determine the rank, branch of service, type of unit, and military experience of a military or paramilitary source. This knowledge is helpful during the planning and preparation and the approach phases discussed in Chapter 3.

OB INFORMATION

OB is defined as the identification, strength, command structure, and disposition of personnel, units, and equipment of any military force. Interrogation OB elements are separate categories by which detailed information is maintained. They are—

- Missions.
- Composition.
- Disposition.
- Strength.
- Training.
- Combat effectiveness.
- Tactics.
- Logistics.
- Electronic technical data.
- Miscellaneous data.

During the questioning phase, OB elements assist the interrogator in verifying the accuracy of the information obtained and can be used as an effective tool to gain new information. Aids which may be used to identify units are—

- Names.
- Commanders.
- Home station identifications.
- Code designations and numbers.
- Uniforms and insignia.
- Guidons.
- Documents.
- Military postal system data.
- Equipment and vehicle markings.

UNDERSTANDING BASIC PSYCHOLOGY

An interrogator can best adapt himself to the EPW's or detainee's personality and control of their reactions when he understands basic psychological factors, traits, attitudes, drives, motivations, and inhibitions. For example, the timely use or promise of rewards and incentives may mean the difference between an interrogation's success or failure and future EPW or detainee exploitation.

NEUROLINGUISTICS

Nuerolinguistics is a behavioral communication model and a set of procedures that improve communication skills. The interrogator should read and react to nonverbal communications. An interrogator can best adapt himself to the source's personality and control his own reactions when he understands basic psychological factors, traits, attitudes, drives, motivations, and inhibitions.

INTERROGATOR CAPABILITIES AND LIMITATIONS

HUMINT collection is capable of obtaining information pertinent to all six IEW tasks:

- Situation development.
- Target development and target acquisition.
- I&W.
- IPB.
- BDA.
- Force protection.

Interrogators are trained as linguists to question EPWs and civilian detainees and to exploit CEDs. During their collection, interrogators attempt to obtain and report any information possessed by these targets that pertains to the IEW tasks. The persistence is determined by comparing the information obtained to the SIR contained in the interrogation element's collection mission.

Interrogators are capable of collecting information on political, economic, and a wide range of military topics. For the most part, interrogators attempt to organize their collection effort according to the OB elements analysts use. In addition to these elements, interrogators also obtain PIR-directed information on the missions assigned to enemy units. Appendix B discusses relevant questioning guides.

ENVIRONMENTAL CONSIDERATIONS

The environment in which interrogation operations are performed affects the degree of success achieved. There are primarily two areas, both having limitations, upon which the interrogators depend:

- The IEW process which gives direction and purpose to their collection efforts.
- The conduct of combat operations which provides them with collection targets; that is, EPWs, detainees, and CEDs.

If the IEW process or combat operations are not ideal, use what you can to capitalize on capabilities.

IEW Process

The IEW process can limit interrogators by assigning collection missions which are not suited to HUMINT collection capabilities; as well as by not disseminating copies of the following reports:

- Intelligence summary (INTSUM).
- Intelligence report (INTREP).
- Daily intelligence summary (DISUM).
- Periodic intelligence report (PERINTREP).
- Supplementary intelligence report (SUPINTREP).
- Other intelligence reports.

Combat Operations

Combat operations can limit interrogators by—

- Delaying evacuation of EPWs or detainees and captured documents, thereby limiting time available to exploit them.
- Allowing prisoners and documents to be mishandled, thereby decreasing their exploitation potential.
- Not providing the equipment, supplies, and secure communications needed for successful operations.

INHERENT LIMITATIONS

Interrogation operations are also limited by the very nature of HUMINT collection. EPWs or detainees and CEDs must actually have the desired information before interrogators can collect it. With EPWs or detainees, there is always the possibility knowledgeable individuals may refuse to cooperate.

The UCMJ, GWS, GPW, and GC set definite limits on measures which can be taken to induce an EPW or detainee to cooperate.

CONFLICTS

HICs are conflicts between two or more nations and their respective allies, where the belligerents employ modern technology complemented by intelligence; mobility; firepower (to include NBC weapons); service support; and C^3 resources.

MICs are conflicts between two or more nations and their respective allies, where the belligerents employ modern technology complemented by intelligence; mobility; firepower (without NBC); C^3; and service support resources for limited objectives under definitive policy limiting employment of destructive power and geography involved.

LICs are political-military confrontations between contending states or groups below conventional war and above the routine, peaceful competition among states. They—

- Frequently involve protracted struggles of competing principles and ideologies.
- Range from subversion to the use of armed force.
- Are waged by combining and employing political, economic, informational, and military instruments.
- Are often localized, generally in the Third World, but contain regional and global security implications.

LIC operational intelligence requirements are HUMINT intensive and demand detailed familiarity with the military, political, and front organizations of the insurgent enemy, and the environment in which he operates.

The interrogator's familiarity with the areas of operations (AOs) must include an understanding of the insurgency, its objectives, history, successes, and failures. This understanding is required not only on a general countrywide basis but also on an expanded basis within the interrogator's particular AO. Therefore, it is essential the interrogator grasps the importance the insurgent organization places on accomplishing political objectives as opposed to military successes.

One measure of the interrogator's effectiveness is his ability to apply appropriate interrogation techniques to the personality of the source. Interrogations associated with LIC operations dictate the need for skill in the full range of interrogation techniques so the interrogator can conduct the many types of interrogations demanded.

Warfighting doctrine IEW principles apply for LIC; however, intelligence indicators for insurgent activity are unique. Anything insurgents can do to influence and direct a society toward overthrowing its government is reflected by some action or indication, no matter how subtle. Some MI advisors may be required to assist paramilitary and nonmilitary elements in developing HUMINT sources and exploiting their information.

As US forces are committed to the LIC operation, interrogation support will more closely adhere to the traditional tactical environment. Typical LIC missions are—

- Counterinsurgency and insurgency support.
- Combatting terrorism.
- Peacekeeping and peacetime contingency operations.

HUMINT is a major LIC source because of the necessity to exploit the local populace and to know and understand enemy intentions. In LIC, interrogators exploit EPWs and CEDs. For example, in addition to conducting EPW operations at collecting points, interrogators may participate in cordon and search and roadblock operations, tactical check points, and low-level collection missions in conjunction with the supporting CI unit (see FM 34-60A(S)). Interrogators may also provide support to drug and law enforcement agency (DLEA) operations.

INTERROGATION MISSIONS

Interrogators perform various types of missions. As discussed previously, the two main missions are personnel and document exploitation. There are other functions for which interrogators are ideally suited because of their language and HUMINT training. These include—

- Linguist support to hostage negotiations, counter-drug, and special operation forces (SOF) operations.
- LLSO linguist support.
- Psychological operations (PSYOP) linguist support.
- Civil Affairs (CA) linguist support.
- Treaty verification and observer duties.

DRUG AND LAW ENFORCEMENT AGENCY OPERATIONS

Army interrogators may assist Federal law enforcement authorities and, where lives are endangered, state and local law enforcement authorities, after concurrence by the Army General Counsel and approval by the Secretary of Defense or his designee. (See AR 381-10, Procedure 12, and AR 500-51.)

Army interrogators may assist law enforcement agencies and security services or foreign governments or international organizations only in accordance with applicable law and policy, including any status of forces agreements. Such assistance will ordinarily constitute security assistance, which must be approved in accordance with AR 12-15.

Under no circumstances will interrogators assist any law enforcement authorities in any manner without prior approval by competent authority after a legal review of the proposal.

CHAPTER 2
COMPOSITION AND STRUCTURE

The interrogation architecture (interrogators and interrogation units) is a seamless system that supports operations from brigade to theater level. The dynamic warfighting doctrine requires interrogation units be highly mobile and have automation and communication equipment to report information to the supported commander.

Regardless of their employment level, interrogation units should be equipped with state-of-the-art automation equipment, necessary HUMINT software, and dedicated and secure communication equipment with skip echelon, digital, voice, facsimile, and optical scanning capability. This equipment enables interrogators to—

- Receive data base information.
- Manipulate that information.
- Incorporate it into their operational data bases.
- Produce tactical information reports.

By using secure communication equipment, interrogators are able to disseminate time-sensitive information to the supported commander as answers to his PIR which facilitates decision-making. The Prisoner of War Information System (PWIS) is a databased system maintained by the provost marshal's office at theater level. It has the capability to recall an EPW's evacuation audit trail.

The prisoner of war interrogation (IPW) communication and automation system facilitates transmission of EPW-derived information from brigade to theater; it precludes duplicated effort in EPW or CED exploitation.

The MI unit commander must ensure interrogators have the necessary equipment to accomplish their wartime mission. The MI unit commander retains overall responsibility for interrogators assigned to his unit. The manner in which these interrogators are controlled depends on how the MI unit is task organized for combat.

If interrogators are deployed in general support (GS) of the division, the MI battalion commander exercises control over them through his S3 and the battalion tactical operations center (TOC). If interrogators are deployed in direct support (DS) of a division's subordinate units, they are tasked by the commanders of those units through their S2s.

TACTICAL OPERATIONS CENTER

Normally, interrogators are a primary source of OB information. The interrogation element chief should ensure that he or someone appointed to this duty has daily personal contact with the division or corps collection management and dissemination (CM&D) section at the TOC. During these visits, all questions and information pertaining to OB and intelligence target priority lists can be discussed and later disseminated to various interrogators.

Interrogator elements must receive all reports and findings made by analysts; in turn, all interrogation reports should reach analysts. Direct contact must be maintained between these two elements, preferably in person or by telephone. This ensures access to important information which may arise between liaison visits.

TASKING RELATIONSHIPS

When interrogators are task-organized under the IEW company, the team leader directs the tasking. The DS and GS teams are under operational control (OPCON) to the IEW company when they are supporting that company. The officers responsible for tasking interrogation elements ensure the following steps are accomplished:

- Collection missions that reflect the capabilities and limitations of interrogators are assigned.
- INTREPs are integrated with information provided by other collectors during the IPB process.
- Copies of the INTSUM, INTREP, PERINTREP, DISUM, and SUPINTREP are disseminated to the interrogation element as they are published.
- Close contact is maintained with the interrogation element.

INTERROGATOR TASK ORGANIZATIONS

Interrogators are not assigned by tables of organization and equipment (TOE) to units below division. However, MI parent units often task interrogators and place them in DS to brigades. For example, in a light division, there are usually enough interrogators assigned to send forward deployed interrogation teams, known as "GO" teams, to the brigades to complement light division operations.

EPW interrogation may be desirable at all echelons, but is not practicable due to limited numbers of interrogators available. As a minimum, there should be an interrogation element at the division central collection point, corps holding areas, and theater internment facility.

Interrogation elements at all echelons are task organized, and may not mirror the TOE organization in their parent unit.

DEPLOYMENT SITES

Interrogation assets are mobile enough to be shifted in response to new developments. The initial deployment of these assets are guided by the exploitation priority established by the commander. Operations are conducted at an echelon that will allow interrogators the best opportunity to satisfy their assigned collection mission. The areas discussed below should be considered when making the deployment decisions.

Number of Interrogators Available

The number of interrogators available limits the number of deployment sites that can be used. MI commanders at corps consider how many interrogators will be available for interrogation operations after augmentation has been provided to subordinate divisions. The number of interrogators also plays a key role in deciding the level of intense or sustained collection operations they can conduct.

Type and Intensity of Combat Operations

Intense collection employs all available interrogators with little or no provision for them to rest. The major disadvantage of intense collection is these interrogators become exhausted quickly. Interrogations amount to prolonged conversations under extreme stress. Once the available interrogators are exhausted, collection stops until they recover or additional assets arrive.

A severe decrease in interrogation effectiveness can be expected between 12 and 18 hours after the onset of intense collection, with 18 hours as the maximum time possible for intense collection. This kind of all-out effort can be justified when critical information must be obtained or confirmed quickly to forestall a major disaster. Similar problems can be expected during intense CED exploitation.

Sustained operations can be maintained indefinitely. They also allow the commander some rested interrogators to use on a contingency basis in a different location. Disadvantages of sustained collection are fewer sources are exploited over a given time and operations are slower.

Support Available

In making deployment decisions, the area where operations are to be conducted must provide the support required by the interrogation element. This support includes—

- MP coordination.
- Priority access to reliable means of secure communications.
- Adequate shelter and security.
- A flow of CEDs and sources to exploit.

INTERROGATION BELOW DIVISION

The first interrogation could take place at brigade. Interrogation teams are attached temporarily to brigades in enemy contact when determined appropriate by the division G2. These teams come from the interrogation section of the parent division. Interrogation personnel are organic to separate brigades and armored cavalry regiments (ACRs). Interrogation at brigade level is strictly tactical and deals with information of immediate value.

Other information the EPW might possess is developed at higher levels. At brigade, the scope of interrogation changes from hour-to-hour as the tactical situation develops. These interrogations must be geared to cope with any tactical possibility at a moment's notice.

Interrogation personnel in DS to brigade will be collocated or immediately adjacent to the division forward EPW collecting point in the brigade support area (BSA). For MI units to receive S2 support, the collecting point and interrogation site will be collocated and accessible to the command post (CP).

DIVISION INTERROGATION ASSETS

An MI battalion is organic to each division. It provides combat intelligence, EW, and OPSEC support to light or heavy infantry and airborne or air assault divisions.

The MI battalion provides special support the G2 needs to produce combat intelligence. Interrogation personnel organic to the MI battalions compose the interrogation support element.

The intelligence and surveillance (I&S) company provides division CI, interrogation, and surveillance support.

The I&S company interrogation team manages the division's interrogation assets, including those interrogation teams attached from corps. Additional team duties are—

- Screen CEDs.
- Provide interpreter and translator support.
- Liaison with PSYOP and G5 personnel.

ORGANIZATION (LIGHT DIVISION)

In a light division, interrogators belong to the I&S Company, MI Battalion. Figure 2-1 shows this structure. Light division MI battalions have 25 interrogators subordinate to the I&S company. Two 5-man DS teams in the interrogation platoon

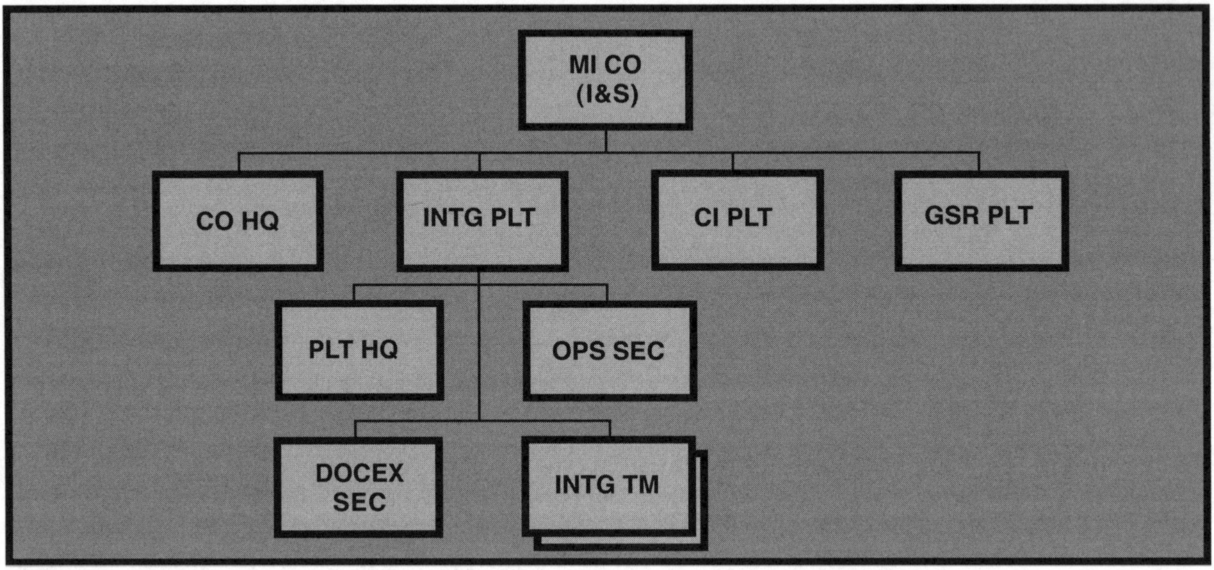

Figure 2-1. MI Company (I&S), MI Battalion, Light Division.

ensure the platoon can provide support to two committed brigades.

Platoon Headquarters

Platoon headquarters provides C^3 for the interrogation element. It consists of a platoon leader and sergeant. The platoon headquarters coordinates with—

- I&S company commander for personnel status, administrative support, and logistical support prior to deployment to the division support area (DSA).
- MI battalion S3 for intelligence tasking and deployment of interrogation assets.
- Division G2 for reporting, enemy situation updates, and PIR, IR, and SIR.
- DISCOM commander for DSA logistical and communications support, and interrogation element location in the DSA.
- MP company commander for division central EPW collecting point location, and EPW processing and evacuation procedures.
- Medical battalion commander for procedures to treat and clear wounded EPW for questioning.
- CI platoon leader for requirements and joint CI and interrogation procedures.
- MI company team leaders for deployment of DS interrogation teams.
- CA and PSYOP elements for requirements and processing of civilian detainees and refugees.

Operations Section

This consists of a section chief (warrant officer), non-commissioned officer in charge (NCOIC), and two 4-member interrogation teams. The operations section chief manages the interrogation effort to ensure interrogations respond to division intelligence requirements.

DOCEX Section

This consists of a section chief (warrant officer) and three document examiners. The DOCEX section may be used as an additional interrogation team when priority of exploitation and EPW capture rate dictate. The division G2 determines whether interrogation or document examination will have priority.

When three brigades are committed in an operation, the DOCEX section may be employed as a third brigade level team.

DOCEX assets may also function in an interrogation role when the number of EPWs at the division central collecting point requires additional division level interrogators or when the CED rate is very low.

Interrogation Teams

Each interrogation team consists of a team leader (warrant officer), NCO assistant team leader, and three team members. Teams are normally employed as part of the MI company teams which provide IEW support to the brigades.

ORGANIZATION (HEAVY DIVISION)

In a heavy division, interrogators are assigned to the I&S Company, MI Battalion. Figure 2-2 shows this structure.

ORGANIZATION (AIRBORNE OR AIR ASSAULT DIVISION)

In an airborne or air assault division, interrogators are assigned to the I&S Company, MI Battalion. Figure 2-3 shows the structure.

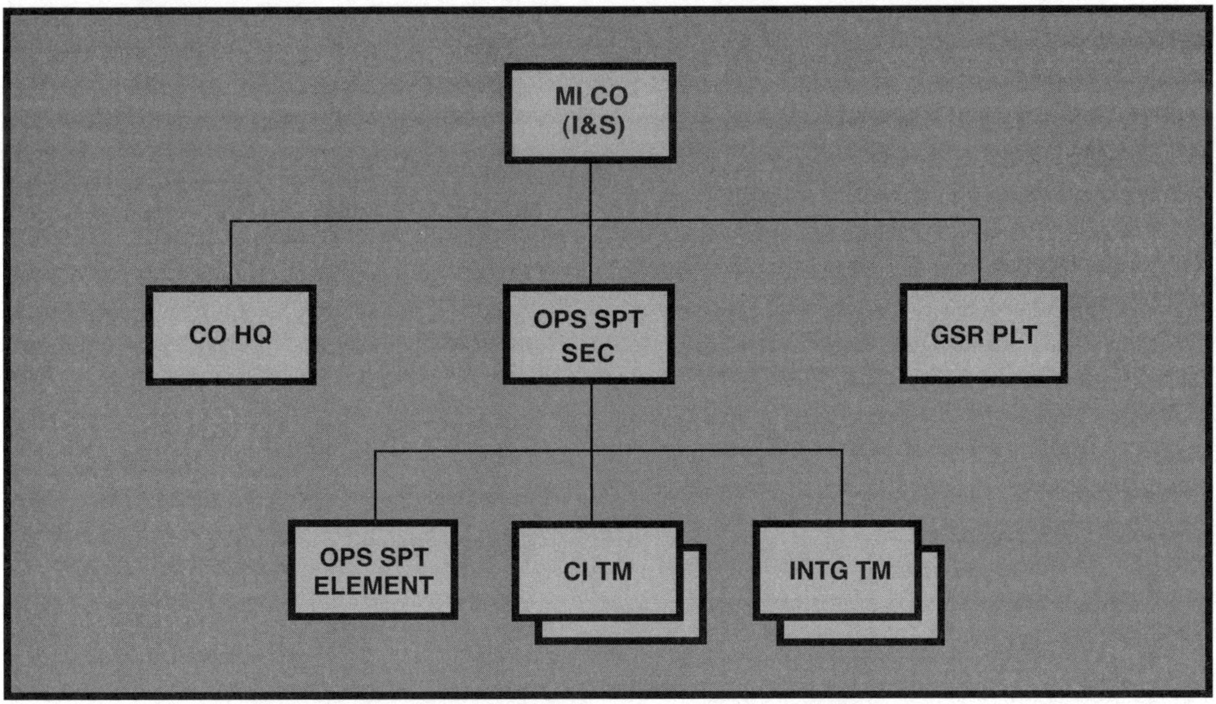

Figure 2-2. I&S Company, MI Battalion, Heavy Division.

ORGANIZATION (ACR AND SEPARATE BRIGADE)

In an ACR or separate brigade, interrogators are assigned to the operations support platoon of the MI company. Figure 2-4 shows this organization.

SPECIAL FORCES GROUP

In a Special Forces Group (Airborne) (SFGA), interrogators are assigned to the Military Intelligence Detachment (MID). Figure 2-5 shows this structure. Interrogation teams may be com-

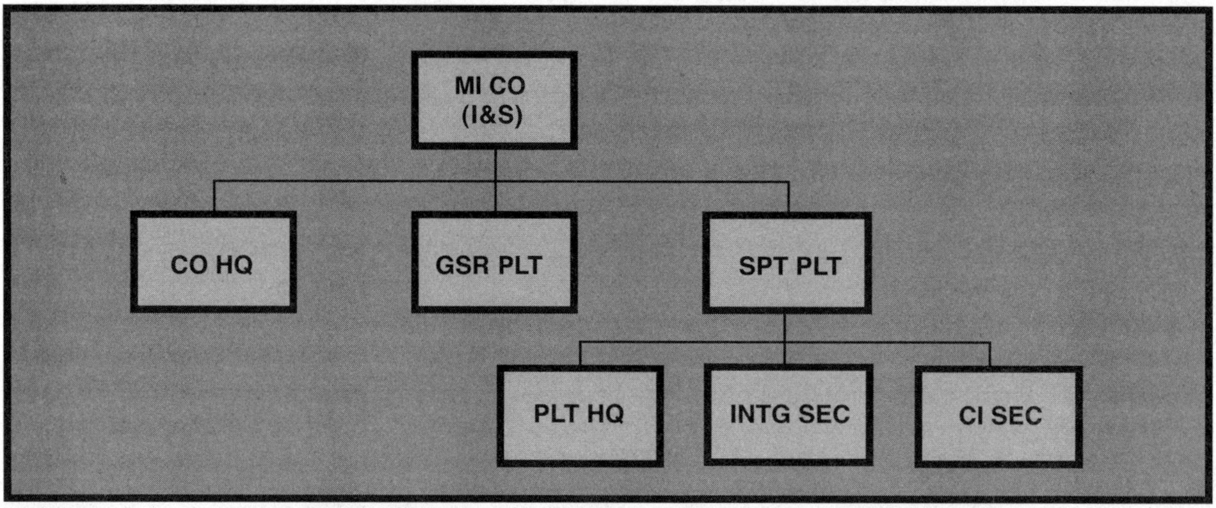

Figure 2-3. I&S Company, MI Battalion, Airborne or Air Assault Division.

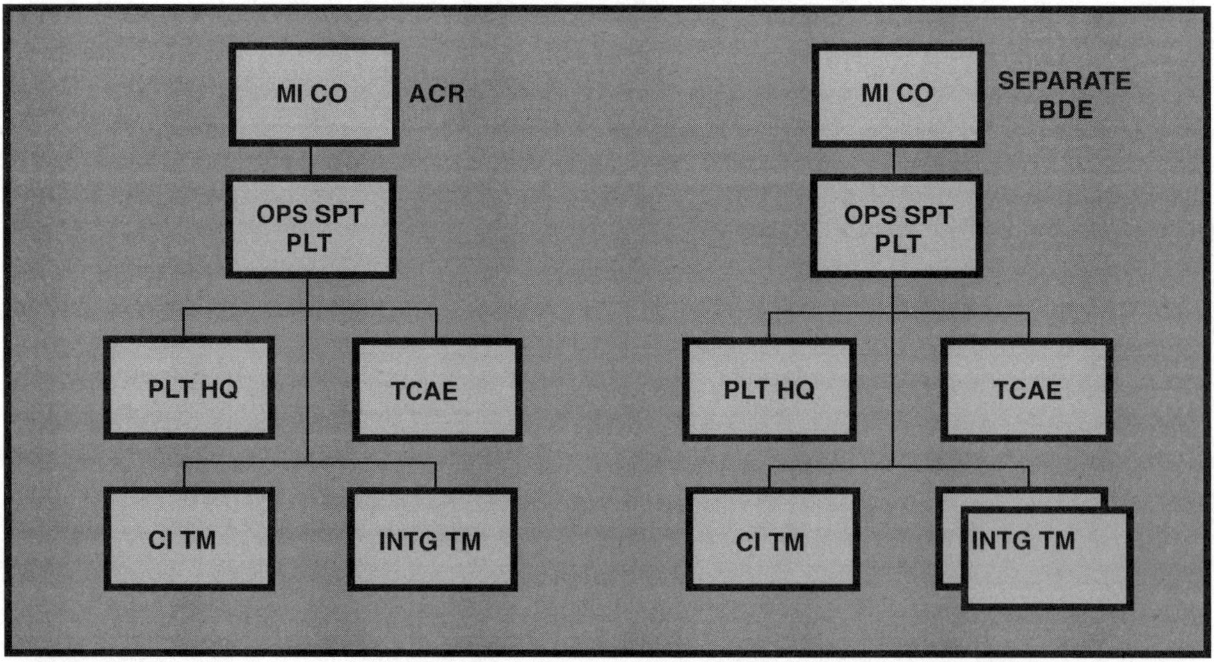

Figure 2-4. MI Company Operations Support Platoon for ACR and Separate Brigade.

bined with the CI section when not conducting operations.

CORPS INTERROGATION ASSETS AND ORGANIZATION

At corps, interrogators are assigned to the MI Battalion (Tactical Exploitation) (TE). Figure 2-6 shows this structure. The CI interrogation company consists of a company headquarters, IPW and CI operation sections, CI and interrogation platoons, and a maintenance section.

The CI platoon has nine teams and the interrogation platoon normally has eight teams. Interrogators can be placed in a DS role to divisions to augment division interrogation assets.

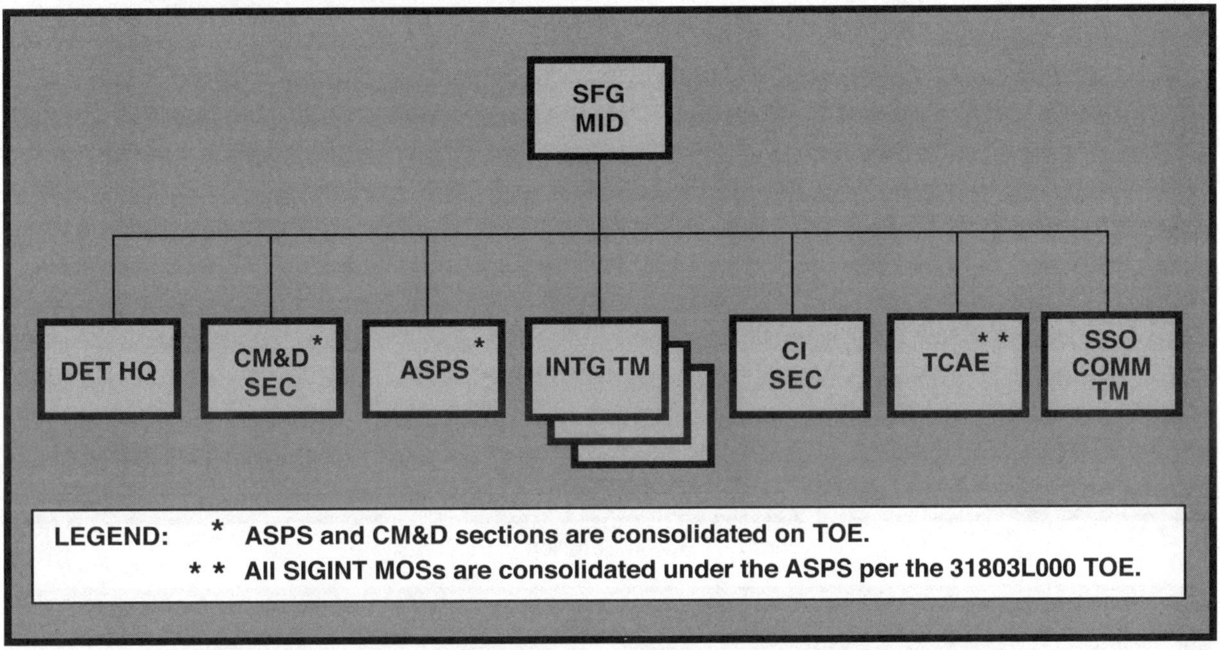

Figure 2-5. Organization, MI Detachment, Support Company, Special Forces Group.

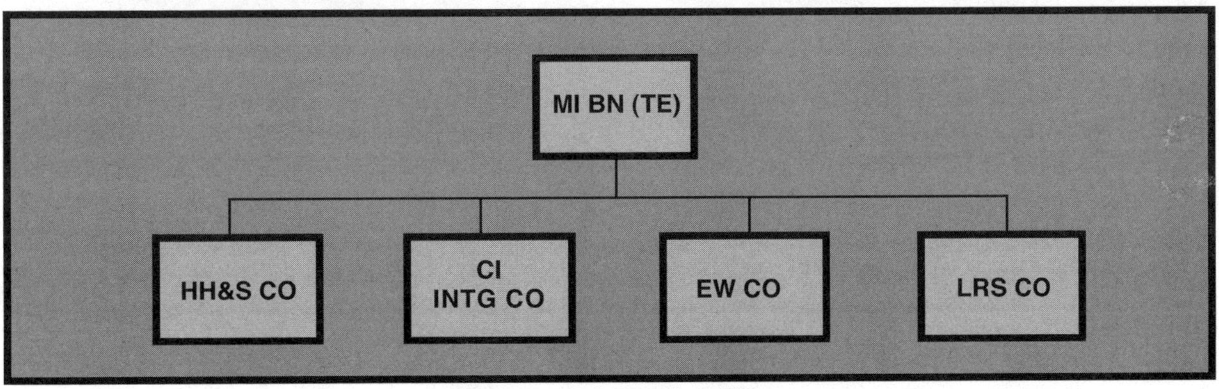

Figure 2-6. MI Battalion (TE).

The corps also has a Reserve Components (RC) MI Battalion (TE), which has a subordinate CI interrogation company. Figure 2-7 shows this structure.

There are also linguist battalions which augment and support Active Component (AC) units in time of hostilities.

ECHELONS ABOVE CORPS INTERROGATION ASSETS AND ORGANIZATION

The MI Battalion (Collection and Exploitation [C&E]), as shown at Figure 2-8, has a headquarters and headquarters company (HHC), MI Com-

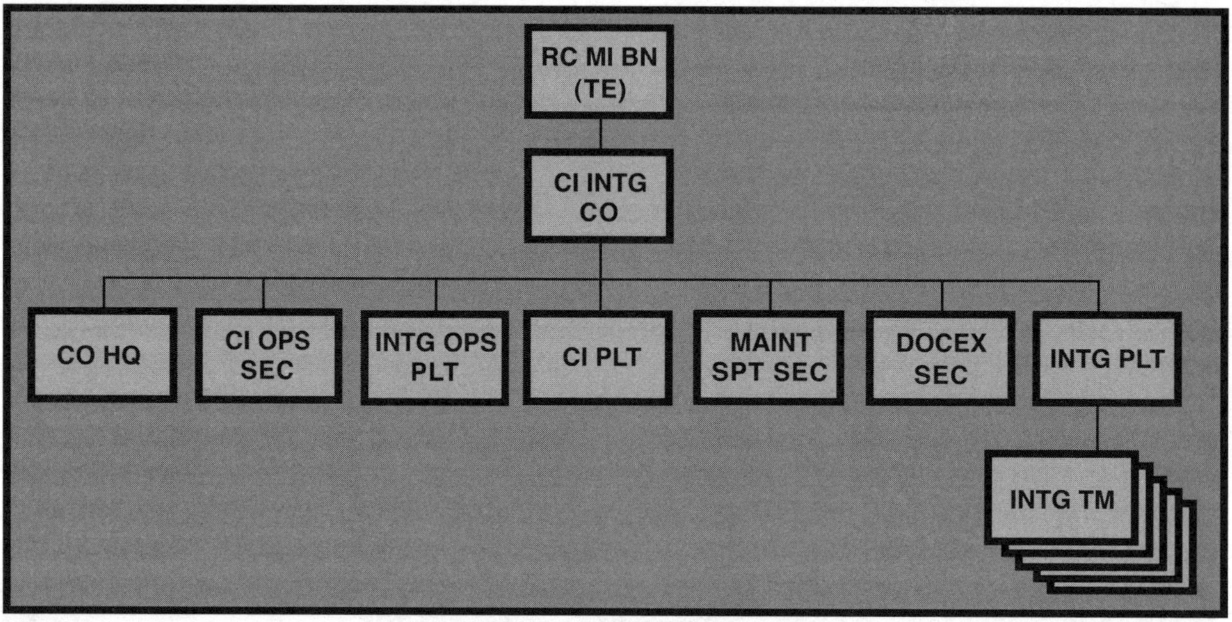

Figure 2-7. RC MI Battalion (TE) Corps.

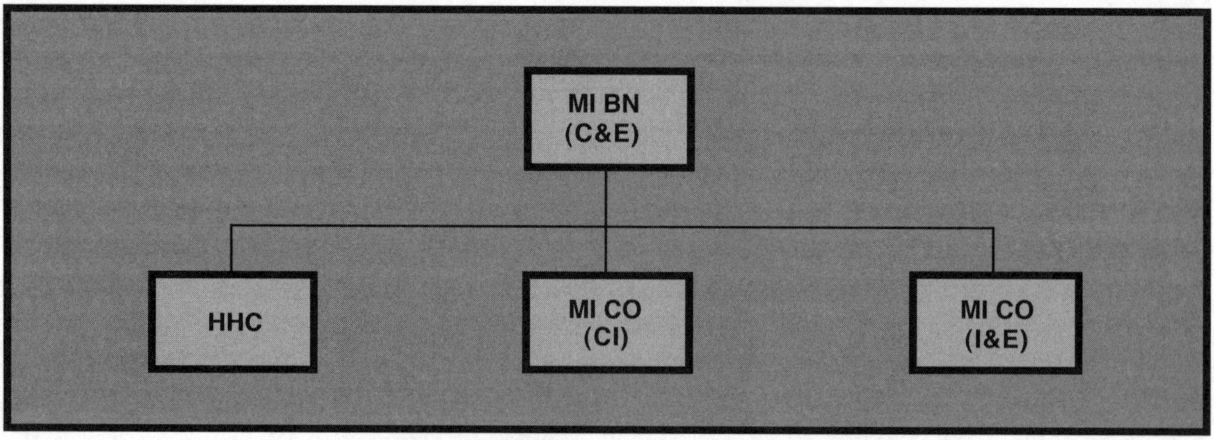

Figure 2-8. MI Battalion (C&E), MI Brigade (EAC).

pany (CI), and MI Company (Interrogation and Exploitation [I&E]).

The MI Battalion (I&E), as shown at Figure 2-9, has an HHC and three MI companies (I&E), of which one is GS. Two MI companies (I&E) (INTG) operate the theater, joint, or combined interrogation facilities, while the MI company (I&E) (GS) is for GS to echelons corps and below (ECB).

The MI Company (Interrogation) of the MI Battalion (C&E) and (I&E), as shown at Figure 2-10, has a company headquarters, operations section, communications section, food service section, and an I&E platoon, consisting of two sections.

The MI company (I&E) (GS), MI Battalion (I&E), has a headquarters section, an operations section, and three interrogation platoons, each with a platoon headquarters and eight sections. Figure 2-11 shows this structure.

ENEMY PRISONER OF WAR AND INTERROGATION FACILITIES

There are significant differences in EPW and interrogation facilities at each echelon; this is due to the numbers of EPWs, the missions of the various echelons, and the size of the interrogation elements.

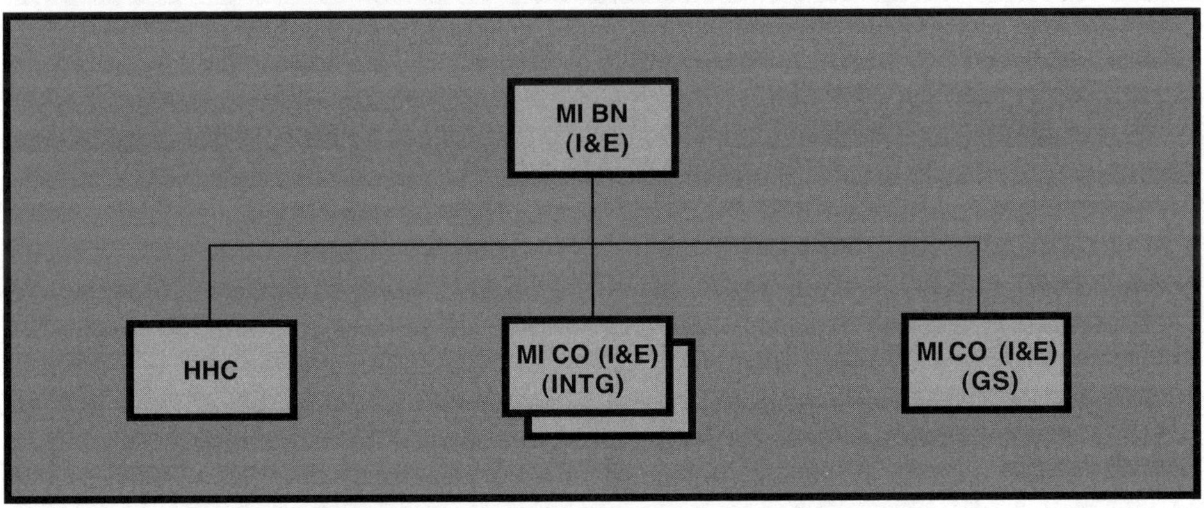

Figure 2-9. MI Battalion (I&E), MI Brigade (EAC).

EVACUATION AND GUARDING EPW

Initially, the capturing unit is responsible for evacuating and guarding EPWs. In brigade-size operations, battalions evacuate prisoners to brigade collecting points as the situation permits. In most cases, EPWs are evacuated rapidly using backhaul transportation from brigade collecting points to departure areas because they require food and guards, both of which are in short supply at brigade. EPW collecting points should be located close to supply routes to speed evacuation.

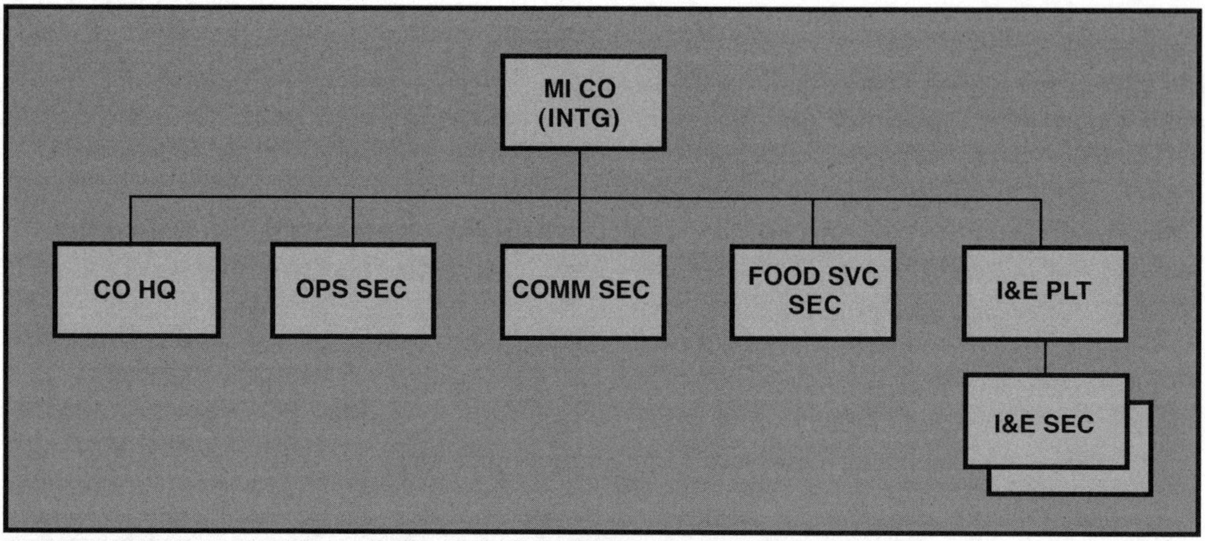

Figure 2-10. MI Company (INTG), MI Battalion (C&E) and (I&E).

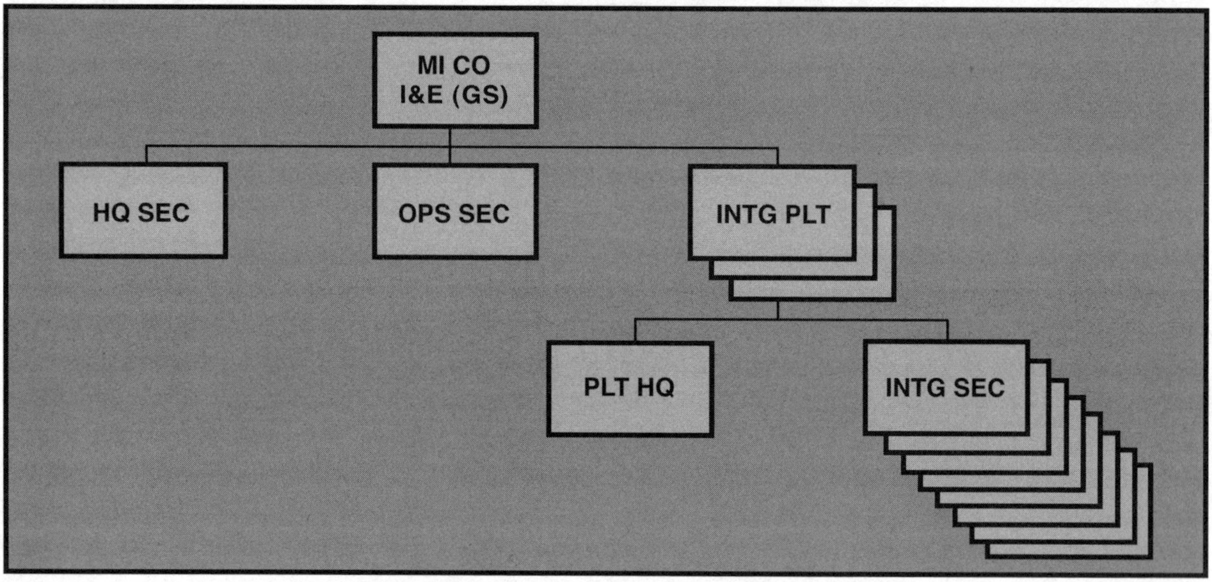

Figure 2-11. MI Company (I&E) (GS), MI Battalion (I&E).

BRIGADE AND LOWER ECHELONS

At brigade level, EPWs can be detained in open fields, courtyards, gardens, jungle clearings, or similar sites if they are hidden from enemy observation. If necessary, these areas can be enclosed with barbed wire for more efficient EPW handling. Because EPWs seldom remain at a forward collecting point for more than a few hours,

EPWs are not usually kept in a building or other shelter.

Interrogation facilities at battalion and brigade are kept to a minimum. Brigade interrogation personnel should be located adjacent to the brigade forward EPW collecting point in the BSA. The collecting point should be out of sight and sound of other BSA activities. It should be close to normal evacuation routes.

The distance between the collecting point and CP is important. When possible, the collecting point and interrogation site should be within walking distance or a few minute's driving distance of the CP.

Interrogators with battalions or brigades should have vehicles equipped with radios for rapid communication with their respective intelligence officers and other intelligence agencies.

DIVISION FACILITIES

The principal EPW tactical interrogation takes place at division. While the procedure is similar to that used at brigade, the interrogation scope is broader.

Previous interrogation reports received from brigade are reviewed. This information is expanded by further interrogations for tactical information to include all OB elements.

The interrogators at division level will prepare and disseminate summary interrogation reports. As dictated by the tactical situation, the interrogation facility at division may be augmented by corps interrogation personnel.

The division's central EPW collecting point is operated by division MP under the supervision of the division provost marshal. The interrogation section should be located immediately adjacent to the division's central EPW collecting point, normally along the main supply route (MSR) within or near the division support command (DISCOM).

The distance between the interrogation facility and G2 section (rear) is not as critical as at brigade level. Personal liaison between the interrogation and intelligence sections, although important, may not be required as frequently as at brigade.

At division, the G2 directs interrogation section collection efforts in conjunction with the CM&D section and the MI battalion commander, who serves as one of his principal assistants.

Compared to brigade facilities, division interrogation facilities are expanded. This is because the division interrogation section handles and interrogates more captured personnel, and interrogations are conducted in greater detail. When practicable, interrogations at division should be conducted in improvised interrogation rooms in buildings adjacent to the division collecting point. If possible, separate rooms should be available to permit several interrogations at once.

CORPS FACILITIES

The corps EPW holding area is established and operated by MP under the supervision of the corps provost marshal. The Corps Interrogation Facility (CIF) will usually be a more permanent type facility than at echelons below corps. It should consist of operations and interrogation areas with separate, enclosed interrogation booths or rooms. If possible, there should be a separate DOCEX area. Figure 2-12 shows a sample CIF.

The commander, CI Interrogation Company, MI Battalion (TE), MI Brigade (Corps), is the CIF commander. CIFs are the principal establishment

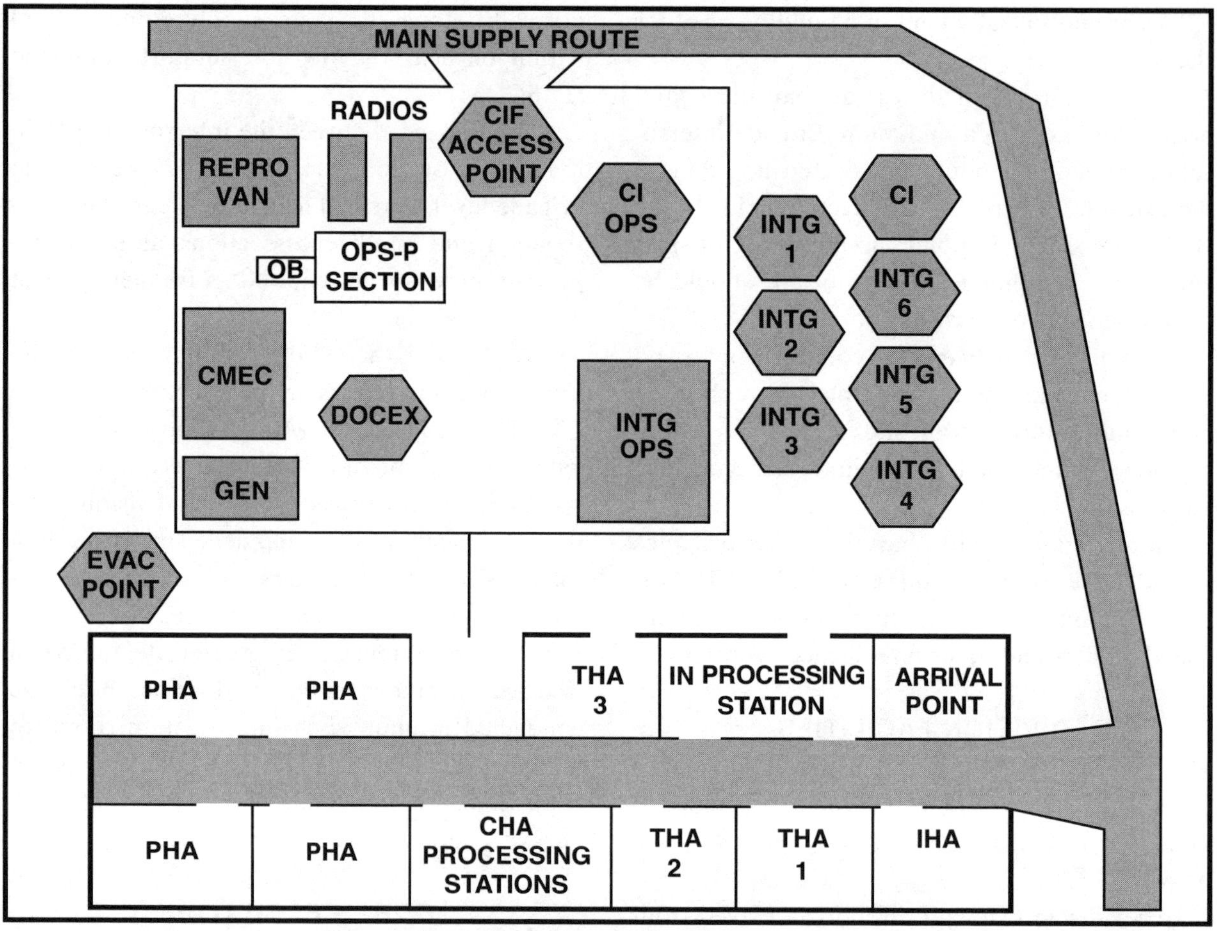

Figure 2-12. Sample Corps Interrogation facility (CIF).

for the exploitation of captured personnel and CEDs. Functions of the centers include—

- Conducting tactical and strategic interrogations based on the intelligence requirements and specific guidance of the corps G2 section.
- Screening to select sources suited for further exploitation at a higher echelon interrogation center.
- Screening of EPW and other sources of specific CI interest.
- Interrogating sources of interest to PSYOP intelligence based on their requirements.
- Preparing and disseminating interrogation reports.

Continuous coordination between the CIF commander and EPW holding area commander is essential. At a sub-level, it is also important for interrogators to maintain a good working relationship with MP at the holding area.

MP, who are in constant contact with EPWs or detainees, can provide interrogators valuable information on individual sources. By properly handling prisoners at all times, they also contribute to the success of interrogation operations by helping to reduce resistance by the sources.

The CIF should be administratively and operationally self-sufficient and located within or adjacent to the EPW holding area, close enough to facilitate operations.

ADEQUATE INTERROGATION FACILITIES

At corps level, particular emphasis should be placed on providing facilities adequate for the interrogation of EPWs of higher positions or rank. Because interrogations will normally last longer than at division, a greater degree of comfort should be provided, if possible. In other respects, the type of interrogation facilities and equipment parallels those found at division.

OB SECTION

OB analysts are a valuable interrogation facility asset. They ensure PIR, IR, and SIR are updated, and reporting is in response to them. In addition, they maintain a situation map (SITMAP) and OB updates to keep interrogators current on tactical situations.

EDITORIAL PERSONNEL

The senior, interrogator may assign interrogators to edit INTREPs. They also may use the organizational chain of command to ensure quality control of reporting. When OB analysts are available, the commander may task them to edit reports.

DOCEX SECTION

The DOCEX section receives documents taken from captured personnel, battlefield casualties, and positions abandoned by the enemy. It processes captured documents; for example, screens for intelligence value, categorizes, and translates. It forwards translation reports on information of immediate tactical value. (Chapter 4 describes document categories.)

SPECIALIZED INFORMATION

The scope of interrogations at corps is widened by the commander's intelligence requirements, SIR of the numerous technical service staff agencies, and other intelligence agencies and services. All such special needs for information are coordinated by the corps G2 section. Interrogators must be aware of these overall intelligence requirements to adequately exploit captured personnel.

Because of the range of specialized information required, interrogation at corps level should be conducted by interrogators who specialize in fields such as armor, engineering, medicine, and other specialized subject areas.

To extract detailed EPW information, the senior interrogator will assign some interrogators as screeners and others to specialized areas. However, he must coordinate, for example, with technical intelligence (TECHINT) assets. This is to prevent duplication or gaps in information obtained.

Continuous coordination is required between all echelon interrogators to ensure a smoothly functioning operation.

The corps MI brigade applies the technical expertise, intelligence manpower, and equipment needed by G2 to produce integrated combat intelligence. The corps commander has OPCON, while the G2 has staff supervision over the MI brigade.

ECHELONS ABOVE CORPS FACILITIES

At echelons above corps (EAC), the MI company (I&E), MI battalion (C&E) or (I&E), MI brigade (EAC), will form the Theater Interrogation Facility (TIF). The TIF, which is command by an MI captain, provides interrogation support to the theater or joint command and to national level intelligence agencies. The TIF will—

- Be located within the main theater EPW internment facility.
- Be tailored organizationally to meet requirements of the theater and situation.
- Include interrogators, CI personnel, and intelligence analysts from the Army, Air Force, Marine Corps, and, in some cases, the Navy.
- Be organized similarly to the CIF; that is, by function.
- Have intelligence analysts to handle requirements and keep interrogators informed of changes in the operational or strategic situation.
- Maintain the capability to deploy "GO" teams to multiple theater EPW camps, as well as to forward deploy them to corps and ECB as needed.
- Provide experienced senior interrogation warrant officers and NCOs who are graduates of the Department of Defense (DOD) Strategic Debriefer Course (additional skill identifier 9N or N7) and physical plant for the Joint Debriefing Center (JDC), where exploitation of high-level (Category A) sources takes places on operational and strategic topics.

MEDICAL COMPANY INTERROGATIONS

Sometimes it may be advantageous to conduct interrogations at the medical company. Wounded prisoners being evacuated through medical channels are frequently valuable sources of information; however, interrogators cannot represent themselves as medical or Red Cross personnel.

The fact the EPW is wounded, and in an "enemy" hospital, puts him in a state of mind conducive to interrogation. The permission of competent medical authority is required before wounded prisoners can be interrogated.

US Army doctors and medics are considered competent medical authorities. In their absence, the interrogation may not commence, even upon direction of nonmedical military authority.

When interrogating a sick or wounded EPW, great care must be taken to avoid implying that treatment will be withheld if cooperation is denied. The interrogation process must not interfere with timely medical treatment, to include administering medication to relieve pain.

INTERROGATION AT BRIGADE AND BELOW

Interrogators are not usually attached below brigade level unless the combat situation requires limited tactical interrogation at battalion or lower. In this event, skilled interrogators from the MI battalion will be attached temporarily to committed battalions. They will assist in exploiting EPW immediately upon capture to extract information needed in support of the capturing unit.

Interrogations at battalion or lower are brief and concerned only with information bearing directly on the combat mission of the capturing unit. The following are examples of circumstances warranting an interrogation:

- A unit or landing force assigned an independent mission in which the S2 is primarily responsible for collecting information necessary to fulfill the unit's mission. Immediate tactical intelligence is necessary for mission accomplishment.

- There is a definite need for interrogation at a lower level to permit rapid reaction based on information obtained.
- It is advantageous to have an EPW point out enemy defenses and installation from observation points in forward areas.

BATTALION S2 CONTROLS

Interrogators employed for temporary periods at battalion level receive PIR, IR, and SIR from the supported battalion S2. This will ensure interrogators are fully oriented to the battalion's collection mission.

In other instances, interrogators may be placed at brigade in an "on-call" status, from which they can proceed to any of the subordinate battalions as circumstances warrant. Upon completion of a low-level, immediate-type interrogation, they can return to brigade and again become available for immediate employment.

Commanders and S2s below brigade level who are unable to obtain interrogator support from higher echelons should include provisions in unit and staff standing operating procedures (SOPs) for the "tactical questioning" (not interrogation) of EPWs or detainees. They should identify assigned personnel for language capability.

Interrogation personnel should provide training in the area of tactical questioning to designated S2 personnel. The potential for abuse of the EPW is greatest at the initial capture and tactical questioning phase. With the excitement and stress of the battlefield, it may become easy for unskilled personnel to resort to illegal techniques to elicit critical information.

You instruction must stress the importance of the proper treatment of EPWs. Emphasize that the abuse of an EPW at the initial stage of contact often renders future interrogation futile.

If you are engaged in, or supervising the tactical questioning of EPWs, you are responsible for ensuring that EPWs are treated in accordance with the requirements of international and US law. Any tactical questioning conducted must be in response to the supported commander's PIR. Appendix C discusses S2 tactical questioning.

At this level the brigade S2 must maintain secure communication with interrogation personnel to ensure requirements are answered. Except under extreme weather conditions, and MP availability, it is not necessary to keep EPWs within the confines of a building or other shelter at battalion level since they will not remain for more than a few hours before being evacuated.

The capturing unit escorts or transports EPWs or detainees to the nearest collecting point, and turns them over to the MP. Interrogators in DS of the brigade will screen and categorize all EPWs or detainees, question them, and report information obtained in response to brigade PIR, IR, and SIR. They will do this under time constraints, as all EPWs or detainees must be evacuated without delay.

In spite of the temporary nature of the forward EPW collecting point, interrogators should maintain enough space between the collecting point and the interrogation site to ensure the privacy of interrogations. EPWs or detainees should not be able to observe or hear interrogations in progress.

INTERROGATIONS IN OTHER OPERATIONS

The functions and basic operational techniques employed by the interrogation element attached to the infantry division apply to interrogation elements supporting armored, amphibious, and airborne operations in any terrain or climate.

Differences arise primarily in the planning stages and interrogation objectives. These differences normally result from the inherent characteristics of each type of unit and terrain and climate involved.

For example, the interrogator engaging in airborne and amphibious operations will be dependent upon intelligence support from higher agencies during the planning stage. This is necessary because the unit does not have actual contact with the enemy until a specific operation begins.

Once H-hour arrives, the interrogator will be faced with a rapidly developing and changing tactical situation. At this time, the degree of success correlates to the preparations made during the planning stage.

Consequently, the interrogator must make a concerted effort to learn everything possible about the objective area—terrain, enemy, and weather—and relate these factors to the mission of the unit supported. Only by taking these steps will the interrogator be able to ensure success, and be prepared to begin interrogations as soon as possible after contact with the enemy is established. Interrogation objectives depend upon the mission assigned and type of unit supported.

SPECIAL FORCES

Special Forces perform five primary missions:

- Unconventional warfare.
- Foreign internal defense.
- Direct action.
- Special reconnaissance.
- Counterterrorism.

The primary role of Special Forces is to influence deep, close, or rear operations beyond the forward limits of conventional military forces. These operations may extend into a hostile nation's homeland or into the territory of hostile states that threaten lines of communication in the friendly strategic rear.

The Special Forces Group (SFG) normally deploys three two-person teams, as required, to support group operations. One of the teams may be attached to the joint interrogation facility (JIF). Special Forces interrogation activities include, but are not limited to—

- Interrogating EPWs, debriefing detainees and returned US personnel, and other persons of intelligence interest to the supported commander.
- Exploiting documents that appear to directly satisfy the supported commanders specific operational requirements (SORs).
- Participating in overt elicitation activities. These activities include liaison, escort, observer, and treaty verification measures.

AMPHIBIOUS OPERATIONS

The assault landing team is the basic subordinate task organization of the assault echelon of a landing force. Regardless of whether a battalion or brigade landing team is the basic element, it will operate independently during the first stages of the landing, and be organized to land, overrun beach defenses, and secure terrain objectives.

The interrogation element, along with CI teams, should participate in all aspects of the planning phase affecting the landing force to which it is attached. Interrogators should conduct specialized training. The chief interrogator should coordinate with the landing force intelligence officer on all matters concerning interrogators after the landing has been made.

The interrogators obtain as much background information about the enemy as possible to interrogate captured enemy personnel. Interrogators should study—

- All maps, charts, and photographs of the terrain and defenses of the landing areas.
- All INTREPs on the enemy armed forces in that area.
- Available information on enemy reserves, as well as on civilians residing in the area.

Interrogators should engage in other phases of training, including rehearsals, to smoothly execute embarkation, movement, and debarkation operations.

The interrogation element attached to an amphibious landing force will be OPCON to the landing force intelligence officer, and employed at his direction. Small interrogation teams may be formed, which will embark on separate ships. Communication silence will place an effective barrier between these teams until that silence is lifted.

When the assault begins, organizational artillery, air support, and naval gunfire depend primarily on shore units for accurate target information. As a result, interrogators may be required to concentrate their efforts on target acquisition.

The importance of information obtained from captured enemy personnel is magnified when establishing a beachhead. This is because the commander is unable to undertake probing actions to "feel out" the enemy as he can during a more conventional land operation.

INITIAL INTERROGATIONS

Interrogators should conduct initial interrogations near the landing beach close to the CP to communicate information without delay. If necessary, interrogators may be sent forward to operate with assault companies. EPW are turned over to the landing force shore party for custody and eventual evacuation.

Further instructions on interrogations and EPW handling are in the intelligence annex of the landing force operations order (OPORD). The interrogation of civilians for information of intelligence value also is an important part of the interrogation mission.

ESTABLISH AND OPERATE

When headquarters of the next higher echelon above the landing force has landed and established its CP, some of the interrogators may be returned to the command level from which they were originally detached. At this time, collecting points and interrogation facilities can be established and operated as in ordinary ground operations.

The shore party of helicopter support teams operate EPW collecting points in the vicinity of the landing beaches. EPW are evacuated from these points to designated ships by landing craft, helicopter, or amphibious vehicle. Retention in the objective areas is begun as increased facilities, supplies, and personnel permit, consistent with reasonable EPW safety from enemy action.

AIRBORNE OPERATIONS

The functions and basic methods of operations by interrogation personnel with airborne operations are similar to that of an infantry division. However, the method of employment of interrogators is somewhat different. Interrogators who are to operate with airborne units must understand the peculiarities in operations, as well as in training.

The most significant difference between airborne and normal ground operations is airborne operations are usually carried out behind enemy lines. Before the operation, airborne qualified interrogators must—

- Gain a realistic and complete picture of the enemy situation.
- Study enemy units identified in the objective area, and those capable of moving to counterattack our forces.
- Locate significant terrain features in the objective area.

The command echelon to which interrogators will be attached depends on each airborne battalion for the assault phase. Interrogators move into the objective area with the unit they are supporting. They are OPCON to the unit intelligence officer.

As soon as the objective areas and the missions of the respective units within an airborne force are designated, the interrogators who are to take part in the operation must receive details on most aspects of the operation. Interrogators must be provided with—

- The SIR and proposed H-hour.
- Maps, photographs, and other data required for interrogations.
- All information on enemy units which are outside the objective area, but are capable of being employed to counterattack US forces.

Interrogators should spend sufficient time coordinating with other intelligence specialists, particularly analysts, to provide a realistic and complete picture of the enemy situation.

They must study enemy units identified in the objective area, as well as significant terrain features, to provide a background for more comprehensive interrogations when the first EPWs are captured. Prior to the actual airborne assault, interrogators must know CP locations of the division and its subordinate units.

Interrogators involved in airborne operations must anticipate the numerous problems which will affect the interrogation mission. For example, it is conceivable during the assault phase that no basic transportation will be available to interrogation personnel; thus, flexibility is critical in planning and executing airborne operations.

COLLECTING POINTS AND INTERROGATION FACILITIES

Collecting points and interrogation facilities are established and operated as in other operations when—

- Headquarters of the next higher echelon above the assault units have been airdropped.
- Assault units have established physical contact with higher headquarters.

AIR ASSAULT (AIRMOBILE) OPERATIONS

Air assault operations are characterized by a high degree of tactical mobility. They are conducted by transporting infantry and field artillery units, with the necessary combat support (CS) and combat service support (CSS), into battle by helicopter. Once deployed on the ground, air assault infantry battalions fight like other infantry battalions. The essence of air assault tactics is a rapid tempo of operations over extended ranges. In division air assault operations, to support more than one brigade, there must be corps augmentation. FM 71-101 describes air assault operations.

Security of aircraft enroute to landing zones (LZs) is a major concern. Friendly aircraft and air defense support must ensure air routes are free of enemy aircraft and air defense systems.

When remotely monitored battlefield sensor systems (REMBASS) are available, friendly ground assets emplace REMBASS along likely enemy ground approach routes in the LZ to detect and report ground movement. Ground surveillance radar (GSR) is employed to warn of enemy movement on friendly flanks.

Air assault operations require extensive HUMINT support in operation planning. CI analysis is critical to ensure OPSEC measures are taken to prevent divulging critical information, such as—

- Date and time of operation.
- Size of force to be employed.
- Air routes to and from planned LZs.
- Planned LZ locations.

CI must also support staging area actions to prevent espionage, sabotage, and acts of terrorism which could adversely affect the operation.

Interrogation is a primary source of information for air assault operations IPB. Interrogation support of initial stages of the operation may be critical to its success.

The assault force commander needs immediate and current enemy intelligence. Lack of immediate questioning of EPWs captured in securing the LZs or in follow-up actions may cause failure of the operation.

Planners must consider the difficulty in getting EPWs back to a support area during the early stages of an air assault operation. Interrogators should support the air assault elements as soon as possible. This may mean an interrogation team is included in the air assault force to operate at a forward EPW collecting point established in the vicinity of the LZ.

Normally, one interrogation team should support each air assault battalion during the assault phase. If the air assault battalion is using more than one LZ, the team may be split to support each LZ.

After assault units have established a ground link-up, some or all of the interrogators may be returned to the echelon of command from which they were detached.

Interrogators supporting the early stages of an air assault operation must be provided with the SIR, which are critical to the operation's success. Interrogators must plan ahead on how to question EPWs to satisfy immediate collection requirements.

ARMORED AND MECHANIZED INFANTRY OPERATIONS

Armored units normally operate on extensive fronts, with deep zones of action and dispersed formations. Because of the mobility and wide range of action of armored units, interrogation normally is not as detailed as in other divisions.

Interrogators must remain mobile, operate with minimum facilities, and be alert for sudden changes in the tactical situation.

Planning and Operation

With a few exceptions, the planning and preparation necessary for interrogators supporting armored units is the same as for those supporting regular infantry units. Since radio is the normal means of communication, all interrogation team members must be familiar with voice radio procedures and know how to operate radio equipment common to armored units.

Interrogator Employment

Interrogator personnel who support armored or mechanized units will come under OPCON of the J2, G2, or S2 of the supported unit. Interrogators at all levels of armored or mechanized units must be able to operate during fluid situations, and remain mobile at all times. Because of this mobility, liaison with the J2, G2, or S2 will not be as frequent as in other units.

Interrogators must operate with maximum efficiency on the basis of radio communications, messages, and written reports. As in other type units, interrogation personnel remain OPCON to the G2 until operations begin. At that time, the division MI battalion will attach interrogation personnel to subordinate units. After an operation is completed, interrogation personnel will revert to division control, pending a future mission.

Normally, interrogations within armored units will be limited to interrogating EPWs for location and deployment of antitank weapons and defenses, enemy roadblocks, and presence of enemy armor. In fast moving offensive operations, interrogators are best employed with the forward elements of the units.

Limited Interrogations

EPWs are questioned briefly at the point of capture (POC), and evacuated to division EPW forward collecting points, or are turned over to division MP for evacuation. Interrogators with battalions and brigades in armored operations should have vehicles equipped with radios so they can communicate with the respective intelligence officers and other intelligence agencies.

General exploitation techniques and procedures are modified to fit the environment and objectives of each interrogation.

EPWs are a primary source of information during tactical operations. The ability to exploit that source is a critical factor in mission success. EPWs are first-hand and last-minute observers of enemy operations. They represent one of the few forms of direct association with the enemy and usually possess valuable information.

Other sources of information are enemy and friendly civilians, refugees, defectors, captured agents, and informers. Because these sources may have lived in or passed through areas occupied or controlled by the enemy, they can provide valuable information.

CEDs are another important source of information which interrogation personnel will exploit in tactical operations. Documents will be found in the possession of EPWs or other detainees and on the battlefield. Often, they provide critical and sometimes detailed enemy information.

CAPTURE RATES

US military involvement in tactical operations during and since World War II has shown that conflict generates large numbers of EPWs, other detainees, and CEDs. The higher the intensity of conflict, the larger the number of EPWs, detainees, and CEDs.

In Operation Desert Storm, EPWs were captured, and surrendered, in such great numbers that many with information had little or no contact with interrogators until they were transported to rear area collecting points. By this time, any tactical information they had was of limited use.

In LIC operations in Grenada and Panama, the EPW capture rate was lower, but the detainee rate was higher. The following factors contri-buted to an extreme challenge for interrogation operations:

- Limited size of US forces.
- Limited number of language-qualified interrogators.
- The focus on local populace.
- Massive amounts of CEDs.

To be successful, interrogation support to tactical operations must be carefully planned. Available interrogation assets must be balanced against the operations objective, enemy situation estimate, and projected EPW capture rates.

The formulas in Table 2-1, are used to estimate the approximate division-level EPW capture rates. These formulas could vary according to type of conflict and mission.

Table 2-1. Division-level EPW capture rate.

Defensive Posture	Offensive Posture
.00035 EPWs* = 9 EPWs/day	.00367 EPWs* = 94 EPWs/day

*per combat soldier per day.

Counterinsurgency Operations

EPW capture rate for counterinsurgency operations may be very low. However, failure of the enemy to wear a uniform or other recognizable insignia results in an identification problem. As a result, large numbers of civilian suspects may also be detained during operations.

This requires individual screening at brigade and division levels of detained personnel to determine their status and appropriate disposition. In Vietnam, the ratio of EPWs approximated one for each six detainees taken into custody.

Terrorists

Terrorists are a fact of contemporary life. They are dedicated, intelligent, well financed, resourceful, and astute planners. They are difficult to identify and are not easily captured or interned. The use of terrorist tactics worldwide has increased significantly over the past 25 years, and this trend is not expected to abate in the future.

Besides peacetime, acts of terrorism should also be expected in time of armed conflict. US forces must be prepared to engage in counterterrorist activities to assist the civil and military police.

Current doctrine states counterterrorist activities may involve use of general purpose forces as well as those specifically organized and trained in counterterrorist techniques. There is no data available on projected terrorist capture rates.

INTERROGATION OF PROTECTED PERSONS

Civilians and refugees caught in the middle of a conflict are protected by the GWS, GPW, and GC. Most of the provisions discussed below apply whether the civilian or refugee is found in the territory of a party to the conflict, or in occupied territory. Civilians and refugees fall into the broadly defined category of protected persons under the GC.

It is important to keep in mind that protected persons, even those who might be detained by you, are not EPWs. They must be treated differently and kept segregated from EPWs. The rights and protections afforded EPWs and protected persons, as well as those control and disciplinary measures that may be used against them, are different. Appendix D provides GWS, GPW, and GC provisions for protecting persons rights.

INTERROGATOR SUPPORTED OPERATIONS

Combat operations which the tactical interrogator supports are discussed below. No matter what the operation is called, it is still incumbent upon the interrogator to gain critical combat information in support of that operation. The interrogator plays a key role to ensure the combat operation is a success.

OFFENSIVE OPERATIONS

Successful offensive operations demand imagination, thorough coordination, and skilled execution. These operations are characterized by—

- Aggressiveness.
- Initiative.
- Rapid shifts in the main effort to take advantage of opportunities.
- Momentum.
- Deep and rapid destruction of enemy forces.

Offenses should move fast, follow successful probes through gaps in the enemy defenses, and shift strength quickly to widen penetrations and reinforce successes to carry the battle deep into the enemy rear operations. They should destroy or control the forces or areas critical to the enemy's overall defensive organization before the enemy can react.

In the offense, certain principles are essential to battlefield success:

- Knowing the battlefield.
- Denying the enemy intelligence.
- Disrupting and destroying enemy command, control, communications, and intelligence (C^3I).
- Maintaining operational integrity.

Interrogation provides a high percentage of information on the enemy and terrain which, along with weather, are the key elements in knowing the battlefield.

Movement to Contact

Movement to contact is a tactical operation to find and engage the enemy. The force is organized to hold the bulk of its combat power in the main body. It moves aggressively toward the enemy, making maximum use of IEW resources to find the enemy before the enemy detects the friendly force.

When contact is made, combat information and intelligence determine where and with what force to attack and overcome enemy resistance. Interrogation is an important source of that information.

In a movement to contact, the friendly force may encounter an enemy defending or moving to contact. Once contact is made, the action must be resolved quickly if the movement to contact operation is to continue. This is normally done by a hasty attack launched as quickly as possible with whatever assets are on hand. No time is available for detailed IPB and analysis, other than what has been done prior to movement to contact. The analyst quickly updates the intelligence analysis for as quickly as possible with whatever assets are on hand. No time is available for detailed IPB and analysis, other than what has been done prior to movement to contact. The analyst quickly updates the intelligence analysis for the commander and continues the update as the attack progresses.

IEW resources look deep to determine second-echelon vulnerabilities. These vulnerabilities form the basis for friendly offensive action, particularly deep interdiction.

While continuing to look deep, IEW resources also support close operations directly. They continue to be sensitive to enemy vulnerabilities which would bring maximum friendly success when exploited. Where possible, IEW resources support deception operations.

In the movement to contact, interrogators should be deployed forward to interrogate EPWs as well as indigenous personnel, particularly refugees, to determine as much as possible about the enemy and terrain which lies in the path of the advancing force.

Meeting Engagement

The meeting engagement may be the result of movement to contact. It occurs when a moving force, incompletely deployed for battle, engages an enemy force about which it has inadequate intelligence. Once contact is made, electronic countermeasures (ECM) are employed against enemy key C^3 and electronic guidance systems.

All available collection resources deploy to determine the size, composition, disposition, capabilities, and intentions of the enemy force. They immediately report critical information, such as the location of assailable flanks and other enemy vulnerabilities, to the force commander. The commander needs this information quickly to decide whether to bypass, attack, or defend against the enemy.

Meeting engagement battles can be avoided if IEW resources are effectively integrated and used. If intelligence is effective, the commander can prepare for battle before encountering the enemy force.

Hasty and Deliberate Attacks

In hasty and deliberate attacks, IEW tasks are virtually the same. MI resources determine as much information as possible about the enemy's defensive posture. Key information determined by IEW assets includes—

- How the enemy's defense is organized.
- Where enemy reserve and counterattack forces are located, and when they move.
- What NBC weapons systems the enemy has, and where they are located.
- Where the enemy's conventional artillery is located.
- Where enemy radio electronic combat (REC) assets are located.

In a hasty attack, the need for rapid collection of combat information is critical. In such an attack it may be advantageous to deploy interrogation teams down to battalion level to operate in a similar manner as in the movement to contact.

In the deliberate attack, intelligence on the enemy is more complete, and interrogation support may not be provided below brigade. However, planning for a deliberate attack should task organize interrogation assets to satisfy the greatest need.

For example, a committed brigade that conducts the main attack receives the support of two interrogation teams; a brigade in a supporting attack receives only one team; and a brigade in reserve receives no interrogation support.

Exploitation and Pursuit

Commanders planning offensive operations must be prepared to conduct exploitation and pursuit actions. Without prior detailed planning for these contingencies, fleeting opportunities to press a successful attack to completion may be missed. IEW resources, particularly MI assets, play an important part in planning for and executing exploitation and pursuit missions.

IPB is critical and helps identify enemy vulnerabilities. Intelligence supports targeting by identifying, locating, and tracking enemy forces which may move to counter exploitation forces.

After the initial assault, MI assets determine the integrity of enemy defenses. They locate gaps, holes, and weak spots that may be exploited. They determine if the enemy intends to defend in place, delay, or withdraw to subsequent defensive positions. ECM are maximized to increase enemy force confusion.

Reconnaissance In Force

A reconnaissance in force (RIF) is a limited objective operation by a substantial force to obtain information and to determine enemy dispositions and strengths. The RIF also tests enemy reactions to friendly force action. Enemy reactions may reveal major defensive weaknesses which could be exploited.

Even when using RIF to gain information, commanders executing it must be alert to seize an opportunity to exploit tactical success. If the enemy situation must be developed across a broad front, a RIF may probe the enemy at selected points.

Recognizing that RIF is primarily an information-gathering operation, commanders must carefully consider the risks involved. Precise plans must be made in advance to extricate the force or to exploit success.

In many respects, MI RIF support is like movement to contact. Interrogation support is critical since EPWs will be an important source of the information the RIF seeks. Interrogation support, described in movement to contact, may be the most efficient means of supporting the RIF.

River Crossing

River-crossing operations are an integral part of land warfare. The objective of any river-crossing operation is to project combat power across a water obstacle while ensuring the integrity and momentum of the force. Because the modern battlefield is so lethal, and small enemy units can be destructive, crossings must be quick and undetected. Therefore, it is essential that rivers be crossed in stride as a continuation of operations.

MI units contribute to the planning and execution phases of river-crossing operations:

- IPB enables the commander to select the best crossing site and know the battlefield beyond, so operations can be sustained without interruption.
- IEW forces deploy forward and continue seeking enemy weaknesses for exploitation, and to warn of enemy forces capable of affecting the operation.
- Other elements guard the flanks to prevent enemy surprise.
- MI resources further help the commander know the battlefield and guard against a surprise attack by identifying, locating, and tracking enemy NBC-capable delivery systems.

Based on the picture of the battlefield drawn by the G2 as a result of IPB, the commander decides whether the crossing will be—

- Hasty or deliberate.
- Day or night.
- Wide or narrow on the front.

MI units normally are not part of the assault force; however, GSR teams may accompany the assault force if surveillance of enemy approaches to the exit bank cannot be conducted from the entry bank. Additionally, interrogators should be included in the assault force if immediate EPW exploitation is deemed critical to developing intelligence on the exit-bank battlefield.

Evacuation of EPWs back over the crossing site to a support area collecting point normally will be delayed. This is due to the need to get the maximum amount of force across the river in the shortest time. Two-way traffic in the early stages of the crossing may be precluded.

A forward collecting point on the exit-bank side of the river may be established immediately behind the assault force, and interrogations can be conducted to obtain information critical to the immediate situation. To accomplish this, organization of interrogation assets as outlined under movement to contact may be employed.

DEFENSIVE OPERATIONS

Defensive operations can retain ground, deny the enemy access to an area, and damage or destroy attacking forces. They cannot, however, win the battle by imposing the will of the commander on the enemy. For this reason, the defense is a temporary expedient, undertaken only when it is impossible to conduct offensive operations, or when attacking in another area. All defensive actions are undertaken in anticipation of ultimately resuming the offense.

Commanders plan the overall defensive effort on the basis of the METT-T. MI assets are allocated within the elements of the organizational framework to support the overall scheme. The IEW principles for supporting offensive operations apply to the defense, as well as to other operations. Interrogation support to defensive operations, likewise, is basically the same as that provided to offensive operations. Listed below are important factors to consider in defensive operations:

- The primary focus of intelligence requirements is on which enemy will attack and when, where, and how they intend to do it.
- The decentralized, fluid nature of the covering force battle requires interrogation support at the lowest possible echelon. This requires DS interrogation teams from the

division MI battalion and the MI brigade (Corps). Questioning of civilians and EPWs is brief and is conducted to obtain information of immediate tactical value. Interrogators gather information about the identification, composition, disposition and direction of movement, strength, and capabilities of enemy forces involved in the immediate covering force battle.

- More interrogation support is required at corps. The enemy has the initiative, and will probably conduct operations in the friendly rear area.

Support of defense operations requires the closest management of interrogation assets. The necessity to support the covering force must be balanced against the increased corps rear operations support. The increased emphasis on rear operations may mean fewer corps interrogation assets available to support division.

The G2, in coordination with the MI unit commander, may determine that an echelon between the covering force and corps will not be supported. For example, EPWs may be interrogated by DS interrogators supporting the covering force, and then be evacuated back to division,

Table 2-2. Interrogation support in LIC.

Insurgency
- Interrogate EPWs and detainees.
- Exploit CEDs.
- Provide PSYOP linguistic support.
- Train insurgent combatants in interrogation techniques.

Combatting Terrorism
- Provide PSYOP linguistic support directed against terrorists.
- Provide CA linguistic support.
- Provide linguistic support for liaison with military or paramilitary HQ.
- Provide linguistic support during PW exchanges.
- Debrief members of US peacekeeping forces for intelligence purposes.

Counterinsurgency
- Interrogate EPWs and detainees.
- Exploit CEDs.
- Train HN forces in interrogation techniques.
- Provide linguistic support to other US forces, advisors, and trainers.
- Provide PSYOP linguistic support.
- Provide CA linguistic support.
- In counter-drug operations—
  —Train HN personnel in interrogation techniques.
  —Exploit and analyze drug-related documents.

Peacetime and Peacekeeping Operations
- Provide PSYOP linguistic support.
- Debrief knowledgeable civilians being evacuated from danger zones during NEO.
- Support counter-drug operations by—
  —Training HN personnel in interrogation techniques.
  —Exploiting and analyzing narcotics-related documents.

bypassing brigade. Additionally, the five-member DS team, which provides flexibility, may have to be reduced to two or three interrogators. Table 2-2 shows interrogation support in LIC.

THEATER INTERROGATION FACILITY

The EAC interrogation facility will normally be designated as the TIF. A TIF is staffed by US Army interrogators and analysts, with support from Air Force, Navy, Marine Corps, and other US national agencies as required. In a multinational operation, a combined interrogation facility may be established with allied interrogator augmentation. In addition to conventional theater Army operations, a TIF may be established to support a joint or unified command to meet theater requirements during crisis or contingency deployments.

MI battalion companies, MI brigade (EAC) provide US Army interrogation support to the EAC TIF. The mission of the TIF is to—

- Establish liaison with host nation (HN) commanders to achieve critical intelligence information in response to theater and national level intelligence collection requirements.
- Ensure communication between HN and US military TIF commanders, and establish rapport with HN interrogation activities.
- Coordinate for national level collection requirements.
- Interrogate PWs, high-level political and military personnel, civilian internees, defectors, refugees, and displaced persons.
- Participate in debriefings of US and allied personnel who have escaped after being captured, or who have evaded capture.
- Translate and exploit selected CEDs.
- Assist in technical support activity (TSA) operations (see FM-34-5(S)).

The MI battalion (I&E) has an HHC for C^3, and three interrogation companies, of which one is Active Component (AC) and the other two are RC. The companies consist of two MI companies, I&E (EPW support) and one MI company, I&E (GS-EAC).

The two MI companies support EPW compound operations. Their elements are primarily for GS at EAC, but may be deployed for DS at corps and division. The MI company (I&E) (GS-EAC) provides priority interrogation and DOCEX support to corps and divisions, to the TIF, and to temporary EPW compounds as required.

A TIF is organized into a headquarters section, operations section, and two interrogation and DOCEX sections. It will normally have an attached TSA section from Operations Group, and a liaison team from the Joint Captured Materiél Exploitation Center (JCMEC). The JCMEC liaison team assists in exploiting sources who have knowledge of captured enemy weapons and equipment.

The headquarters section provides all command, administrative, logistical, and maintenance support to the TIF. It coordinates with—

- Commander, MI Battalion (I&E) for personnel status, administrative support, and logistical support prior to deployment.
- Battalion S3 for deployment of interrogation assets.
- Theater J2 for reporting procedures, operational situation update, and theater and national level intelligence requirements.

- Provost marshal for location of theater EPW camps, and for procedures to be followed by interrogators and MP for processing, interrogating, and internment.
- Commanders of theater medical support units and internment facility for procedures to treat, and clear for questioning, wounded EPWs.
- Commander, CI company, for CI requirements and joint interrogation and CI procedures.

OPERATIONS SECTION

This section (where ideally the officer in charge [OIC] has the 3Q additional skill identifier) is organized into the operations, OB, and communications elements. The operations section—

- Designates work areas for all TIF elements.
- Establishes and maintains TIF functional files.
- Establishes interrogation priorities.
- Maintains a daily log and journal.
- Disseminates incoming and outgoing distribution.
- Conducts liaison with local officials, adjacent and subordinate intelligence activities, CI, MP, PSYOP, the JCMEC, Plans and Policy Directorate (J5), and provost marshal.
- Conducts coordination with holding area OIC or enclosure commander for screening site, medical support, access, movement, and evacuation procedures for EPWs.
- Conducts operations briefings when required.
- Manages screening operations.
- Manages EPW access for intelligence collection.
- Assigns control numbers (see DIAM 58-13).
- Supervised all intelligence collection activities within the TIF.

OB ELEMENT

This element—

- Obtain the initial data base and updates and maintains it.
- Establishes and maintains OB workbooks and files to include data generated by intelligence information which has not been verified.
- Maintains SITMAPs displaying enemy and friendly situation.
- Catalogs, cross-references, and disseminates collection requirements to TIF collection elements.
- Reviews INTREPs for inclusion into data base.
- Conducts OB briefings when required.

OTHER MI ELEMENTS

Collection missions are tailored and assigned by the CM&D section subordinate to the G2 at corps and division. The same functions are performed at brigade and battalion by the battlefield information control center (BICC). These elements must ensure the assigned collection mission is passed by secure means, through established channels, to the interrogation element.

If interrogators are deployed in a GS role, the CM&D section will pass its interrogator taskings to the MI battalion TOC. If interrogators are deployed in a DS role, they will receive taskings directly from the BICC.

The CM&D section (through the MI battalion TOC) or the BICC must maintain close contact with the interrogation element. This contact allows a two-way flow of communication.

The CM&D or BICC element needs the contact to accomplish the preceding three steps. They also use the contact to revise the interrogation element's collection mission as required. The interrogation element requires the contact to ensure it receives current guidance, direction, and assistance in solving collection problems.

ALL SOURCE ANALYSIS SYSTEM (ASAS)

This system provides assistance to the J2, G2, or G3 and MI unit commanders who collect and analyze intelligence and perform CI and EW functions. The following elements feed into the ASAS.

Imagery Exploitation

Interrogators should maintain close contact with imagery exploitation elements. Interrogators may be required to identify items on air photographs and should report information of interest to the imagery analysts. Imagery analysts can aid interrogation personnel by furnishing photographs for use in connection with interrogation and by verifying leads originally obtained through interrogation.

TECHINT Personnel

Normally, interrogation elements coordinate with the TECHINT sections of the RC battalion (TE). The TECHINT section, and its field teams, furnishes guidance and requirements to the interrogation elements through questionnaires and interrogation guides. These are valuable aids to the interrogator in obtaining specific TECHINT information.

Interrogators notify the nearest TECHINT personnel to obtain detailed technical information and guidance. At tactical levels, this is the exception rather than the rule, but it may be necessary when information is of immediate tactical value.

COUNTERINTELLIGENCE

Coordination between CI and interrogation elements is always necessary. This coordination is effected continuously, directly or indirectly, and at the discretion of the intelligence officer. CI elements are active in the security screening of refugees and civilians in the combat zone.

CI personnel and interrogators must work together to ensure proper interrogation of enemy civilians or personnel speaking the enemy's language. Interrogator personnel can further assist the CI effort by—

- Furnishing leads on suspected enemy agents and intelligence personnel.
- Informing CI elements concerning enemy personnel dressed in other than enemy uniforms.
- Referring to CI elements, or making available to them for interrogation, all EPWs and other sources of CI interest. CI personnel are trained for interrogation in cases of suspected espionage, sabotage, or subversion. Their knowledge of the CI situation (to include hostile intelligence activities) enhances full exploitation of appropriate sources.

MILITARY POLICE

The corps MP commander operates the corps EPW holding area and provides escort guard support to divisions for EPW evacuation in routine or medical channels. EPWs are evacuated from the corps holding area to the next higher echelon with the least possible delay.

The MP commander also arranges and coordinates transportation requirements to include rations and water, if required, for the movement to include a number of vehicles, railroad or passenger cars, or aircraft with the time and place of departure.

Expeditious EPW evacuation is provided by the prior dispatch of escort guards to establish a ready reserve at the supported divisions. This reserve evacuation capability is maintained by sending additional escort guards on a continuing or as required basis. These guards may also be attached to EPW and processing reception camps as needed.

EPW administrative processing is done by MP PW processing units. Processing includes personnel record preparation, fingerprint and identity cards (if needed), and internment serial number assignment.

PSYOP

Normally, interrogation elements coordinate with PSYOP elements to obtain information concerning the motivational factors and cultural value systems of the individuals to be interrogated.

PSYOP units, as a part of their normal operations, develop detailed analysis concerning psychological and cultural factors of friendly and hostile elements in the AO. Such information will help interrogation personnel to understand the source's attitude, value system, and perception; it will also help to obtain information more rapidly, and at the same time, PSYOP information on current conditions in enemy country or among enemy forces. A PSYOP PIR would be established to cover this requirement.

SUPPORT RELATIONSHIPS

Successful interrogation operations require support from elements within their echelon of assignment, including all major staff organizations. These elements are collectively responsible for the planning that creates the overall environment for interrogators. The intelligence staff's (J2, G2, or S2) direct contribution to interrogation operations has already been discussed. Its general responsibilities are outlined below, along with those of other staff and support elements.

PERSONNEL (G1 AND S1)

The G1 and S1 are responsible for—

- Supervising the medical support furnished to sources.
- Maintaining a list (by language and proficiency) of qualified linguists within their command.
- Coordinating with the G5 for procurement and payment of other interpreters and translators needed to perform intelligence and nonintelligence duties.

The G1 and S1 ensure the echelon's operations plan (OPLAN) contains complete provisions for source handling and evacuation. This plan must satisfy the interests of all other staff officers and provide for—

- Humane treatment of all sources.
- Prompt evacuation from the combat zone.
- Opportunities to interrogate sources.
- Integration of procedures for the evacuation, control, and administration of sources with

other CS and CSS operations (through the provost marshal).

- Training for all troops on the provisions of international agreements and regulations relating to sources.
- Ensuring delivery of EPW and detainee mail.
- Maintaining EPW and detainee statistics.
- Administration and control of EPW currency and pay records, to include coordination with appropriate intelligence authorities about investigation of large sums of money.

INTELLIGENCE (J2, G2, AND S2)

The J2, G2, and S2 are responsible for supervising appropriate censorship activities relating to sources. They also—

- Coordinate with the G3 to ensure plans for interrogation, CI, PSYOP, and CA operations are included in unit training plans and OPLANs.
- Draft instructions for MI handling, evacuating, and exploiting captured enemy personnel and CEDs. (They coordinate with the G3 to ensure draft instructions are included in the command SOP, OPLANs, and supplementary orders.)
- Project source capture flows.
- Determine the number of interpreters and translators needed to perform intelligence duties.
- Control the procedures used to process and grant clearance to the interpreters and translators who need them.
- Coordinate with G5 on screening of nonsuspect local nationals and displaced persons.

OPERATIONS (G3 AND S3)

The G3 and S3 are responsible for operations, plans, organization, and training. Where MP assets are not available, or insufficient, they are responsible for obtaining, organizing, and supervising employment of additional personnel as guards. The G3 and S3—

- Prepare, coordinate, and publish the command SOP, OPLANs, and supplementary orders. This includes instructions for handling, evacuating, and exploiting captured enemy personnel and CEDs, which are drafted by the G2.
- Incorporate interrogation operations into future plans and operations.
- Ensure subordinate units are trained in proper handling and evacuation of captured enemy personnel, captured enemy materiél (CEM), and CEDs.
- Train guard personnel.
- Provide G2 and S2 with details of planned operations.
- Plan and supervise all PSYOP activities in support of tactical operations.
- Evaluate, in coordination with the G2 and G5, enemy PYSOP efforts and effectiveness of friendly PSYOP on target groups.

SUPPLY (G4 AND S4)

The G4 and S4 are responsible for storing and maintaining supplies and equipment needed by subordinate units to conduct source handling operations, as well as delivering them to subordinate units as they are needed. The G4 and S4 also supervise—

- Command policy for evacuation and internment of captured enemy personnel, and evacuation and safekeeping of CEM and CEDs.
- Real estate acquisition and construction of source holding area facilities.
- Collection and distribution of captured enemy supplies. (This is coordinated with the intelligence and operations staffs.)
- Procurement and distribution of rations to source holding areas. (Captured enemy rations will be used when possible.)
- EPW and detainee transportation.
- Determination of requirements for use of source labor for the logistical support needed in source handling operations.
- Logistical support to interpreter personnel.

CIVIL-MILITARY OPERATIONS (G5 AND S5)

The G5 and S5 are responsible for CA. They—

- Advise, assist, and make recommendations that relate to civil-military operations (CMO) and CA aspects of current or proposed operations.
- Prepare estimates and conduct studies and analyses for CMO activities.
- Prepare the portions of operations, administrative, and logistics plans and orders for CMO activities.
- Determine requirements for resources to accomplish command CMO activities, including CA units and personnel.
- Coordinate with local US government, G1 and S1 representatives, and HN armed forces for procuring native linguists for interpreter support.
- Recommend command policy on obligations between civil and military authorities; on the AO population; and on the works and activities arising from treaties, agreements, international law, and US policy.
- Provide civil support for tactical and CSS operations and prevent civilian interference with these operations.
- Coordinate military support of populace and resource control programs.
- Provide technical advice and assistance in reorientation of sources and enemy defectors.
- Coordinate MI aspects of CMO activities with the G2 or S2.

ADDITIONAL SUPPORT

Besides the major staff elements, an interrogation element requires support from several other elements in order to conduct operations. These elements are discussed below.

Communications

Secure, reliable communication must be available at or near the interrogation element's deployment site. Priority access to these communications must be arranged to support contact with collection management.

Staff Judge Advocate

This element can provide legal support and advice on the interpretation and application of international regulations and agreements about handling sources. It is also a channel for reporting known or suspected war crimes.

Health Service Support

This element must clear all sick and wounded sources before they can be interrogated. Seriously sick or wounded sources are evacuated through medical channels. If adequate facilities are not available in EPW hospitals, EPWs are admitted to military or civilian medical facilities where treatment can be obtained.

Each EPW is medically examined and weighed at least once a month. Provisions are made for the isolation of communicable cases, disinfection, and inoculations. Retained medical personnel and EPWs with medical training are used to care for their own sick an wounded.

NBC Protection

All EPWs will be provided NBC protection. If EPWs do not have their own NBC protection equipment, or their equipment is not usable, the detaining forces must provide them with proper NBC gear.

Chaplain Support

The unit ministry team, consisting of the chaplain and chaplain assistant, provides religious support. The team coordinates with the G5 and S5 to provide religious support for refugees, displaced persons, and indigenous civilians. It provides services for EPWs or assists detained clergy of enemy forces and other detained clergy. The team provides burial rites according to the religious rites of combatants. Religious preference of EPWs will be obtained from DA Form 4237-R (Detainee Personnel Record) (see Chapter 3).

Inspector General

This element is a channel for reporting known or suspected war crimes.

Public Affairs officer

The public affairs officer advises and informs the commander of public affairs impact inherent in planned or implemented EPW operations.

Engineer Officer

The engineer officer assists in planning the construction of EPW enclosures. He also assists the G2 and S2 in developing obstacle intelligence (OBSTINTEL) during the IPB. OBSTINTEL requirements are reflected in the PIR and IR. Much of the IR is technical in nature and warrants direct coordination with the interrogator to ensure the right questions are asked. Through the J2, G2, and S2, he will also analyze the information collected and its impact on the maneuver and engineer plan.

Military Band Unit

At division and corps, the band may augment the MP by providing security at central collecting points and corps holding areas.

CHAPTER 3

THE INTERROGATION PROCESS

Criteria for selecting personnel to be interrogated vary with the—

- Commander's collection requirements.
- Time limitations.
- Number and types of potential sources available.
- Exact circumstances surrounding the employment of US Forces.

In this regard, source selection is important in conducting interrogation at tactical echelons of command because of the proximity to enemy elements, number and conditions of detainees, and time restrictions.

The interrogation process involves screening of sources for interrogation and the use of interrogation techniques and procedures. Screening and interrogation involve complex interpersonal skills, and many aspects of their performance are subjective. Each screening and interrogation is unique because of the interaction between the interrogator and the source.

The five interrogation phases—planning and preparation, approach, questioning, termination, and reporting—are discussed later in this chapter.

COLLECTION PRIORITY

Interrogators are trained to exploit sources and CEDs. This allows the all-source collection manager three exploitation options for interrogation assets: They may exploit sources alone, exploit CEDs, or exploit both simultaneously.

In the past, it was assumed interrogators could accomplish the dual collection mission no matter what type of combat operations were being supported. This may no longer be true. Unit staffing coupled with the amount of CEDs and sources, may prevent exploitation of sources and CEDs simultaneously.

The density of interrogation assets and command emphasis on the collection effort determine mission requirements. The feasibility of a dual collection mission may also be the result of initial IPB by the commander's intelligence staff. If an echelon cannot conduct a dual collection effort, interrogating sources receives the priority for two reasons:

- The greater intelligence potential of a source.
- The rate at which people forget detailed information.

An individual's value system is easier to bypass immediately after undergoing a significant traumatic experience. The circumstances of capture are traumatic for most sources. Many former PWs indicated extreme disorientation immediately after capture. Capture thrusts them into a foreign environment over which they have no control. Their mores were of no use to them during this period. Most of them survived this phase by clinging to very basic values (love of family and loyalty to friends or comrades).

Since humans are adaptable, this initial vulnerability passes quickly. An individual's established values begin to assert themselves again within a day or two. When this happens, much of an individual's susceptibility to interrogation is gone.

Memory stores information in two areas: short-term and long-term memory. The five senses constantly transmit information to the brain's short-term memory temporarily and then shifts to the brain's long-term memory. The time at which this transfer takes place varies, but research shows a great amount of detail is lost during that transfer. The percentage of information lost beyond recall varies from study to study, but 70 percent is a conservative estimate.

Much of the information of value to the interrogator is information the source is not aware he has. Although no research data is available in this area, it is likely this type of information will be lost quickly.

CEDs, while not affected by memory loss, are often time-sensitive and thus are screened quickly for possible exploitation (see Chapter 4).

The supported echelon's intelligence officer determines the guidelines for priority of exploitation. The commander's intelligence needs and the J2's, G2's, or S2's estimate of the enemy's intentions dictate the extent to which these guidelines can be applied. Exploitation priorities are reviewed and changes when needed.

SCREENING

Screening is the selection of sources for interrogation. It must be conducted at every echelon to—

- Determine source cooperativeness and knowledgeability.
- Determine which sources can best satisfy the commander's PIR and IR in a timely manner.

PREPARE TO CONDUCT SCREENINGS

Screeners should obtain a copy of the element's overall objective statement from the PIR, IR, and SIR and become familiar with the intelligence indicators listed there. Screeners must use their experience and imagination to devise ways to identify EPWs and detainees who might possess information pertinent to these indicators.

For example, one group of indicators may concern new enemy units moving along a specific avenue of approach. In this case, a screener may want to concentrate first on screening EPWs and detainees captured near that location. When he questions those EPWs or detainees, the screener might try to determine what units are due to arrive in that area in the near future. The ability to recognize branch of service and rank insignia can be of great assistance to screeners.

Screeners coordinate with MP holding area guards on their role in the screening process. The guards are told where the screening will take place, how EPWs and detainees are to be brought there from the holding area, and what types of behavior on their part will facilitate the screenings.

DOCUMENT SCREENING

If time permits, screeners should go to the holding area and examine all available documents pertaining to the EPWs and detainees. They should look for signs that certain EPWs and detainees are willing, or can be induced, to cooperate with the interrogator. Previous screening and interrogation reports and EPW personnel records are important.

Interrogation reports identify EPWs and detainees who have been cooperative in the past. Prior screening reports indicate EPWs and detainees who appear cooperative. During EPW inprocessing, MPs prepare a DA Form 4237-R, which is prescribed by AR 190-8. A sample is shown at Figure 3-1. DA Form 4237-R contains additional information not required by the GWS, GPW, and GC, but which the EPWs and detainees may have volunteered during inprocessing. The volunteering of information is one indicator of EPW's or detainee's cooperation.

When examining documents, screeners should identify topics on which EPWs and detainees have pertinent information. Screeners should make a note of any documents captured with specific EPWs and detainees that may contain indications of pertinent knowledge and potential cooperation.

PERSONNEL SCREENING

If time permits, screeners should question holding area personnel about the EPWs and detainees. Since these personnel are in almost constant contact with the EPWs and detainees, their descriptions of specific ones can help identify sources who might answer the supported commander's PIR and IR.

Screeners should identify and note those EPWs and detainees whose appearance and behavior indicate they are willing to cooperate immediately or are unlikely to cooperate ever. Unless time is critically short, screeners should—

- Personally observe the EPWs and detainees.
- Pay attention to rank and branch of service insignias, and condition of uniform and equipment.
- Carefully observe the behavior demonstrated by other EPWs and detainees.
- Look for things like attempts to talk to the guards, intentional placement in the wrong segregation group, or any overt signs of nervousness, anxiety, or fright.
- Note any EPW or detainee whose appearance or behavior indicates willingness to talk.

CI SCREENING

Before initiating the screening process, the interrogator establishes liaison with supporting CI agents. The CI element, through the CM&D, provides PIR of CI interest. During the screening process, interrogators identify sources of CI interest. After these sources have been interrogated for any information of immediate tactical value (as needed), they are turned over to CI. CI is interested in sources who—

- Have no identification documents.
- Have excessive or modified identification documents.
- Possess unusually large amounts of cash or valuables.
- Possess knowledge of critical interest (for example, nuclear power or chemical plant operations, weapons test and development).
- Are illegal border crossers.
- Attempt to avoid checkpoints.
- Are on the black, gray, or white list (FM 34-60A(S)).
- Request to see CI or US Army Intelligence personnel.
- Have family in the denied area.

Screeners should always try to screen cooperative knowledgeable EPWs and detainees first. These include EPWs and detainees identified during the screener's review of documents, questioning of holding area personnel, and their own personal observations. Based on screener notes

DETAINEE PERSONNEL RECORD

For use of this form, see AR 190-8, the proponent agency is ODCSPER.

PART I – TO BE COMPLETED AT TIME OF PROCESSING

CARD I	1. INTERNMENT SERIAL NO. (1-13)	2. NAME (Last, first, middle) (14-34)	3. RANK (35-37)
	US-1501-23176	CH'OE, HYON-SIK	SRSGT

4. ENEMY SVC NO. (38-46)	5. TYPE (47)	6. DATE OF CAPTURE (48-53)	7. DATE OF BIRTH (54-59)
5611642	REG	8 OCT 99	24 FEB 77

8. NATIONALITY (60-61)	9. EDUCATION (62)	10. RELIGION (63-64)	11. MARSTA (65)	12. PW CAMP UIC (66-71)	13. PW PROCESS DATE (72-77)
KOREAN (DPRK)	10 year compulsory	None	Single	US-AA3CU	8 Oct 99

CARD II (Keypuncher will pick up Item 1 above)	14. SEX (14)	15. LANGUAGE I (15-16)	16. LANGUAGE II (17-18)
	M	KOREAN	KOREAN

17. PHYSICAL CONDITION (19)	18. PW CAMP LOCATION (20-22)	19. ENEMY UNIT (23-34)
Good	AB654321	3BN, 34REGT, 17INF DIV.

20. ARM OF SVC (35)	21. MOSC (36-39)	22. CIVILIAN OCCUPATION (40-45)	23. UIC-CAPTURE UNIT (46-51)
Army	IIA(INF)	FARMER	US-ARA7DD

24. CORPS AREA OF CAPTURE (52)	25. PLACE OF CAPTURE	26. POWER SERVED	27. PLACE OF BIRTH
IV	AB123456	DPRK	KAESONG

28. ADDRESS TO WHICH MAIL FOR PW MAY BE SENT
3 DONG 5 BAN
KAESONG,
DPRK

29. FATHER/STEPFATHER
CH'OE, KANG-T'AE

30. MOTHER'S MAIDEN NAME
YI, NYONG-CHA

31. PERMANENT HOME ADDRESS OF PW
See Item 28.

32. NAME, ADDRESS, AND RELATIONSHIP OF PERSON TO BE INFORMED OF CAPTURE
See Items 29 and 30.

33. OTHER PARTICULARS FROM ID CARD:
HT - 1.70 meters HAIR - Black
WT - 65 Kilos EYES - Brown

34. DISTINGUISHING MARKS
Scar on left knee.

35. IMPOUNDED PERSONAL EFFECTS AND MONEY
26 WON

THE ABOVE LIST OF IMPOUNDED ITEMS IS CORRECT Choe Hyon-Sik
(Signature of Detainee)

SAMPLE

36. REMARKS
None.

37. PHOTO
PHOTO (Front View) PHOTO (Right Profile)

38. PREPARED BY (Individual and unit)
SFC D.C. SMITH, 17th MP Co.

39. SIGNATURE
SFC D.C. Smith

40. DATE PREPARED
8 Oct 99

41. PLACE
29th INF DIV REAR INTERNMENT FACILITY

DA FORM 4237-R, Aug 85 EDITION OF MAY 82 IS OBSOLETE

Figure 3-1. DA Form 4237-R (Detainee Personnel Record) (front).

PART II – TO BE MAINTAINED BY UNIT HAVING CUSTODY

42a. LAST NAME	b. FIRST NAMES
CH'OE	HYON-SIK

43. INTERNMENT SERIAL NUMBER
US-1501-23176

44. MEDICAL RECORD

a. IMMUNIZATION *(Vaccinations and Innoculations with Dates)*
Smallpox - 15 APR 98

b. MAJOR ILLNESSES AND PHYSICAL DEFECTS *(With Dates)*	c. BLOOD GROUP
NONE.	B POS

45. INTERNMENT EMPLOYMENT QUALIFICATIONS
FARMER

46. SERIOUS OFFENSES, PUNISHMENTS, AND ESCAPES *(With Dates)*
NONE.

47. TRANSFERS

FROM *(Location)*	TO *(Location)*	DATE

SAMPLE

48. REMARKS

49. FINANCIAL STATUS AT TIME OF FIRST INTERNATIONAL TRANSFER

a. CERTIFICATE OF CREDIT BALANCE ISSUED TO EPW *(Amount in words)*	b. AMT IN FIGURES
c. LOCATION	d. DATE

50. FINANCIAL STATUS AT TIME OF SECOND INTERNATIONAL TRANSFER

a. CERTIFICATE OF CREDIT BALANCE ISSUED TO EPW *(Amount in words)*	b. AMT IN FIGURES
c. LOCATION	d. DATE

51. REPATRIATION

a. REASON

b. MODE	c. DATE

52. FINANCIAL STATUS AT TIME OF REPATRIATION

a. CERTIFICATE OF CREDIT BALANCE ISSUED TO EPW *(Amount in words)*	b. AMT IN FIGURES
c. LOCATION	d. DATE

REVERSE OF DA FORM 4237-R, AUG 85

Figure 3-1. DA Form 4237-R (Detainee Personnel Record) (reverse).

and recommendations, they establish the order which EPWs and detainees will be questioned. The holding area guards are then told to bring these EPWs and detainees, in order, to the screening site one at a time.

A screener must use a screening report to record information as it is obtained from the source. Figure 3-2 is a format for a screening report. All information shown is rarely obtained from any one source. The blocks save the screener as much additional writing as possible. If PIR, IR, and SIR information is obtained, it is spot reported in SALUTE format. When this type of information is obtained during screening, it must be exploited fully and reported as soon as possible.

Source screening ends when the screener is sure he can make an accurate assessment of the source's potential cooperation and pertinent knowledge. At this time, the source is returned to the control of the guards, and the screener records his assessment on the screening report.

The assessment is recorded using a screening code. The screening code is an alphanumeric designation which reflects the level of cooperation expected from the source and the level of knowledgeability the source may possess. Table 3-1 shows the codes for assessing sources.

Those sources who have been assigned to the same category may be interrogated in any order deemed appropriate by the senior interrogator. Category 1A sources normally should be the first to be interrogated; Category 1B, next; followed by those assigned to categories 2A, 1C, 2B, 3A, 2C, and 3B. Category 3C sources are normally interrogated last.

This order ensures the highest probability of obtaining the greatest amount of pertinent information within available time. Screening codes may change with the echelon. The higher the echelon, the more time is available to conduct an approach.

Figure 3-3 shows the order in which sources will be interrogated. The term "screening category" should not be confused with the categories that are assigned to EPWs and detainees based on their intelligence value.

There are five interrogation phases which take place after the screening process.

- Planning and preparation.

Table 3-1. Instructions for assessing sources.

CODE	COOPERATION LEVEL
1	Responds to direct questions.
2	Responds hesitantly to questioning.
3	Does not respond to questioning.
	KNOWLEDGEABILITY LEVEL
A	Very likely to possess PIR information.
B	Might have IR information.
C	Does not appear to have pertinent information.

MP NUMBER: **EVACUATION DATE:**

PERSONAL

LNAME (P): KHRAIS
LNAME (M):
FNAME: HAITHAM
MNAME: ABDULLAH
SVC/ID NO: 1234567
DOB: 24 OCT 80
LANGUAGES: ARABIC
MARITAL STATUS: M (S) W D

****

STATUS: (M) = Military C = Civilian P = Paramilitary ? = Other

CAPTURE DATA

DATE: 7 Aug 99
TIME: 1417
PLACE: ZA 123456
CAP UNIT: 1Co/2/3/4 REGT
CIRCUMSTANCES: AFTER FIRE FIGHT
DOCUMENTS: NONE
WPNS/EQUIP: AK-47

MILITARY

BRANCH: AF (AR) CG MC NV
RANK: PVT
FULL UNIT DSG: 1SQD/2PLT/3Co
DUTY PSN: DUTY SOLDIER
JOB: RIFLEMAN
STATION:
SKILLS: SHARPSHOOTER
EXPERIENCE: IN SVC 9 Mos.

CIVILIAN

JOB: STUDENT
ORG:
DUTIES:
SKILLS: NONE.

ASSESSMENT DATA

PHYSICAL CONDITION: SEX: (M) F
WOUNDED: Y (N)
REMARKS:

MENTAL CONDITION:
EDUCATION = 8 YRS
INTELLIGENCE: AVG + AVG (AVG –)
MENTAL STATE: NERVOUS

SCREENER: SFC ROYCE
DATE: TIME:
COOPERATION: (1) (High) 2 3 (low)
KNOWLEDGE: A (High) (B) C (low)
BGW LIST: Y (N) BGW CODE:
SOURCE CATEGORY: A B (C) D
APPROACH: DIRECT, INCENTIVE

SPECIAL HANDLING REQUIREMENT CODES:

PIR & IR

REMARKS

Figure 3-2. Screening report format.

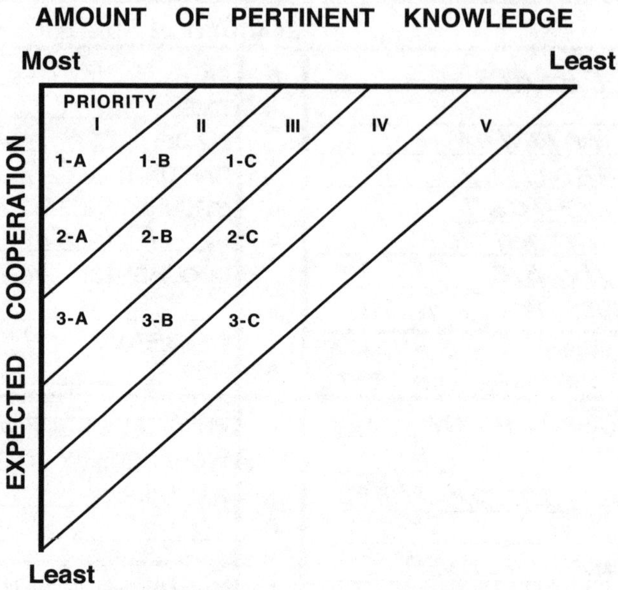

Figure 3-3. Interrogation priorities by screening category.

- Approach.
- Questioning.
- Termination.
- Reporting.

PLANNING AND PREPARATION

Once the senior interrogator has assigned specific sources to his subordinates, the interrogators develop a plan for their interrogations. These plans reflect the supported commander's PIR, IR, and SIR and current tactical situation. If they do not, subsequent interrogations will not help the element to satisfy its assigned collection mission, and information needed by the supported unit will be missed.

Each interrogator, where feasible, begins his preparation by examining the SITMAP, OB data base, and pertinent information contained in the interrogation element's files.

Screening reports (Figure 3-2) and DA Form 5976 (Enemy Prisoner of War Capture Tag) are excellent sources of information the interrogator needs. Figure 3-4 shows a sample of DA Form 5976. There should be at least one of these documents available on each EPW and detainee. Additional sources of information may be—

- Documents captured with the EPW or detainee.
- Reports from interrogation elements at previous echelons.
- DA Form 4237-R (Figure 3-1).

The planning and preparation phase and the approach phase (discussed later) are interrelated. In the planning and preparation phase, the interrogator gathers—

- Information on the source's circumstances of capture.
- Comments from others who have been with the source.
- Information on the source's observed behavior and personal traits.
- Peculiarities from the screening sheet.

This information helps the interrogator develop a picture of the source and enables him to select approaches most likely to work.

There are four primary factors that must be considered when selecting tentative approaches:

- The source's mental and physical state. Is the source injured, angry, crying, arrogant, cocky, or frightened? If so, how can this state be best exploited during interrogation.
- The source's background. What is the source's age and level of military or civilian experience.
- The objective of the interrogation. How much time is available for the interrogation? Is the commander interested only in specific areas (PIR, IR, SIR)? Is this source knowledgeable enough to require a full OB interrogation?
- The interrogator himself. What abilities does he have that can be brought into play? What weaknesses does he have that may interfere with the interrogation? Can his personality adapt to the personality of the source?

The interrogation may require the interrogator conduct research to obtain detailed data on a specific geographic area, political group, weapons system, or technical field. In the technical field, TECHINT personnel assist the interrogator.

There are various weapons identification guides to assist the interrogator in identifying any weapons mentioned by the source. However, the source should not be shown this guide until he has thoroughly described the items, or has drawn a picture of the weapons.

The interrogator may require maps, documents, recording and photographic equipment, screening reports, and other aids to facilitate the interrogation. From these aids, he must select those best suited to accomplish the objective, determine their availability, and arrange for their procurement well in advance of the interrogation. Some aids the interrogator may use are—

- DA Form 5976.
- Previous interrogation reports.
- Documents found on an EPW or detainee or on the battlefield.
- Maps.
- Imagery or aerial photographs.
- OB data.
- Guards.
- CA and PSYOP personnel.
- Informants.
- Physical aids (such as lights, tables, drafting tools).
- Interrogation guides.

The interrogator must consider in advance obstacles and limitations which may affect the interrogation. These obstacles and limitations may include—

- EPW or detainee legal status.
- Time and facilities available for interrogation.
- The military situation.
- Knowledgeability.

1. DATE AND TIME OF CAPTURE	2. SERIAL NO.
111300Z JAN 91	XXXXXX1A

3. NAME	4. DATE OF BIRTH
STEWART L. HOOD	12 MAY 56

5. RANK	6. SERVICE NO.
MAJ	XXX-XX-XXXX

7. UNIT OF EPW	8. CAPTURING UNIT
122nd REGIMENTAL GUARDS	401ST MP Co.

9. LOCATION OF CAPTURE (Grid coordinates)
MA 132456

10. CIRCUMSTANCES OF CAPTURE	PHYSICAL CONDITION OF EPW	WEAPONS EQUIPMENT, DOCUMENTS
-Mass Surrender -Fire fight -Deserter, -Gave Up, etc.	-Wounded; -Broken foot; -Knee injury, - etc.	Rifle-AK47; Protective Mask; Maps, personal papers

ENEMY PRISONER OF WAR (*EPW*) CAPTURE TAG (*PART A*)

For use of this form see AR 190-B. The proponent agency is DCSOPS

Attach this part of the tag to EPW. (*Do not remove from EPW*)

1. Search - For weapons, military documents, or special equipment
2. Silence - Prohibit talking among EPWs for ease of control.
3. Segregate - By rank, sex, and nationality.
4. Safeguard - To prevent harm or escape.
5. Speed - Evacuate from the combat zone.
6. Tag - Prisoners and documents or special equipment.

DA FORM 5976, JAN 91

---

1. DATE AND TIME OF CAPTURE	2. SERIAL NO.
111300Z JAN 91	XXXXXX1B

3. NAME	4. DATE OF BIRTH
STEWART L. HOOD	12 MAY 56

5. RANK	6. SERVICE NO.
MAJ	XXX-XX-XXXX

7. UNIT OF EPW	8. CAPTURING UNIT
122nd REGIMENTAL GUARDS	401ST MP Co.

9. LOCATION OF CAPTURE (Grid coordinates)
MA 132456

10. CIRCUMSTANCES OF CAPTURE	PHYSICAL CONDITION OF EPW	WEAPONS EQUIPMENT, DOCUMENTS
-Mass Surrender -Fire fight -Deserter, -Gave Up, etc.	-Wounded; -Broken foot; -Knee injury, - etc.	Rifle-AK47; Protective Mask; Maps, personal papers

UNIT RECORD CARD (*Part B*)
Forward to Unit
(*Capturing unit retains for records.*)

Use string, wire, or other durable material to attach the appropriate section of this form to the EPW's equipment or property.

SAMPLE

DA FORM 5976, JAN 91

---

1. DATE AND TIME OF CAPTURE	2. SERIAL NO.
111300Z JAN 91	XXXXXX1C

3. NAME	4. DATE OF BIRTH
STEWART L. HOOD	12 MAY 56

5. RANK	6. SERVICE NO.
MAJ	XXX-XX-XXXX

7. UNIT OF EPW	8. CAPTURING UNIT
122nd REGIMENTAL GUARDS	401ST MP Co.

9. LOCATION OF CAPTURE (Grid coordinates)
MA 132456

10. DESCRIPTION OF WEAPONS, SPECIAL EQUIPMENT, DOCUMENTS
AK-47 Rifle, Protective Mask, MA, 00 800 Rounds 7.62 Ammunition; 3 Fragmentation grenades, personal papers.

DOCUMENTS/SPECIAL EQUIPMENT/ WEAPONS CARD (*Part C*)

Attach this part of the tag to EPW's retained property. (*Do not remove from property.*)

As a minimum, the tag must include the following information:

– Item 1. date and time of capture
– Item 8. capturing unit
– Item 9. place of capture (*Grid coordinates*).
– Item 10. circumstances of capture (*how the EPW was captured*)

DA FORM 5976, JAN 91

Figure 3-4. DA Form 5976 (Enemy Prisoner of War Capture Tag).

- Language restrictions.
- Physical condition.
- Psychological aspects.
- Other issues which may appear during the course of the interrogation.

Logistical requirements include—

- Billets.
- Office space.
- Heat.
- Light.
- Messing and detention facilities.
- Transportation which may be required in support of the interrogation.

The various staff sections of the supported command may be called upon to furnish the necessary logistical items mentioned above. All support requests will be coordinated with the appropriate staff officer by the EPW or detainee camp or collecting point commander.

Interrogators should question guards about the sources, time permitting, as part of preparation. Since the guards are in constant contact with the sources, they may be able to provide information on—

- Their physical condition.
- Demonstrated attitude and behavior.
- Contact made with other guards or sources.
- How the source has been handled since capture.
- Hearsay (H/S) information from others who have handled the source.
- Confirmation of capture data, especially the circumstances under which the source was captured.

Time permitting, each interrogator should unobtrusively observe the source to personally confirm his identity and to check his personal appearance and behavior.

After the interrogator has collected all information available about his assigned source, he analyzes it. He looks for indicators of psychological or physical weakness that might make the source susceptible to one or more approaches, which facilitates his approach strategy. He also uses the information he collected to identify the type and level of knowledge possessed by the source pertinent to the element's collection mission.

The interrogator uses his estimate of the type and extent of knowledge possessed by the source to modify the basic topical sequence of questioning. He selects only those topics in which he believes the source has pertinent knowledge. In this way, the interrogator refines his element's overall objective into a set of specific interrogation subjects.

The major topics that can be covered in an interrogation are shown below in their normal sequence. However, the interrogator is free to modify this sequence as necessary.

- Missions.
- Composition.
- Weapons, equipment, strength.
- Dispositions.
- Tactics.
- Training.
- Combat effectiveness.
- Logistics.
- Electronic technical data.
- Miscellaneous.

As a result of the planning and preparation phase, the interrogator develops a plan for conducting his assigned interrogation. He must review this plan with the senior interrogator, when possible. Whether written or oral, the interrogation plan must contain at least the following items:

- Interrogation objective.
- EPW's or detainee's identity, to include visual observation of the EPW or detainee by the interrogator.
- Interrogation time and place.
- Primary and alternate approaches.
- Questioning techniques to be used or why the interrogator selected only specific topics from the basic questioning sequence.
- Means of recording and reporting information obtained.

The senior interrogator reviews each plan and makes any changes he feels necessary based on the commander's PIR and IR. After the plan is approved, the holding compound is notified when to bring the source to the interrogation site. The interrogator collects all available interrogation aids needed (maps, charts, writing tools, and reference materials) and proceeds to the interrogation site.

APPROACH PHASE

The approach phase begins with initial contact between the EPW or detainee and interrogator. Extreme care is required since the success of the interrogation hinges, to a large degree, on the early development of the EPW's or detainee's willingness to communicate. The interrogator's objective during this phase is to establish EPW or detainee rapport, and to gain his willing cooperation so he will correctly answer pertinent questions to follow: The interrogator—

- Adopts an appropriate attitude based on EPW or detainee appraisal.
- Prepares for an attitude change, if necessary.
- Begins to use an approach technique.

The amount of time spent on this phase will mostly depend on the probable quantity and value of information the EPW or detainee possesses, the availability of other EPW or detainee with knowledge on the same topics, and available time. At the initial contact, a businesslike relationship should be maintained. As the EPW or detainee assumes a cooperative attitude, a more relaxed atmosphere may be advantageous. The interrogator must carefully determine which of the various approach techniques to employ.

Regardless, of the type of EPW or detainee and his outward personality, he does possess weaknesses which, if recognized by the interrogator, can be exploited. These weaknesses are manifested in personality traits such as speech, mannerisms, facial expressions, physical movements, excessive perspiration, and other overt indications that vary from EPW or detainee.

From a psychological standpoint, the interrogator must be cognizant of the following behaviors. People tend to—

- Talk, especially after harrowing experiences.
- Show deference when confronted by superior authority.
- Rationalize acts about which they feel guilty.
- Fail to apply or remember lessons they may have been taught regarding security if confronted with a disorganized or strange situation.
- Cooperate with those who have control over them.

- Attach less importance to a topic about which the interrogators demonstrates identical or related experience or knowledge.
- Appreciate flattery and exoneration from guilt.
- Resent having someone or something they respect belittled, especially by someone they dislike.
- Respond to kindness and understanding during trying circumstances.
- Cooperate readily when given material rewards such as extra food or luxury items for their personal comfort.

Interrogators do not "run" an approach by following a set pattern or routine. Each interrogation is different, but all interrogation approaches have the following in common. They—

- Establish and maintain control over the source and interrogation.
- Establish and maintain rapport between the interrogator and source.
- Manipulate the source's emotions and weaknesses to gain his willing cooperation.

The successful application of approach techniques eventually induces the source to willingly provide accurate intelligence information to the interrogator. The term "willingly" refers to the source's answering the interrogator's questions, not necessarily his cooperation.

The source may or may not be aware he is providing the interrogator with information about enemy forces. Some approaches may be complete when the source begins to answer questions. Others may have to be constantly maintained or reinforced throughout the interrogation.

The techniques used in an approach can best be defined as a series of events, not just verbal conversation between the interrogator and the source. The exploitation of the source's emotion can be harsh or gentle in application. Some useful techniques used by interrogators are—

- Hand and body movements.
- Actual physical contact such as a hand on the shoulder for reassurance.
- Silence.

RAPPORT POSTURES

There are two types of rapport postures determined during planning and preparation: stern and sympathetic.

In the stern posture, the interrogator keeps the EPW or detainee at attention. The aim is to make the EPW or detainee keenly aware of his helpless and inferior status. Interrogators use this posture with officers, NCOs, and security-conscious enlisted men.

In the sympathetic posture, the interrogator addresses the EPW or detainee in a friendly fashion, striving to put him at ease. This posture is commonly used in interrogating older or younger EPWs. EPWs may be frightened and confused. One variation of this posture is when the interrogator asks about the EPW's family. Few EPWs will hesitate to discuss their family.

Frightened persons, regardless of rank, will invariably talk in order to relieve tension once they hear a sympathetic voice in their own tongue. To put the EPW at ease, the interrogator may allow the EPW to sit down, offer a cigarette, ask whether or not he needs medical care, and otherwise show interest in his case.

There are many variations of these basic postures. Regardless of the one used, the interrogator must present a military appearance and show character and energy. The interrogator must control his temper at all times, except when a display is planned. The interrogator must not waste time in pointless discussions or make promises he cannot keep; for example, the interrogator's granting political asylum.

When making promises in an effort to establish rapport, great care must be taken to prevent implying that rights guaranteed the EPW under international and US law will be withheld if the EPW refused to cooperate.

Under no circumstances will the interrogator betray surprise at anything the EPW might say. Many EPWs will talk freely if they feel the information they are discussing is already known to the interrogator. If the interrogator acts surprised, the EPW may stop talking immediately.

The interrogator encourages any behavior that deepens rapport and increases the flow of communication. At the same time, the interrogator must discourage any behavior that has the opposite effect.

The interrogator must always be in control of the interrogation. If the EPW or detainee challenges this control, the interrogator must act quickly and firmly. Everything the interrogator says and does must be within the limits of the GPW, Article 17.

DEVELOPING RAPPORT

Rapport must be maintained throughout the interrogation, not only in the approach phase. If the interrogator has established good rapport initially and then abandons the effort, the source would rightfully assume the interrogator cares less and less about him as the information is being obtained. If this occurs, rapport is lost and the source may cease answering questions. Rapport may be developed by—

- Asking about the circumstances of capture. By doing this, the interrogator can gain insight into the prisoner's actual state of mind and, more importantly, he can ascertain his possible breaking points.
- Asking background questions. After asking about the source's circumstances of capture, apparent interest can be built by asking about the source's family, civilian life, friends, like, and dislikes. This is to develop rapport, but nonpertinent questions may open new avenues for the approach and help determine whether tentative approaches chosen in the planning and preparation phase will be effective. If these questions show that the tentative approaches chosen will not be effective, a flexible interrogator can shift the approach direction without the source being aware of the change.

Depending on the situation, and requests the source may have made, the interrogator also can use the following to develop rapport.

- Offer realistic incentives, such as—
  - —Immediate comfort items (coffee, cigarettes).
  - —Short-term (a meal, shower, send a letter home).
  - —Long-term (repatriation, political asylum).
- Feign experience similar to those of the source.
- Show concern for the source through the use of voice vitality and body language.

- Help the source to rationalize his guilt.
- Show kindness and understanding toward the source's predicament.
- Exonerate the source from guilt.
- Flatter the source.

After having established control and rapport, the interrogator continually assesses the source to see if the approaches—and later the questioning techniques—chosen in the planning and preparation phase will indeed work.

Approaches chosen in planning and preparation are tentative and based on the sometimes scanty information available from documents, guards, and personal observation. This may lead the interrogator to select approaches which may be totally incorrect for obtaining this source's willing cooperation. Thus, careful assessment of the source is critical to avoid wasting valuable time in the approach phase.

The questions can be mixed or separate. If, for example, the interrogator has tentatively chosen a "love of comrades" approach, he should ask the source questions like "How did you get along with your fellow squad members?" If the source answers they were all very close and worked well as a team, the interrogator can use this approach and be reasonably sure of its success.

However, if the source answers, "They all hated my guts and I couldn't stand any of them," the interrogator should abandon that approach and ask some quick, nonpertinent questions to give himself time to work out a new approach.

Smooth Transitions

The interrogator must guide the conversation smoothly and logically, especially if he needs to move from one approach technique to another. "Poking and hoping" in the approach may alert the prisoner to ploys and will make the job more difficult.

Tie-ins to another approach can be made logically and smoothly by using transitional phrases. Logical tie-ins can be made by including simple sentences which connect the previously used approach with the basis for the next one.

Transitions can also be smoothly covered by leaving the unsuccessful approach and going back to nonpertinent questions. By using nonpertinent conversation, the interrogator can move the conversation in the desired direction and, as previously stated, sometimes can obtain leads and hints about the source's stresses or weaknesses or other approach strategies that may be more successful.

Sincere and Convincing

If an interrogator is using argument and reason to get the source to cooperate, he must be convincing and appear sincere. All inferences of promises, situations, and arguments, or other invented material must be believable. What a source may or may not believe depends on the interrogator's knowledge, experience, and training. A good source assessment is the basis for the approach and vital to the success of the interrogation effort.

Recognize the Breaking Point

Every source has a breaking point, but an interrogator never knows what it is until it has been reached. There are, however, some good indicators the source is near his breaking point or has already reached it. For example, if during the approach, the source leans forward with his facial expression indicating an interest in the proposal or is more hesitant in his argument, he is probably nearing the breaking point. The interrogator must be alert to recognize these signs.

Once the interrogator determines the source is breaking, he should interject a question pertinent to the objective of the interrogation. If the source answers it, the interrogator can move into the questioning phase. If the source does not answer or balks at answering it, the interrogator must realize the source was not as close to the breaking point as thought. In this case, the interrogator must continue with his approach, or switch to an alternate approach or questioning technique and continue to work until he feels the source is near breaking.

The interrogator can tell if the source has broken only by interjecting pertinent questions. This process must be followed until the EPW or detainee begins to answer pertinent questions. It is possible the EPW or detainee may cooperate for a while and then balk at answering further questions. If this occurs, the interrogator can reinforce the approaches that initially gained the source's cooperation or move into a different approach before returning to the questioning phase.

At this point, it is important to note the amount of time spent with a particular source depends on several factors:

- The battlefield situation.
- Expediency which the supported commander's PIR and IR requirements needs to be answered.
- Source's willingness to talk.

The number of approaches used is limited only by the interrogator's skill. Almost any ruse or deception is usable as long as the provisions of the GPW, as outlined in Figure 1-4, are not violated.

An interrogator must not pass himself off as a medic, chaplain, or as a member of the Red Cross (Red Crescent or Red Lion). To every approach technique, there are literally hundreds of possible variations, each of which can be developed for a specific situation or source. The variations are limited only by the interrogator's personality, experience, ingenuity, and imagination.

APPROACH COMBINATIONS

With the exception of the direct approach, no other approach is effective by itself. Interrogators use different approach techniques or combine them into a cohesive, logical technique. Smooth transitions, sincerity, logic, and conviction almost always make a strategy work. The lack of will undoubtedly dooms it to failure. Some examples of combinations are—

- Direct—futility—incentive.
- Direct—futility—love of comrades.
- Direct—fear-up (mild)—incentive.

The number of combinations are unlimited. Interrogators must carefully choose the approach strategy in the planning and preparation phase and listen carefully to what the source is saying (verbally or nonverbally) for leads the strategy chosen will not work. When this occurs, the interrogator must adapt to approaches he believes will work in gaining the source's cooperation.

The approach techniques are not new nor are all the possible or acceptable techniques discussed below. Everything the interrogator says and does must be in concert with the GWS, GPW, GC, and UCMJ. The approaches which have proven effective are—

- Direct.
- Incentive.
- Emotional.
- Increased fear-up.
- Pride and ego.

Direct Approach

The interrogator asks questions directly related to information sought, making no effort to conceal the interrogation's purpose. The direct approach, always the first to be attempted, is used on EPWs or detainees who the interrogator believes will cooperate.

This may occur when interrogating an EPW or detainee who has proven cooperative during initial screening or first interrogation. It may also be used on those with little or no security training. The direct approach works best on lower enlisted personnel, as they have little or no resistance training and have had minimal security training.

The direct approach is simple to use, and it is possible to obtain the maximum amount of information in the minimum amount of time. It is frequently employed at lower echelons when the tactical situation precludes selecting other techniques, and where the EPW's or detainee's mental state is one of confusion or extreme shock. Figure C-3 contains sample questions used in direct questioning.

The direct approach is the most effective. Statistics show in World War II, it was 90 percent effective. In Vietnam and Operations Urgent Fury, Just Cause, and Desert Storm, it was 95 percent effective.

Incentive Approach

The incentive approach is based on the application of inferred discomfort upon an EPW or detainee who lacks willpower. The EPW or detainee may display fondness for certain luxury items such as candy, fruit, or cigarettes. This fondness provides the interrogator with a positive means of rewarding the EPW or detainee for cooperation and truthfulness, as he may give or withhold such comfort items at his discretion. Caution must be used when employing this technique because—

- Any pressure applied in this manner must not amount to a denial of basic human needs under any circumstances. [Note: Interrogators may not withhold a source's rights under the GPW, but they can withhold a source's privileges.] Granting incentives must not infringe on these rights, but they can be things to which the source is already entitled. This can be effective only if the source is unaware of his rights or privileges.
- The EPW or detainee might be tempted to provide false or inaccurate information to gain the desired luxury item or to stop the interrogation.

The GPW, Article 41, requires the posting of the convention contents in the EPW's own language. This is an MP responsibility.

Incentives must seem to be logical and possible. An interrogator must not promise anything that cannot be delivered. Interrogators do not make promises, but usually infer them while sidestepping guarantees.

For example, if an interrogator made a promise he could not keep and he or another interrogator had to talk with the source again, the source would not have any trust and would probably not cooperate. Instead of clearly promising a certain thing, such as political asylum, an interrogator will offer to do what he can to help achieve the source's desired goal; as long as the source cooperates.

As with developing rapport, the incentive approach can be broken down into two incentives. The determination rests on when the source expects to receive the incentive offered.

- Short term—received immediately; for example, letter home, seeing wounded buddies.
- Long term—received within a period of time; for example, political asylum.

Emotional Approach

Through EPW or detainee observation, the interrogator can often identify dominant emotions which motivate. The motivating emotion may be greed, love, hate, revenge, or others. The interrogator employs verbal and emotional ruses in applying pressure to the EPW's or detainee's dominant emotions.

One major advantage of this technique is it is versatile and allows the interrogator to use the same basic situation positively and negatively.

For example, this technique can be used on the EPW who has a great love for his unit and fellow soldiers. The interrogator may take advantage of this by telling the EPW that by providing pertinent information, he may shorten the war or battle in progress and save many of his comrades' lives, but his refusal to talk may cause their deaths. This places the burden on the EPW or detainee and may motivate him to seek relief through cooperation.

Conversely, this technique can also be used on the EPW or detainee who hates his unit because it withdrew and left him to be captured, or who feels he was unfairly treated in his unit. In such cases, the interrogator can point out that if the PEW cooperates and specifies the unit's location, the unit can be destroyed, thus giving the EPW an opportunity for revenge. The interrogator proceeds with this method in a very formal manner

This approach is likely to be effective with the immature and timid EPW.

Emotional Love Approach. For the emotional love approach to be successful, the interrogator must focus on the anxiety felt by the source about the circumstances in which he finds himself. The interrogator must direct the love the source feels toward the appropriate object: family, homeland, or comrades. If the interrogator can show the source what the source himself can do to alter or improve his situation, the approach has a chance of success.

This approach usually involves some incentive such as communication with the source's family or a quicker end to the war to save his comrades' lives. A good interrogator will usually orchestrate some futility with an emotional love approach to hasten the source's reaching the breaking point.

Sincerity and conviction are critical in a successful attempt at an emotional love approach as the interrogator must show genuine concern for the source, and for the object at which the interrogator is directing the source's emotion.

If the interrogator ascertains the source has great love for his unit and fellow soldiers, the interrogator can effectively exploit the situation. This places a burden on the source and may motivate him to seek relief through cooperation with the interrogator.

Emotional Hate Approach. The emotional hate approach focuses on any genuine hate, or possibly a desire for revenge, the source may feel. The interrogator must ascertain exactly what it is the source may hate so the emotion can be exploited to override the source's rational side. The source may have negative feelings about his country's regime, immediate superiors, officers in general, or fellow soldiers.

This approach is usually most effective on members of racial or religious minorities who have suffered discrimination in military and civilian life. If a source feels he has been treated unfairly in his unit, the interrogator can point out that, if the source cooperates and divulges the location of that unit, the unit can be destroyed, thus affording the source revenge.

By using a conspiratorial tone of voice, the interrogator can enhance the value of this technique. Phrases, such as "You owe them no loyalty for the way they treated you," when used appropriately, can expedite the success of this technique.

Do not immediately begin to berate a certain facet of the source's background or life until your assessment indicates the source feels a negative emotion toward it.

The emotional hate approach can be used more effectively by drawing out the source's negative emotions with questions that elicit a thought-provoking response. For example, "Why do you think they allowed you to be captured?" or "Why do you think they left you to die?" Do not berate the source's forces or homeland unless certain negative emotions surface.

Many sources may have great love for their country, but may hate the regime in control. The emotional hate approach is most effective with the immature or timid source who may have no opportunity up to this point for revenge, or never had the courage to voice his feelings.

Fear-Up Approach

The fear-up approach is the exploitation of a source's preexisting fear during the period of capture and interrogation. The approach works best with young, inexperienced sources, or sources who exhibit a greater than normal amount of fear or nervousness. A source's fear may be justified or unjustified. For example, a source who has committed a war crime may justifiably fear prosecution and punishment. By contrast, a source who has been indoctrinated by enemy propaganda may unjustifiably fear that he will suffer torture or death in our hands if captured.

This approach has the greatest potential to violate the law of war. Great care must be taken to avoid threatening or coercing a source which is in violation of the GPW, Article 17.

It is critical the interrogator distinguish what the source fears in order to exploit that fear. The way in which the interrogator exploits the source's fear depends on whether the source's fear is justified or unjustified.

Fear-Up (Harsh). In this approach, the interrogator behaves in an overpowering manner with a loud and threatening voice. The interrogator may even feel the need to throw objects across the room to heighten the source's implanted feelings of fear. Great care must be taken when doing this so any actions would not violate the prohibition on coercion and threats contained in the GPW, Article 17.

This technique is to convince the source he does indeed have something to fear; that he has no option but to cooperate. A good interrogator will implant in the source's mind that the interrogator himself is not the object to be feared, but is a possible way out of the trap.

Use the confirmation of fear only on sources whose fear is justified. During this approach, confirm to the source that he does indeed have a legitimate fear. Then convince the source that you are the source's best or only hope in avoiding or mitigating the object of his fear, such as punishment for his crimes.

You must take great care to avoid promising actions that are not in your power to grant. For example, if the source has committed a war crime, inform the source that the crime has been reported to the appropriate authorities and that action is pending. Next inform the source that, if he cooperates and tells the truth, you will report that he cooperated and told the truth to the appropriate authorities. You may add that you will also report his lack of cooperation. You may not promise that the charges against him will be dismissed because you have no authority to dismiss the charges.

Fear-Up (Mild). This approach is better suited to the strong, confident type of interrogator; there is generally no need to raise the voice or resort to heavy-handed table-banging.

For example, capture may be a result of coincidence—the soldier was caught on the wrong side of the border before hostilities actually commenced (he was armed, he could be a terrorist)—or as a result of his actions (he surrendered contrary to his military oath and is now a traitor to his country, and his forces will take care of the disciplinary action).

The fear-up (mild) approach must be credible. It usually involves some logical incentive.

In most cases, a loud voice is not necessary. The actual fear is increased by helping the source realize the unpleasant consequences the facts may cause and by presenting an alternative, which, of course, can be brought about by answering some simple questions.

The fear-up (harsh) approach is usually a dead end, and a wise interrogator may want to keep it in reserve as a trump card. After working to increase the source's fear, it would be difficult to convince him everything will be all right if the approach is not successful.

Fear-Down Approach

This technique is nothing more than calming the source and convincing him he will be properly and humanely treated, or telling him the war for him is mercifully over and he need not go into combat again. When used with a soothing, calm tone of voice, this often creates rapport and usually nothing else is needed to get the source to cooperate.

While calming the source, it is a good idea to stay initially with nonpertinent conversation and to avoid the subject which has caused the source's fear. This works quickly in developing rapport and communication, as the source will readily respond to kindness.

When using this approach, it is important the interrogator relate to the source at his perspective level and not expect the source to come up to the interrogator's level.

If the EPW or detainee is so frightened he has withdrawn into a shell or regressed to a less threatening state of mind, the interrogator must break through to him. The interrogator can do this by putting himself on the same physical level as the source; this may require some physical contact. As the source relaxes and begins to respond to kindness, the interrogator can begin asking pertinent questions.

This approach technique may backfire if allowed to go too far. After convincing the source he has nothing to fear, he may cease to be afraid and may feel secure enough to resist the interrogator's pertinent question. If this occurs, reverting to a harsher approach technique usually will bring the desired result quickly.

The fear-down approach works best if the source's fear is unjustified. During this approach, take specific actions to reduce the source's unjustified fear. For example, if the source believes that he will be abused while in your custody, make extra efforts to ensure that the source is well cared for, fed, and appropriately treated.

Once the source is convinced that he has no legitimate reason to fear you, he will be more inclined to cooperate. The interrogator is under no duty to reduce a source's unjustified fear. The only prohibition is that the interrogator may not say or do anything that directly or indirectly communicates to the source that he will be harmed unless he provides the requested information.

These applications of the fear approach may be combined to achieve the desired effect. For example, if a source has justified and unjustified fears, you may initially reduce the source's unfounded fears, then confirm his legitimate fears. Again, the source should be convinced the interrogator is his best or only hope in avoiding or mitigating the object of his fear.

Pride and Ego Approach

The strategy of this approach is to trick the source into revealing desired information by goading or flattering him. It is effective with sources who have displayed weakness or feelings of inferiority. A real or imaginary deficiency voiced about the source, loyalty to his organization, or any other feature can provide a basis for this technique.

The interrogator accuses the source of weakness or implies he is unable to do a certain thing. This type of source is also prone to excuses and reasons why he did or did not do a certain thing, often shifting the blame to others. An example is opening the interrogation with the question, "Why did you surrender so easily when you could have escaped by crossing the nearby ford in the river?"

The source is likely to provide a basis for further questions or to reveal significant intelligence information if he attempts to explain his surrender in order to vindicate himself. He may give an answer such as "No one could cross the ford because it is mined."

This technique can also be employed in another manner—by flattering the source into admitting certain information in order to gain credit. For example, while interrogating a suspected saboteur, the interrogator states: "This was a smooth operation. I have seen many previous attempts fail. I bet you planned this. Who else but a clever person like you would have planned it? When did you first decide to do the job?"

This technique is especially effective with the source who has been looked down upon by his superiors. The source has the opportunity to show someone he is intelligent.

A problem with the pride and ego approach is it relies on trickery. The source will eventually realize he has been tricked and may refuse to cooperate further. If this occurs, the interrogator can easily move into a fear-up approach and convince the source the questions he has already answered have committed him, and it would be useless to resist further.

The interrogator can mention it will be reported to the source's forces that he has cooperated fully with the enemy, will be considered a traitor, and has much to fear if he is returned to his forces.

This may even offer the interrogator the option to go into a love-of-family approach where the source must protect his family by preventing his forces from learning of his duplicity or collaboration. Telling the source you will not report that he talked or that he was a severe discipline problem is an incentive that may enhance the effectiveness of the approach.

Pride and Ego-Up Approach. This approach is most effective on sources with little or no intelligence, or on those who have been looked down upon for a long time. It is very effective on low-ranking enlisted personnel and junior grade officers, as it allows the source to finally show someone he does indeed have some "brains."

The source is constantly flattered into providing certain information in order to gain credit. The interrogator must take care to use a flattering somewhat-in-awe tone of voice, and speak highly of the source throughout this approach. This quickly produces positive feelings on the source's part, as he has probably been looking for this type of recognition all of his life.

The interrogator may blow things out of proportion using items from the source's background and making them seem noteworthy or important. As everyone is eager to hear praise, the source will eventually reveal pertinent information to solicit more laudatory comments from the interrogator.

Effective targets for a successful pride and ego-up approach are usually the socially accepted reasons for flattery, such as appearance and good military bearing. The interrogator should closely watch the source's demeanor for indications the approach is working. Some indications to look for are—

- Raising of the head.
- A look of pride in the eyes.
- Swelling of the chest.
- Stiffening of the back.

Pride and Ego-Down Approach. This approach is based on attacking the source's sense of personal worth. Any source who shows any real or imagined inferiority or weakness about himself, loyalty to his organization, or captured under embarrassing circumstances, can be easily broken with this approach technique.

The objective is for the interrogator to pounce on the source's sense of pride by attacking his loyalty, intelligence, abilities, leadership qualities, slovenly appearance, or any other perceived weakness. This will usually goad the source into becoming defensive, and he will try to convince the interrogator he is wrong. In his attempt to redeem his pride, the source will usually involuntarily provide pertinent information in attempting to vindicate himself.

A source susceptible to this approach is also prone to make excuses and give reasons why he did or did not do a certain thing, often shifting the blame to others. If the interrogator uses a sarcastic, caustic tone of voice with appropriate expressions of distaste or disgust, the source will readily believe him. Possible targets for the pride and ego-down approach are the source's—

- Loyalty.
- Technical competence.
- Leadership abilities.

- Soldierly qualities.
- Appearance.

The pride and ego-down approach is also a dead end in that, if unsuccessful, it is difficult for the interrogator to recover and move to another approach and reestablish a different type of rapport without losing all credibility.

Futility

In this approach, the interrogator convinces the source that resistance to questioning is futile. When employing this technique, the interrogator must have factual information. These facts are presented by the interrogator in a persuasive, logical manner. He should be aware of and able to exploit the source's psychological and moral weaknesses, as well as weaknesses inherent in his society.

The futility approach is effective when the interrogator can play on doubts that already exist in the source's mind. There are different variations of the futility approach. For example:

- Futility of the personal situation—"You are not finished here until you answer the questions."
- Futility in that "everyone talks sooner or later."
- Futility of the battlefield situation.
- Futility in the sense if the source does not mind talking about history, why should he mind talking about his missions, they are also history.

If the source's unit had run out of supplies (ammunition, food, or fuel), it would be somewhat easy to convince him all of his forces are having the same logistical problems. A soldier who has been ambushed may have doubts as to how he was attacked so suddenly. The interrogator should be able to talk him into believing that the interrogator's forces knew of the EPW's unit location, as well as many more units.

The interrogator might describe the source's frightening recollections of seeing death on the battlefield as an everyday occurrence for his forces. Factual or seemingly factual information must be presented in a persuasive, logical manner, and in a matter-of-fact tone of voice.

Making the situation appear hopeless allows the source to rationalize his actions, especially if that action is cooperating with the interrogator. When employing this technique, the interrogator must not only have factual information but also be aware of and exploit the source's psychological, moral, and sociological weaknesses.

Another way of using the futility approach is to blow things out of proportion. If the source's unit was low on, or had exhausted, all food supplies, he can be easily led to believe all of his forces had run out of food. If the source is hinging on cooperating, it may aid the interrogation effort if he is told all the other sources have cooperated.

The futility approach must be orchestrated with other approach techniques (for example, love of comrades). A source who may want to help save his comrades' lives may be convinced the battlefield situation is hopeless and they will die without his assistance.

The futility approach is used to paint a bleak picture for the prisoner, but it is not effective in and of itself in gaining the source's cooperation.

We Know All

This approach may be employed in conjunction with the "file and dossier" technique (discussed below) or by itself. If used alone, the interrogator must first become thoroughly familiar with available data concerning the source. To begin the interrogation, the interrogator asks questions based on this known data. When the source hesitates, refuses to answer, or provides an incorrect or incomplete reply, the interrogator provides the detailed answer.

When the source begins to give accurate and complete information, the interrogator interjects questions designed to gain the needed information. Questions to which answers are already known are also asked to test the source's truthfulness and to maintain the deception that the information is already known. By repeating this procedure, the interrogator convinces the source that resistance is useless as everything is already known.

After gaining the source's cooperation, the interrogator still tests the extent of cooperation by periodically using questions to which he has the answers; this is very necessary. If the interrogator does not challenge the source when he is lying, the source will know everything is not known, and he has been tricked. He may then provide incorrect answers to the interrogator's questions.

There are some inherent problems with the use of the "we know all" approach. The interrogator is required to prepare everything in detail, which is time consuming. He must commit must of the information to memory, as working from notes may show the limits of the information actually known.

File and Dossier

The file and dossier approach is used when the interrogator prepares a dossier containing all available information obtained from documents concerning the source or his organization. Careful arrangement of the material within the file may give the illusion it contains more data than actually there. The file may be padded with extra paper, if necessary. Index tabs with titles such as education, employment, criminal record, military service, and others are particularly effective.

The interrogator confronts the source with the dossiers at the beginning of the interrogation and explains intelligence has provided a complete record of every significant happening in the source's life; therefore, it would be useless to resist. The interrogator may read a few selected bits of known data to further impress the source.

If the technique is successful, the source will be intimidated by the size of the file, conclude everything is known, and resign himself to complete cooperation. The success of this technique is largely dependent on the naivete of the source, volume of data on the subject, and skill of the interrogator in convincing the source.

Establish Your Identity

This approach is especially adaptable to interrogation. The interrogator insists the source has been correctly identified as an infamous individual wanted by higher authorities on serious charges, and he is not the person he purports to be. In an effort to clear himself of this allegation, the source makes a genuine and detailed effort to establish or substantiate his true identity. In so doing, he may provide the interrogator with information and leads for further development.

The "establish your identity" approach was effective in Vietnam with the Viet Cong and in Operations Just Cause and Desert Storm.

This approach can be used at tactical echelons. The interrogator must be aware if it is used in conjunction with the file and dossier approach, as it may exceed the tactical interrogator's preparation resources.

The interrogator should initially refuse to believe the source and insist he is the criminal wanted by the ambiguous higher authorities. This will force the source to give even more detailed information about his unit in order to convince the interrogator he is who he says he is. The approach works well when combined with the "futility" or "we know all" approach.

Repetition

This approach is used to induce cooperation from a hostile source. In one variation of this approach, the interrogator listens carefully to a source's answer to a question, and then repeats the question and answer several times. He does this with each succeeding question until the source becomes so thoroughly bored with the procedure he answers questions fully and candidly to satisfy the interrogator and gain relief from the monotony of this method.

The repetition technique must be judiciously used, as it will generally be ineffective when employed against introverted sources or those having great self-control. In fact, it may provide an opportunity for a source to regain his composure and delay the interrogation. In this approach, the use of more than one interrogator or a tape recorder has proven effective.

Rapid Fire

This approach involves a psychological ploy based upon the principles that—

- Everyone likes to be heard when he speaks.
- It is confusing to be interrupted in midsentence with an unrelated question.

This approach may be used by one of simultaneously by two or more interrogators in questioning the same source. In employing this technique, the interrogator asks a series of questions in such a manner that the source does not have time to answer a question completely before the next one is asked.

This confuses the source and he will tend to contradict himself, as he has little time to formulate his answers. The interrogator then confronts the source with the inconsistencies causing further contradictions.

In many instances, the source will begin to talk freely in an attempt to explain himself and deny the interrogator's claims of inconsistencies. In this attempt, the source is likely to reveal more than he intends, thus creating additional leads for further exploitation. This approach may be orchestrated with the pride and ego-down or fear-up approaches.

Besides extensive preparation, this approach requires an experienced and competent interrogator, with comprehensive case knowledge and fluency in the source's language.

Silent

This approach may be successful when used against the nervous or confident source. When employing this technique, the interrogator says nothing to the source, but looks him squarely in the eye, preferably with a slight smile on his face. It is important not to look away from the source but force him to break eye contact first.

The source may become nervous, begin to shift in his chair, cross and recross his legs, and look away. He may ask questions, but the interrogator should not answer until he is ready to break the silence. The source may blurt out questions such as "Come on now, what do you want with me?"

When the interrogator is ready to break silence, he may do so with some nonchalant questions such as, "You planned this operation for a long time, didn't you? Was it your idea?" The interrogator must be patient when using this technique. It may appear the technique is not succeeding, but usually will when given a reasonable chance.

Change of Scene

The idea in using this approach is to get the source away from the atmosphere of an interrogation room or setting. If the interrogator confronts a source who is apprehensive or frightened because of the interrogation environment, this technique may prove effective.

In some circumstances, the interrogator may be able to invite the source to a different setting for coffee and pleasant conversation. During the conversation in this more relaxed environment, the interrogator steers the conversation to the topic of interest. Through this somewhat indirect method, he attempts to elicit the desired information. The source may never realize he is being interrogated.

Another example in this approach is an interrogator poses as a compound guard and engages the source in conversation, thus eliciting the desired information.

QUESTIONING PHASE

The interrogation effort has two primary goals: To obtain information and to report it. Developing and using good questioning techniques enable the interrogator to obtain accurate and pertinent information by following a logical sequence.

The questioning phase starts when the source begins to answer questions pertinent to interrogation objectives.

QUESTIONING TECHNIQUES

Good questioning techniques must be used throughout the interrogation. The interrogator must know when to use different types of questions. Good questioning techniques enable the interrogator to extract the maximum amount of information in the minimum amount of time. The interrogator must be able to use the following types of questions:

- Direct.
- Follow-up.
- Nonpertinent.
- Repeated.
- Control.
- Prepared.

Direct Questions

Questions should be presented in a logical sequence to avoid neglecting significant topics. A series of questions following a chronological sequence of events is frequently employed, but this is not the only logical method of asking questions. Adherence to a sequence should not deter the interrogator from exploiting informational leads as they are obtained.

The interrogator must consider the probable response of the source to a particular question or line of questioning and should not, if at all possible, ask direct questions likely to evoke a refusal to answer or to antagonize the source.

Experience has shown that in most tactical interrogations, the source is cooperative. In such instances, the interrogator should proceed with direct questions. Good, direct questions—

- Begin with a basic interrogative: Who, What, When, Where, Why, and How.

(CLASSIFICATION)

SPOT REPORT

TO: G2, X Corp DATE: 171105FEB99
FROM: Team 2, IPW Section, 213th MI Bn REPORT NO: 02-314
25th Div (Armd), X Corps

1. SIZE/WHO: Squad.
2. ACTIVITY/WHAT: Reconnaissance.
3. LOCATION/WHERE: NB 576472 (Hwy intersection).
4. UNIT/WHO: 1 MRS/3 MRC/2 MRB/44 MRR/56 MRD.
5. TIME/WHEN: No later than 171800FEB99.
6. EQUIPMENT/HOW: Using assigned weapons and equipment, recon forward areas to determine avenues of approach for elements of 2 MRB.
7. REMARKS:
   a. SOURCE: EPW, Interrogation serial number US-AR-23.035.73.
   b. MAP DATA: GERMANY, EISENACH-HUNFELD, 1:50,000, USACGSC 50-242, Edition 5.
   c. H/S, CPT ANRUF, CO, 3 MRC/2 MRB/44 MRR/56 MRD, DOI: 170100FEB99.

(CLASSIFICATION)

Figure 3-5. Sample spot report (SALUTE).

- Require a narrative answer. One which cannot be answered by a simple Yes or No. This type of question requires the source to think about his answer in order to respond correctly.
- Provide a maximum amount of information in the least amount of time, and the greatest number of leads to other information.
- Are brief, precise, and simply worded to avoid confusion.

(Note: The source may not be on the same intellectual level as the interrogator and some may be illiterate. Some words or phrases in English do not translate into a foreign language.)

Follow-Up Questions

Follow-up questions are used to obtain complete information on a topic that pertains to the interrogation objective. They are used to exploit leads obtained from the source on information not directly related to the primary interrogation objective. Exploitation of these leads is discussed later. There are two types of leads:

- Hot—information that could affect the immediate tactical situation in your AO. This type of lead should be exploited immediately, and a spot report submitted as soon as possible. FIGURE 3-5 is a sample of a spot report in a SALUTE format.
- Cold—information of intelligence value that will not affect the immediate tactical situation. This type of lead is recorded and exploited after the interrogation objective has been satisfied or at the appropriate time during the interrogation sequence.

Nonpertinent Questions

Nonpertinent questions are used to conceal the interrogation's objectives or to strengthen rapport with the source. They may also be used to break the source's concentration, particularly, if the interrogator suspects the source is lying. It is hard for a source to be a convincing liar if his concentration is frequently interrupted.

Repeated Questions

Repeated questions ask the source for the same information obtained in response to earlier questions. They may be exact repetitions of the previous question, or the previous question may be rephrased or otherwise disguised. The use of repeated questions may develop a topic the source had refused to talk about earlier. Repeated questions may also be used to—

- Check source reliability.
- Ensure accuracy of important details such as place names, dates, and component parts of technical equipment.
- Return to a topical area for further questioning.

Control Questions

Control questions are developed from recently confirmed information that is not likely to have changed. They are used to check the truthfulness of the source's responses and should be mixed in with other questions throughout the interrogation.

Prepared Questions

Prepared questions are used primarily when dealing with information of a technical nature, or specific topic, which requires the interrogator to formulate questions beforehand; the interrogator prepares them in writing to be used during the interrogation. The interrogator may have to research technical material or contact TECHINT personnel to assist him in preparing questions. Interrogators must not allow the use of prepared questions to restrict the scope and flexibility of the interrogations.

The interrogator must use the different type of questions effectively. Active listening and maximum eye-to-eye contact with the source will provide excellent indicators for when to use follow-up, repeated, control, and nonpertinent questions.

The interrogator must use direct and follow-up questions to fully exploit subjects pertinent to his interrogation objectives. He should periodically include control, repeated, and nonpertinent questions in order to check the sincerity and consistency of the source's responses and to strengthen rapport.

A response which is inconsistent with earlier responses or the interrogator's available data is not necessarily a lie. When such a response is obtained, the interrogator should reveal the inconsistency to the source and ask for an explanation. The source's truthfulness should then be evaluated based on the plausibility of his explanation.

QUESTIONS TO AVOID

Interrogators should avoid the following types of questions.

Leading Questions

Leading questions require the source to answer Yes or No. They do not elicit narrative answers. They also prompt the source to answer the question in a way he thinks the interrogator wants to hear it; for example, "Did you go to the command post last night?" Although normally avoided during the interrogation, leading questions may be used to—

- Verify facts.
- Pinpoint map locations.
- Confirm information obtained during map tracking. Leading questions are used sparingly during map tracking.

Negative Questions

Negative questions should never be used during an interrogation. They imply the source should reply in the negative, and this sometimes confuses or leads the source to provide false information; for example, "You're not in the 1st Company, are you?" Negative questions usually require additional questions to clarify the source's responses.

Compound Questions

Compound questions are never used during an interrogation. They are two questions asked at the same time; for example, "Before you were captured today, were you traveling north or south?" They are easily misunderstood and may confuse the source or force him to give an ambiguous answer. Compound questions allow the source to evade a part of the question or to give an incomplete answer. They may confuse the source or cause the interrogator to misunderstand the response.

Vague Questions

Vague questions do not have enough information for the source to understand exactly what is being asked by the interrogator. They may be incomplete, general, or otherwise nonspecific and create doubt in the source's mind. Vague questions confuse the source, waste time, are easily evaded, and result in answers that may confuse or mislead the interrogator.

INTERROGATORS GUIDE

An Interrogators Guide is a pamphlet or notebook designed to guide the interrogator through the interrogation. The IPW senior interrogator should ensure team members prepare an interrogators guide, which could be included in the unit's SOP. The guides are made based on the AO and supported command intelligence requirements. They should be jointly prepared by the interrogator and available intelligence analysts. The guides contain information such as—

- PIR and IR.
- Topical sequence question format.
- Actual prepared questions to be used during the interrogation.
- Guidelines for employing the various approach techniques.
- Formats or samples of completed interrogation reports used by interrogators.

SPOT REPORTABLE INFORMATION

Spot reportable information is critical to the successful accomplishment of friendly COAs. Information may be spot reportable even when an interrogator cannot determine its immediate intelligence value. Spot reportable information is always time sensitive in that its value depends on the speed with which it is reported and processed.

If an interrogator obtains information he thinks is spot reportable, he must compare the information with his element's overall objective statement. Items of information relating to any of the intelligence indicators listed in the objective statement are spot reportable. Information relating to indicators not listed may still be spot reportable.

The key to identifying spot reportable information is recognizing its potential value. If the information indicates a significant change in the enemy's capabilities or intentions, it is spot reportable. Information inconsistent with current OB holdings should be spot reported if the inconsistency concerns an important item and the source has given a plausible explanation for it.

If an interrogator cannot decide if a piece of information is spot reportable, he should act as though it is. This means he should exploit it fully and record all pertinent information. The interrogator should then consult the senior interrogator for a final determination of the information's value. Spot reportable information is transmitted by the interrogator either written or orally in the SALUTE format (Figure 3-5).

LEADS

Leads are signs which tell the interrogator the source has additional pertinent information that can be obtained through further questioning. Hot and cold leads are provided by a source in response to interrogator questions.

A hot lead, when exploited, may obtain spot reportable information. A cold lead, when exploited, may obtain information not spot reportable, but still of intelligence value.

The use of follow-up questions to fully exploit hot and cold leads may require an interrogator to cover topics he did not list in his interrogation plan. An interrogator must exploit hot leads as soon as he identifies them.

Once the interrogator is sure he has obtained and recorded all the details known to the source, he issues a spot report. The interrogator then resumes his questioning of the source at the same point where the hot lead was obtained. An interrogator should note cold leads as they are obtained, and exploit them fully during his questioning on the topics to which the cold lead apply.

Cold leads may expand the scope of the interrogation because they may indicate the source possesses pertinent information in areas not previously selected for questioning. If the interrogator does not fully exploit all cold leads he obtains, he must include information on all leads he did not exploit in his interrogation report.

HEARSAY INFORMATION

H/S information must include the most precise data possible of its source. This will include—

- Name, rank, and duty position.
- Full unit designation of the person who provided the information.
- Date-time group (DTG) when the source obtained the information.

QUESTIONING SEQUENCE

The interrogator begins the questioning phase with the first topic in the sequence he tentatively established as part of his interrogation plan. He obtains all the source's pertinent knowledge in this topical area before moving on to the next topic in his sequence. He maintains his established questioning sequence to ensure no topics are missed. The only exception is exploiting a hot lead.

Map Tracking

During the questioning phase, the interrogator will attempt to pinpoint locations of any enemy dispositions known to the source. He will attempt to determine the whereabouts of the source, and will compare the source's description of terrain features with maps, aerial photographs, and pictomaps. Some map tracking advantages are—

- The source is led through his memory in a logical manner.
- A valid reliability scale can be determined by comparing the source's information with a map or aerial photographs.
- Discrepancies in the source's statements are easier to detect.

The interrogator asks the source if he can read the map being used. If so, he should be asked to show the location of routes and dispositions. If the source cannot read the interrogator's map, he must be asked if he knows compass directions. If not, the interrogator must explain them to him. This can be done by having the source picture himself facing the rising or setting sun and then establishing compass points.

The interrogator may find the source is most confident when expressing himself in terms other than compass directions. When this happens, the interrogator should allow the source to use his own frames of reference. However, the interrogator must ensure he understands the source.

The first location the interrogator should try to establish as the initial common point of reference (ICPR) is the source's POC. The POC cannot be used, however, unless the source can describe it well enough for the interrogator to be certain of its location. If the POC cannot be used, the interrogator must review locations previously mentioned by the source and ask him to describe each of them in turn.

Once the source describes a location well enough for the interrogator to be certain of its position on the map, an ICPR has been established. The interrogator then marks that position.

The interrogator reviews the source's past missions to identify those points he actually visited. The interrogator determines how long ago the source was at each point, and approximately how far each point is from the ICPR.

The interrogator wants to select as the destination common point of reference (DCPR) that point visited by the source which provides the longest route of travel to the ICPR, and is still within the supported command's AI. The DCPR selected must be a location the source can describe well enough for it to be plotted on the map, even if it is nothing more than a general vicinity.

Establish a Route

The interrogator establishes the route the source traveled between the DCPR and ICPR. When the DCPR is a specific point, the interrogator can establish the route from it to the ICPR, tracing the route in the same direction which the source actually traveled.

When the DCPR is an undefined point, the interrogator establishes the route from ICPR to the DCPR. This means the interrogator must trace the route in the opposite direction from that traveled by the source. The interrogator should establish the route traveled by using the following procedures in the sequence shown:

- Obtain the direction in which the source would travel when leaving the ICPR.
- Obtain a description of the surface on which the source would be traveling.
- Obtain the distance the source would travel in this direction.
- Obtain a description of the prominent terrain features the source would remember while traveling in this direction.
- Repeat the questions and plot responses until the entire route between the ICPR and DCPR has been plotted.

The interrogator can follow the same sequence when establishing the route actually traveled by the source by beginning with the DCPR.

Exploit the DCPR

The interrogator must obtain the exact location and description of each enemy disposition the source knew about at the DCPR. The interrogator does this by having the source—

- Identify and describe all items of military significance belonging to his forces which are located at the DCPR.
- Provide the full unit designation of enemy units to which these items belong.
- Identify and describe all collocated enemy units.
- Describe security measures employed at each identified disposition.
- Identify the source of his information.
- Provide the date and time he obtained his information.
- Provide name, rank, duty position, and full unit designation of each person who provided H/S information to the source.

The interrogator must repeat these questions, and plot or record the information as it is provided by the source, until he obtains all dispositions knows by the source to be in the vicinity of the DCPR.

Segment and Exploit the Route

The interrogator begins exploiting the source's route with the segment closest to the ICPR or DCPR. The interrogator will segment closest to the DCPR, but either can be used.

The interrogator will exploit each segment of the route by asking the question: "From (description of common point of reference [(CPR)] to (description of next CPR) back along your route of travel, what of military significance belonging to your forces do you know of, have seen, or heard?" The interrogator will continue from segment to segment, fully exploiting each, until he has exploited the entire route traveled.

Exploit Dispositions Not On Route

If the interrogator obtains a disposition which is not located on the established route, he must establish the route the source would have taken to that disposition. The interrogator then treats this new route the same way he does any other route segment, exploiting it fully before moving on the to the next segment of the original route.

The sequence above organizes map tracking so information obtained from the source can be plotted and recorded accurately. The description of each disposition must be recorded preferably near the site of the disposition on the map.

Recording Information

There are several reasons for recording information obtained during interrogations. The most important is to ensure information can be reported completely and accurately. Recorded information may also be used to—

- Refresh the interrogator's memory on a topic covered earlier, such as when returning to a topic after exploiting a hot lead.
- Check responses to repeated questions.
- Point out inconsistencies to the source.
- Gain the cooperation of other sources.
- Compare with information received from other sources.

Taking Notes

There are several methods of recording information used during interrogations. Two are listed below, along with their advantages and disadvantages. These methods may be used separately, or in combination with each other.

Using His Own Notes. The interrogator's own notes are the primary method of recording information. When the interrogator takes his own notes, he has a ready reference to verify responses to repeated questions or to refresh his memory. They also provide him with the means to record cold leads for later exploitation.

Using his own notes expedites the interrogator's accurate transferral of information into a report format. When taking his own notes, however, he cannot observe the source continuously. This may cause him to miss leads or fail to detect losses in rapport or control that are detectable only through clues provided by the source's behavior.

It is possible to lose control, and the source's willing cooperation, by concentrating too much on note taking. The interrogator must avoid distracting the source while taking notes. They should be taken in such a way that maintains maximum eye-to-eye contact with the source.

The interrogator will not have enough time to record each word the source says. Thus, he must—

- Be able to summarize information into a few words.
- Use past experiences to decide which items of information should be recorded.
- Organize his materials to avoid having to flip back and forth between references.

The only information that should be recorded during the approach phase is that required by Part I of DA Form 4237-R (Figure 3-1). All other information should not be recorded until after the source's cooperation has been obtained.

All notes must be complete, accurate, and legible. Notes should be organized by topical areas. A separate piece of paper should be used to record cold leads. The interrogator should use authorized military abbreviations and brevity codes (see AR 310-50). Notes should be in a recognizable format and complete for other interrogators to use. Situations may arise that require one interrogator to finish another's interrogation.

Using a Sound or Video Recorder. This method allows the interrogator to continually observe the source. When compared with note taking, this method allows more information to be obtained in less time. However, more time is required for report writing because the entire tape must be replayed to transfer information to the report.

Record names, numbers, and other pertinent, detailed information that may be unclear on the tape. Sound recorders cannot provide a quick reference that can be used to compare answers to a repeated question, and the equipment may malfunction.

Another method which has proven successful during exercises is to have linguist qualified intelligence analysts view interrogations or debriefings by using video cameras and monitors. This method allows the intelligence analyst to immediately pass additional questions to the interrogator to follow up on possible source knowledge.

TERMINATION PHASE

When it is necessary or prudent, the interrogator will terminate the interrogation. There are many ways to conduct a termination, but the following points must be conveyed to the source:

- The approaches used to "break" the source must be reinforced. Any promised incentives should be rendered. The reinforcement must be sincere and convincing, as the source may be interrogated again.
- The source must be told the information he gave will be checked for truthfulness and accuracy. His reaction to this statement should be closely monitored.
- The source must be told he will be spoken to again by the same or another interrogator.
- Any identification or other documents, personal property, or other material must be returned to the source or be given to the evacuation guard, as appropriate.

REASONS FOR TERMINATION

Some reasons for termination are—

- The source remains uncooperative during the approach phase.
- The source could be wounded, sick, or elderly, and his condition might force the interrogator to terminate until a later time.
- The interrogation objective requires several questioning periods to obtain all the information.
- The source may change his attitude during the interrogation, and may become more alert, belligerent, bored, or too talkative, thus indicating termination until later.
- The interrogator fails to maintain rapport and loses control of the interrogation.
- Interrogation objectives have been satisfied.
- The interrogator becomes physically or mentally unable to continue.
- Information possessed by the source is of such value his immediate evacuation to the next echelon is required.
- The interrogator's presence is required elsewhere.

TERMINATION PROCEDURES

Whatever the reason for terminating, the interrogator must remember there is a possibility someone may want to question the source at a

EPW IDENTITY CARD For use of this form, see AR 190-8; the proponent agency is DCSPER		DATE ISSUED 8 OCT 99
(Photograph)	LAST NAME CH'OE	
	FIRST NAME HYON-SIK	GRADE Sr SGT
	SERVICE NUMBER 5611642	POWER SERVED DPRK
PLACE OF BIRTH KAESONG		DATE OF BIRTH 24 FEB 67
SIGNATURE OF BEARER Hyon Sik Choe		

DA FORM 2662-R, May 82 EDITION OF 1 JUL 63 IS OBSOLETE.

FRONT

SAMPLE

OTHER MARKS OF IDENTIFICATION	LEFT INDEX / RIGHT INDEX	FINGERPRINTS	WEIGHT 65 K	COLOR OF EYES BROWN
			HEIGHT 1.70 m	COLOR OF HAIR BLACK
			BLOOD TYPE B POS	RELIGION NONE
			NOTICE This card is issued to prisoners of war in the custody of the United States Army. This card must be carried at all times by the EPW to whom it is issued.	

Reverse of DA Form 2662-R, May 82

REVERSE

Figure 3-6. DA Form 2662-R (United States Army EPW Identification Card).

later date. For that reason, he should terminate without any loss of rapport when possible. He offers the opportunity for the source to change or add to any information he has given.

During termination, the interrogator must properly dispose of any documents captured with the source. A source's military identity document must be returned to him.

If a source does not hold an identity card issued by his government, the MP will issue a DA Form 2662-R (United State Army EPW Identification Card). This form, shown at Figure 3-6, will accompany the source at all times. AR 190-8 is the prescribing directive of this form.

Some captured documents will contain information that must be exploited at higher echelons. These documents may be impounded by the interrogator and evacuated through intelligence channels. The interrogator must issue a receipt to the source for any personal documents he decides to impound. He must comply with the accounting procedures established for captured documents by the MP in accordance with AR 190-8.

These procedures are time-consuming but necessary. The interrogator can save time by preparing receipts and document tags during the planning and preparation phase.

The interrogator completes the termination phase by instructing the escort guard to return the source to the holding compound and to keep him away from sources who have not been interrogated.

REPORTING INFORMATION

The last portion of the interrogation process is reporting information obtained. The most brilliantly executed interrogation becomes a wasted effort if not reported properly. To aid military operations, information obtained must be transmitted as quickly as the situation permits in a usable form to an agency capable of taking action.

Although the interrogator normally takes notes during the interrogation, he will have to rely on his memory, to some degree, while reporting information received from the source. The more distractions that occur between the interrogation and the reporting, the greater the chance the interrogator will lose some of the information obtained. The reporting normally is done in the format appropriate for the information being reported.

Appendix E contains formats of reports. Initial reports are submitted electronically when possible to ensure the information reaches the intelligence analysts in the least amount of time.

Written reports are prepared to document electronic reports. They are used as initial means of reporting only when electronic reporting is impossible. Any information of intelligence value that will diminish with the passage of time must be SALUTE reported.

Electronic SALUTE reports are formatted and submitted according to the procedures established during the senior interrogator's initial coordination. Information not SALUTE reportable is electronically reported with a lower priority.

The aim of any interrogation is to obtain information which will help satisfy a commander's intelligence requirements. Since these requirements will differ in scope at each level, when conducting PIR or IR interrogations, nonapplicable paragraphs may be deleted. Part I must always be included and distribution made according to STANAG 2033.

Regardless of the report format used, information must be reported accurately according to the following criteria:

- Each item of information reported which has a different date of information from the overall report must be accompanied by its correct date.
- Each item of information not obtained as a direct result of the source's personal experiences must be accompanied by a description of how he obtained that information.
- All dispositions, towns, and other specific geographic locations must be accompanied by a correct, complete set of at least 6-digit universal transverse mercator (UTM) coordinates, to include the correct 100,000-meter grid zone identifier. The UTM coordinates are in STP 34-97E24-SM-TG.
- The information is reported exactly as it was obtained from the source. No information is deleted or added without explanatory comments.
- The report contains no errors in spelling, punctuation, or grammar that affect the meaning of the information reported.

Each report must include the interrogator's assessment of the source's value. This assessment addresses the source's intelligence, experience, cooperation, and reliability. Any areas of special knowledge possessed by the source should be identified.

The assessment codes are established by STANAG 2033. The codes assigned, and a written statement supporting these assignments, must be included on each report.

INTERROGATION WITH AN INTERPRETER

Interrogating through an interpreter is time consuming because the interpreter must repeat everything said by the interrogator and source. The interrogator must brief the interpreter before the interrogation can begin. An interrogation with an interpreter will go through all five phases of the interrogation process. After the interrogation is over, the interrogator will evaluate the interpreter.

INTERPRETATION METHODS

During the planning and preparation phase, the interrogator selects a method of interpretation. There are two methods: Simultaneous and alternate. The interrogator obtains information about his interpreter from the senior interrogator. He analyzes this information and talks to the interpreter before deciding which method to use.

With the alternate method, the interpreter listens to an entire phrase, sentence, or paragraph. He then translates during natural pauses in the interrogation.

The simultaneous method should be selected only if all the following criteria are met:

- The sentence structure of the target language is parallel to English.
- The interpreter can understand and speak English as well as the target language with ease.
- The interpreter has special vocabulary skills for the topics to be covered.
- The interpreter can easily imitate the interrogator's tone of voice and attitude for the approaches selected.

- Neither interrogator nor interpreter tends to get confused when using the simultaneous method of interpretation.

With the simultaneous method, the interpreter listens and translates at the same time as the person for whom he is interpreting, usually just a phrase or a few words behind.

If any of the criteria in the simultaneous method cannot be met, the interrogator must use the alternate method. The alternate method should also be used when a high degree of precision is required.

INTERPRETER BRIEFING

Once the interrogator has chosen a method of interpretation, he must brief his interpreter. This briefing must cover—

- Current tactical situation.
- Background information obtained on the source.
- Specific interrogation objectives.
- Method of interpretation to be used.
- The conduct of the interrogation: For example—
  - —Statements made by the interpreter and source should be interpreted in the first person, using the same content, tone of voice, inflection, and intent. The interpreter must not inject his own personality, ideas, or questions into the interrogation.
  - —The interpreter should inform the interrogator if there are any inconsistencies in the language used by the source. The interrogator will use this information in his assessment of the source. One example is a source who claims to be an officer, but uses excessive slang and profanity.
- Selected approach techniques and how they are to be applied.
- Physical arrangements of the interrogation site. Ideally, the interrogator and the source should face each other with the interpreter behind the source. This enhances interrogator control by allowing him to simultaneously observe the source and interpreter.
- Need for the interpreter to assist with preparing reports.

Throughout the briefing, the interrogator fully and clearly answers questions the interpreter may have. This helps ensure the interpreter completely understands his role in the interrogation.

CONDUCT THE INTERROGATION

During the interrogation, the interrogator corrects the interpreter if he violates any standards on which he was briefed. For example, if the interpreter injects his own ideas into the interrogation, he must be corrected.

Corrections should be made in a low-key manner. At no time should the interrogator rebuke his interpreter sternly or loudly while they are with the source. The interrogator should never argue with the interpreter in the presence of the source. If a major correction must be made, the interrogator and interpreter should leave the interrogation site temporarily, and only when necessary.

When initial source contact is made, the interpreter must instruct him to maintain eye contact with the interrogator. Since rapport and control must be established, the interpreter should be able to closely imitate the attitude, behavior, and tone of voice used by the interrogator and source. The questioning phase is conducted in the same way it would be if no interpreter were used.

During the termination phase, too, the interpreter's ability to closely imitate the interrogator and source is important. The approaches used are reinforced, and necessary sincerity and conviction must be conveyed to the source.

The interpreter assists the interrogator in preparing reports. He may be able to fill in gaps and unclear areas in the interrogator's notes. He may also assist in transliterating, translating, and explaining foreign terms.

After submitting all reports, the interrogator evaluates the performance of his interpreter. The evaluation must cover the same points of information the interrogator received from the senior interrogator.

The interrogator submits the results of his evaluation to the senior interrogator, who uses this evaluation to update information about the interpreter. This evaluation may also be used to develop training programs for interpreters.

STRATEGIC INTERROGATIONS AND DEBRIEFINGS

Strategic debriefing is questioning of individuals who are sources of information in a strategic or operational environment. This is done to obtain usable information in response to command and national level intelligence needs. Strategic intelligence—

- Provides support to national level planners and operational commanders across the operational continuum, and is useful for long-range planning.
- Is collected in peacetime as well as wartime; it often fills intelligence gaps on extremely sensitive topics or areas.

The objective of the strategic debriefing process is to obtain information of the highest degree of credibility to satisfy outstanding information objectives (IO). This avoids surprises of a strategic nature and consequences.

The types of sources encountered in strategic debriefing are emigres, refugees, resettlers, defectors, and selected US personnel. While there are other types, these represent the majority. Strategic debriefing guidance is provided in DIAM 58-13 and FM 34-5(S), Chapter 4.

DUTIES AND RESPONSIBILITIES OF DEBRIEFERS

Specific duties and responsibilities peculiar to a particular operation will be detailed in unit SOPs. This is due to the diverse nature of the various operations using debriefers outside continental United States (OCONUS) and within the continental United States (CONUS). However, debriefers have the following common duties and responsibilities regardless of assignment.

Notification

Proper response to notification of the availability of a source will depend upon unit operations. The debriefer may have to respond spontaneously as in the case of walk-in sources. He may have the luxury of advance notice as in the case of an invitational interview.

Planning the Debriefing

The process for planning a strategic debriefing is similar to conducting a tactical interrogation, with the following considerations peculiar to the strategic environment. The debriefer should—

- Determine source's area of knowledgeability, personality traits, and potential intelligence value.
- Review IOs.
- Assemble and organize necessary maps, technical reference manuals, city plans, photographs, and handbooks in anticipated debriefing sequence.
- Select an appropriate debriefing site with consideration to host country legal agreements or particular unit SOP directives.

Initial Contact

The debriefer will usually use a friendly rapport posture with sources, who have a status far different from EPWs or detainees.

Questioning

Good questioning techniques, rapport, and effective lead follow-up ensure answering specific IO.

Reporting Information Obtained

Comprehensive and logical note taking is translated into objective reporting within the parameters of intelligence report procedures in DIAM 58-13.

Concluding the Debriefing

An interview is concluded in a manner which enables any debriefer to contact a source at a later date and resume the debriefing process. The debriefer ensures the source receives all promised incentives. It is often necessary to provide source transportation and lodging. Such considerations demand the debriefer be familiar with procedures for using Intelligence Contingency Funds (ICFs).

Operational Security

There is an obvious need for OPSEC before, during, and after any debriefing. Source confidentiality and handling of classified materials demand constant and special attention.

Language Ability

Maintaining a language proficiency is a basic requirement; improvement of dialects, slang, technical terminology, and military vocabulary is a must.

Liaison

A debriefer may have the added responsibility of maintaining local liaison with host-government agencies while OCONUS. Unit SOPs usually dictate necessary and proper procedures.

S&T Enhancement

The debriefer keeps abreast with target country S&T developments. Intelligence agencies publish numerous reports and summaries which are readily available to the strategic debriefer.

STRATEGIC INTELLIGENCE COMPONENTS

Information gathered as strategic intelligence may be categorized into eight components. An easy way to remember these components is the acronym "BEST MAPS":

- Biographic intelligence.
- Economic intelligence.

- Sociological intelligence.
- Transportation and telecommunications intelligence.
- Military geographic intelligence.
- Armed forces intelligence.
- Political intelligence.
- S&T intelligence.

Each of these components can be divided into subcomponents. These components and subcomponents are not all-encompassing nor mutually exclusive. This approach enhances familiarization with the types of information included in strategic intelligence.

Biographic Intelligence

Biographic intelligence is the study of individuals of actual or potential importance through knowledge of their personalities and backgrounds. This component can be divided into subcomponents:

- Educational and occupational history—civilian and military backgrounds of individuals.
- Individual accomplishment—notable accomplishments of an individual's professional or private life.
- Idiosyncrasies and habits—mannerisms and unusual life styles.
- Position, influence, and potential—present future positions of power or influence.
- Attitudes and hobbies—significant interests that may affect an individual's accessibility.

Biographic information is reported by a message intelligence report in accordance with the format in DIAM 58-13.

Economic Intelligence

Economic intelligence studies economic strength and weaknesses of a country. Its subcomponents are—

- Economic warfare—information on the diplomatic or financial steps a country may take to induce neutral countries to cease trading with its enemies.
- Economic vulnerabilities—the degree to which a country's military would be hampered by the loss of materials or facilities.
- Manufacturing—information on processes, facilities, logistics, and raw materials.
- Source of economic capability—any means a country has to sustain its economy.

Sociological Intelligence

Sociological intelligence deals with people, customs, behaviors, and institutions. The subcomponents are—

- Population—rates of increase, decrease, or migrations.
- Social characteristics—customs, morals, and values.
- Manpower—divisions and distribution within the workforce.
- Welfare—health and education.
- Public information—information services within the country.

Transportation and Telecommunications Intelligence

Transportation and telecommunications intelligence studies systems dedicated to and used during military emergencies and peacetime. The subcomponents are too varied and numerous to cover.

Military Geographic Intelligence

Military geographic intelligence studies all geographic factors (physical and cultural) which may impact on military operations. Physical geography is concerned with natural or manmade geophysical features. Cultural geography provides demographics information.

Armed Forces Intelligence

Armed forces intelligence is the integrated study of the ground, sea, and air forces of the country. This is often referred to as OB. It is concerned with—

- Strategy—military alternatives in terms of position, terrain, economics, and politics.
- Tactics—military deployments and operations doctrine.
- OB—location, organization, weapons, strengths.
- Equipment—analysis of all military materiél.
- Logistics—procurements, storage, and distribution.
- Training—as carried out at all echelons to support doctrine.
- Organization—detailed analysis of command structures.
- Manpower—available resources and their conditioning.

Political Intelligence

Political intelligence studies all political aspects which may affect military operations. Its subcomponents are—

- Government structure—organization of departments and ministries.
- National policies—government actions and decisions.
- Political dynamics—government views and reactions to events.
- Propaganda—information and disinformation programs.
- Policy and intelligence services—organization and functions.
- Subversion—subversive acts sponsored by the government.

S&T Intelligence

S&T intelligence studies the country's potential and capability to support objectives through development of new processes, equipment, and weapons systems. The subcomponents are—

- Weapons and weapon systems.
- Missile and space programs.
- Nuclear energy and weapons technology.
- NBC developments.
- Basic applied science.
- Research and development systems.

STRATEGIC INTELLIGENCE CYCLE

Equally important to strategic intelligence components is awareness of the strategic intelligence cycle, and the debriefer's role within that 5-step cycle.

The debriefers—

- Identify intelligence gaps.
- Translate these gaps into IO.
- Answer those IO.
- Prepare intelligence reports.
- Prepare intelligence evaluation by the IO originator.

These evaluations measure information and report writing quality (see Appendix E). Evaluations provide vital feedback and guidance to strategic debriefers.

Appendix F contains information on the command language program (CLP) and Appendix G, on individual and collective training.

CHAPTER 4

PROCESSING AND EXPLOITING CAPTURED ENEMY DOCUMENTS

STANAG 2084 defines a document as any piece of recorded information, regardless of form, obtained from the enemy, which subsequently comes into the hands of a friendly force. CEDs can be US or allied documents that were once in the hands of the enemy. CEDs are—

- Typed, handwritten, printed, painted, engraved, or drawn materials.
- Sound or voice recordings.
- Imagery such as videotapes, movies, or photographs.
- Computer storage media including, but not limited to, floppy disks.
- Reproductions of any of the items listed above.

CEDs are mainly acquired two ways: Some are taken from sources; most, however, are captured on the battlefield from former enemy locations and enemy dead.

Documents found on EPWs or detainees or on the battlefield—which can be exploited more efficiently when combined with interrogation—are forwarded with the EPW or detainee to the next echelon in the evacuation channel.

In exceptional cases, documents may be evacuated ahead of the EPW or detainee for advance study by intelligence agencies. A notation should be made on the prisoner's captive tag (Figure 3-6), or accompanying administrative papers, about the existence of such documents and their location if they become separated from the EPW or detainee.

EPW or detainee interrogation has its disadvantages. The main disadvantage is prisoner-derived information usually has to be confirmed from other sources; for example, OB, CEDs, and other EPWs or detainees.

A prisoner may lie to further his army's cause or to ingratiate himself with the interrogator, by telling him what the prisoner believes he wants to hear. A prisoner may lack the background knowledge needed to interpret what he has seen or to pass it on accurately. He may misunderstand or misinterpret the interrogator's question because of language barriers or fright.

An EPW or detainee may have been misinformed or misled concerning the true situation for any number of reasons. This does not mean EPW or detainee interrogation is fruitless; however, it should not be considered absolutely reliable.

In contrast, a CED is something which the enemy has written for its own use. For this reason, CEDs are usually truthful and accurate. Spectacular cases have occurred in which falsified documents have been permitted to fall into enemy hands as a means of deception. However, these cases are exceptions and thus are usually famous. Because deceptive documents are unusual, a commander tends to believe in the authenticity of captured documents.

Information contained in CEDs can prove to be of intelligence value to commanders at all levels. CEDs are important because they provide information directly from the enemy. Only rarely will a single document or group of documents provide vital information. Usually, each document provides a small bit of a larger body of information. Each CED, much like a single piece of a puzzle, contributes to the whole.

In addition to their tactical intelligence value, technical data and political indicators can be extracted from CEDs that are important to strategic and national level agencies. CEDs can be helpful in exploiting sources.

The handling methods and reporting procedures to be used by US personnel acquiring CEDs are contained in STANAG 2084. It states CEDs, except those belonging to captured enemy equipment (CEE), will be forwarded for exploitation to the appropriate captured DOCEX center (normally organic to major North Atlantic Treaty Organization [NATO] commands). There are three types of documents:

- Official—documents of governmental or military origin (such as overlays, field orders, maps, codes, field manuals, and reports).
- Identity—personal items (such as cards or books, passport, and driver's license).
- Personal—documents of a private or commercial origin (such as letters, diaries, and photographs).

The volume of CEDs in combat will overwhelm an interrogation element of the size projected for a heavy division. A flow of CEDs similar to those encountered in Operations Urgent Fury, Just Cause, and Desert Storm would supply enough targets to keep a light division's interrogators busy around-the-clock screening and categorizing CEDs. Any attempt to conduct deeper exploitation would result in a tremendous evacuation delay and the end of timely reporting.

Experience shows a division involved in a HIC may have to process between 525 and 5,300 sources per week. While these figures are estimates, they demonstrate the inability of a division's own interrogators to simultaneously exploit sources and CEDs.

Divisions may receive additional interrogation assets from corps, depending on their mission. Prior planning must be conducted to establish the availability of these assets and their deployment within the division.

The density of interrogation assets and command emphasis on the collection effort determine mission requirements. The feasibility of a dual collection mission may also be the result of initial IPB by the commander's intelligence staff. If an echelon cannot conduct a dual collection effort, EPW interrogation receives priority.

CEDs, while not affected by memory loss, are often time sensitive; therefore, they are quickly screened for possible exploitation. Interrogators are given the CED exploitation mission because of their linguistic ability. This makes printed and typed material readily exploitable, but many handwritten documents are illegible.

Information contained in undeveloped imagery and recordings is inaccessible to most interrogation elements. The intelligence value of painted, drawn, or engraved material cannot be exploited by many elements unless it is accomplished by explanatory information in writing. An example of this would be an overlay prepared without map data, registration points, or identifying terrain features.

In spite of these limitations, an estimated 90 percent of all the information contained in CEDs can be exploited.

Figure 4-1 shows a comparison along a timeline of the amounts of information available to the interrogator from the two collection targets.

The comparison assumes the CEDs and sources initially had the same amount of information, and it was of equal intelligence value. The figures used are conservative estimates, and the time between the two target types might be even greater between 24 and 72 hours.

The percentage of information available from sources drops sharply during the first 24 hours after capture. This represents the rapid loss of what sources would consider to be insignificant details. A slower drop in the percentage begins at 48 hours to represent the resurgence of established value systems. The resurgence makes it harder for interrogators to obtain what information the source still remembers.

DOCUMENT CATEGORIES

The category assigned to each CED must be recorded as part of the Captured Document Log entry for that CED. Interrogators should also enter a brief description of that CED. This description should identify the type of document (such as sound recording, written material, painting, engraving, imagery); and what language was used in the CED.

This entry should also specify the physical construction of the CED (such as typed, printed, handwritten, tape cassette, photographs, film) and give some indication of its size (such as the number of pages, rolls of film, cassettes). The categories are discussed below.

CATEGORY A

Category A documents—

- Contain spot reportable information.
- Are time sensitive.
- Contain significant intelligence information.
- May be critical to successfully accomplishing friendly COAs.

Significant intelligence topics include enemy OB, new weapons or equipment on the battlefield, and may contain information that indicates a significant change in the enemy's capabilities or intentions.

When a document is identified as Category A, the document examiner immediately ceases screening operations and submits a spot report in SALUTE format of the critical information from the document. The examiner then resumes screening operations.

CATEGORY B

Category B documents contain information pertaining to enemy cryptographic or communication systems. Once a document is identified as Category B, it is classified Secret. This is done to limit the number of people having knowledge of the capture or contents.

Category B documents may contain spot reportable information, thereby requiring immediate exploitation. In every case, these documents will be transferred through secure channels to the technical control and analysis element (TCAE) or TSA as soon as possible.

CATEGORY C

Category C documents contain no spot reportable or time-sensitive information, but do contain information of general intelligence value that does not indicate significant changes in enemy capabilities or intentions. Category C documents may be of interest or value to other agencies. When

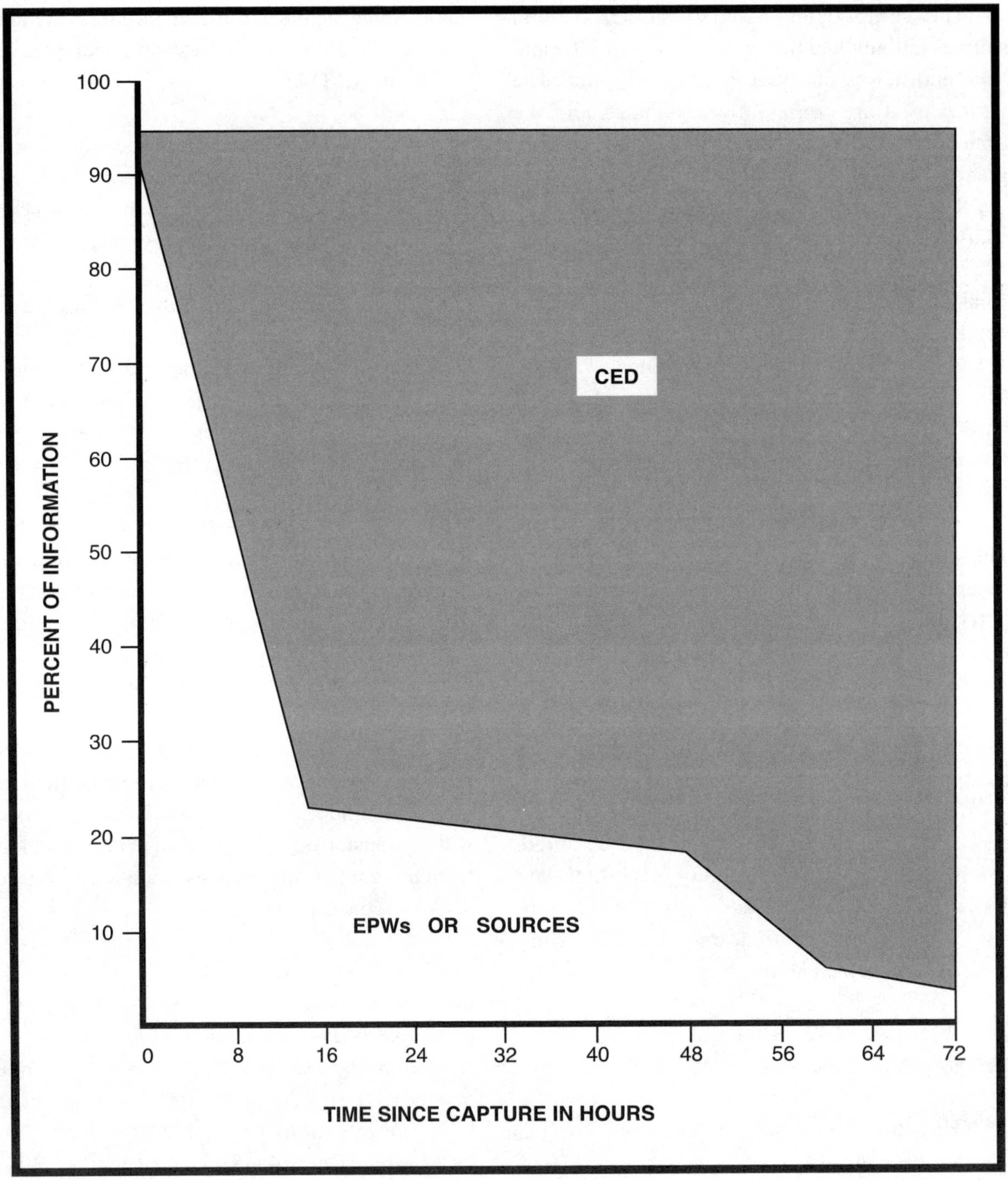

Figure 4-1. Comparison timelines.

identified as Category C, they require exploitation, regardless of content.

CATEGORY D

Category D documents appear to contain information of no intelligence value. Documents are not identified as Category D until after a thorough examination by document translation specialists at the highest command interested. This is accomplished at EAC. Category D documents are to be disposed of as directed by the appropriate authority.

DOCUMENT HANDLING

The accountability phase begins at the time the document is captured. Original documents must not be marked, altered, or defaced in any way. Documents must be clearly tagged. The capturing unit attaches a captured document tag (DA Form 5976, Part C) to each document; multiple CEDs are bundled or bagged together. The capture data is always recorded on a captured document tag. Figure 4-2 shows a format to use when a capture tag is not available; record the required data on any paper.

The captured document tag should be assigned a sequential number at the first formal exploitation point, showing the nationality of the capturing force by national letters prescribed in STANAG 1059. The capturing unit will record the information as follows:

- Time document was captured, recorded as a DTG.
- Place document was captured, including the six- or eight-digit coordinate, and description of the location of capture.
- Identity of the capturing unit.
- Identity of the source from whom the document was taken, if applicable.
- Summary of the circumstances under which the document was found.

EVACUATION

CED intelligence value will be determined and exploited as early as possible. The document

CAPTURED DOCUMENT TAG

____
NATIONALITY OF CAPTURING FORCE
(STANAG 1059)

1. DATE/TIME CAPTURED: 091756Z APR 99
2. PLACE CAPTURED: TA 123456
3. CAPTURING UNIT: 1CO/2/3/4 Regt
4. IDENTITY OF SOURCE (IF APPLICABLE): __________
5. CIRCUMSTANCES OF CAPTURE: FOUND IN ABANDONED ENEMY CP.

Figure 4-2. Captured document tag format.

must be forwarded immediately to higher headquarters.

Custody of CEDs transfers (normally from the MP) to MI when MI identifies a document as having intelligence interest. When MI interest in an EPW-related CED stops, MI gives it back to the MP.

Echelon Responsibilities

There is no set time for how long any particular echelon may keep a document for study. The primary aim of speedy evacuation to the rear for interrogator examination remains. During evacuation, escorts carefully guard CEDs to prevent recapture, loss, or destruction.

Capturing Unit Responsibilities

The capturing unit is responsible for properly tagging and securing CEDs found on an EPW or on the battlefield. It forwards CEDs found on the battlefield directly to its S2. Documents found on an EPW stay with him. If the capturing unit takes CEDs from a captured person, it does so in accordance with the GPW and unit SOPs.

The capturing unit must clearly tag CEDs to show which EPW it was taken from so they can be matched up later. Specific responsibilities are discussed below.

Capture Unit's S2. This officer is responsible for tagging all untagged CEDs. The S2 performs battlefield DOCEX as practicable and ensures speedy CED evacuation to brigade.

Escort or Guards, Brigade and Below. The brigade provides escorts and guards to transport EPWs and CEDs from subordinate battalions to the division forward collecting point. The guards—

- Assume accountability for transported CEDs.
- Ensure each item transported has a completed captured document tag attached.
- Ensure items gathered from different battalions are not mixed.

Brigade IPW Team. This 2- to 4-person team's mission, when placed in DS, is to collect information of critical interest to the supported brigade commander. It concentrates whatever DOCEX efforts it can on CEDs found with EPWs. MP evacuate all examined CEDs, along with unexamined CEDs, via EPW evacuation channels.

Division IPW Section. This interrogation section's mission is similar to that of the brigade IPW team. At this stage, priority evacuation of high value EPWs and CEDs direct to EAC is possible. Most EPWs and CEDs of intelligence interest go to the corps EPW holding facility.

MP Escorts. MP assume responsibility for evacuating CEDs and EPWs from the brigade's capturing units at the division's forward collecting point. They escort EPWs and CEDs through EAC. MI assumes control from the MP when interrogators determine a captured item or EPW is of intelligence value.

Corps CED Team. The CIF commander may task-organize a team of interrogators at the corps EPW holding facility to screen incoming CEDs for examination by the CIF DOCEX element.

The CED screening team—

- Sorts incoming CEDs.
- Identifies those of possible intelligence value.
- Separates them.
- Assumes custody from the MP.
- Batches selected CEDs and delivers them to the CIF DOCEX element.

CIF DOCEX Element. At the CIF or combined corps interrogation facility (CCIF), interrogators scan selected CEDs and decide their intelligence category. They assign serial numbers and examine CEDs to answer corps collection requirements, filing spot reports in SALUTE format as necessary.

CIF interrogators batch and forward Category B documents to specialized collection activities. Interrogators label, batch, and direct evacuation of all other documents to EAC via MP and EPW evacuation channels. Examples are the TECHINT team, CI team for espionage items, and Criminal Investigation Division (CID) or SJA for war crimes information.

Theater Document Examiners. Theater level interrogators, normally at a TIF, perform a final examination of all documents of possible theater intelligence value before storing or evacuating them. The Defense Intelligence Agency (DIA) sets procedures for exploitation of documents above theater Army level. The following procedures have been devised to aid timely exploitation:

- Technical documents (TECHDOCs) found with materiél that relate to their design or operation should be evacuated with the materiél. When the materiél cannot be evacuated, the documents should be identified with the materiél by attaching a sheet marked "TECHDOC." This should list the precise location, time, circumstance of capture, and a detailed description of the materiél. If possible, photographs should be taken of the equipment and evacuated with the document. An object of known size such as a ruler should be placed close to the materiél and photographed with it to provide a size reference.
- CEDs containing communications or cryptographic information are handled as secret material and are evacuated through secure channels to the TCAE at division and the TSA at EAC.

ACCOUNTABILITY

At each echelon, starting with the capturing unit, steps are taken to ensure CED accountability is maintained during document evacuation. To establish accountability, the responsible element inventories all incoming CEDs. Thorough accountability procedures at each echelon ensure CEDs are not lost. To record each processing step as it occurs helps correct mistakes in CED processing.

Accountability is accomplished by anyone who captures, evacuates, processes, or handles CEDs. All CEDs should have completed captured document tags. An incoming batch of documents includes a CED transmittal. Figure 4-3 shows this format. The exact format for a document transmittal is a matter of local SOP, but it should contain the information listed below:

- The identity of the element to which the CEDs are to be evacuated.

- The identity of the unit forwarding the CEDs.
- The identification number of the document transmittal.
- Whether or not CEDs in the package have been screened and the screening category. (If not screened, NA is circled.)
- A list of the document serial numbers of the CEDs in the package.

When a batch is received without a transmittal, the interrogation element contacts the forwarding unit and obtains a list of document serial numbers.

The interrogation element records all trace actions in its journal. Accountability includes—

- Inventorying the CEDs as they arrive.
- Initiating necessary trace actions.
- Maintaining the CED log.

When intelligence derived from a CED is included in a unit or information INTREPs, the identification letters and number of the document concerned are quoted to avoid the false confirmation. All CEDs are shipped with any associated documents.

INVENTORY

An inventory of incoming CEDs is conducted initially by comparing the CED to the captured document tag and accompanying transmittal documents. This comparison identifies—

CAPTURED ENEMY DOCUMENT TRANSMITTAL:

TO: G2, X CORPS **DATE/TIME:** 04

FROM: G2, 25 TNF DIV **TRANSMITTAL NO:** 010

SCREENED: YES NO **CATEGORY:** A B (C) D NA

DOCUMENT SERIAL NUMBERS:

TR-AR-091 thru 100
SY-AR-8.1 thru 9.7

Figure 4-3. Sample CED transmittal.

- Transmittals that list missing CEDs.
- Document tags not attached to CEDs.
- CEDs not attached to document tags.
- CEDs not listed on the accompanying transmittal documents.

LOG

The captured document log, shown at Figure 4-4, is a record of what an element knows about a CED. After trace actions are initiated, the CEDs are entered in the remarks section of the captured document log. This log must contain the following:

- Name of capturing unit.
- File number (a sequential number to identify the order of entry).
- DTG the CED was received at this element.
- Document serial number of the captured document tag.
- Identification number of the transmittal document accompanying the CED.
- Full designation of the unit that forwarded the CED.
- Name and rank of individual that received the CED.
- DTG and place of capture (as listed on the captured document tag).
- Identity of the capturing units (as listed on the captured document tag).
- Document category (after screening).
- Description of the CED (at a minimum the description includes the original language; number of pages; type of document such as a map, letter, or photograph; and the enemy's identification number for the CED, if available).
- Destination and identification number of the outgoing transmittal.
- Remarks (other information that can assist the unit in identifying the CED to include processing codes. These are set up by local SOPs to denote all actions taken with the document while at the element, including spot (SALUTE) reports, translations, reproductions, or return of the CED to the source from whom it was taken).

Accountability for the CED should be established at each echelon once the actions described above have been done.

TRACE ACTIONS

When necessary, the receiving unit initiates a CED trace action. Trace actions are initiated on all missing CEDs, captured document tags, and all information missing from the captured document tag. Trace actions are initiated by contacting elements from which the documents were received. This corrective action can be completed swiftly if that unit's captured document log was filled out completely.

If necessary, the trace action continues to other elements that have handled the document. If a captured document tag is unavailable from elements that have previously handled the CED, the document examiner fills out a captured document tag for the document using whatever information is available. Attempts to obtain missing CEDs are critical because of the information those CEDs might contain.

DOCUMENT EXPLOITATION

As incoming CEDs are accounted for, the exploitation phase for intelligence information begins. Exploitation includes—

UNIT: 16 INF DIV (L)

FILE NUMBER	RECEIVED DTG	DOCUMENT SERIAL NUMBER	INCOMING TRANS-MISSION NUMBER	FORWARDING UNIT	RECEIVED BY	TIME AND PLACE OF CAPTURE (DTG)
0001	1119107	US-AR-1910-1	NA	4th Bde	ROYCE	110719ZNC123456
0002	111917Z	US-AF-WAV6	NA	1st Bde	JONES	111314ZBC654321

CAPTURING UNIT	SCREENING CATEGORY	DESCRIPTION OF DOCUMENT	OUTGOING TRANSMITTAL	REMARKS
B/1/2/3	C	PERSONAL LETTER	011.17	NONE
D/2/3/4	A	OPLAN	019.44	NONE

Figure 4-4. Captured document log format.

- CED screening to determine potential intelligence value.
- Extracting pertinent information from the CED.
- Reporting the extracted information.

CEDs are processed and exploited as soon as possible within the constraints of the unit's mission. The main mission of some units is to exploit human sources rather than to translate CEDs; therefore, manpower constraints may limit time for translation.

However, translating CEDs is necessary at any echelon where interrogators and translators are assigned. Therefore, it is important that interrogation elements possess qualified personnel to provide the translation support required. Intelligence units ensure there is no delay in CED exploitation.

Qualified personnel or document copying facilities should be available to handle CEDs; personnel should be available to exploit the volume or type of documents concerned. If not, documents are forwarded immediately to the next higher echelon. Copying availability is determined by the echelon in question, as well as mission and mobility considerations.

CED SCREENING

Document exploitation begins when CEDs are screened for information of immediate intelligence interest. As each document is screened, it is assigned one of four category designations. The category assigned determines the document's priority for exploitation and evacuation.

CED screening procedures include receiving the latest PIR, IR, and SIR; current friendly and enemy situation update; relevant OB; and review.

Brigade and division interrogators get this information from the supported J2, G2, or S2. Corps and theater DOCEX elements receive this information from their parent MI battalion or brigade. The DOCEX elements are responsible for obtaining and providing such operational intelligence information to their DOCEX teams.

SPECIAL DOCUMENT HANDLING

TECHDOCs are given special handling to expedite exploitation and evacuation. TECHDOCs are handled as Category A CEDs until screened by TECHINT personnel. Generally, TECHDOCs accompany the captured equipment until the intelligence exploitation is completed. TECHDOCs include maintenance handbooks, operational manuals, and drawings. Examples of TECHDOCs include—

- Air Force documents (AIRDOCs). These are documents of any category captured from crashed enemy aircraft, particularly if related to enemy anti-aircraft defense or air control and reporting systems. AIRDOCs are transmitted to the nearest Air Force headquarters without delay.
- Navy documents (NAVDOCs). These are documents taken from ships (for example, code books, call signs, frequency tables, and identification symbols). NAVDOCs are forwarded without delay to the nearest Navy headquarters.
- Maps and charts of enemy forces. Captured maps and charts containing any operational graphics are evacuated immediately to the supporting all-source analysis center. Captured maps and charts without graphics may be transmitted to the topographical intelligence section attached to corps.

SCREENING AT HIGHER ECHELONS

CEDs can be recategorized during screening conducted at higher echelons. The information may have become outdated, or the echelon currently exploiting the document may have different intelligence requirements.

TRANSLATING

Once a CED has been screened, the document must be exploited. The translation must be clearly and accurately typed or handwritten; this ensures usability. Also, as part of interrogation duties, the interrogator may have previously translated a document by sight to help gain a source's cooperation.

TYPES OF TRANSLATIONS

There are three types of translations:

- Full—one in which the entire document is translated. It is time-intensive and requires manpower, especially for lengthy documents or TECHDOCs. It is unlikely many full translations will be performed at corps or below. Even when dealing with Category A documents, it may not be necessary to translate the entire document to gain the information it contains.
- Extract—one in which only a portion of the document is translated. For instance, a TECHINT analyst may decide a few paragraphs in the middle of a 600-page helicopter maintenance manual merit translation, and a full translation is not necessary. The analyst would request only what he needed.
- Summary—one in which a translator begins by reading the entire document. He then summarizes the main points of information instead of rendering a full or extract translation.

A summary translation requires a translator have more analytical abilities. The translator must balance the need for complete exploitation of the document against time available in combat operations.

A summary translation may also be used by translators working in languages in which they have not been formally trained. For instance, a Russian linguist may not be able to accurately deliver a full translation of a Bulgarian language document. However, he can probably render a usable summary of the information it contains.

TRANSLATION REPORTS

Except for SALUTE spot reports, all information resulting from document exploitation activities will be reported in a translation report. After all required SALUTE reports have been submitted, the translator will prepare required translation reports.

CEDs that contain information of intelligence value that was not SALUTE reported are the subject of translation reports. Translation reports are prepared on all Category C CEDs and include portions of Category A, TECHDOCs, and Category B CEDs not SALUTE reported.

The priorities for preparing translation reports are—

- Category A.
- TECHDOCs.
- Category B.
- Category C.

A translation report, shown at Figure 4-5, should contain the following information:

(CLASSIFICATION)

TRANSLATION REPORT

TO: G2, 23d Inf Div (MECH) DATE: 291130ZAUG99
FROM: IPW Sec, I&S Co, 231st MI Bn REPORT NUMBER: 08-0356

PART I. CONTROL DATA:

1. DOCUMENT NUMBER: US-WAIBVO-03093.
2. DOCUMENT DESCRIPTION: Personal letter, 1 page, handwritten.
3. DOCUMENT'S ORIGINAL LANGUAGE: Russian.
4. DATE AND TIME RECEIVED: 290510ZAUG99.
5. DATE AND TIME OF CAPTURE: 290120ZAUG99.
6. PLACE OF CAPTURE: vic NB146122.
7. CAPTURING UNIT: Co. A, 2d Bn, 1st Inf Bde, 23d Inf Div.
8. CIRCUMSTANCES OF CAPTURE: During ambush.
9. TRANSLATOR: SGT Royce.
10. TRANSLATION TYPE: Full.

PART II. TRANSLATION TEXT:

My dear Serezhen'ka:

It has been a long time since I received a letter from you. How are you and where are you? The last time you wrote that fighting was going on around you all the time, and this worries me a lot. Take care of yourself. There have been many changes at home. Your mother, despite her age, had to go to work in the factory. They make tanks there, but the sign over the entrance says this is a sugar plant. I don't know why they do this. At the school where I work, we were also told to go and work at the same plant. They are going to close the school. Everyone has to go to the front or work in the war industry. I would be more at ease if I knew you are alive and well. Please write as soon as you can.

Your KATHY.

PART III: REMARKS: None.

(CLASSIFICATION)

Figure 4-5. Sample translation report.

- Destination, which is the element to which the report will be forwarded.
- Originator, which is the element that prepared the report.
- Date of preparation showing the DTG.
- Report number as designated by local SOP.
- Document number taken from the captured document tag.
- Document description including type of document, number of pages, physical construction of document, and enemy identification number, if applicable.
- Original CED language.
- DTG document was received at element preparing the report.
- DTG document was captured.
- Place document was captured.
- Identity of capturing unit.
- Circumstances under which document was captured.
- Rank and last name of translator.
- Type of translation: full, extract, or summary.
- Remarks for clarification or explanation, including the identification of the portions of the document translated in an extract translation.
- Classification and downgrading instructions, according to AR 380-5.

DISSEMINATION AND RECORDS

The translator records each exploitation step taken in the captured document log. Transmission of spot and translation reports is entered in the element's journal.

At least two copies are prepared for each spot (SALUTE) and translation report. One copy is placed in the interrogation element's files. The other accompanies the CED when it is evacuated. When the CED cannot be fully exploited, a copy of the CED should be made and retained. The original CED is forwarded through evacuation channels. Even when copies of an unexploited CED cannot be made, the original CED is still forwarded through evacuation channels without delay.

EVACUATION PROCEDURES

For friendly forces to benefit fully from a document, send CEDs to the element most qualified to exploit them as quickly as possible. Information gained from a CED is frequently time-sensitive. If a document is not sent to the element most capable of exploiting it, time will be lost. Time lost in exploiting the document may reduce or even negate the value of the information. The CED evacuation procedures in use at any element must ensure documents are shipped to their proper destinations in a timely manner.

NORMAL EVACUATION

CEDs are normally evacuated from echelon to echelon through the intelligence organizational chain. Depending on the type of documents, they may eventually be evacuated to the National Center for Document Exploitation. Interrogators and translators can exploit CEDs at every echelon; they will make an attempt to exploit CEDs within their expertise and technical support constraints.

DIRECT EVACUATION

Some CEDs are evacuated to different elements based upon the information contained and the type of document concerned. Direct evacuation to an element outside the chain of command takes place at the lowest practical echelon. Specific evacuation guidelines contained in local unit SOPs are followed when dealing with documents requiring special handling.

EVACUATION PRIORITIES

When transportation assets are limited, CEDs are evacuated according to priority. The priority is the category assigned to the CED. All Category A CEDs will be evacuated first, TECHDOCs will be considered Category A CEDs until examined by the captured materiél exploitation center (CMEC), followed in order by Categories B, C, and D.

Category B documents are evacuated to the TCAE, which maintains a SIGINT and EW data base. Category B documents pertaining to communications equipment are duplicated, if possible; the duplicate documents are sent to the CMEC.

CEDs not evacuated are held until the next transportation arrives. These remaining CEDs are combined with any other CEDs of the same category that have arrived and have been processed.

When determining evacuation priorities, interrogators consider CEDs ready for evacuation. Lower priority CEDs, no matter how old, are never evacuated ahead of those with higher priority. A package of documents contains CEDs of only one category. All unscreened CEDs are handled as Category C documents, but they are not packaged with screened Category C documents. CEDs in a single package must have the same destination.

TRANSMITTAL DOCUMENTS

When CEDs are evacuated from any echelon, a document transmittal is used (see Figure 4-3). A separate document transmittal is prepared for each group of CEDs to be evacuated.

When second copies of Category B CEDs are being sent to a TECHINT element, a separate document transmittal is required.

The transmittal identification number is recorded in the captured document log as part of the entry for each CED.

All CEDs being evacuated must be accompanied with the appropriate—

- TECHDOC cover sheet.
- SECRET cover sheet on Category B documents.
- Translation reports and hard-copy spot reports in SALUTE format accompanying translated documents.
- Captured document tags.

ASSOCIATED DOCUMENTS

Preparations for further CED evacuation begin with verifying document serial numbers. This is done by comparing the entry in the captured document log with the entry on the captured document tag attached to each CED.

Once all CEDs are present, copies of all reports derived from the CEDs are assembled. A copy of all SALUTE and translation reports is placed with the CEDs that were the sources of those reports. When possible, all Category B CEDs and their captured document tags should be copied.

GROUP DOCUMENTS

CEDs are first grouped according to their assigned screening category. Personnel must be careful when sorting CEDs to ensure no CED is separated from its associated documents. These large groupings can be broken down into smaller groups. Each of these smaller groupings consists of CEDs that were—

- Captured by the same unit.
- Captured in the same place.
- Captured on the same day at the same time.
- Received at the interrogation element at the same time.

DOCUMENTS CAPTURED WITH A SOURCE

The documents captured with a source play an important role in the interrogation process and can contain reportable information the same as with a CED obtained on the battlefield. During source screening operations, for instance, documents can indicate a specific source may have information pertaining to the commander's intelligence requirements.

The interrogator uses various pieces of information in forming his interrogation plan. Documents captured with the source may provide the key to the approach necessary to gain the source's cooperation.

Guidelines for the disposition of the source's documents and valuables are set by international agreement and discussed in more detail in AR 190-8 and FM 19-4.

One way the source's trust and continued cooperation can be gained is through fair and equitable handling of his personal possessions. In some instances, such treatment can make it more likely the source will cooperate during interrogation. Furthermore, fair treatment by the interrogator and holding area personnel can ease tensions in the confinement facility.

DOCUMENT DISPOSAL

The disposition of documents captured with a source is normally an MP function. Because of their language capabilities, interrogators at the compound probably will be required to provide assistance.

The MP sign for all documents taken from sources. To ensure proper handling and expeditious disposition of these documents, the interrogation element should sign for any documents captured with a source. When the interrogation element assumes control of documents, they process them according to established procedures.

When documents are captured with a source, it is recommended that they be taken away from him so he cannot destroy them. However, under no circumstances is a source's identification card to be permanently taken from him.

When documents are taken from a source, it is necessary to ensure the source from whom they were taken can be identified. The best way to do this is with the source's captive tag. The bottom portion of the tag is designed to be used for marking equipment or documents. Three possible actions may be taken with documents captured with a source. The documents may be confiscated, impounded, or returned to the source.

Confiscation

Documents confiscated from a source are taken away with no intention of returning them. Official documents, except identification documents, are confiscated and appropriately evacuated. The intelligence value of the document should be weighed against the document's support in the interrogation of the source.

Category A documents require exploitation and should be copied. One copy should be translated and exploited separately, and the other copy should be evacuated with the source. If copying facilities are not available, a decision should be made on whether to evacuate the document with the source or separately.

Category B CEDs should be evacuated to the TCAE for appropriate exploitation. Category C official documents can best be used in the interrogation of the source. Therefore, these CEDs and Category D official documents should be evacuated with the source.

Impounded

Impounded CEDs are taken away with the intention of returning them later. When a document is impounded, the source must be given a receipt. The receipt must contain a list of the items impounded and the legible name, rank, and unit of the person issuing the receipt. All personal effects, including monies and other valuables, will be safeguarded.

An inventory of personal effects that have been impounded will be entered on DA Form 4237-R (see Figure 3-1). Also, the officer in charge or authorized representative will complete and sign DA Form 1132-R (Prisoner's Personal Property List—Personal). A copy will be provided the source. See AR 190-8 for procedures on handling personal effects.

Returned

Returned CEDs are usually personal in nature, taken only for inspection and information of interest, and immediately given back to the source. Personal documents belonging to a source will be returned to the source after examination in accordance with the GPW. Copies of such papers may be made and forwarded if considered appropriate. An identification document must be returned to the source.

RECOGNITION AND EVACUATION OF DOCUMENTS

In a fast-moving tactical situation, it is possible documents captured with sources will not be handled expeditiously. Final disposition of these documents may not be made until the source is evacuated at least as far as the corps holding area.

Some documents captured with a source will aid in the interrogation of the source. Others, particularly Category A, should be copied and evacuated separately. One copy can remain with the source to aid in the interrogation, and the other can be translated and exploited separately.

It is essential that the capturing unit correctly identify the documents captured with the source. This is more easily done when the interrogation element, rather than the MP element, signs for the documents captured with sources.

EVACUATION OF SIGNIFICANT DOCUMENTS

To efficiently exploit CEDs and sources, documents captured with a source are normally evacuated with the source. A document of great significance may be evacuated ahead of the source, but a reproduction should be kept with the source. If reproduction is not possible, note on the captured document tag where the document was sent.

Significant documents such as Categories A and B, TECHDOCs, maps, charts, AIRDOCs and NAVDOCs are evacuated directly.

APPENDIX A
UNIFORM CODE OF MILITARY JUSTICE EXTRACT

Article 78, Accessory after the fact

Text of the offense: Any person subject to this chapter who, knowing that an offense punishable by this chapter has been committed, receives, comforts, or assists the offender in order to hinder or prevent his apprehension, trial, or punishment shall be punished as a court-martial shall direct.

Article 80, Attempts

Text of the offense:

(a) An act, done with specific intent to commit an offense under this chapter, amounting to more than mere preparation and tending, even though failing, to effect its commission, is an attempt to commit that offense.

(b) Any person subject to this chapter who attempts to commit any offense punishable by this chapter shall be punished as a court-martial may direct, unless otherwise specifically prescribed.

(c) Any person subject to this chapter may be convicted of an attempt to commit an offense although it appears on the trial that the offense was consummated.

Article 81, Conspiracy

Text of the offense: Any person subject to this chapter who conspires with any other person to commit an offense under this chapter shall, if one or more of the conspirators does an act to effect the object of the conspiracy, be punished as a court-martial may direct.

Article 93, Cruelty and maltreatment

Elements of the offense:

(1) That a certain person was subject to the orders of the accused; and

(2) That the accused was cruel toward, or oppressed, or maltreated that person. (The cruelty, oppression, or maltreatment, although not necessarily physical, must be measured by an objective standard.)

Article 118, Murder

Text of the offense: Any person subject to this chapter who, without justification or excuse, unlawfully kills a human being, when he—

(1) has a premeditated design to kill;

(2) intends to kill or inflict great bodily harm;

(3) is engaged in an act that is inherently dangerous to others and evinces a wanton disregard of human life; or

(4) is engaged in the perpetration or attempted perpetration of a burglary, sodomy, rape, robbery, or aggravated arson;

is guilty of murder, and shall suffer punishment as a court-martial shall direct, except that if found guilty under clause (1) or (4), he shall suffer death or imprisonment for life as a court-martial may direct.

Article 119, Manslaughter

Text of the offense:

(a) Any person subject to this chapter who, with an intent to inflict great bodily harm, unlawfully kills a human being in the heat of sudden passion caused by adequate provocation is guilty of voluntary manslaughter and shall be punished as a court-martial may direct.

(b) Any person subject to this chapter who, without an intent to kill or inflict great bodily harm, unlawfully kills a human being—

(1) by culpable negligence; or

(2) while perpetrating or attempting to perpetrate an offense, other than those named in clause (4) of Article 118, directly affecting the person; is guilty of involuntary manslaughter and shall be punished as a court-martial may direct.

Article 124, Maiming

Text of the offense: Any person subject to this chapter who, with intent to injure, disfigure, or disable, inflicts upon the person of another an injury which—

(1) seriously disfigures his person by any mutilation thereof;

(2) destroys or disables any member or organ of his body; or

(3) seriously diminishes the physical vigor by the injury of any member or organ;

is guilty of maiming and shall be punished as a court-martial may direct.

Article 127, Extortion

Text of the offense: Any person subject to this chapter who communicates threats to another person with the intention thereby to obtain anything of value or any acquittance, or immunity is guilty of extortion and shall by punished as a court-martial may direct.

Article 128, Assault

Text of the offense:

(a) Any person subject to this chapter who attempts or offers with unlawful force or violence to do bodily harm to another person, whether or not the attempt or offer is consummated, is guilty of assault and shall be punished as a court-martial may direct.

(b) Any person subject to this chapter who—

(1) commits an assault with a dangerous weapon or other means or force likely to produce death or grievous bodily harm; or

(2) commits an assault and intentionally inflicts grievous bodily harm with or without a weapon;

is guilty of aggravated assault and shall be punished as a court-martial may direct.

Article 134, Homicide, negligent

Elements of the offense:

(1) That a certain person is dead;

(2) That this death resulted from the act or failure to act of the accused;

(3) That the killing by the accused was unlawful;

(4) That the act or failure to act of the accused which caused the death amounted to simple negligence; and

(5) That, under the circumstances, the conduct of the accused was to the prejudice of good order and discipline in the armed forces or was of a nature to bring discredit upon the armed forces.

Article 134, Misprision of a serious offense

Elements of the offense:

(1) That a certain serious offense was committed by a certain person;

(2) That the accused knew that the said person had committed the serious offense;

(3) That thereafter, the accused concealed the serious offense and failed to make it known to civilian or military authorities as soon as possible;

(4) That the concealing was wrongful; and

(5) That, under the circumstances, the conduct of the accused was to the prejudice of good

order and discipline in the armed forces or was of a nature to bring discredit upon the armed forces.

Article 134, Soliciting another to commit an offense

Elements of the offense:

(1) That the accused solicited a certain person or persons to commit a certain offense under the code other than one of the four offenses named in Article 82;

(2) That the accused did so with the intent that the offense actually be committed; and

(3) That, under the circumstances, the conduct of the accused was to the prejudice of good order and discipline in the armed forces or was of a nature to bring discredit upon the armed forces.

Article 134, Threat, communicating

Elements of the offense:

(1) That the accused communicated certain language expressing a present determination or intent to wrongfully injure the person, property, or reputation of another person, presently or in the future;

(2) That the communication was made known to that person or a third person;

(3) That the communication was wrongful; and

(4) That, under the circumstances, the conduct of the accused was to the prejudice of good order and discipline in the armed forces or was of a nature to bring discredit upon the armed forces.

APPENDIX B
QUESTIONING GUIDES

This appendix contains sample tactical questions and topics for specific EPWs and detainees. It also contains a sample overall objective statement for an interrogation element and a sample overall objective statement with IEW tasks.

RIFLEMEN

Depending on assignment and experience, riflemen can be expected to have tactical information concerning mission, organization, and locations of enemy infantry units. Topics for interrogation include—

- Identification of source's squad, platoon, company, battalion, regiment, and division.
- Organization, strength, weapons, and disposition of squad, platoon, and company.
- Number of newly assigned personnel in unit within last 30 days.
- Location and strength of men and weapons at strongholds, outposts, and observation posts in source's immediate area.
- Source mission immediately before capture as well as mission of source's squad, platoon, company, and higher echelons.
- Location and description of defensive installations, such as missile sites, antitank ditches, and emplacements, minefields, roadblocks, and barbed wire entanglements in source's area before capture. Description of weapons in which these locations are covered.
- Names and personality information of small unit commanders known to source.
- Possible identifications of support mortar, artillery, and armored units.
- Status of food, ammunition, and other supplies.
- Troop morale.
- Casualties.
- Defensive and protective items of NBC equipment; status of NBC training and defensive NBC instructions, and offensive capability of NBC operations.
- Status of immunizations; new shots, booster shots more frequently than normal.
- Stress on care and maintenance of NBC protective equipment.
- Issuance of new or different NBC protective equipment.
- Morale and esprit de corps of civilians.
- Civilian supply.
- Health of civilians, and medicine availability.
- Night maneuvers, rehearsals, unit size, night vision devices, and special equipment.

MESSENGERS

Messengers are frequently chosen on the basis of above-average intelligence, ability to observe, and to remember oral messages and instructions. Messengers, who have an opportunity to travel within the immediate combat zone, generally, will have a good picture of the current situation, and are excellent prospects for tactical interrogation on the following:

- Nature and exact contents of messages he has been carrying over a reasonable period of time, as well as names of persons who originated these messages, and names of persons to whom messages were directed. Description of duty positions of such personalities.

- Information as to extent which messengers are used in the applicable enemy unit, routes of messengers, and location of relay posts.
- Locations of message center and communications lines.
- Conditions of roads, bridges, and alternate routes.
- Location of CPs and names of commanders and staff officers.
- Location of artillery, mortars, and armor seen during messenger's movement through the combat area.
- Location of minefields and other defensive installations.
- Location of supply and ammunition dumps.
- Description of terrain features behind enemy lines.
- NBC weapons, installations, and units.
- Morale and esprit de corps of civilians.
- Relocation of movement of civilians.
- Civilian supply.
- Health of civilians and medicine availability.
- Use of radio equipment in applicable enemy units.

SQUAD AND PLATOON LEADERS AND COMPANY COMMANDERS

Squad and platoon leaders, as well as company commanders, generally possess information on a broader level than discussed to this point. In addition to the information possessed by the riflemen, they may be able to furnish information on the following:

- Plans and mission of their respective units.
- Organization of their units as well as their regiment and battalion.
- Number of newly assigned unit personnel within last 30 days.
- Disposition of companies, regiments, and reserves of each.
- Identification and general organization of supporting units such as artillery, armor, and engineer units.
- Location, strength, and mission of heavy weapons units.
- Offensive and defensive tactics of small units.
- Quality and morale of subordinate troops.
- Doctrine for employment of NBC weapons.
- Doctrine for defense against NBC weapons.
- Status of NBC defense SOPs and current NBC training.
- Communications procedures and equipment.
- Issuance of NBC detection equipment and detector paints or paper.
- Morale of civilians.
- Relocation or movement of civilians.
- Civilian supply.
- Health of civilians and availability of medicine.
- Instructions on handling and evacuating US and allied prisoners.
- Night maneuvers, rehearsals, unit size, night vision devices, and special equipment.

RADIO AND TELEPHONE OPERATORS

Radio and telephone operators, like messengers, are frequently familiar with the plans and instructions of their commanders. In general, they can be expected to know the current military situation even more thoroughly because of the greater volume of information which they normally transmit. The following questions could be asked:

- Nature and exact contents of messages sent and received during a given tactical situation.
- Code names or numbers of specific enemy units—those appearing in enemy telephone directories—and in other signal operations instructions (SOI), such as unit identification panel codes.
- Major enemy units to your front and their code names.
- Units and individuals in radio nets, their call signs, call words, and operating frequencies.
- Names and code names of commanders and their staff officers.
- Types, numbers, and basic characteristics of radios and telephone equipment used at company, regiment, and division levels.
- Identification and location of units occupying front-line positions.
- Location of artillery and mortar positions.
- Information on enemy codes and ciphers.
- Code names given to operations or specially designated supply points such as for special weapons.
- Names and signals designating various types of alerts.

DRIVERS

Questions directed to captured EPW drivers of command and staff vehicles, supply vehicles, and vehicles drawing weapons should concern the aspects of the enemy situation which the prisoner would know because of his driving assignments. The following questions could be asked:

- Identification and location of CPs of higher, lower, and supporting units.
- Names and personal character traits of commanders and staff officers.
- Plans, instructions, orders, and conversations of commanders and staff officers.
- Attitudes of commanders and staff officers toward each other, civilians, units under their command, and the general military situation.
- Routes of communications and their condition.
- Tactical doctrine of commanders.
- Command and staff organization.
- Supply routes and road conditions.
- Location of supply points and types of military and civilian vehicles carrying supplies.
- Sufficiency or lack of civilian and military supplies.
- Types, numbers, and condition of military and civilian vehicles carrying supplies.
- Location of artillery and mortar positions.
- Troop movements and assembly areas.
- Location of truck parks and motor pools.
- Organization of antitank and air defense artillery (ADA) units. Include their weapons and strength.
- Location of antitank and ADA positions.
- Names of commanders of antitank and ADA units.
- Mission of antitank and ADA.
- Types and status of ammunition.
- Voluntary or forced evacuation or movement of civilians.
- Morale and health of civilians.

PATROL LEADERS AND MEMBERS

The degree of patrol activity on the enemy's part is often a good indication of enemy plans. The following can be asked:

- Specific mission of the patrol.
- Exact routes used, and time of departure and return of patrol.
- Location of enemy forward edge of the battle area (FEBA), general outpost, combat outpost, and outposts.
- Location of platoon, company, battalion, regiment, or division headquarters.
- Routes of approach and enemy positions.
- Enemy strongholds and fields of fire.
- Machine gun and mortar positions of the enemy.
- Observation and listening posts.
- Condition of bridges and location of fords.
- Description of key terrain features.
- Location and description of defensive positions such an antitank weapons, roadblocks, mines, barbed wire entanglements, gaps in wire and safe lanes, trip flares, booby traps, tank traps, and ambushes.
- Other reconnaissance objectives, agencies, and patrols.
- Organization and equipment of tactical reconnaissance agencies in regiments and divisions.
- Passwords and countersigns of patrols and line units.
- Patrol communications system and range of radios.
- Names of commanders, staff officers, and, particularly, enemy unit intelligence officers.
- Coordination of patrol activities with other units such as rifle companies and mortar and artillery units.
- Morale and esprit de corps of civilians.
- Relocation or movement of civilians.
- Civilian supply.
- Health of civilians and availability of medicine.

MEMBERS OF MACHINE GUN AND MORTAR UNITS

Members of machine gun and mortar units can be expected to know, on the basis of their experience or observation, the following:

- Location of their own, as well as other, machine gun and mortar positions and projected alternate positions.
- Organization, strength, casualties, and weapons of the source's unit.
- Targets for machine guns and mortars.
- Names of small-unit leaders.
- Status of weapons crew training.
- Disposition of small rifle units, squads, and platoons.
- Supply of ammunition to include type of ammunition in the basic load or on hand; for example, chemical and biological ammunition.
- Location of forward ammunition points.
- Characteristics of weapons used.
- Food and other supplies.
- Morale.
- Effect of our firepower upon their positions.
- Availability of nuclear capability.
- Number of newly assigned personnel to the unit within last 30 days.

LIAISON OFFICERS

The liaison officer is the commander's agent for accomplishing coordination among the headquarters of lower, adjacent, and higher units. The liaison officer also may be called upon to effect coordination between infantry units and supporting or supported armor and artillery, engineer, and reconnaissance units.

- Contents of field orders, such as composition of attacking forces—location and direction of attack; missions of individual units; objectives; plans for attack, defense, or withdrawals; and plans for communication and coordination among units.
- Location of lower, adjacent, higher, and supporting unit CPs as well as location of supply and communications installations.
- Locations of observation posts and outposts.
- Assembly areas for troops and location of supply points.
- Disposition of regiments, battalions, and companies of a division.
- Identification and disposition of reserves.
- Status of supplies of all types.
- Civilian social and economic conditions.
- Evacuation or movement of civilians.

ARMORED TROOPS

Armored troops are good interrogation prospects concerning enemy tank tactics, communications, logistics, and based on combat experience, mines, traps, and ambushes. Topics for interrogation should cover—

- Unit identifications.
- Designation and strength of supporting or supported infantry units.
- Types and characteristics of tanks employed.
- Mechanical and tactical weaknesses of these tanks.
- Means of communications between tanks and between tanks and infantry.
- Missions and objectives.
- Routes of approach.
- Armored units in reserve.
- Location of tank parks and assembly areas.
- Location of impassable terrain features.
- Methods of mortar, artillery, and tank coordination.
- Location of tank repair depots and petroleum, oils, and lubricants (POL) dumps (to include resupply and refueling techniques).
- Effect of weather on tank operations.
- Armored reconnaissance missions.
- Number of newly assigned personnel in unit within last 30 days.
- Morale and esprit de corps of civilians.
- Relocation or movement of civilians.
- Civilian supply.
- Health of civilians and availability of medicine.
- Status of ammunition and POL resupply.
- Location of ammunition supply points.
- Ammunition supply to include type in the basic load or on hand; for example, chemical ammunition.
- Measures for defense against NBC and radiological attack, to include type of NBC defensive equipment installed in the tank.
- Night maneuvers, rehearsals, unit size, night vision devices, and special equipment.

ARTILLERYMEN

Topics to be covered when questioning captured artillerymen are broken down as follows by forward observers, artillery firing battery personnel, and air defense artillerymen.

FORWARD OBSERVERS

- Location, organization, and number of guns of the battery or battalion whose fire the source was observing and directing.
- Location of front lines, outposts, and observation posts.
- Location of alternate observation posts.
- Location and probable time of occupation of present or alternate gun positions.
- Deployment of artillery.
- Characteristics of guns, including caliber and range.
- Targets for various types of fire during different phases of combat.
- Nature of the infantry artillery communication net.
- Type and location of artillery fire requested by infantry units.
- Identification of corps or other supporting artillery units.
- Plan of attack, defense, or withdrawal of enemy units.
- Methods of coordinating artillery fire with infantry maneuver.
- Mission and objectives of source's unit as well as of supported units.
- Routes of approach and their condition. Characteristics of terrain features.
- Methods of observing and directing artillery fire, including information such as types of aircraft employed.
- Methods of counterbattery fire and protecting enemy positions from counterbattery fire.
- Use and location of dummy artillery positions.
- Types of artillery ammunition used for various targets, new types of ammunition, conservation of fires and reasons for conservation.
- Location of artillery and infantry unit CPs.
- Trafficability of routes appropriate for movement of heavy artillery.
- Names of commanders, staff officers, and their attitudes toward each other and infantry commanders.
- Number of newly assigned personnel to the unit within last 30 days.
- Effect of our artillery upon enemy units.
- Location and numbering of defensive concentrations.
- Location of ammunition supply points.
- Radio channels used for fire control nets.
- Identification and location of supporting battalions.
- Availability of nuclear fire support.
- Morale and esprit de corps of civilians.
- Relocation or movement of civilians.
- Civilian supply.
- Health of civilians and availability of medicine.

ARTILLERY FIRING BATTERY PERSONNEL

- Measures of defense against friendly artillery fire.
- Counterbattery protection for artillery installations.
- Effect of friendly counterbattery fire.
- Location of battery ammunition points.
- Disposition of local security weapons.
- Direction and elevation of fire.
- Instructions concerning ammunition use.
- Names of battery and other commanders.
- Detailed description of artillery weapons used.
- Status of weapons crew training.
- Information on food supplies and morale of military and civilians.

- Measures for defense against NBC attack.
- Types and amount of ammunition, to include chemical and nuclear, in basic load or on hand.
- Location of chemical and biological ammunition.
- Location targets marked for chemical and biological fires.

AIR DEFENSE ARTILLERYMEN

- Location and number of air defense weapons.
- Detailed description and characteristics of air defense guns and missiles used.
- Shape, size, and location of ground radars.
- Organization of air defense units.
- Types of areas defended.
- Nuclear capability.
- Methods of attack against friendly aircraft, by type of aircraft.
- Avenues of approach and altitudes most and least advantageous to enemy air defense.
- Methods of identifying unknown aircraft.

MEDICAL CORPSMEN

Although medical personnel are entitled to special protective measures under international agreements, they can be and are interrogated without infringement of any existing laws or rules of warfare. The following questions could be asked:

- Number of casualties over a given phase of combat operations.
- Weapons accounting for most casualties.
- Key personnel who have been casualties.
- Conditions of health and sanitation in enemy units.
- Ratio of dead to wounded.
- Commander's tactics in relation to number of casualties.
- Adequacy and efficiency of casualty evacuation.
- Weapons most feared by the enemy.
- Location and staffing of aid stations and hospitals.
- Organization of division, regiment, and battalion medical units.
- Status and types of medical supplies.
- Use and characteristics of newly developed medicine or drugs.
- Data on wounded, sick, or dead in enemy hands.
- Skill of enemy medical personnel.
- Information on mass sickness or epidemics in the enemy forces.
- Types of treatment and medication for NBC casualties.
- Supply and availability of materials used in treatment of NBC casualties.
- Special training or treatment of NBC casualties.
- New or recent immunizations.
- Morale and esprit de corps of civilians.
- Relocation or movement of civilians.
- Civilian supply.
- Health of civilians and availability of medicine.
- Location and present condition of civilian hospitals, factories producing medical supplies, and warehouse and stores containing medical supplies.

ENGINEER TROOPS

Engineer personnel are prime interrogation candidates for information concerning bridges, fortifications, minefields, and coordination between infantry and supported units. Topics to be covered are—

- Mission of supported unit.
- Exact location and pattern of existing minefields, location of bridges, buildings, airfields, and other installations prepared for demolition, and types of mines or explosives used.
- Doctrine pertaining to the use of mines and booby traps to include types of mines, characteristics of firing devices, and minefields' patterns.
- Location of roadblocks and tank traps and how they are constructed.
- Conditions of roads, bridges, and streams or rivers for trafficability of personnel, vehicles, and armor; weight-carrying capacity of bridges and location and description of fords.
- Location of engineer materials and equipment such as road material, bridge timber, lumber, steel, explosives, quarries, rock crushers, sawmills, and machine shops.
- Location of dummy vehicles and tank and gun positions.
- Location of camouflaged positions and installations.
- Water supply and locations of water points.
- Organization, strength, and weapons of engineer units.
- Presence of other than organic engineer units at the front, and mission of such units.
- Number of trucks, tractors, and other engineer vehicles available.
- Location of new or repaired bridges.
- Use of demolitions.
- Morale and esprit de corps of civilians.
- Relocation or movement of civilians.
- Civilian supply.
- Health of civilians and availability of medicine.
- Location and present conditions of civilian power plants, water works, and sewage disposal plants.
- Night maneuvers, rehearsals, unit size, night vision devices, and special equipment.

RECONNAISSANCE TROOPS

Reconnaissance personnel and degree of activity are good indicators on enemy intentions. Topics for questioning are—

- The reconnaissance plan, march order, time schedule, and specific missions of all elements, means of coordination and communication between elements, and unit and higher headquarters.
- Nature of orders received from higher headquarters.
- Identification, organization, composition, strength, means of transportation, and weapons of the unit.
- Routes of approach used by the unit.
- Identification, composition, organization, strength, and disposition of the main body of troops and reinforcements. Routes to be used.
- General quality of troops of the reconnaissance unit and of the main body.
- Radio communication equipment and frequencies used.
- Night maneuvers, rehearsals, unit size, night vision devices, and special equipment.

LOCAL CIVILIANS

Civilians who recently left enemy-held areas normally have important information, and often give this information readily.

This information is usually important to CA and PSYOP personnel. The following questions could be asked:

- Location of enemy front lines and major defensive positions.
- Location of artillery positions.
- Location and nature of minefields in enemy rear area.
- Description of key terrain.
- Condition of roads, bridges, and major buildings.
- Enemy policy and attitude toward local civilians.
- Human and material resources of the area.
- Morale and esprit de corps of local civilians.
- Data on important civilian personalities remaining in enemy areas.
- Health and medical status of local populace.
- Effect of friendly operations on civilian populace.
- Instructions to prepare for defensive measures against NBC attack.
- Recent immunizations.

POLITICAL AND PROPAGANDA PERSONNEL

Personnel recently acquired through combat operations and identified as involved with political and PSYOP should be questioned as follows:

- Policy, plans, and objectives.
- Organization and training.
- Current and past activities, to include themes of any propaganda programs.
- Enemy analysis of our weaknesses and strengths.
- Target audiences for propaganda, including priorities.
- Effects of our PSYOP.
- Analysis of enemy weaknesses and strengths.
- Enemy counterpropaganda activities.

GUERRILLA PERSONNEL

Guerrilla personnel, depending on assignment, can be expected to have information concerning activities, strength, equipment, leadership, and local influence or support. Topics to be covered are—

- Area of activities.
- Nature of activities.
- Strength.
- Equipment.
- Motivation.
- Leadership.
- Reliability.
- Contacts.
- External direction or support.

NBC OPERATIONS

The following topics are of interest when interrogating personnel about NBC operations:

- What items of NBC protective equipment have been issued to troops? Is there any differentiation in issue of items for particular areas? If so, what items for what areas?
- Are there any new or recent immunizations indicated by sources during interrogations?
- What immunizations have troop units received, as indicated in captured immunization records?
- Are troops equipped with protective masks? Is the individual required to carry the mask on his person? Are there any sectors where

the mask is not required equipment for the individual? What accessory equipment is issued with the mask?

- Is protective equipment issued to troops? If so, what type of clothing or articles? If special clothing is used, is it for any particular geographic area?
- Have troop units constructed NBC protective shelters? If so, what type?
- Are fortifications, individual and collective, provided with overhead cover?
- Are troops issued any protective footwear or other means to provide protection against penetration by liquid agents?
- Are tanks and armored vehicles provided with specially installed protective equipment to protect the crew in case of chemical attack?
- Are troops issued any type of individual protective items for first aid, such as antidotes or protective ointment?
- Are there any areas for which additional or unusual NBC safety precautions have been established?
- What is the size and composition of NBC specialist troop units? Where are they located? Why?
- Have troops been issued any special precautionary instructions concerning consumption of food and water or handling of livestock in areas that may be overrun by enemy forces?
- What training, if any, have troops received in the use of incapacitating-type agents and their dissemination?
- What items of chemical detection equipment have been issued to troops? Are the items operated continuously, irregularly, or not at all? Is there any differentiation made regarding their use in certain areas?
- What type radiation-measuring instruments are issued to troop units and what is their range or limit? How are they distributed?
- How many hours of training with radiation-measuring instruments have monitoring and survey personnel received?
- How many hours of NBC training have troops received? How many hours of individual training are devoted to chemical, biological, and radiological operations? Have troops received any special or accelerated training above what is considered routine?
- Do units have decontamination materials on hand? If so, what type and quantity?
- Have you observed decontamination stations or installations established in your area? If so, what are their location and composition?
- Are troop units issued biological sampling kits or devices? If so, what is their type and composition?
- Have you observed any cylinders or containers which might contain bulk chemical agents?
- Have you observed any tactical aircraft equipped with accessory tanks which indicated a spray capability?
- Are you aware of location of dumps of chemical-filled ammunition, bombs, clusters, and bulk chemical agents?
- Do artillery, mortar, or rocket units have chemical ammunition on hand?
- At what radiological exposure or dose are troops required to relocate?
- Are there any problem areas or shortcomings in NBC material?

Note: The following are applicable or internal defense operations in appropriate theaters of operations.

- What types of tunnels, caves, and modifications are used in defense against riot control agents and explosive gases?
- What defensive material and instructions are issued for defense against riot control agents?
- What defensive measures are taken against defoliation and anticrop agents?

OVERALL OBJECTIVE STATEMENT

Figure B-1 shows a sample overall objective statement for an interrogation element in division GS. It is not all inclusive. PIR and IR shown are not comprehensive and are used as subheadings with intelligence indicators grouped under each. Figure B-2 contains an overall objective statement that includes the six IEW tasks.

PRIORITY INTELLIGENCE REQUIREMENTS

I. NBC WEAPONS.

1. Are NBC weapons present in any of the brigade sectors?
2. When will these NBC weapons be used?
3. Where will these NBC weapons be used?
4. How many of these NBC weapons will be used against each target?
5. What systems will deliver these NBC weapons?

II. ENEMY ATTACK.

1. When will the enemy attack?
2. Where will the enemy attack?
3. What is the attack's main objective?
4. What units will conduct the attack?
5. What is the combat effectiveness of attack units?
6. What artillery groups, regimental or divisional, will support the attack?
7. Where are these artillery groups located?

III. ENEMY DEFENSE.

1. Where will the enemy establish lines of defense?
2. What enemy units have been assigned to each defensive belt?
3. What is the combat effectiveness of the units assigned to each defensive belt?
4. What types of antitank weapons have been assigned to each defensive belt?
5. What obstacles have been emplaced in each defensive belt?
6. What minefields have been emplaced in each defensive belt?
7. What enemy units comprise the reaction force to counter friendly armor or heliborne assaults?
8. What types of artillery are assigned to support the defense?
9. Where is this artillery located?

IV. ENEMY RETREAT.

1. What units will take part in the retreat?
2. What are the current positions of the retreating units?
3. When will each of the retreating units begin its movement?
4. What routes will be taken by the retreating units?
5. What units have been designated the rear guard for the retreat?
6. What units have been designated the covering force for the retreat?

Figure B-1. Sample overall objective statement.

7. Where will each of the retreating units establish new positions?
8. What types of artillery have been assigned to support the retreat?
9. What deception efforts will be made to conceal the retreat?

V. ENEMY REINFORCEMENT.

1. What units comprise the enemy's second echelon?
2. What is the combat effectiveness of the units in the enemy's second echelon?
3. What is the direction of travel for each unit in the enemy's second echelon?
4. How soon will units in the enemy's second echelon begin to enter each brigade's AO?
5. What units within the enemy's fist echelon will receive reinforcements of personnel or equipment?
6. To what extent will these units be reinforced?
7. How soon will these reinforcements arrive?
8. By what routes will these reinforcements arrive?

INFORMATION REQUIREMENTS

I. SUPPLY POINTS.

1. What types of ammunition is the enemy stockpiling?
2. What are the types of POL the enemy is stockpiling?
3. Where are these supply points located?
4. What units are serviced by these supply points?
5. How much materiél is currently stockpiled at these locations?

II. VULNERABILITIES.

1. What malfunctions are occurring with the enemy's—
   a. Weapons?
   b. Vehicles?
   c. Communications?
   d. Ammunition?
2. What are the enemy's major supply routes?
3. How often are supplies transported over these routes?
4. What transportation priority has the enemy assigned to each category of supplies?
5. What choke points has the enemy identified along his own lines of communications?

Figure B-1. Sample overall objective statement (continued).

I. SITUATION DEVELOPMENT.

1. Are NBC weapons present in any of the brigade sectors?
    a. Have any tracked, self-propelled rocket launchers been sighted within any of the brigade sectors?
    b. Have any small convoys been sighted traveling under unusually heavy security within any of the brigade sectors?
    c. Have light aircraft been sighted circling over convoys moving in any of the brigade sectors?
    d. Have any noncommunications emitters normally associated with NBC weapons been identified in any brigade sector?
    e. Have any installations with unusually heavy security been identified within any of the brigade sectors?
    f. Have any tall, slender objects (such as towers, chimneys, or narrow trees) suddenly appeared in any of the brigade sectors?
2. When will these NBC weapons be used?
    a. Have contingency orders been received by any enemy units in any of the brigade sectors which indicate circumstances under which NBC weapons will be used?
    b. Have code words been disseminated to alert troops that NBC weapons will be used in any of the brigade sectors?
    c. What procedures are to be followed by enemy troops in any brigade sector immediately following receipt of alert codes?
    d. Have any front-line enemy troops in any brigade sector inexplicably slowed or halted their advance?
    e. Has any very heavy artillery been moved to within supporting distance of front-line enemy troops within any brigade sector?
    f. Has random firing of very heavy artillery occurred within any of the brigade sectors?
3. Where will these NBC weapons be used?
    a. Have all known enemy agents suddenly disappeared from any areas within any of the brigade sectors?
    b. Has enemy air activity suddenly increased in any areas within any of the brigade sectors?
    c. Is unusual enemy air activity taking place in any areas within any of the brigade sectors?
    d. Is smoke being used or planned for use as cover for any front-line enemy troops in any of the brigade sectors.

Figure B-2. Sample overall objective statement (IEW tasks).

e. Have specific areas within any brigade sector been identified as targets for NBC weapons?

f. Have orders been received by any enemy units in any brigade sector which indicate that NBC weapons might be used in support of their activities?

4. How many of these NBC weapons will be used against each target?

a. How many very heavy artillery dispositions have been identified within each brigade sector?

b. How many noncommunications emitters associated with NBC weapons have been identified within each brigade sector?

c. How many transporter-erector-launchers (TELs) have been sighted within each brigade sector?

d. How many enemy units within each brigade sector have been notified that NBC weapons might be used to support them?

e. How many front-line enemy units within each brigade sector have inexplicably slowed or stopped their advance?

5. What types of systems will be used to deliver these NBC weapons?

a. What calibers of very heavy artillery have been identified within each of the brigade sectors?

b. What types of TELs have been identified within each brigade sector?

c. What types of chemical agents have been identified within each brigade sector?

d. What types of biological agents have been identified within each brigade sector?

e. What types of noncommunications emitters have been identified within each brigade sector?

6. When will the enemy attack?

a. Have any enemy units in any of the brigade sectors received orders to conduct assault operations?

b. Is the enemy massing mechanized infantry units in any of the brigade sectors?

c. Is the enemy massing armor units in any of the brigade sectors?

d. Is the enemy massing artillery units in any of the brigade sectors?

e. Are front-line enemy troops disposed along relatively narrow fronts in any areas within any of the brigade sectors?

f. What rumors indicating future offensive operations are circulating within enemy units in each brigade sector?

7. Where will the enemy attack?

a. What avenues of approach will be used by specific enemy units within each brigade sector?

Figure B-2. Sample overall objective statement (IEW tasks) (continued).

   b. How many enemy units will use each avenue of approach within each brigade sector?
   c. Where are the enemy's large concentrations of mechanized infantry units within each brigade sector?
   d. Where are the enemy's large concentrations of armor units within each brigade sector?
   e. Where are the enemy's large concentrations of artillery units within each brigade sector?

8. What is the attack's main objective?
   a. What objectives have been assigned to specific enemy units in each brigade sector for their offensive operations?
   b. How many objectives have been assigned to specific enemy units in each brigade sector for their offensive operations?
   c. How many enemy units within each brigade sector have been assigned the same objectives?
9. What units have been assigned to conduct the attack?
   a. What enemy units in any of the brigade sectors have received orders to conduct assault operations?
   b. What enemy units are rumored to be preparing to conduct offensive operations within any of the brigade sectors?
   c. What enemy units have been assigned to use specific avenues of approach within each brigade sector?
   d. What specific enemy units have been assigned the same objectives within each brigade sector?
10. What is the combat effectiveness of the units assigned to conduct the attack?
   a. How many personnel are currently fit for duty within the specific enemy units assigned to conduct offensive operations in any of the brigade sectors?
   b. How many vehicles are currently operational within the specific enemy units assigned to conduct offensive operations in any of the brigade sectors?
   c. How many weapon systems are currently operational within the specific enemy units assigned to conduct offensive operations in any of the brigade sectors?
   d. What is the morale of the personnel assigned to the specific enemy units assigned to conduct offensive operations in any of the brigade sectors?
11. What artillery groups, regimental or divisional, have been assigned to support the attack?
   a. What artillery units have been ordered to support the enemy regiments or divisions assigned to conduct offensive operations in each of the brigade sectors?

Figure B-2. Sample overall objective statement (IEW tasks) (continued).

   b. What artillery assets have been identified within supporting distance of the enemy regiments or divisions assigned to conduct offensive operations?
   c. What types of noncommunications emitters associated with regimental or divisional artillery groups have been identified within each of the brigade sectors?

12. Where will the enemy establish lines of defense?
    a. Where are enemy units preparing extensive field fortifications within each brigade sector?
    b. Where are enemy units establishing antitank strong points within each brigade sector?
    c. To which front-line enemy units within each brigade sector are antitank units being attached?
    d. Where are alternate artillery positions being prepared within each brigade sector?
    e. Where are obstacles being emplaced within each brigade sector?
    f. Where are mines being emplaced within each brigade sector?
13. What enemy units have been assigned to each defensive belt?
    a. What specific enemy units are preparing extensive field fortifications within each brigade sector?
    b. What specific enemy units are establishing antitank strong points within each brigade sector?
    c. What specific enemy units within each brigade sector are receiving attached antitank units?
    d. What specific enemy units within each brigade sector are preparing alternate artillery positions?
    e. What specific enemy units are emplacing obstacles within each brigade sector?
    f. What specific enemy units are emplacing mines within each brigade sector?
14. What is the combat effectiveness of the units assigned to each defensive belt?
    a. How many personnel are currently fit for duty within the specific enemy units assigned to the defensive belts in each brigade sector?
    b. How many vehicles are currently operational within the specific enemy units assigned to the defensive belts in each brigade sector?
    c. How many weapons systems are currently operational within the specific enemy units assigned to the defensive belts in each brigade sector?
    d. What is the morale of the personnel assigned to the specific enemy units assigned to the defensive belts in each brigade sector?

Figure B-2. Sample overall objective statement (IEW tasks) (continued).

15. What types of antitank weapons have been assigned to each defensive belt?
    a. What types of antitank weapons are possessed by the specific enemy units assigned to the defensive belts in each brigade sector?
    b. What types of antitank units have been attached to specific enemy units assigned to the defensive belts in each brigade sector?
16. What obstacles have been emplaced in each defensive belt?
    a. What natural obstacles have been incorporated into the defensive belts in each brigade sector?
    b. What manmade antipersonnel obstacles have been emplaced by the specific enemy units assigned to the defensive belts within each brigade sector?
    c. What manmade anti-vehicular obstacles have been emplaced by the specific enemy units assigned to the defensive belts within each brigade sector?
17. What minefields have been emplaced in each defensive belt?
    a. What types of antipersonnel mines are being emplaced by the specific enemy units assigned to the defensive belts in each brigade sector?
    b. What types of antitank mines are being emplaced by the specific enemy units assigned to the defensive belts in each brigade sector?
18. What units comprise the reaction force to counter friendly armor or heliborne assaults?
    a. What enemy units have received orders to act as the reaction force for defensive positions in each brigade sector?
    b. What enemy units are rumored to be the reaction force for defensive positions in each brigade sector?
    c. What enemy units are located behind, but in proximity to, the defensive positions in each brigade sector?
19. What types of artillery are assigned to support the defense?
    a. What enemy artillery units have received orders to support the defensive positions in each brigade sector?
    b. What enemy artillery units are rumored to be supporting the defensive positions in each brigade sector?
    c. What types of artillery have been identified within each brigade sector?
20. Where is the artillery located?
    a. What is the current location of the enemy artillery units ordered to support the defensive positions in each brigade sector?

Figure B-2. Sample overall objective statement (IEW tasks) (continued).

   b. What is the current location of the enemy artillery units rumored to be supporting the defensive positions in each brigade sector?
   c. What is the current location of all artillery identified within each brigade sector?

21. What units will take part in the retreat?
    a. What enemy units in each brigade sector have received orders to participate in a retreat?
    b. What enemy units in each brigade sector are rumored to be participating in a retreat?
    c. What enemy units within each brigade sector are disposed along an extended front?
    d. What enemy units in each brigade sector have been notified their artillery support is moving to the rear?
    e. What enemy units in each brigade sector have been notified their logistical support is moving to the rear?
22. What are the current positions of the retreating units?
    a. What is the current location of enemy units in each brigade sector ordered to participate in a retreat?
    b. What is the current location of enemy units in each brigade sector rumored to be participating in a retreat?
    c. What is the current location of enemy units within each brigade sector disposed along an extended front?
    d. What is the current location of artillery units supporting enemy units in each brigade sector?
    c. What is the current location of logistical units supporting enemy units in each brigade sector?
23. When will each of the retreating units begin its movement?
    a. At what time have specific enemy units in each brigade sector been ordered to begin their retreat?
    b. What start times are being mentioned in rumors about the retreat of specific enemy units in each brigade sector?
24. What routes will be taken by the retreating units?
    a. What movement routes have been assigned for the retreat of specific enemy units in each brigade sector?
    b. What movement routes are being cited in rumors about the retreat of specific enemy units in each brigade sector?

Figure B-2. Sample overall objective statement (IEW tasks) (continued).

c. What movement routes are being used or planned for use during the retreat of enemy artillery units in each brigade sector?

d. What movement routes are being used or planned for use during the retreat of enemy logistical units in each brigade sector?

25. What units have been designated the rear guard for the retreat?

a. What specific enemy units have been ordered to act as rear guard for the retreat in each brigade sector?

b. What specific enemy units are rumored to be rear guard for the retreat in each brigade sector?

26. What units have been designated the covering force for the retreat?

a. What specific enemy units have been ordered to act as covering force for the retreat in each brigade sector?

b. What specific enemy units are rumored to be covering force for the retreat in each brigade sector?

27. Where will each of the retreating units establish new positions?

a. Where are the new positions assigned to retreating enemy units in each brigade sector?

b. What are the new positions being cited in rumors about the retreat of enemy units in each brigade sector?

c. Where are the new positions assigned to retreating enemy artillery units in each brigade sector?

d. Where are the new positions assigned to retreating enemy logistical units in each brigade sector?

28. What types of artillery have been assigned to support the retreat?

a. What specific enemy artillery units have been assigned to support the retreat in each brigade sector?

b. What specific enemy artillery units are rumored to be supporting the retreat in each brigade sector?

29. What deception efforts will be made to conceal the retreat?

a. What deception efforts have been ordered in conjunction with the retreat in each brigade sector?

b. What specific enemy units are conducting deception efforts in conjunction with the retreat in each brigade sector?

c. What deception efforts are being cited in rumors about the retreat in each brigade sector?

d. What enemy units are rumored to be conducting deception efforts in conjunction with the retreat in each brigade sector?

Figure B-2. Sample overall objective statement (IEW tasks) (continued).

30. What units comprise the enemy's second echelon?
    a. What specific units are known to be part of the enemy's second echelon in each brigade sector?
    b. What specific units are rumored to be part of the enemy's second echelon in each brigade sector?
    c. How many units comprise the enemy's second echelon in each brigade sector?
    d. What type of units comprise the enemy's second echelon in each brigade sector?
31. What is the combat effectiveness of the units in the enemy's second echelon?
    a. How many personnel are currently fit for duty within the specific enemy units comprising the second echelon in each brigade sector?
    b. How many vehicles are currently operational within the specific enemy units comprising the second echelon in each brigade sector?
    c. How many weapons systems are currently operational within the specific enemy units comprising the second echelon in each brigade sector?
    d. What is the morale of the personnel assigned to the specific enemy units comprising the second echelon in each brigade sector?
32. What is the direction of travel for each unit in the enemy's second echelon?
    a. What is the known direction of travel for units comprising the enemy's second echelon in each brigade sector?
    b. What are the known movement routes for units comprising the enemy's second echelon in each brigade sector?
    c. What is the rumored direction of travel for units comprising the enemy's second echelon in each brigade sector?
    d. What are the rumored movement routes for units comprising the enemy's second echelon in each brigade sector?
33. How soon will units in the enemy's second echelon begin to enter each brigade's AO?
    a. What is the current known location of units comprising the enemy's second echelon in each brigade sector?
    b. What is the current rumored location of units comprising the enemy's second echelon in each brigade sector?
    c. What is the known rate of travel for units comprising the enemy's second echelon in each brigade sector?
    d. What is the rumored rate of travel for units comprising the enemy's second echelon in each brigade sector?

Figure B-2. Sample overall objective statement (IEW tasks) (continued).

34. What units within the enemy's first echelon will receive reinforcements of personnel or equipment?
    a. What personnel or equipment replacements have been ordered for specific front-line enemy units in each brigade sector?
    b. What specific front-line enemy units in each brigade sector are rumored to be receiving personnel or equipment replacements?
35. To what extent will these units be reinforced?
    a. How many personnel replacements have been ordered for specific enemy units in each brigade sector?
    b. How many personnel are cited in the rumors concerning replacements for specific enemy units in each brigade sector?
    c. How much lost equipment has been ordered replaced in specific enemy units in each brigade sector?
    d. How much equipment is cited in the rumors concerning replacements for specific enemy units in each brigade sector?
36. How soon will these reinforcements arrive?
    a. At what time will scheduled personnel replacements arrive at specific enemy units in each brigade sector?
    b. At what time will scheduled equipment replacements arrive at specific enemy units in each brigade sector?
    c. What time is cited in rumors concerning personnel replacements for specific enemy units in each brigade sector?
    d. What time is cited in rumors concerning equipment replacements for specific enemy units in each brigade sector?
37. By what routes will these reinforcements arrive?
    a. What is the current known location of personnel and equipment replacements for specific enemy units in each brigade sector?
    b. What is the current rumored location of personnel and equipment replacements for specific enemy units in each brigade sector?
    c. What are the known movement routes of personnel and equipment replacements for specific enemy units in each brigade sector?
    d. What are the rumored movement routes for personnel and equipment replacements for specific enemy units in each brigade sector?
38. What type of ammunition is the enemy stockpiling?
    a. What type of small arms ammunition is the enemy stockpiling in each brigade sector?

Figure B-2. Sample overall objective statement (IEW tasks) (continued).

b. What type of ammunition is the enemy stockpiling for crew-served weapons in each brigade sector?
c. What type of ammunition is the enemy stockpiling for armored vehicles in each brigade sector?
d. What type of artillery ammunition is the enemy stockpiling in each brigade sector?

39. What type of POL is the enemy stockpiling?
    a. What type of fuel is the enemy stockpiling in each brigade sector?
    b. What type of oil is the enemy stockpiling in each brigade sector?
    c. What type of lubricants is the enemy stockpiling in each brigade sector?
40. Where are these supply points located?
    a. Where are the enemy's ammunition supply points located in each brigade sector?
    b. Where are the enemy's POL supply points located in each brigade sector?
41. What units are serviced by these supply points.
    a. What ammunition supply points support specific enemy units in each brigade sector?
    b. What POL supply points support specific enemy units in each brigade sector?
42. How much material is currently stockpiled at these locations?
    a. How much ammunition is stockpiled at specific supply points in each brigade sector?
    b. How much POL are stockpiled at specific supply points in each brigade sector?
43. What malfunctions are occurring with the enemy's weapons?
    a. What malfunctions are occurring with the enemy's small arms in each brigade sector?
    b. What malfunctions are occurring with the enemy's crew-served weapons in each brigade sector?
    c. What malfunctions are occurring with the enemy's artillery in each brigade sector?
44. What malfunctions are occurring with the enemy's vehicles?
    a. What malfunctions are occurring with the enemy's tracked vehicles in each brigade sector?
    b. What malfunctions are occurring with the enemy's wheeled vehicles in each brigade sector?

Figure B-2. Sample overall objective statement (IEW tasks) (continued).

45. What malfunctions are occurring with enemy communications?
    a. What malfunctions are occurring with enemy vehicle-mounted communications equipment in each brigade sector?
    b. What malfunctions are occurring with enemy manpacked communications equipment in each brigade sector?
    c. What malfunctions are occurring with enemy pyrotechnic means of communication in each brigade sector?
46. What malfunctions are occurring with enemy ammunition?
    a. What malfunctions are occurring with enemy small arms ammunition in each brigade sector?
    b. What malfunctions are occurring with enemy artillery ammunition in each brigade sector?
    c. What malfunctions are occurring with enemy ammunition for armored vehicles in each brigade sector?
    d. What malfunctions are occurring with enemy ammunition for crew-served weapons in each brigade sector?
47. What are enemy main supply routes?
    a. What are the known movement routes used by enemy supply convoys in each brigade sector?
    b. What movement routes are rumored to be used by enemy supply convoys in each of the brigade sectors?
    c. What is the known direction of travel for enemy supply convoys passing named areas of interest (NAIs) in each brigade sector?
    d. What direction of travel is rumored for enemy supply convoys passing NAIs in each brigade sector?
48. How often are supplies transported over these routes?
    a. How often are specific enemy units in each brigade sector resupplied?
    b. How often are enemy supply convoys sighted along established movement routes in each brigade sector?
49. What transportation priority has the enemy assigned to each category of supplies?
    a. What is the enemy's known transportation priority for each category of supplies in each brigade sector?
    b. What is rumored to be the enemy's transportation priority for each category of supplies in each brigade sector?

Figure B-2. Sample overall objective statement (IEW tasks) (continued).

c. What is the frequency with which specific enemy units in each brigade sector receive each category of supplies?

50. What choke points has the enemy identified along his own LOCs?
  a. What choke points are known to exist along the enemy's LOCs in each brigade sector?
  b. What choke points are rumored to exist along the enemy's LOCs in each brigade sector?

II. TARGET DEVELOPMENT AND ACQUISITION.

1. Are NBC weapons present in any of the brigade sectors?
  a. Where have tracked, self-propelled rocket launchers been sighted within any of the brigade sectors?
  b. What was the direction of travel of any small convoys sighted traveling under unusually heavy security in any of the brigade sectors?
  c. Where have light aircraft been sighted circling over convoys moving in any of the brigade sectors?
  d. Where have noncommunications emitters normally associated with NBC weapons been identified in any brigade sectors?
  e. Where have installations with unusually heavy security been identified within any of the brigade sectors?
  f. Where have tall, slender objects (such as towers, chimneys, or narrow trees) suddenly appeared in any of the brigade sectors?
2. Where will these NBC weapons be used?
  a. Where has enemy air activity suddenly increased within any of the brigade sectors?
  b. Where is unusual enemy air activity taking place within any of the brigade sectors?
  c. Where is smoke being used or planned for use as cover for any front-line enemy troops in any of the brigade sectors?
  d. Where has very heavy artillery been moved to within supporting distance of front-line enemy troops within any brigade sector?
  e. Where has random firing of very heavy artillery occurred within any of the brigade sectors?
3. Where will the enemy attack?
  a. Where are the enemy's large concentrations of mechanized infantry units within each brigade sector?

Figure B-2. Sample overall objective statement (IEW tasks) (continued).

  b. Where are the enemy's large concentrations of armor units within each brigade sector?
  c. Where are the enemy's large concentrations of artillery units within each brigade sector?

4. What artillery groups, regimental or divisional, have been assigned to support the attack?
  a. What artillery units have been ordered to support the enemy regiments or divisions assigned to conduct offensive operations in each of the brigade sectors?
  b. How many artillery dispositions have been identified within supporting distance of the enemy regiments or divisions assigned to conduct offensive operations?
5. Where will the enemy establish lines of defense?
  a. Where are enemy units preparing extensive field fortifications within each brigade sector?
  b. Where are enemy units establishing antitank strong points within each brigade sector?
  c. Where are alternate artillery positions being prepared within each brigade sector?
  d. Where are obstacles being emplaced within each brigade sector?
  e. Where are mines being emplaced within each brigade sector?
6. What units comprise the reaction force to counter friendly armor or heliborne assaults?
  a. What is the location of the enemy units ordered to act as the reaction force for defensive positions in each brigade sector?
  b. What is the location of the enemy units rumored to be the reaction force for defensive positions in each brigade sector?
7. What is the location of artillery units assigned to support the enemy's defense?
  a. What is the current location of the enemy artillery units ordered to support the defensive positions in each brigade sector?
  b. What is the current location of the enemy artillery units rumored to be supporting the defensive positions in each brigade sector?
8. What are the current positions of retreating enemy units?
  a. What is the current location of enemy units in each brigade sector that have been ordered to participate in a retreat?
  b. What is the current location of enemy units in each brigade sector that are rumored to be participating in a retreat?

Figure B-2. Sample overall objective statement (IEW tasks) (continued).

c. What is the current location of enemy units within each brigade sector disposed along an extended front?

d. What is the current location of artillery units supporting enemy units in each brigade sector?

e. What is the current location of logistical units supporting enemy units in each brigade sector?

9. What routes will be taken by retreating enemy units?

   a. What movement routes have been assigned for the retreat of specific enemy units in each brigade sector?

   b. What movement routes are being cited in rumors about the retreat of specific enemy units in each brigade sector?

   c. What movement routes are being used or planned for use during the retreat of enemy—

      (1) Artillery units in each brigade sector?

      (2) Logistical units in each brigade sector?

10. Where will each retreating enemy unit establish its new position?

    a. Where are the new positions assigned to retreating enemy units in each brigade sector?

    b. What are the new positions being cited in rumors about the retreat of enemy units in each brigade sector?

    c. Where are the new positions assigned to retreating enemy artillery units in each brigade sector?

    d. Where are the new positions assigned to retreating enemy logistical units in each brigade sector?

11. How soon will units in the enemy's second echelon begin to enter each brigade's AO?

    a. What is the current known location of units comprising the enemy's second echelon in each brigade sector?

    b. What is the current rumored location of units comprising the enemy's second echelon in each brigade sector?

    c. What is the known rate of travel for units comprising the enemy's second echelon in each brigade sector?

    d. What is the rumored rate of travel for units comprising the enemy's second echelon in each brigade sector?

12. By what routes will enemy reinforcements arrive?

    a. What is the current known location of personnel and equipment replacements for specific enemy units in each brigade sector?

Figure B-2. Sample overall objective statement (IEW tasks) (continued).

b. What is the current rumored location of personnel and equipment replacements for specific enemy units in each brigade sector?

c. What are the known movement routes of personnel and equipment replacements for specific enemy units in each brigade sector?

d. What are the rumored movement routes of personnel and equipment replacements for specific enemy units in each brigade sector?

13. Where are the enemy's supply points located?

a. Where are the enemy's ammunition supply points located in each brigade sector?

b. Where are the enemy's POL supply points located in each brigade sector?

14. What are the enemy's main supply routes?

a. What are the known movement routes used by enemy supply convoys in each brigade sector?

b. What movement routes are rumored to be used by enemy supply convoys in each of the brigade sectors?

c. What is the known direction of travel for enemy supply convoys passing NAIs in each brigade sector?

d. What direction of travel is rumored for enemy supply convoys passing NAIs in each brigade sector?

15. What choke points has the enemy identified along his own LOCs?

a. Where are choke points along the enemy's LOCs in each brigade sector known to exist?

b. Where are choke points rumored to exist along the enemy's LOCs in each brigade sector?

III. INTELLIGENCE PREPARATION OF THE BATTLEFIELD.

1. Are NBC weapons present in any of the brigade sectors?

a. Have any noncommunications emitters normally associated with NBC weapons been identified in any brigade sector?

b. What is the circular area in each brigade sector within which these noncommunications emitters are probably located?

c. What is the nomenclature or operating frequency of the noncommuncations emitters identified in each brigade sector?

2. Where will these NBC weapons be used?

a. Have specific areas within any brigade sector been identified as targets for NBC weapons?

Figure B-2. Sample overall objective statement (IEW tasks) (continued).

b. Have orders been received by any enemy units in any brigade sector which indicate NBC weapons might be used in support of their activities?

3. What types of systems will be used to deliver these NBC weapons?
   a. What noncommunications emitters associated with very heavy artillery have been identified within each brigade sector?
   b. What noncommunications emitters associated with TELs have been identified in each brigade sector?
   c. What is the nomenclature or operating frequency of any noncommunications emitters identified in each brigade sector?
4. When will the enemy attack?
   a. What rumors indicating future offensive operations are circulating within enemy units in each brigade sector?
   b. Is the enemy massing mechanized infantry units in any of the brigade sectors?
   c. Is the enemy massing armor units in any of the brigade sectors?
   d. Is the enemy massing artillery units in any of the brigade sectors?
   e. What is the nomenclature or operating frequency of any electronic emitters belonging to enemy units preparing to conduct offensive operations in each brigade sector?
5. Where will the enemy attack?
   a. What avenues of approach will be used by specific enemy units within each brigade sector?
   b. Where are the enemy's large concentrations of mechanized infantry units within each brigade sector?
   c. Where are the enemy's large concentrations of armor units within each brigade sector?
   d. Where are the enemy's large concentrations of artillery units within each brigade sector?
   e. What is the nomenclature or operating frequency of any electronic emitters belonging to enemy units preparing to conduct offensive operations in each brigade sector?
6. What units have been assigned to conduct the attack?
   a. What enemy units are rumored to be preparing for offensive operations within any of the brigade sectors?
   b. What enemy units have been assigned to use specific avenues of approach within each brigade sector?

Figure B-2. Sample overall objective statement (IEW tasks) (continued).

   c. What is the nomenclature or operating frequency of any electronic emitters belonging to enemy units preparing to conduct offensive operations in each brigade sector?

7. What artillery groups, regimental or divisional, have been assigned to support the attack?
   a. What artillery units have been ordered to support the enemy regiments or divisions assigned to conduct offensive operations in each of the brigade sectors?
   b. What is the nomenclature or operating frequency of noncommunications emitters belonging to the regimental or divisional artillery groups identified within each of the brigade sectors?
   c. What is the nomenclature or operating frequency of communications emitters belonging to the regimental or divisional artillery groups identified within each of the brigade sectors?
8. Where will the enemy establish lines of defense?
   a. Where are enemy units preparing extensive field fortifications within each brigade sector?
   b. Where are alternate artillery positions being prepared within each brigade sector?
9. What enemy units have been assigned to each defensive belt?
   a. What specific enemy units are preparing extensive field fortifications within each brigade sector?
   b. What specific enemy units within each brigade sector are preparing alternate artillery positions?
   c. What is the nomenclature or operating frequency of electronic emitters belonging to enemy units establishing lines of defense within each brigade sector?
10. What units comprise the reaction force to counter friendly armor or heliborne assaults?
   a. What enemy units are rumored to be the reaction force for defensive positions in each brigade sector?
   b. What enemy units are located behind, but in proximity to, the defensive positions in each brigade sector?
   c. What is the nomenclature or operating frequency of electronic emitters belonging to the units which are part of the enemy's reaction force within each brigade sector?

Figure B-2. Sample overall objective statement (IEW tasks) (continued).

11. What types of artillery are assigned to support the defense?
    a. What artillery units are rumored to be supporting the enemy's defensive positions in each brigade sector?
    b. What is the current location of the enemy artillery units rumored to be supporting the defensive positions in each brigade sector?
    c. What is the nomenclature or operating frequency of electronic emitters belonging to the artillery units rumored to be supporting the enemy's defensive positions in each brigade sector?
12. What enemy units will take part in a retreat?
    a. What enemy units in each brigade sector are rumored to be participating in a retreat?
    b. What enemy units in each brigade sector have been notified their—
        (1) Artillery support is moving to the rear?
        (2) Logistical support is moving to the rear?
    c. What is the nomenclature and operating frequency of electronic emitters belonging to retreating enemy units in each brigade sector?
13. What are current positions of retreating units?
    a. What is the current location of enemy units in each brigade sector rumored to be participating in a retreat?
    b. What is the current location of artillery units supporting enemy units in each brigade sector?
    c. What is the current location of logistical units supporting enemy units in each brigade sector?
14. When will each of the retreating units begin its movement?
    a. At what time have specific enemy units in each brigade sector been ordered to begin their retreat?
    b. What start times are being mentioned in rumors about the retreat of specific enemy units in each brigade sector?
15. What routes will be taken by the retreating units?
    a. What movement routes are being cited in rumors about the retreat of specific enemy units in each brigade sector?
    b. What movement routes are being used or planned for use during the retreat of enemy artillery units in each brigade sector?
    c. What movement routes are being used or planned for use during the retreat of enemy logistical units in each brigade sector?

Figure B-2. Sample overall objective statement (IEW tasks) (continued).

16. Where will each of the retreating units establish new positions?
    a. Where are the new positions being cited in rumors about the retreat of enemy units in each brigade sector?
    b. Where are the new positions assigned to retreating enemy artillery units in each brigade sector?
    c. Where are the new positions assigned to retreating enemy logistical units in each brigade sector?
17. What units comprise the enemy's second echelon?
    a. What specific units are rumored to be part of the enemy's second echelon in each brigade sector?
    b. How many units comprise the enemy's second echelon in each brigade sector?
    c. What type of units comprise the enemy's second echelon in each brigade sector?
    d. What is the nomenclature and operating frequency of electronic emitters belonging to units in the enemy's second echelon in each brigade sector?
18. What is the direction of travel for each unit in the enemy's second echelon?
    a. What is the rumored direction of travel for units comprising the enemy's second echelon in each brigade sector?
    b. What are the rumored movement routes for units comprising the enemy's second echelon in each brigade sector?
19. How soon will units in the enemy's second echelon begin to enter each brigade's AO?
    a. What is the current rumored location of units comprising the enemy's second echelon in each brigade sector?
    b. What is the rumored rate of travel for units comprising the enemy's second echelon in each brigade sector?
20. How soon will enemy reinforcements arrive?
    a. What times are being cited in rumors about the arrival of personnel replacements at specific enemy units in each brigade sector?
    b. What times are being cited in rumors about the arrival of equipment replacements at specific enemy units in each brigade sector?
21. By what routes will enemy reinforcements arrive?
    a. What are the current locations of replacement personnel and equipment cited in rumors about specific enemy units in each brigade sector?
    b. What are the movement routes of replacement personnel and equipment cited in rumors about specific enemy units in each brigade sector?

Figure B-2. Sample overall objective statement (IEW tasks) (continued).

22. What specific enemy units are serviced by enemy supply points?
    a. What ammunition supply points support specific enemy units in each brigade sector?
    b. What POL supply points support specific enemy units in each brigade sector?
    c. What is the nomenclature or operating frequency of electronic emitters belonging to enemy supply points in each brigade sector?
23. What malfunctions are occurring with enemy communications?
    a. What malfunctions are occurring with enemy vehicle-mounted communications equipment in each brigade sector?
    b. What malfunctions are occurring with enemy manpacked communications equipment in each brigade sector?
    c. What is the nomenclature or operating frequency of enemy communications equipment which is malfunctioning?
24. What are major enemy supply routes?
    a. What are the known movement routes used by enemy supply convoys in each brigade sector?
    b. What movement routes are rumored to be used by enemy supply convoys in each of the brigade sectors?
    c. What is the known direction of travel for enemy supply convoys passing NAIs in each brigade sector?
    d. What direction of travel is rumored for enemy supply convoys passing NAIs in each brigade factor?
25. What choke points has the enemy identified along their own LOCs?
    a. What choke points along enemy LOCs in each brigade sector are known to exist?
    b. What choke points are rumored to exist along enemy LOCs in each brigade sector?

IV. FORCE PROTECTION.

1. Where will NBC weapons be used?
    a. Have specific areas within any brigade sector been identified as targets for NBC weapons?
    b. Have orders been received by any enemy units in any brigade sector which indicate that NBC weapons might be used in support?
    c. Where has enemy air activity suddenly increased within any of the brigade sectors?

Figure B-2. Sample overall objective statement (IEW tasks) (continued).

   d. Where is unusual enemy air activity taking place within any of the brigade sectors?
   e. Where has very heavy artillery been moved to within supporting distance of front-line enemy troops within any brigade sector?
   f. Where has random firing of very heavy artillery occurred within any of the brigade sectors?
2. What is the main objective of enemy attack?
   a. What objectives have been assigned to specific enemy units in each brigade sector for their offensive operations?
   b. How many enemy units within each brigade sector have been assigned the same objectives?
   c. What measures are the enemy using to conceal the offensive's objectives in each brigade sector?
3. What units have been assigned to conduct the attack?
   a. What enemy units are rumored to be preparing for offensive operations within any of the brigade sectors?
   b. What special operations elements are attached to enemy units preparing for offensive operations in each brigade sector?
   c. What is the nomenclature or operating frequency of any electronic emitters belonging to enemy units preparing to conduct offensive operations in each brigade sector?
4. What enemy units have been assigned to defensive belts?
   a. What specific enemy units are preparing extensive field fortifications in each brigade sector?
   b. What special operations elements have been attached to enemy units establishing lines of defense in each brigade sector?
   c. What is the nomenclature or operating frequency of electronic emitters belonging to enemy units establishing lines of defense within each brigade sector?
   d. What measures are employed to conceal defensive preparations in each brigade sector?
5. What units comprise the reaction force to counter friendly armor or heliborne assaults?
   a. What enemy units are rumored to be the reaction force for defensive positions in each brigade sector?
   b. What enemy units are located behind, but in proximity to, the defensive positions in each brigade sector?

Figure B-2. Sample overall objective statement (IEW tasks) (continued).

   c. What special operations elements have been attached to the units in enemy reaction force in each brigade sector?
   d. What is the nomenclature or operating frequency of electronic emitters belonging to the units which are part of the enemy's reaction force within each brigade sector?

6. What enemy units will take part in a retreat?
   a. What enemy units in each brigade sector are rumored to be participating in a retreat?
   b. What special operations elements are attached to retreating enemy units in each brigade sector?
   c. What enemy units in each brigade sector have been designated as stay-behind elements?
   d. What efforts have been made to recruit stay-behind agents from the local populace in each brigade sector?
   e. What is the nomenclature or operating frequency of electronic emitters belonging to retreating enemy units in each brigade sector?
7. What deception efforts will be made to conceal the retreat?
   a. What deception efforts have been ordered in conjunction with the retreat in each brigade sector?
   b. What specific enemy units are conducting deception efforts in conjunction with the retreat in each brigade sector?
   c. What special operations elements are involved in the deception efforts being conducted in each brigade sector?
   d. What deception efforts are being cited in rumors about the retreat in each brigade sector?
   e. What enemy units are rumored to be conducting deception efforts in conjunction with the retreat in each brigade sector?
8. What units comprise the enemy's second echelon?
   a. What specific units are rumored to be part of the enemy's second echelon in each brigade sector?
   b. How many units comprise the enemy's second echelon in each brigade sector?
   c. What type of units comprise the enemy's second echelon in each brigade sector?
   d. What special operations elements are attached to units in the enemy's second echelon?
   e. What is the nomenclature and operating frequency of electronic emitters belongs to units in the enemy's second echelon in each brigade sector?

Figure B-2. Sample overall objective statement (IEW tasks) (continued).

V. BATTLE DAMAGE ASSESSMENT.

1. What production loss has the enemy sustained?
    a. How long will it take to recuperate?
    b. What was the extent of battle damage?
    c. What was the attack's total effect?
    d. How much warfighting stock was lost?
    e. How many personnel were lost?
    f. What type, and how many pieces, of warfighting equipment were destroyed or damaged?
    g. How many craters are visible?
    h. Where was the detonation point?
    i. What contingency plans have been put into effect?

VI. INDICATIONS AND WARNING.

1. How stable is the current government?
    a. What anti-allied demonstrations are planned?
    b. Who, or what organization, is responsible for the unrest?
    c. How well financed is the opposition?
    d. What outside help is the opposition receiving?
    e. What is the current economic situation?
    f. What kind of treatment can foreign citizens expect?

Figure B-2. Sample overall objective statement (IEW tasks) (continued).

APPENDIX C

S2 TACTICAL QUESTIONING GUIDE AND BATTLEFIELD EXPLOITATION OF CAPTURED ENEMY DOCUMENTS AND EQUIPMENT

History shows that EPWs, CEDs, and CEE are critical sources of combat intelligence. It has also shown the usefulness of information is directly proportionate to how fast a commander can get it.

Operations Urgent Fury, Just Cause, and Desert Storm proved that without workable procedures to handle captured persons or items, our combat effectiveness suffers because the evacuation chain jams the forward resupply effort. We also suffer because we have not exploited combat information sources at a low enough echelon to do that commander any good.

This guide is for battalion and brigade S2s. It explains standard procedures on what to do when the S2—

- Receives an enemy soldier.
- Detains a civilian.
- Finds an enemy document.
- Discovers an unusual enemy weapon during tactical operations.

PERSONNEL HANDLING

There are two types of persons captured on the battlefield: combatants and noncombatants. FM 27-10 defines the two types. The capturing unit treats all combatants and noncombatants as EPWs until the division forward collecting point segregates them by category. This is whether they are soldiers, clergy, or medics (see Chapter 3).

Noncombatants are handled, questioned, detained, evacuated, and released in accordance with theater policy.

At the EPW's capture point, the capturing element performs the following steps, with the senior soldier responsible for ensuring they are done. The steps are referred to as the "five S's."

STEP 1. SEARCH

The POC unit's first job is to disarm, then search all EPW or detainees, and tie their hands behind their back. They gather all loose enemy documents and equipment in the area. They evacuate them with the EPW. Documents and personal and protective military equipment stay with the prisoner unless otherwise directed by the battalion S2.

STEP 2. SILENT

The capturing unit instructs or signals EPWs to be silent. If that does not work, the EPW is gagged. Guards give orders to EPWs, but do not talk nor give them comfort items.

STEP 3. SAFEGUARD

The POC unit immediately moves the EPWs out of the fire zone. They protect EPWs from reprisals and give them medical care as necessary. The POC unit tries to preserve the shock of capture until brigade interrogators have a chance to question the EPWs.

STEP 4. SEGREGATE

The POC unit orders the EPWs to sit on the ground. It separates officers from enlisted, senior from junior, male from female, and civilian from soldier. It prepares a captive tag and puts one on each EPW (Figure 3-4). Tagging procedures are discussed under equipment handling procedures below.

STEP 5. SPEED TO THE REAR

Lastly, the POC unit moves EPWs to the unit supply point for evacuation. All captured documents, personal effects, and portable enemy equipment go with EPW. Also, one escort guard should know the EPW's circumstances of capture.

CAPTURED ENEMY DOCUMENTS FOUND ON ENEMY PRISONER OF WAR

The battalion S2, and subordinate unit commander, ensures CEDs found on EPWs are handled as follows. The POC unit will—

- Search each EPW.
- Return identification documents to EPW.
- Write the following on the top and bottom half of the EPW captive tag: Number of documents taken; date and time, location and circumstances of capture; capturing unit's designation.
- Put CED in a waterproof bag, one per EPW.
- Affix Part C of the captive tag to the bag (see Figure 3-4).
- Give CEDs to senior escort.
- Direct senior escort to evacuate CEDs with the EPW.

CAPTURED ENEMY DOCUMENTS FOUND ON THE BATTLEFIELD

An example of CEDs found on the battlefield is paperwork discovered in an overrun CP, but not on an EPW's person. The POC unit will—

- Put CEDs in a waterproof bag.
- Follow the same procedures described above, and tag the bag.
- Evacuate to battalion S2.
- Battalion S2 evacuates all CEDs along EPW evacuation channels.

EQUIPMENT HANDLING PROCEDURES

CEE includes all types of foreign material found on an EPW or on the battlefield that may have military application. The POC unit—

- Evacuates equipment with the EPW.
- Confiscates, tags, and evacuates weapons and other equipment found on an EPW the same as CEDs.

ITEMS OF TECHINT VALUE

The capturing unit may recognize certain CEE as having possible TECHINT value. Such items include—

- New weapons.
- Radios.
- Track vehicles.
- Associated manuals.
- All CEE known or believed to be of TECHINT interest.

The capturing unit's primary job when capturing a TECHINT item is to secure and report the capture to its S2 for disposition instructions. Figure C-1 provides a scenario for TECHINT items.

FIRST ECHELON BATTLEFIELD TECHINT EXPLOITATION

It is conceivable, although not likely, that the capturing unit leader of S2 may need to do field exploitation of a piece of CEE. If this happens—

- It will usually be at the request of the battlefield TECHINT team attached to corps headquarters.
- The small-unit leader or S2 follows the same procedures used to exploit a CED.

TAGGING PROCEDURES

There are two capture tags: A CEE tag and an EPW tag with a smaller tear-off document tag. The POC unit tags all captured personnel, CEDs, and CEE at the POC.

The battalion S2 or company commander is responsible for having sufficient CEE and EPW document tags as well as waterproof bags prior to an operation.

When no standard tag forms are available, the following procedures will be used for expediency:

- Use meals, ready-to-eat (MRE) cardboard or other type of paper.
- Write the capturing unit's designation.
- Write date and time of capture.
- Write POC coordinates.
- Write circumstances of capture.
- Identify EPW, CED, or CEE captured.
- Put tag, without damaging the CED, in a waterproof bag.
- Attach EPW and CEE tags so they will not come off.

TACTICAL QUESTIONING

This section provides "how to" instructions to enable the S2 to do tactical questioning (TQ) on EPWs. Following these will—

- Achieve usable results.
- Preserve the source for subsequent formal interrogation.
- Keep the S2 from breaking the law.

Warning

Improper, unlawful, or inept attempt at field exploitation can harm or destroy possible critical intelligence sources, and send US soldiers to prison. Any decision to attempt these procedures is a command responsibility, and only done by the S2.

Figure C-2 is an example of the front and reverse sides of a CEE tag. It should be included as a tab to the TECHINT appendix in the intelligence annex of an OPLAN plan or operations order (OPORD).

The purpose of TQ is to obtain combat information of immediate use to the battalion or subordinate unit by the S2. Sources of information can be an EPW and local or friendly civilians encountered in the operational area. (S2s use established procedures when questioning local or friendly civilians.)

LANGUAGE REQUIREMENT

TQ can be done only under one of the following circumstances:

- The S2 speaks the EPW's language well enough to ask direct questions and understand the answers.
- A language qualified interpreter is available to assist the S2.

FROM THE FOXHOLE TO THE CMEC

The solider either captures or observes an item of possible TECHINT interest. The solider quickly reports the encounter through his or her command to the Battalion S2. The soldier then either safeguards the item or continues the mission as directed.

Upon learning that a forward platoon or company has captured or encountered an item of possible TECHINT interest, the Battalion S2 promptly—

- Coordinates security or continued observation of the item with the S3 and ensures the item is not tampered with in any way. Components, control knobs, and switches on C-E equipment should not be touched until the equipment is photographed or positions recorded.
- Examines and screens the item against PIR and IR and determines whether the item is known or believed to be of TECHINT interest; or, whether, in the soldier's opinion, the item deserves initiative reporting.
- Spot reports the capture or encounter in the SALUTE format through higher headquarters to the first Battlefield TECHINT element in the chain of command.
- Coordinates continued security or observation of the item until receipt of further instructions.
- Identifies items requiring immediate screening for combat information by other supporting MI elements. This could include C-E system items like code books, radios, or technical documents such as operator manuals.

Intermediate echelons of command continue forwarding the spot reported encounter or capture to their supporting Battlefield TECHINT element.

The supporting Battlefield TECHINT element receives the spot report and compares the information to requirements and the existing data base to see if collection is necessary. The element then decides further action and notifies the capturing unit accordingly. The CMEC or Battlefield TECHINT team's options at this point include, but are not limited to—

- Requesting the capturing unit to provide further information, such as detailed descriptions, sketches, photographs, or documents captured with the item.
- On-site screening or exploiting.
- Destroying the item.
- Abandoning the item unharmed.
- TECHINT team-supervised or routine evacuating.
- Priority evacuating to EAC.
- Recommending turning over initial exploitation to other MI elements, such as target exploitation or interrogators, for immediate tactical information screening.

Figure C-1. Disposition of TECHINT items scenario.

WHERE TQ IS DONE

TQ is done as soon as possible after removing the EPW from fire zones. However, battalion or brigade commanders forced to deal with heavy EPW input may set up an organized TQ effort at the unit's EPW collecting point.

WHO ASKS THE QUESTIONS

Only the S2 is authorized to conduct TQ. The S2 asks every question himself, even when using another soldier or local national as an interpreter. If augmented by interrogators, the interrogation team supervises the TQ effort.

TIME CONSIDERATIONS

TQ is designed to be a quick procedure, lasting from 5 to 20 minutes. A command decision is required if source questioning interferes with mission accomplishment or delays a priority evacuation.

ITEMS NEEDED FOR TQ

TQ is authorized for collection of combat information critical to successful mission accomplishment. The questioner needs to know what information headquarters requires. Other items required for TQ are—

- Maps.
- Vehicle and aircraft identification guides.
- Target language dictionary.
- Report forms, stationery, capture tags, waterproof bags.
- Interpreter or translator.

THE EXPLOITATION PROCESS

The exploitation process, discussed in Chapter 3, is the basis for all personnel examinations, to include TQ. It consists of three parts: screening, questioning, and reporting.

SCREENING

If there is more than one EPW, the quickest method to pick who to question first is to—

- Check the captive tag to see if your unit recently captured the EPW with unusual equipment; for example, a sniper rifle or booby trap in an area of operational interest.
- Observe for high rank, key enemy unit patches, and unusual behavior.
- Use established guidelines and rank the most likely EPWs first for questioning.

QUESTIONING

The key to questioning is brevity. Tactical questioners work fast until they find an EPW who will give useful combat information. To do this, the tactical questioner—

- Ensures the EPW is under guard.
- Briefs interpreter as necessary.
- Has the EPW searched and obtains identity document.
- Looks over EPW's identity document and CEDs.
- Makes a mental questioning plan.
- Presents military bearing. Preserves the shock of capture.
- Asks military questions, intermixing biographical questions so as not to arouse the EPW's security training.
- Compares answers given on the identity card and other items found on the EPW to check for truthfulness.

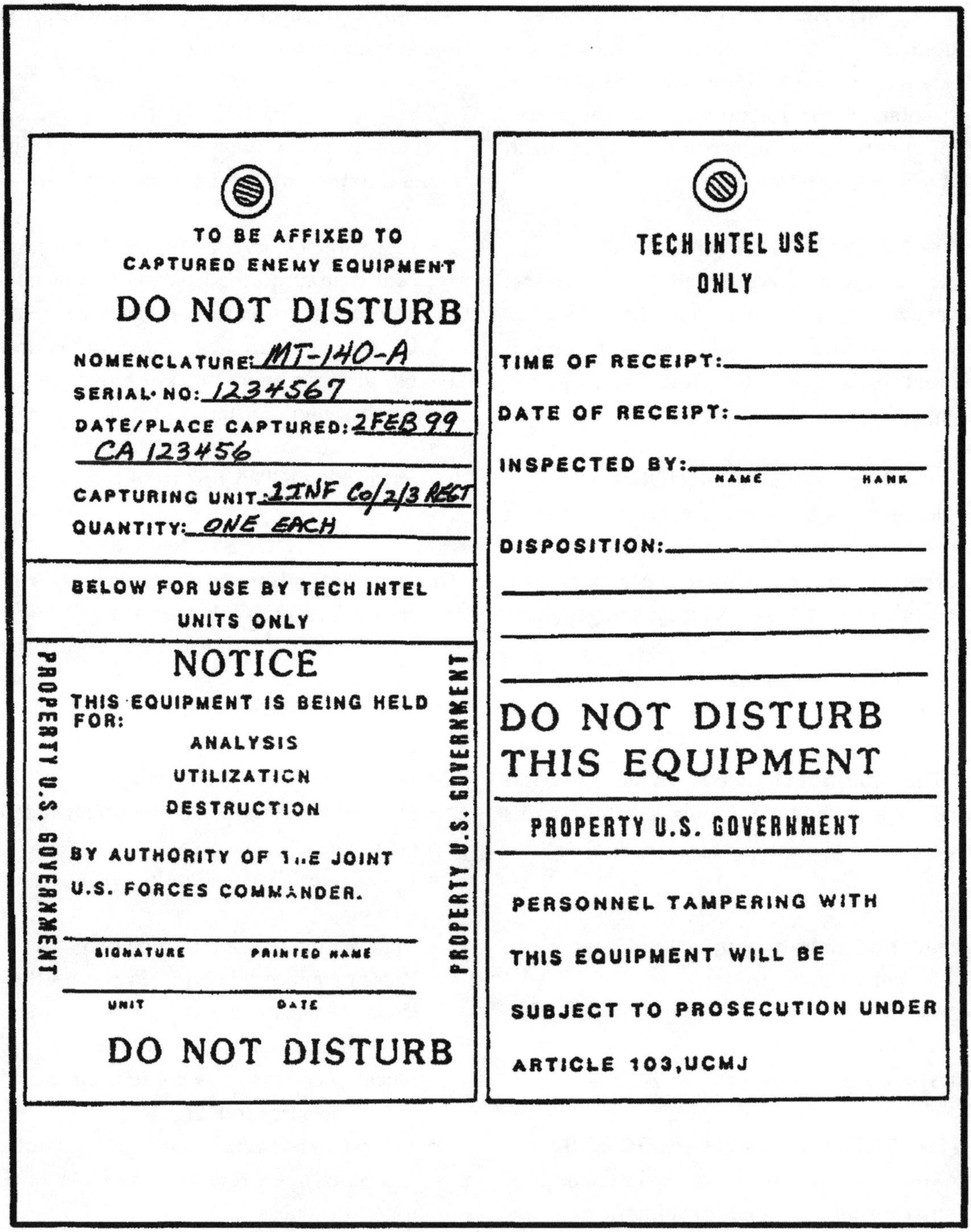

TO BE AFFIXED TO
CAPTURED ENEMY EQUIPMENT

DO NOT DISTURB

NOMENCLATURE: MT-140-A
SERIAL NO: 1234567
DATE/PLACE CAPTURED: 2FEB99
CA 123456
CAPTURING UNIT: 2 INF Co/2/3 REGT
QUANTITY: ONE EACH

BELOW FOR USE BY TECH INTEL
UNITS ONLY

PROPERTY U.S. GOVERNMENT

NOTICE

THIS EQUIPMENT IS BEING HELD FOR:

ANALYSIS
UTILIZATION
DESTRUCTION

BY AUTHORITY OF THE JOINT
U.S. FORCES COMMANDER.

SIGNATURE PRINTED NAME

UNIT DATE

DO NOT DISTURB

PROPERTY U.S. GOVERNMENT

TECH INTEL USE
ONLY

TIME OF RECEIPT:
DATE OF RECEIPT:
INSPECTED BY:
NAME RANK
DISPOSITION:

DO NOT DISTURB
THIS EQUIPMENT

PROPERTY U.S. GOVERNMENT

PERSONNEL TAMPERING WITH
THIS EQUIPMENT WILL BE
SUBJECT TO PROSECUTION UNDER
ARTICLE 103, UCMJ

Figure C-2. Front and reverse sides of CEE tag.

- Ends questioning if the EPW stops or refuses to answer military questions.
- Ends questioning if the EPW intentionally or unintentionally provides so much irrelevant military information instead of information pertinent to the tactical questioner's combat mission.
- Never promises anything that cannot be delivered.

REPORTING

Tactical questioners report acquired information in SALUTE format (Figure 3-5). To do this, they—

- Obtain combat information using the direct questioning technique (see Chapter 3).
- Record combat information of interest to headquarters. This is recorded in SALUTE format as relevant answers are obtained.
- Attempt to fill in all SALUTE report blanks before moving to another collection requirement or before ending the questioning.
- End questioning by telling the EPW they will talk again, and return required items, such as the EPW's ID.

THE TACTICAL QUESTIONING PLAN

The questioning plan used during TQ is short, simple, and standard. The questioner can use it to uncover spot reportable information on any subject. An easy way to remember it is through the phrase "BIG 4 and JUMP."

- BIG 4 is a nickname for the Geneva Convention's "name, rank, service number, and date of birth."
- JUMP is an acronym for job, unit, mission, PIR, IR, and SIR, which is the sequence of the TQ plan.

More specifically, the TQ plan covers the following topics in sequence. Figure C-3 shows examples of the BIG 4 and JUMP questions.

- EPW biographical data.
- EPW duty position or job.
- EPW unit or employer.
- EPW present and future mission at time of capture.
- Commander's collection requirements in order of priority.

BATTLEFIELD DOCUMENT EXPLOITATION

Battlefield DOCEX is a capturing unit procedure done by the S2 before interrogator exploitation. A combat unit without language-qualified personnel can perform limited battlefield DOCEX, mainly on maps and overlays. Units with linguists have the advantage of being able to do more.

After capturing an EPW or enemy CP, the capturing unit needs to look for maps, encrypted items, OPORDs, overlays, and other documents. The capturing unit then notifies headquarters to request disposition instructions.

The small-unit leader safeguards the items pending disposition instructions. At the same time he—

- Looks over the document.
- Does not mark or harm it in any way.
- Uses whatever resources are available to

What is your last name? First name? Middle name?
What is your rank? Service number? Date of Birth?

* * *

What is your position (or job) in your unit (or firm)?
What unit are you in (or who do you work for)?
What was your mission (or what type of work were you doing) when you were captured?
What would your future mission have been (or what jobs or projects would you have had) had you not been captured? What other missions would you have had if you had not been captured?

* * *

Follow up on all given information items; in particular, ensure you have the source's full unit designation and thoroughly follow up on the source's missions. A good rule of thumb is to ask Who, What, When, Where, How, and Why to fully develop whatever information you obtain.

Note: Continue to ask questions based on collection requirements, phrasing them as direct questions. For example, "Where are the GATO cell's arm caches?" or "When will your unit attack San Pablo?

Figure C-3. BIG 4 and JUMP question examples.

decipher it; for example, dictionaries and enemy map symbol guides. An example of Soviet and non-NATO symbols is at Figure C-4.

- Looks for information that has a direct bearing on his current mission.

After finding information of possible value to the mission, the S2 extracts the combat information and uses the SALUTE format as a template to organize the information (see Figure 3-5).

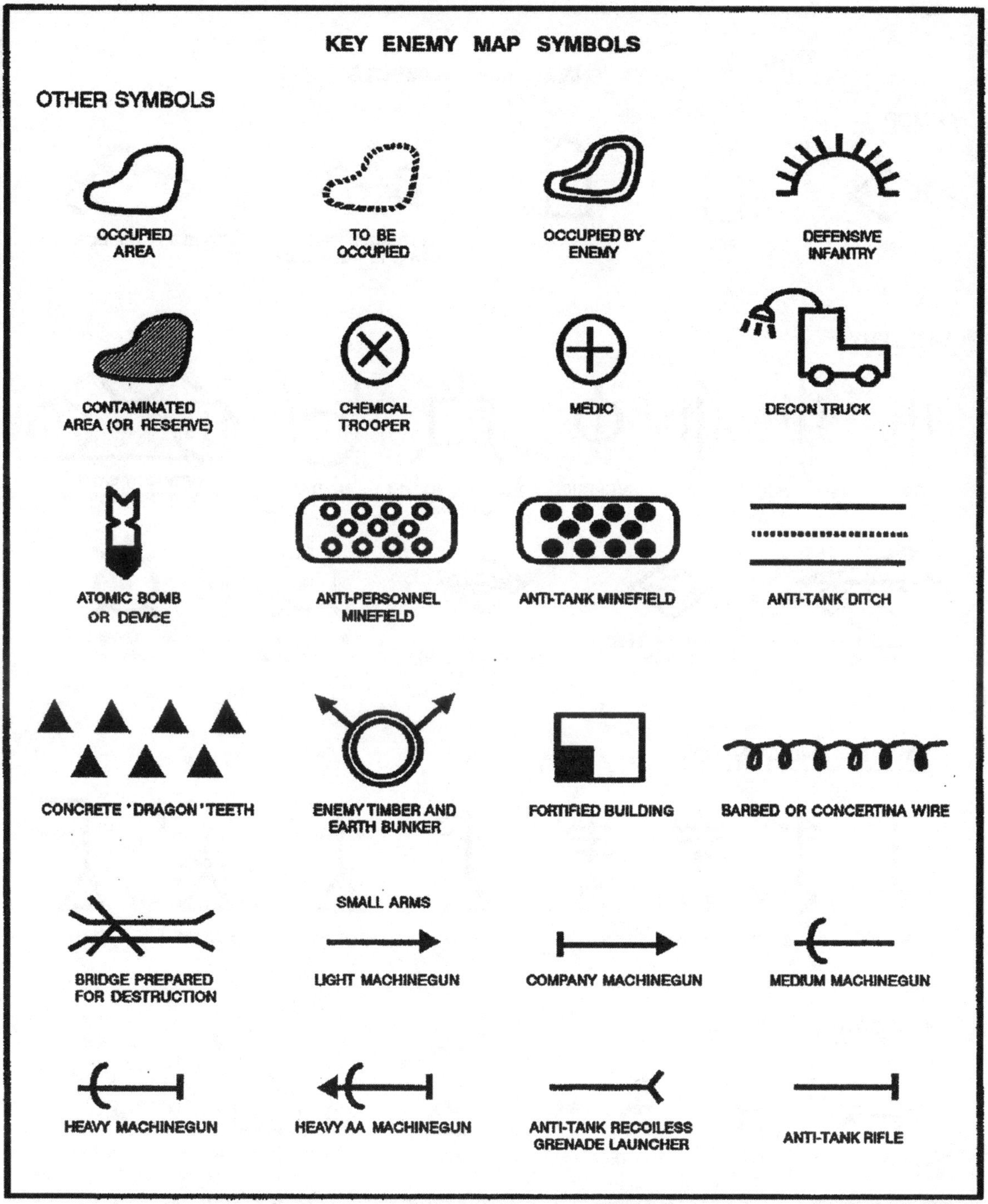

Figure C-4. Soviet and non-NATO map symbols.

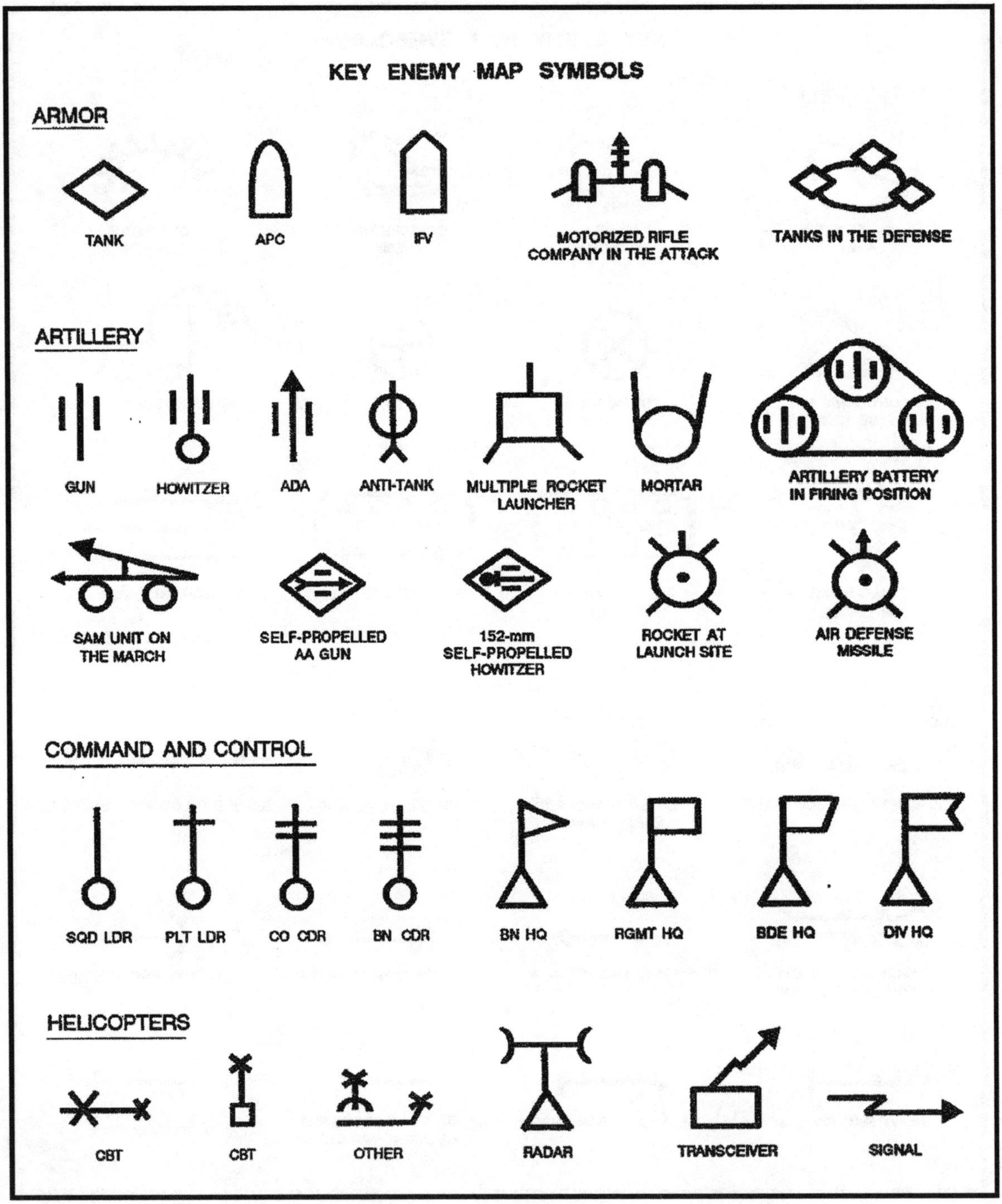

Figure C-4. Soviet and non-NATO map symbols (continued).

APPENDIX D

PROTECTED PERSONS RIGHTS VERSUS SECURITY NEEDS

The articles in the Appendix are extracted from the Geneva Convention Relative to the Protection of Civilian Persons in Time of War of August 12, 1949.

The GC attempts to balance the necessity of the proper treatment of protected persons with the needs of security by the Detaining or Occupying Power. The GC applies to the whole of the populations of the countries in conflict, without any adverse distinction based, in particular, on race, nationality, religion, or political opinion. It is the design of the Convention to alleviate the sufferings caused by war (Article 13).

At the outbreak of a conflict, many protected persons become displaced persons. They move within their own country to areas where hostilities are not a threat or a power is able to protect them. They may become refugees, fleeing into neighboring countries seeking a safe haven. The GC provides that protected persons who desire to leave at the outset of, or during, a conflict should be allowed to do so, unless their departure is contrary to the national interest of the State (Article 35). However, in light of possible threats to the security of the State receiving the refugees or a Detaining Power, the Geneva Convention does recognize a State's right to take appropriate action to insure security.

The most typical security measure taken in such cases is the establishment of some manner of screening camps where the people may be identified and screened. During the process, useful intelligence may be obtained from legitimate displaced persons or refugees, and from potential threats, such as covert agents, who may be identified and interrogated.

In most cases, interrogators or linguists will conduct the screening operations while working closely with CI personnel to identify those protected persons of CI interest. Other military intelligence personnel may be required to participate in this screening process because of the large numbers of refugees and/or the lack of other qualified personnel.

Internment of a protected person occurs when the Detaining Power determines that confinement or assignment of residences to certain protected persons is absolutely necessary to the security of the Detaining Power (Articles 41 and 42). A civilian internee is defined by the Department of Defense (DOD) as a civilian who is interned during an armed conflict or occupation for security reasons or for protection or because he has committed an offense against the Detaining Power.

GENEVA CONVENTION PROVISIONS CONCERNING PROTECTED PERSONS

It is critical that the GC provisions concerning protected persons be strictly adhered to in the quest to identify legitimate threats and gain needed intelligence. Specifically:

(a) Article 5 provides that if a Party to the conflict is satisfied that an individual protected person is suspected of or engaged in activities hostile to the security of the State, such individual shall not be entitled to claim rights or privileges under the convention, if the exercise of that right would be prejudicial to that State. However, such individuals must be humanely treated during internment and the pendency of any investigation and/or prosecution. A limitation of rights or privileges may include the withholding of the right to communicate with members of their family or representatives of their government. Such restrictions would be appropriate in a case involving spying.

(b) Article 29 places the responsibility for the treatment accorded protected persons upon the Party in whose hands they are found. This is in addition to any personal responsibility incurred by an agent of that Party. This is an affirmative duty upon commanders to insure their subordinates are not mistreating protected persons or their property. The command and the government will ultimately be held responsible for any mistreatment.

(c) Article 31 prohibits physical or moral coercion against protected persons to obtain information from them or from third parties. Prohibited coercion may be obvious, such as physically abusing the subject of the screening or interrogation. It may also be more subtle, such as threats to turn the individual over to hostile forces; subjecting the individual to humiliating or degrading treatment; implying harm to the individual or his property, or implying a deprivation of rights guaranteed by international law because of a failure to cooperate; threatening to separate parents from their children; or forcing a protected person to perform guide services.

(d) Article 32 prohibits, corporal punishment, torture, or taking any measure of such character as to cause the physical suffering or extermination of protected persons in your control. This prohibition not only applies to actions taken by the Detaining Party against the protected persons, but also any adverse action that others may take.

(e) Article 33 prohibits collective punishments, penalties, reprisals, or pillaging of protected persons and their property. The principle behind this provision is that protected persons should only be held liable for offenses they personally commit. This prohibition includes all measures of intimidation or terrorism.

(f) Article 41 allows the Power, in whose hands the protected persons are found, to intern or force assigned residence to protected persons, if the other measures of control permitted by the convention are inadequate. Some persons may demand internment (for example, protected persons who may be threatened by others). Internment must be provided when the situation renders this step necessary (Article 42).

(g) If interned or forced into assigned residences, protected persons have the right to have any such determination reconsidered and reviewed on a periodic basis (Article 43).

(h) In connection with the above, Article 44 prohibits the Detaining Power from automatically interning or forcing an assigned residence against refugees who are nationals of an Enemy State, exclusively on the basis of their nationality, who do not, in fact, enjoy the protection of any government. The purpose of this article is to insure that refugees, who may only technically remain enemy aliens, are not, on that basis alone, automatically subject to control measures, notwithstanding the fact that they are not protected by their government. An example of this would be interning Iraqi refugees based solely on their status as Iraqis. This prohibition, however, does not in any way deny the right of a State to intern such persons or subject them to legitimate controls when there is an additional basis for taking such action in the interest of security of the State.

(i) Article 45 prohibits the transfer of protected persons into the custody of a Power not a signatory to the convention. The transferring Power must insure that protected persons transferred from their custody will be treated in accordance with the conventions. In the event that the transferring Power discovers that the protected persons are not being treated in accordance with the convention, they shall request that the protected persons be returned to their custody.

APPENDIX E

REPORTS

In addition to reports previously covered, there are other reports prepared or used by interrogators in tactical and strategic units. DIAM 58-13 is the authority for format and preparation of intelligence information reports (IIRs), biographic reports, and knowledgeability briefs (KBs). Local SOPs guide the interrogator in preparing other reports.

Message Text Format (MTF) Editor is software used by the military services, National Security Agency (NSA), and Defense Intelligence Agency (DIA).

MTF Editor—

- Creates, formats, edits, stores, prints, and transmits United States Message Text Formatting (USMTF) messages.
- Is designed to run on Z-150, AN/UYK-83, Z-248, IBM PC compatibles, and other standard and non-standard systems.
- Requires minimum 320K random access memory (RAM), microsoft (MS) or personal computer (PC) disk operating system (DOS) version 2.1 or higher, and 5.25-inch disk drive.
- Is "user friendly," as it employs many of the same commands available in commercial word processors.

The SALUTE report format contains relevant information necessary to alert higher commands of an incident or relevant information obtained. It answers all basic interrogatives: Who, What, When, Where, How, and Why.

Figures of sample reports, formats, and tags used by interrogators are listed below:

- Figure E-1, Spot report voice message template.
- Figure E-2, Battlefield TECHINT spot report.
- Figure E-3, Tactical interrogation report.
- Figure E-4, Captive tag (STANAG 2044).
- Figure E-5, IIR.
- Figure E-6, Biographic report.
- Figure E-7, Knowledgeability brief.
- Figure E-8, Interrogation report.

TACTICAL INTERROGATION REPORT

The TIR (Figure E-3) serves as written summary of initial or subsequent interrogations. The term "tactical interrogation report" was adopted under NATO STANAG 2033. The TIR—

- Eliminates information duplication of effort in later EPW interrogations.
- Disseminates information to the intelligence officers of the immediate command, those of other appropriate commands, and interrogators who will conduct further interrogations.
- Serves as an intelligence value assessment of EPWs, documents, and equipment carried by him at time of capture.
- Consists of Part I, Intelligence Potential of EPW, and Part II, information obtained.

In the heading, the EPW will be classified according to one of four categories explained in Chapter 4 under document exploitation.

The first section of the report contains the source's name and category, interrogation serial number, date, report number, interrogator's name and unit, maps and language used, and interpreter's name (if one is used).

The second section, Part I, contains the EPW's personal particulars, career, assessment of intelligence value, capture data from the captive tag, and documents and equipment found on the EPW.

The third section, Part II, lists information obtained from the EPW during the interrogation regarding missions, composition, strength, dispositions, tactics, training, logistics, combat effectiveness, electronic technical data, and miscellaneous data.

BIOGRAPHIC DATA ENTRIES

The following data prosigns are used in biographic reporting. If available, biographic information will fit in the summary of the IIR; the text entry will be None.

Should the reportable information exceed the limitations of the summary, entries will be made in the text. When making entries, ensure that the numbers and prosigns shown here are those used in the biographic report; if you have no data for a particular item, skip it and list the next item for which you have a data entry. Items skipped are not listed on the report.

The paragraph classification follows the biographic prosign. Do not use colons to separate the prosign and data entries. Minimum essential data (MED) prosigns are asterisked.

SUMMARY INTERROGATION REPORT

The rationale behind the summary interrogation report, shown at Figure E-8, is to preclude duplication of effort. In Desert Storm, as EPWs were being evacuated up the chain, the gaining interrogator would ask questions only to be told the same questions had already been asked by somebody else at a previous location. This is embarrassing, and does not foster rapport building, because the gaining interrogator had no previous EPW screening or interrogation reports. It was assumed this was the first time the EPW was questioned.

If the previous echelon received EPW information pertaining only to their immediate tactical situation, with no reports being forwarded, it would have been to the gaining interrogators advantage to be apprised of what transpired at the lower echelon; hence the summary interrogation report. This report is simple in design and purpose, but reveals EPW information that gives the gaining interrogator insight as to what was developed at the previous echelon.

VOICE MESSAGE TEMPLATE FOR A SPOT (SALUTE) REPORT

G2, X Corps THIS IS G2, 25th INF DIV SALUTE. OVER
addressee originator

THIS IS SEND SALUTE. OVER
originator addressee

THIS IS SALUTE PROBLEMS
addressee originator

FLASH IMMEDIATE PRIORITY ROUTINE (Underline and transmit the precedence of this message.)

TOP SECRET SECRET CONFIDENTIAL CLEAR UNCLASSIFIED (Underline and transmit the security classification of this message.)

SALUTE REPORT

1. SIZE SQUAD (Enter the size of the unit or target.)
2. ACTIVITY RECON (Enter a description of the activity detected.)
3. LOCATION CR 123456 (Enter the target location [UTM].)
4. UNIT 1 MRS/2/3/44/59 MRD (Enter the unit identity or type.)
5. TIME NLT 171800ZFEB99 (Enter the time of the sighting.)
6. EQUIPMENT NA (Enter the name of any equipment sighted.)
7. DIRECTION NA (Enter the direction if target is moving in degrees or mils.)
8. TIME 1105T (Enter hour-minute-zone. See NOTE.)
9. AUTHENTICATION IS 170225 (Enter message authentication See NOTE.)
10. OVER

NOTE: The message DTG is used when required to identify message time of origin. Authentication will be in accordance with joint task force procedures.

Figure E-1. Spot report voice message template.

BATTLEFIELD TECHINT SPOT REPORT

TO: VI CORPS TECHINT TEAM
THRU: RS2, 14th ACR
FROM: SS2, 3/14th ACR
DTG: 300700ZJAN99 REPORT NO: 07-0623

SIZE: 3xMissiles, 1xSuitcase, 1xControl Box with periscope sight, 1xSpent missile round.

ACTIVITY: Capture of antitank wire-guided missile system. NATO nomenclature AT-3/SAGGER Mannpack.

LOCATION: Capture at coordinates //32UNB538331//.

TIME: Time of capture was 300530ZJAN99.

EQUIPMENT/HOW:

System captured intact after overrunning enemy ambush position. No associated enemy captured. Equipment secure. Awaiting disposition instructions.

REMARKS:

SOURCE DATA: Captured Enemy Equipment.

MAP DATA: GERMANY, 1:50,000, LAUTERBACH, L5322, EDITION 5

MISC DATA: REPORT NO: 07-0623

Figure E-2. Sample battlefield TECHINT spot report.

(CLASSIFICATION)

TACTICAL INTERROGATION REPORT

NAME OF PRISONER: KLEYMENOV

CATEGORY: A (B) C D

INTG SERIAL NO: US-AR-1234-1

DTG OF INTG: 221700ZNOV99

INTG REPORT NO: PT-001

INTERROGATOR: SGT ROYCE.

UNIT/FORMATION TO WHICH INTERROGATOR ATTACHED: Intg Sec, Intel-Surv Co, 231st MI Bn, 23d Inf Div

MAPS USED: GERMANY, 1:50,000, EISENAC HUNFELD, Ed #2.

LANGUAGE USED: Russian

INTERPRETER: None

PART I—INTELLIGENCE POTENTIAL OF ENEMY PRISONER OF WAR (EPW)

A. PERSONAL PARTICULARS:

1. Rank, full name, service number, and position: JrLT, Dimitar KLEYMENOV, No. 0506031, Plt Ldr.
2. Date and place of birth: 23 May 72, TBILISI, Georgian SSR, USSR.
3. Nationality: Soviet (Ethnic Rumanian) (Religion: Orthodox).
4. Knowledge of languages and proficiency: Russian (N).
5. Unit, formation, or organization: 2 MR Plt (MRP), 2 MR Co (MRC), 3 MR Bn (MRB), 62 MR Regt (MRR), 34 MR Div (MRD)(2MRP/2/3/62/34MRD).
6. Date/time, place/grid references, capturing unit and circumstances of capture: 221330ZNOV99, Hill 457 (NB625305), A/1/2/3, captured after taking Hill 457.

B. CAREER:

1. Premilitary: Gymnasium graduate, attended 1 year at University of Moscow.
   Vocational training: None.
   Paramilitary training: None.
2. Military: 5 years military service, attended OCS Oct97; previous military jobs: Assistant Platoon Leader.

DOWNGRADING/DECLASSIFICATION DATA:
(NOTE: This report is UNCLASSIFIED. The word "CLASSIFICATION" is used for training purposes to denote lines which may carry classification markings on an actual report.)

(CLASSIFICATION)

Figure E-3. Sample TIR.

(CLASSIFICATION)

C. ASSESSMENT OF INTELLIGENCE VALUE:

1. Intelligence, experience, cooperation, reliability: EPW seemed cooperative in that he did not hesitate to answer questions. EPW has 5 years' military experience. EPW appeared reliable in that no discrepancies were noted through the use of control and repeated questions. EPW was of average intelligence as he attended 1 year University of Moscow.
2. Specialist knowledge: None.
3. Discussion of approach techniques: EPW cooperated on the orchestration of the Incentive (better treatment) and Pride and Ego Up (too good to do mundane EPW work) approaches.

D. DOCUMENTS CARRIED AT TIME OF CAPTURE:

1. List of documents: 1xID card No. 0506031 (returned to EPW).
2. Details of money and valuables: 18xrubles (impounded and receipted).

E. EQUIPMENT OF INTELLIGENCE INTEREST CARRIED AT TIME OF CAPTURE:

1. Personal equipment: 1xShMK protective mask (returned to EPW).
2. Weapons: 1x9mm PM pistol, 2xempty magazines, 1xfull magazine (all evacuated through supply channels).

PART II—INFORMATION OBTAINED

A. SUMMARY:

1. DOI is 221330ZNOV99 unless otherwise indicated in the body of this report.
2. This report contains information pertaining to the 34th MRD, or units subordinate thereto.

B. TEXT:

1. Missions:
    a. EPW:
        (1) TOC: To establish Plt OP and defensive position for 2MRP/2/3/62/34MRD.
        (2) Future: To assist calling in artillery fire on enemy positions.
        (3) Past: Participated in assault against Hill 457 (NB625305).
    b. Unit: (2MRP/2/3/62/34MRD).
        (1) Present: To establish and maintain OP and defensive positions.
        (2) Future: To monitor convoy traffic, use position as jumping off point for future operations.

(CLASSIFICATION)

Figure E-3. Sample TIR (continued).

(CLASSIFICATION)

(3) Past: Assaulted Hill 457 (NB625305).

c. Unit: (2MRC/3/62/34MRD).

(1) Present: To continue offensive operation east on highway.

(2) Future: To link up with the 3MRB in ALSFELD (NB1922) NLT 27NOV99.

(3) Past: Crossed international border 18NOV99 to liberate oppressed populace.

2. <u>COMPOSITION:</u> (62MRR/34MRD).

a. 62MRR had 2xMRB, dsg 1 and 3. 1xArty Btry, dsg unk. 2xEngr Bn, dsg unk.

b. 2MRB/62MRR had 3xMRC dsg, 1, 2, and 3.

c. 2MRC/3/62MRR had 1xHq Section and 3xMRP dsg 1, 2, 3.

d. Ea MRP/2/3/62MRR had 3xMRS, dsg 1, 2, 3.

3. <u>STRENGTH:</u> (2MRC).

a. Personnel: (2MRC).

(1) 2MRC had 93xpersonnel(6xOff/87xEM).

(2) Hq Sec/2MRC had 6xpersonnel (3xOff - CO, PO, TO/3xEM 1SG, BMP driver/mechanic, BMP commander/gunner).

(3) Ea MRP/2MRC had 29xpersonnel(1xOff - Plt Ldr/28xEM - 1xPlt SGT and 27xPlt mbrs).

(4) Ea MRS/ea MRP/2MRC had 9xEM (1xSqd Ldr, 8xSqd mbrs).

b. WEAPONS AND EQUIPMENT: (2MRP/2MRC).

(1) Individual Weapons: (2MRP).

(a) 7x9mm pistol (1xPlt Ldr, 1xea RPG-16 gunner, 1xea BMP driver/mechanic).

(b) 16x5.45mm AK-74 rifles (1xea remaining EM except RPK-74 gunners).

(c) 1x7.62mm SVD sniper rifle carried by sniper, 2MRP.

(2) Crew-served Weapons: (2MRP).

(a) 6x5.45mm RPK-74 LMG (2xea MRS/2MRP).

(b) 3x58mm RPG-16 ATGL (1xea MRS/2MRP).

(3) Other Weapons: (2MRP) Ea mbr/2MRP carried unk no RGD-5 and F-1 hand grenades.

(4) Armored Vehicles: (2MRP) (3xBMP, ea armed with 1x73mmsmoothbore gun, 1x7.62mm coaxial MG, and 1xAT-3 SAGGER, ATGM, 1xea MRS/2MRP).

(5) Other Vehicles: Unk.

(CLASSIFICATION)

Figure E-3. Sample TIR (continued).

(CLASSIFICATION)

(6) Communication Equipment: (2MRP).
  (a) 3xR-123 transceivers, 1xea BMP/2MRP.
  (b) 1xR-126 transceivers, 1xPlt Hq/2MRP.
(7) NBC Equipment: (2MRP)
  (a) Individual:
    (1) 29xSHM protective masks (1xea mbr/2MRP).
    (2) 29xU/I protective clothing sets (1xea mbr/2MRP).
    (3) 29xU/I individual decon kits (1xea mbr/2MRP).
  (b) Vehicular: (2MRP) 3xU/I air filtration systems (1xea BMP/2MRP).
(8) Specialized equipment: None.

4. <u>DISPOSITIONS:</u>
  (a) CP, 3MRB/62/34MRD loc vic NB673344 in abandoned 2xstory building in HEIMBOLDSHAUSEN (NB6734) (II/S, CO, 2MRC/3MRB, DOI: 211200ZNOV99).
  (b) CP, 2MRC/3/62/34MRD loc vic NB639310 in building at road intersection in RANSBACH (NB6331) (DOI: 211130ZNOV99).
  (c) CP, 1MRP/2/3/62/34MRD loc vic NB626291, in building N of road junction WEHRSHAUSEN (NB6229) (DOI: 210800ZNOV99).
  (d) CP, 3MRP/2/3/62/34MRD loc vic NB608324 in one-story, white building in HILMES (NB6032) (DOI: 210800NOV99).
  (e) CP, artillery battery, FUD UNK, loc vic NB626334, (H/S, CO, 2MRC/3/62/34MRD DOI: 220400NOV99).
  (f) CP, 2MRP/2/3/62/34MRD, Hill 457, loc vic NB625305. (DOI: 221330ZNOV99).
5. <u>TACTICS:</u> (2MRC/3/62/34MRD) To continue rapid advance toward ALSFELD (NB1922) where various U/I units will consolidate and then advance SW.
6. <u>TRAINING:</u> (2MRC/3/62/34MRD) Practiced small unit and company-size attack formation along with ground control of attack formations.
7. <u>COMBAT EFFECTIVENESS:</u> (2MRC/3/62/34MRD).
  a. Losses: (2MRC).
    (1) Personnel: 10xKIA in 2MRS/1/2/MRC due to artillery barrage on 20NOV99.
    (2) Equipment: 1xBMP in 2MRS/1/2MRC due to artillery barrage on 20NOV99.
  b. Replacements: (2MRC).

(CLASSIFICATION)

Figure E-3. Sample TIR (continued).

(CLASSIFICATION)

(1) Personnel: 5xEM received by 2MRS/1/2MRC to replace losses.

(2) Equipment: 1xBMP received by 2MRS/1/2MRC within 8 hours of loss.

c. Reinforcements: Unk to EPW.

d. Combat experience: Unk to EPW.

e. Morale: (2MRP/2MRC) Morale was good due to offensive going as planned and faith in leaders. PO, 3MRB/62/34MRC gives good political indoctrination.

f. Electronic technical data: Unk to EPW.

8. <u>LOGISTICS:</u> (2MRP/2/3/62/34MRD).

(a) Weapons and Ammunition: (2MRP).

(1) Weapons: (2MRP) All weapons were in excellent condition due to inspection in early Nov99. Spare parts for all weapons were stored in BMPs. No shortages of weapons or spare parts.

(2) Ammunition: (2MRP) All ammunition was in excellent condition as it was issued new and also was inspected in early Nov99. No shortages.

(b) Vehicles and POL: (2MRP).

(1) Vehicles: (2MRP) All BMPs were in good conditions due to regular maintenance. Ea BMP/2MRP carried its own spare parts and tool kit. No shortages of vehicle spare parts.

(2) POL: (2MRP) POL was resupplied ea evening by a U/I tanker truck at approximately 1800. Nor shortages.

(c) Food/Water: (2MRP).

(1) Food: (2MRP) All personnel eating field rations since offensive began. Each member eats 2xcanned rations each day. Resupply every 3xdays. Last resupply on 20NOV99. No shortages.

(2) Water: (2MRP) Water was obtained from local sources. Each member/2MRP has purification tablets to be used as necessary. No shortages.

(d) Communication Equipment: (2MRP) All transceivers are in good working order as they were inspected in early Nov99. Spare parts are stored in BMPs.

(e) Medical: (2MRP) Each member had 1xfirst-aid kit.

(f) NBC Equipment: (2MRP) All NBC gear was in excellent condition as it was inspected in late Oct99.

9. MISCELLANEOUS: (3MRB).

a. Personalities: (3MRB/62/34MRD).

(CLASSIFICATION)

Figure E-3. Sample TIR (continued).

(CLASSIFICATION)

Last Name	First Name	MN/I	Rank	Psn	FUD
GARNOV	W.	MNU	MAJ	PO	3MRB
PANKRATOV	A.	MNU	CPT	CO	2MRC/3MRB
ZAGORSKIY	H.	MNU	SrSGT	1SG	2MRC/3MRB
MEL'NIKOV	C.	MNU	SrLT	Plt Ldr	1MRP/2/3MRB
KOVALEV	I.	MNU	SGT	Plt Ldr	2MRP/2/3MRB
KHOLODNOV	M.	MNU	JrLT	Plt Ldr	3MRP/2/3MRB

b. Code names/numbers: Unk to EPW.

c. Radio frequencies: (2MRC/3MRB) Frequencies for the R-123 transceiver on 22NOV99 were: Primary - 14.70MHz. Alternate - 18.36MHz. Frequencies changed daily at 2400 per unit SOI. Effective date: 22NOV99.

d. Call Signs: (2MRC/3MRB) Call signs for 22NOV99 were CO, 2MRC TASC 20; 1MRP/2MRC - PZQN 11; 2MRP/2MRC - PZQN 12; 2MRP/2MRC - PZQN 13. Call signs changed daily at 2400 per unit SOI. Effective date: 22NOV99.

e. Passwords: (2MRC/3MRB) Challenge for 22NOV99 was NOS; Countersign was UTROM. Passwords changed daily at 2400 per unit SOP.

f. Obstacles: Unk to EPW.

g. PSYOP: Unk to EPW.

PART III—REMARKS

Recommend EPW for further interrogation on annual training competition at battalion and regimental levels.

(CLASSIFICATION)

Figure E-3. Sample TIR (continued).

Attach to PW

Part A

Serial No. of Tag: 026AR17

Nationality of Capture Unit: US

Capturing Unit: US- A/1/2/3

DTG of Capture: 1106452AUG99

Location of Capture: CA123456

PW Name: Flores , Juan
(Last Name, First, MI)

PW Rank: PVT

PW DOB: 15 MAY 79

PW Service Number: 6543210

Power Served by PW: REPUBLIC OF ARMANDA

Part B attached to Equipment or Documents: (YES)/ NO

Comments or remarks on reverse

REMARKS:
Include any information that may assist in the intelligence effort; eg, special circumstances of capture. Associated PW captured at same time/location. PW Power Served, etc.

Perforation

Part B

Serial Number of Tag: 026AR17

Nationality of Capture Unit: US

PW Name: Flores , Juan
(Last Name, First, MI)

PW Rank: PVT

Power Served by PW: REPUBLIC OF ARMANDA

DTG of Capture: 1106452AUG99

Location of Capture: CA123456

Attach to PW equipment documents. Ensure all documents/equipment are secure in one package. Mark with X in box below if of particular intelligence importance.

Figure E-4. Standardized EPW and personal equipment and document captive tag (STANAG 2044).

(CLASSIFICATION)

FM G2, 12 INF DIV

TO G2, XII CORPS

INFO G2, X CORPS

CLASSIFICATION/CAVEATS

–

SERIAL: (U).

–

PASS: (U) OPTIONAL.

–

COUNTRY: (U).

–

SUBJ: IIR COMBAT/ LOSSES (U)

–

WARNING: (U) THIS IS AN INFORMATION REPORT, NOT FINALLY EVALUATED INTELLIGENCE. REPORT CLASSIFIED (CLASSIFICATION/CAVEATS, WITH CAVEATS ABBREVIATED).

–

DOI: (U).

–

REQS: (U).

–

SOURCE: (U).

–

SUMMARY: (U).

–

TEXT: (U).

–

COMMENTS: (U).

//IPSP: (U) BT //.

//COMSOBJ: (U) BT //.

PROJ: (U).

COLL: (U) (OPTIONAL).

PREP: (U).

ENCL: (U) TO FOLLOW: 1 ENCLOSURES. (OPTIONAL) WARNING: (U) REPORT CLASSIFIED (CLASSIFICATION/CAVEATS WITH CAVEATS SPELLED OUT).

–

DECL: OADR ##

NOTE: LEFT MARGIN DASHES ENSURE PROPER SPACING BETWEEN PROSIGNS.

(UNCLASSIFIED)

Figure E-5. Format for intelligence information report (IIR).

*1. NAME OF COUNTRY
2. DATE OF INFORMATION (for example, YYMMDD or YYMMDD-YYMMDD)
3. DATE OF REPORT (for example, YYMMDD)
*4.A. FULL NAME (Must be listed in Roman letters in the order normally used by the individual, with surname in capital letters; accent on last name, if known; phonetic pronunciation, as appropriate.)
4.B. NAME(S) BY WHICH INDIVIDUAL PREFERS TO BE ADDRESSED
(1) IN OFFICIAL CORRESPONDENCE
(2) ORALLY AT OFFICIAL GATHERINGS
4.C. FULL NAME IN NATIVE ALPHABET (Include standard telegraphic code or other transcription code.)
4.D. VARIANTS, ALIASES, OR NICKNAMES
*5. RANK (List complete official rank)
5.A. ENGLISH LANGUAGE (List American equivalent.)
5.B. NATIVE
6. DATE OF RANK (for example, YYMMDD)
7. POSITION/BILLET
*7.A. PRESENT POSITION (List what the person is and where.)
7.B. MILITARY ADDRESS
7.C. DATE ASSUMED POSITION (for example, YYMMDD)
7.D. SCHEDULED DATE OF DEPARTURE (for example, YYMMDD)
7.E. NAME OF PREDECESSOR
(1) PREDECESSOR'S RANK
(2) PREDECESSOR'S BRANCH OF ARMED SERVICE
(3) DATE PREDECESSOR ASSIGNED (for example, YYMMDD)
(4) DURATION OF PREDECESSOR'S ASSIGNMENT (List from and to date in YYMMDD order.)
*8. BRANCH OF ARMED SERVICE (for example, Army, Navy, Air Force, Special Branch)
9. SPECIALITY/OTHER ORGANIZATIONS (List affiliation with Ministry of Defense, a space program, or other specialized agencies or programs.)
10. DATE OF BIRTH (for example, YYMMDD)
11. PLACE OF BIRTH (List town, state, province, country.)
12. SEX
13. HOME ADDRESS

Figure E-6. Format for biographic report.

14. TELEPHONE NUMBER (Include area code, if applicable.)
14.A. HOME
14.B. WORK
15. MARITAL STATUS (List married, single, divorced, widowed, or separated.)
16. CITIZENSHIP (List country or countries where citizenship is held.)
17. ETHNIC GROUP (for example, Caucasian)
18. NATIONALITY
19. RELIGIOUS AFFILIATION
19.A. NAME (for example, Roman Catholic)
19.B. PRACTICING OR NON-PRACTICING
20. TITLES, HONORIFICS
21. HIGH ORDER DECORATIONS (List native, US, other country awards, by what government awarded, and when.)
22. PHYSICAL DESCRIPTION
22.A. FACIAL HAIR (List beard, mustache, other.)
22.B. TEETH (Yes or No. Note whether teeth are natural.)
22.C. HARD OF HEARING (Yes or No)
22.D. GLASSES (Yes or No)
22.E. COLOR OF EYES
22.F. BALD (Yes or No)
22.G. COLOR OF HAIR
22.H. WRITING HAND
22.I. POSTURE (List whether erect or round-shouldered.)
22.J. HEIGHT (List in inches.)
22.K. WEIGHT (List in pounds.)
22.L. BUILD (List small, medium, or large.)
23. MEMBERSHIP IN ORGANIZATIONS (List professional, social, military, and other organizations and inclusive date in YYMMDD order.)
24. PREFERENCES (List preferences for food, drink, tobacco, entertainment, sports, and hobbies.)
25. PUBLISHED WORKS—BY OR ABOUT INDIVIDUAL (List title and publication date of article or book. If an article, list name of publication in which article appeared.)
26. CIVIL EDUCATION (List college or highest level schools, locations, major courses, degrees, honors, and inclusive dates in YYMMDD order.)

Figure E-6. Format for biographic report (continued).

27. LANGUAGES (List proficiency, dialects, degree of fluency, and ability to act as a translator or interpreter.)

28. INTERNATIONAL TRAINING/TRAVEL (List countries, purpose, and inclusive dates in YYMMDD order.)

29. PHOTOGRAPH SUBMITTED (Yes or No)

30. DATE OF PHOTOGRAPH, IF SUBMITTED (for example, YYMMDD)

31. MILITARY SERVICE (Chronologically, list inclusive dates in YYMMDD order and locations. List all military schools, in-country and foreign; promotions an demotions by listing rank to which moved and effective date in YYMMDD order; foreign service; units served and position held; retired or reserve status; and involvement with programs, activities, and key people.)

32. FULL NAME OF SPOUSE

32.A. MAIDEN NAME (for example, Escobal)

32.B. DATE OF BIRTH (for example, YYMMDD)

32.C. PLACE OF BIRTH (List town, state, province, and country.)

32.D. CITIZENSHIP (List country or countries in which citizenship held.)

32.E. ETHNIC GROUP

32.F. NATIONALITY

32.G. RELIGIOUS AFFILIATION

(1) NAME (for example, Roman Catholic)

(2) PRACTICING OR NON-PRACTICING

32.H. BACKGROUND (List education; languages; preferences in food, drink, hobbies, and entertainment; special interests; and professional societies and groups.)

33. NAMES OF CHILDREN (Include sex, date of birth in YYMMDD order, marital status, and any other items of interest such as schools, health, or military service.)

34. SIGNIFICANCE:

The following paragraphs are classified, except number 40.

35. POLITICS

36. MILITARY REPUTATION

37. CHARACTER

38. ACQUAINTANCES/RELATIONS INFLUENCE

39. PERSONAL CHARACTERISTICS

40. POLICE RECORD (Not a classified paragraph.)

41. EVALUATION

42. ADDITIONAL INFORMATION ON SPOUSE

Figure E-6. Format for biographic report (continued).

PRECEDENCE/DTG
FM
TO
INFO
BT OR ZEN
CLASSIFICATION/CAVEATS/CODEWORDS
CITE:
SERIAL:
SUBJ: KNOWLEDGEABILITY BRIEF (Classification)
REF:
SUMMARY: (Classification) (Source description limited to 414 characters, 6 message lines)
TEXT:

1. (Classification) PERSONAL DATA:
1A. NAME:
1B. SRCNO: (14-characters)
1C. SRCNO1: (14-characters)
1D. SRCNO2: (14-characters)
1E. SRCNO3: (14-characters)
1F. CITIZEN: (2-characters)
1G. BIRTCITY: (2-characters)
1H. BIRTCRTY: (2-characters)
1I. BIRTDT: (YYMMDD—6-characters)
1J. PCO: (2-characters)
1K. LEFTDT: (YYMMDD—6-characters)
1L. INITCTDT: (YYMMDD—6-characters)
1M. LASTCTDT: (YYMMDD—6-characters)
1N. LASTCTRY: (YYMMDD—6-characters)
1O. LANGCOMP: (3-characters, 3 occurrence limit.)
2. (Classification) EDUCATION:
2A. C or M (1 character; YY-YY; educational institution in 76-characters including blanks; geographic coordinates in 15-characters without blanks; city name in 30-characters including blanks; country code in 2-characters; degree/certificate/diploma and major in 32-characters including blanks.
2B-2E. (Include these subparagraphs as needed using format above.)
3. (Classification) EMPLOYMENT:

Figure E-7. Format for a knowledgeability brief.

3A. YY-YY: (Employment installation in 76-characters including blanks; geographic coordinates in 15-characters without blanks; city name in 30-characters including blanks; country code in 2-characters; employment position and duties in 30-characters including blanks; security clearance in 1 character.)

3B-3G. (Include these subparagraphs as needed using format above.)

4. (Classification) MIL SERVICE:

4A. YY-YY: (Military installation in 76-characters including blanks; geographic coordinates in 15-characters without blanks; service component in 2-characters; rank in 2-characters; unit in 30-characters including blanks; city name in 30-characters including blanks; country code in 2-characters; military specialty and duties in 30-characters including blanks; security clearance in 1 character.

4B-4T. (Include these subparagraphs as needed using format above.)

5. (Classification) SPECIFIC KNOWLEDGEABILITY: Free/text variable length (maximum 6,900-characters or 100 message lines) to address full source knowledgeability. The last two elements or paragraph, list applicable military equipment and IPSP codes, as follows:

//MILEQUIP: Two 8-CHARACTER CODE; CODE; CODE; CODE; CODE// (6-CODE LIMIT).

//IPSP: Six 7-CHARACTER CODE; CODE; CODE; CODE; CODE; CODE; CODE; CODE// (8-CODE LIMIT).

6. (Classification) COLLECTOR'S COMMENTS: Free text/variable length (maximum 1,380-characters or 20 message lines) to address collection capability.

7. (Classification) GUIDE: Free text/variable length (maximum 1,380-characters or 20 message lines) to address desired method of intelligence tasking.

DECL: OADR

Figure E-7. Format for a knowledgeability brief (continued).

(CLASSIFICATION)

SOURCE NAME YUSSEF MAGRIM AL-MUFAJIR DATE 7 OCT 99

SOURCE's RANK AND SERVICE/SERIAL NO. PVT 1234567

SOURCE's DPOB 29 SEP 80, MEDINA

SOURCE's UNIT 1SQD/2/3/MRC INTG SEQUENCE 017

DOC/EQUIP CAPTURED W/SOURCE AK-47, PICTURE OF FATHER

CIVILIAN CAREER STUDENT

MILITARY CAREER RIFLEMAN

SPECIALIST KNOWLEDGE NONE

DURATION OF INTG 30 MIN INTG LOCATION AB 123456

REPORTS GENERATED PERS LOSSES

INFO OBTAINED SUMMARY SOURCE UNIT SUFFERED 60% CASUALTIES DURING COALITION ATTACK.

INTG NAME AND UNIT SFC SMITH

LANGUAGE USED ARABIC SOURCE's MP SERIAL No. US-2307.912

(CLASSIFICATION)

Figure E-8. Sample summary interrogation report.

APPENDIX F
COMMAND LANGUAGE PROGRAM

Foreign language knowledge is a perishable skill. Without constant reinforcement, this knowledge quickly fades. In a combat situation, this knowledge will be most critical. It is incumbent on the commander to establish and maintain an effective CLP.

STANDARDS

The goal for any language maintenance program is to have all linguists perform critical wartime mission tasks proficiently. Scoring 2/2/2 or better on the listening, reading, and speaking portion of the Defense Language Proficiency Test (DLPT) is the minimum standard for foreign language proficiency. However, there are several reasons why this should not be the sole criteria for judging the effectiveness of a language maintenance program nor an individual's proficiency.

Languages have different degrees of difficulty. The Defense Language Institute, Foreign Language Center (DLIFLC) has divided languages into four categories according to difficulty for an English speaker. The romance languages belong to Category I (easiest), while most of the Asian languages belong to Category IV (hardest). Therefore, a 2 on the DLPT for Korean does not correspond to a 2 for French.

There are several versions of the DLPT for each language. A 2 result on a version I examination is not the same as a 2 result on a version III examination, even in the same language. There are different forms (For example, A, B, or C) within each examination version.

Nevertheless, unless there is a qualified native speaker who can evaluate language proficiency, the DLPT can be used to evaluate language maintenance program effectiveness.

METHODS

The best method of learning and maintaining a foreign language is total immersion. Opportunities for total immersion include in-country temporary duty and teaching institutions. Unfortunately, in-country experience is not readily available for all languages, and immersion courses can be cost prohibitive.

A substitute for immersion training is one-on-one instruction or conversation with a native speaker. This can be part of the formal instruction at DLIFLC, Presidio of Monterey, CA; at the Foreign Language Training Center, Europe (FLTCE), Garmisch, Germany; and university refresher training courses or a DA-sponsored institute. It can also be done through hiring native speakers at unit locations.

The most prevalent, but probably least effective, method is through self-study materials, such as US Army Forces Command Language Maintenance Refresher and Improvement Course (FLAMRIC) and foreign language tapes. Most of these materials are available from DLIFLC or local language learning centers.

There is satellite communications for learning which transmits in-language news broadcasts from countries around the world.

An effective CLP begins with the commander. He must have a clear and accurate picture of his language mission requirements and be accountable for the CLP.

A command language council is formed to assist the commander. Council recommendations should become policy following command endorsement. This council—

- Consists of unit members who have a CLP interest.
- Consists of members who are appointed on orders.
- Should meet at least quarterly and follow an agenda.
- Should prepare and disseminate meeting minutes to unit linguists.

The CLP manager (CLPM) chairs the CLP council. Units commanded by a colonel should have a full-time CLPM. In lieu of rank and duty position, the CLPM should be appointed based on academic credentials or experience. The CLPM's tenure should be at least one year or longer.

The CLPM should maintain an individual linguist data base, with the following information:

- Duty assignment.
- Primary military occupational specialty (MOS).
- On-going language training.
- Post-DLIFLC language training.
- Expiration term of service (ETS) date.
- Permanent change of station (PCS) and date eligible for return from overseas (DEROS) date (if applicable).
- Foreign language proficiency pay (FLPP) status.
- DLPT dates and scores, to include which version.
- Required DLPT test.
- Individual training plan.
- Year-to-year test results.
- Current DA Form 330 (Language Proficiency Questionnaire).

The command should have a detailed SOP covering all CLP aspects. It should be specific in task assignments and self-explanatory. It is updated regularly and becomes an integral part of the unit or command SOP.

Unit language training time, governed by AR 611-6, is designated at regular intervals on the training schedule, and should take priority over competing and unscheduled training. Each linguist should have the opportunity to attend a specified amount of language training with established objectives and goals.

Units should have a refresher language training program. Self-study materials should be available, and off-duty use encouraged.

The CLPM should be aware of adult language education courses in the community. Both duty-hour and off-duty hour attendance are encouraged.

Opportunities for operational readiness training (REDTRAIN) should be used in support of the CLP. These opportunities include, but are not limited to, forward area training, live environment training, and summer language programs.

Monetary support for language maintenance programs comes mainly from REDTRAIN funds. These funds are normally located at major Army commands and are available to subordinate units. However, this should not preclude use of a unit's regular funds to support language sustainment when available.

Funding to support CLPs must be identified and documented regularly. These requirements must be addressed in annual budget planning. The CLP should also be represented in long-range budget planning. CLP requirements should be separate from other training budgets.

A good incentive is the FLPP for qualified linguists, depending on how they score on their DLPT. Only qualified linguists are eligible to receive FLPP.

A state-of-the-art language training vehicle is the teletraining network, or commonly referred to as video teletraining (VTT).

The VTT system was used by DLIFLC to teach Arabic to troops being deployed to Southwest Asia. DLIFLC broadcasts Arab language instruction to Fort Hood and Fort Huachuca. Other critical instruction was passed through the system.

The VTT is versatile and has many applications. Video and audio can be transmitted from one site to any number of receiving sites. In a two-way interactive mode, two sites can hold a bidirectional video and audio conference. In the multipoint mode, up to eight locations can hold a conference. The host site transmits the video and audio, while other locations receive the host's audio and video, plus all audio from the remaining sites. Any site can request, during the conference, to become the host site.

DLIFLC is committed to the VTT concept. It is ready to assist units having VTT capability with their remedial foreign language sustainment and enhancement programs.

For information concerning VTT language training, contact DLIFLC's Distance Education Division at DSN 878-5746/5747; Commercial (408) 647-5746/5747; or Fax at DSN 878-5512 or Commercial (408) 647-5512.

VTT is a proven cost effective and viable language training tool; for example, training soldiers in their units with qualified native speakers, which dramatically reduces travel and per diem costs.

APPENDIX G

INDIVIDUAL AND COLLECTIVE TRAINING

"In no other profession are the penalties for employing untrained personnel so appalling or so irrevocable as in the military."

—General Douglas MacArthur.

Interrogator employment during Operation Desert Storm demonstrated that units whose mission training plans (MTPs) were battle focused and based on the principles of training outlined in FM 25-100 and FM 25-101, accomplished the EPW and DOCEX mission more efficiently and timely.

The commander bears the ultimate responsibility for training his soldiers to fight and win. This appendix is designed to make the interrogation unit commander aware of aspects to consider when developing unit training programs.

There are no commissioned interrogation officers. The commissioned interrogation specialty was eliminated in 1970. The Interrogation Warrant Officer (351E) and the Senior Enlisted Interrogator (97E4L) advise the commander on the training and employment of interrogators. They provide the technical expertise required to develop the unit mission-essential task list (METL) and training plans and exercises to support that METL.

MISSION-ESSENTIAL TASK LIST

To train interrogators in the areas critical to the unit's mission accomplishment, the commander (CI/Interrogation Company or I&S Company) develops a complete and accurate METL. During the METL development process, the commander—

- Analyzes the MI battalion commander's restated wartime mission and approved METL; identifies specified and implied tasks.
- Uses situation training exercises (STXs) and field training exercises (FTXs) in ARTEP 34-298-10-MTP to determine collective tasks in support of critical wartime missions.
- Sequences collective tasks as he expects them to occur during the execution of the company's wartime mission.
- Obtains battalion commander's approval of the company METL.
- Briefs company leadership (officers and NCOs); uses soldiers training publications, soldiers manuals, and MTPs to identify leader and soldier tasks to support the collective critical tasks which comprise the METL.

When developing the METL, the commander keeps in mind, regardless of echelon, that interrogators have a mission to perform at the next lower echelon as GS or DS. For this reason, they must train and practice performing their mission at the assigned and lower echelon, and deploy with both echelons.

In addition to understanding the METL of your unit, you must be familiar with the METL of supported staffs and units. Other unit METLs to consider are—

- Supported S2s and the maneuver brigade and battalion staffs to which they belong. Train with these staffs during FTXs and command post exercises (CPXs) to facilitate team cohesiveness for combat. The S2 should know and train with his interrogation support team to prepare for wartime operations.

- Train and deploy with CI personnel. Interrogation and CI personnel should cross-train on each other's respective wartime critical tasks.
- Train with combat arms units. Interrogators should train and emphasize the importance of tagging and evacuating EPWs and CEDs. Stress that EPWs and CEDs provide information that saves lives.

JOINT MILITARY INTELLIGENCE AND MILITARY POLICE TRAINING

Operations Urgent Fury, Just Cause, and Desert Storm demonstrated the need for interrogators and MP to conduct integrated training with regard to EPW and civilian internee operations.

For effective, meaningful training to occur, commanders must plan, develop, and coordinate many tasks. Interrogators must be familiar with the METL of the MP unit assigned to your echelon with regard to EPW operations. Without integrating the two METLs, you cannot develop scenarios that allow soldiers to train in a battle-focused environment. Two units must learn to work together and understand the requirements and functions each unit will have to perform in wartime. Members of the band are trained and may be employed as augmentees to the holding area perimeter security force.

EXERCISE REQUIREMENTS

In addition to normal personnel and equipment required of any unit exercise, the following must be planned for and considered.

SCENARIO

The most time consuming and complicated portion of an interrogation exercise is scenario development. Included in the scenario must be reasonable actions of enemy and friendly forces.

Stories must be developed for EPWs and civilian internees; for example, as in the technical support packages and interrogator comprehensive evaluation. These stories should be entered into an automated HUMINT data base, and should interact with each other at least minimally. For example:

- Units should cross match.
- Missions should fit together.
- Some degree of personality (names of leaders and soldiers) should be shared by personnel.

It is not necessary that all EPWs and civilian internees have stories that include information of intelligence value nor that stories be complete in all aspects. There should be enough material in the stories to provide a realistic "skeleton" on which role players can build.

If possible, interrogators should develop or assist with story development. The stories should tie into real world exercise play and provide indicators of enemy COAs to the G2. Tying EPW and CI stories to exercise play facilitates incorporating EPW play into G2 exercise planning and execution. This will help identify and fix many shortcomings in the stories.

PERSONNEL

Additional personnel must be employed to make an interrogation exercise successful. Personnel will be needed to serve as EPWs, civilian internees, medical personnel, interpreters, CI teams, and EPW civilian internee guards for lower echelon units. The numbers of personnel needed can be varied and personnel may be reinserted any number of times, in any number of roles.

The minimum number of personnel serving as EPWs and civilian internees at any one time should not be allowed to go below 10 to 15. Personnel should be able to speak a foreign language; preferably, languages of assigned interrogators. This allows for optimum training and practice in performing the actual job of an interrogator.

Possible sources for linguistically capable EPW and civilian internee role players include—

- Other interrogation units.
- EW and CI personnel.
- PYSOP personnel.
- MP personnel.
- CA personnel.

Linguistically capable personnel may also be in other MOSs and units not normally associated with foreign language capabilities.

Another source of linguistic support is the US Army Reserve (USAR) and the Army National Guard (ARNG) units for AC units and vice versa. A few personnel with languages not indigenous to the unit should be included so interpreters can be trained when used.

If possible, at least one insertion of mass numbers of EPWs and civilian internees should occur. The number of personnel should be at least double the number of available interrogators. One way of simulating this is to—

- Insert a large quantity of individuals.
- Allow a short time for MP and interrogator personnel to work with this.
- Remove a portion of the personnel.
- Immediately reinsert them as new EPWs and civilian internees.

The knowledgeability and cooperativeness of the sources should be mixed; for example, some may be of CI interest, some may have no information, and a few may refuse to break.

DOCUMENTS

Documents present another time consuming and difficult consideration for interrogation operation exercises. Documents should be in foreign languages; numerous documents should be relevant to scenario documents which are developed to interact with the EPWs and civilian internees and as stand-alone intelligence sources.

The number of documents used during an exercise should be excessive; large quantities of documents should be input into the scenario at the same time EPWs are being inputted. This allows simulation of EPWs and civilian internees, and documents arriving on the same sources of transportation.

MULTIPLE EXERCISE LOCATIONS

In order to exercise evacuation of EPWs and civilian internees, support to lower echelons' multiple exercise locations is necessary. These locations do not need to be drastically separated, but should not be within sight of each other.

For example, location to simulate a medical aid station should also be included along with personnel to simulate medical personnel. This allows personnel to practice interrogating EPWs and civilian internees in the medical evacuation system. Having multiple locations serves several purposes.

- Both interrogation and MP units have functions that must be performed at a lower echelon.
- Interrogators must be able to support the lower echelons with interrogations. This means teams must be able to deploy and act without normal unit leadership.
- Coordination must be affected with the supported lower echelon unit.
- Reports must be transmitted to the supported unit and accompany EPWs being evacuated.
- MP must receipt and receive EPW and civilian internees from lower echelons and guard them during the evacuation process from lower echelon to assigned echelon.

There is also a need to practice having multiple EPW and civilian internee facilities at the assigned echelon. When these are established, MP and interrogation assets must be divided in order to operate the additional facilities.

An additional aspect of using additional locations is training of interrogation and MP units to function with reduced staffing necessitated by performing multiple missions simultaneously.

OTHER SUPPORT

For corps interrogation platoon exercises, a food services section of the HHS company should be deployed in support of the exercise. This allows the food service section to practice operating two separate mess facilities required by doctrine.

GLOSSARY

AC	Active Component
ACE	analysis and control element
ACR	armored cavalry regiment
ADA	air defense artillery
AI	area of interest
AIRDOC	Air Force document
AO	area of operations
armd	armored
ARNG	Army National Guard
ARTEP	Army Training Evaluation Program
ASAS	All-Source Analysis System
ASPS	all-source production section
ATGM	antitank guided missile
BICC	battlefield information control center
BIRTCITY	birth city
BIRTCRTY	birth country
BIRTDT	birth date
bn	battalion
BSA	brigade support area
BT	message break indicator
CA	Civil Affairs
CAP	civic action program
C^3	command, control, and communications
C^3I	command, control, communications and intelligence
C-E	communications-electronics
C&E	collection and exploitation
CCIF	combined corps interrogation facility
CED	captured enemy document
CEE	captured enemy equipment
CEM	captured enemy materiél
CHA	central holding area
CI	counterintelligence
CID	Criminal Investigation Division

CIF	Corps Interrogation Facility
CLP	Command Language Program
CLPM	Command Language Program Manager
CM&D	collection management and dissemination
CMEC	Captured Materiél Exploitation Center
CMO	civil-military operations
co	company
COA	course of action
coll	collection
CONUS	continental United States
CP	command post
CPR	common point of reference
CPT	captain
CPX	command post exercise
CS	combat support
CSS	combat service support
DA	Department of Army
DCPR	destination common point of reference
DECL	declassify
DEROS	date eligible for return from overseas
DIA	Defense Intelligence Agency
DISCOM	division support command
DISUM	daily intelligence summary
div	division
DLEA	drug and law enforcement agency
DLIFLC	Defense Language Institute Foreign Language Center
DLPT	Defense Language Proficiency Test
doc	document
DOCEX	document exploitation
DOD	Department of Defense
DOI	date of information
DOS	disk operating system

DPOB	date and place of birth
DPRK	Democratic People's Republic of Korea
DS	direct support
DSA	division support area
dsg	designation
DSN	digital support network
DST	decision support template
DTG	date-time group
ea	each
EAC	echelons above corps
ECB	echelon corps and below
ECM	electronic countermeasures
EM	enlisted member
encl	enclosure
engr	engineer
EPW	enemy prisoner of war
equip	equipment
ETS	expiration term of service
EW	electronic warfare
FAX	facsimile
Feb	February
FEBA	forward edge of the battle area
FIS	foreign intelligence and security
FLAMRIC	US Army Forces Command Language Maintenance Refresher and Improvement Course
FLPP	foreign language proficiency pay
FLTCE	Foreign Language Training Center, Europe
FM	field manual
FS	fire support
FTX	field training exercise
G1	Assistant Chief of Staff (Personnel)
G5	Assistant Chief of Staff (Civil Affairs)
GAZ	Soviet truck
GC	Geneva Convention Relative to the Protection of Civilian Persons in Time of War of August 12, 1949
GPW	Geneva Convention Relative to the Treatment of Prisoners of War of August 12, 1949
GS	general support
GSR	ground surveillance radar
GWS	Geneva Convention for the Amelioration of the Wounded and Sick in Armed Forces in the Field of August 12, 1949
hq	headquarters
HHC	headquarters and headquarters company
HHS	headquarters, headquarters and service
HIC	high-intensity conflict
HPT	high-payoff target
H/S	hearsay
HUMINT	human intelligence
HVT	high-value target
hwy	highway
ICF	Intelligence Contingency Fund
ICPR	initial common point of reference
I&E	interrogation and exploitation
IEW	intelligence and electronic warfare
IHA	initial holding area
IIR	intelligence information report
IMINT	imagery intelligence
info	information
intg	interrogation
INTREP	intelligence report
INTSUM	intelligence summary
IO	information objectives
IPB	intelligence preparation of the battlefield
IPW	prisoner of war interrogation
IR	intelligence requirements

I&S	intelligence and surveillance
I&W	indications and warning
J5	Plans and Policy Directorate
JCMEC	Joint Captured Materiél Exploitation Center
JIF	Joint Interrogation Facility
jr	junior
JTF	joint task force
JUMP	job, unit, mission, and PIR, IR, and SIR
k	thousand
KB	knowledgeability briefs
LANGCOMP	language competency
ldr	leader
LIC	low-intensity conflict
LLSO	low-level source operations
loc	location
LN	local national
LRS	long-range surveillance
LZ	landing zone
MASINT	measurement and signature intelligence
mbr	member
MDCI	multidiscipline counterintelligence
MED	minimum essential data
METL	mission essential task list
METT-T	mission, enemy, troops, terrain, and time available
MHz	megahertz
MI	military intelligence
MIC	mid-intensity conflict
MID	military intelligence detachment
mil	military
misc	miscellaneous
MN/I	middle name or initial
MOS	military occupational specialty
MP	military police
MRC	motorized rifle company
MRD	motorized rifle division
MRR	motorized rifle regiment
MRS	motorized rifle squad
MS	microsoft
MSR	main supply route
MTF	Message Text Format
NA	not applicable
NAI	named area of interest
NATO	North Atlantic Treaty Organization
NAVDOC	Navy document
NBC	nuclear, biological, and chemical
NCA	national command authority
NCO	noncommissioned officer
NCOIC	noncommissioned officer in charge
NEO	noncombatant evacuation operations
no	number
NSA	National Security Agency
OADR	Originating Agency's Determination Required
OB	order of battle
OBSTINTEL	obstacle intelligence
OCONUS	outside continental United States
OCS	officer candidate school
off	officer
OP	observation post
OPCON	operational control
OPLAN	operations plan
OPORD	operations order
OPSEC	operations security
PC	personal computer
PCS	permanent change of station
PERINTREP	periodic intelligence report
pers	personnel
PHA	permanent holding area
PIR	priority intelligence requirements

plt platoon
PM Makarov pistol (Soviet)
PO political officer
POC point of capture
POL petroleum, oils, and lubricants
prep preparation
proj project
PSA post-strike assessment
PSYOP psychological operations
PW prisoner of war

QSTAG Quadripartite Standardization Agreement

RAM random access memory
RC Reserve Components
REC radio electronic combat
recon reconnoiter
REDTRAIN readiness training
RIF reconnaissance in force

S&T scientific and technical
S2 Intelligence Officer
SALUTE size, activity, location, unit, time equipment
sec section
SFG Special Forces Group
SFGA Special Forces Group (Airborne)
SIGINT signals intelligence
SIR specific information requirements
SITMAP situation map
SJA staff judge advocate
SOF special operations forces
SOI signal operation instruction
SOP standing operating procedure
SOR specific operational requirement
sqd squad
sr senior
srchno search number
SSO special support office
STANAG Standardization Agreement
STX situation training exercise
SUPINTREP supplementary intelligence report
SVD Soviet rifle
SW southwest

TCAE technical control and analysis element
TE tactical exploitation
TECHDOC technical document
TECHINT technical intelligence
TEL transporter-erector-launcher
THA temporary holding area
TIF Theater Interrogation Facility
TIR tactical interrogation report
TOC tactical operations center
TOE tables of organization and equipment
TQ tactical questioning
TRADOC United States Army Training and Doctrine Command
TSA technical support activity

UCMJ Uniform Code of Military Justice
U/I unit of issue
unk unknown
USAR United States Army Reserve
USMTF United States Message Text Format
UTM universal transverse mercator (grid)

vic vicinity
VTT videoteletraining

w with

XO executive officer

REFERENCES

SOURCES USED

These are the sources quoted or paraphrased in this publication.

Army Publications

AR 310-50. Authorized Abbreviations and Brevity Codes. 15 November 1985.

DA Form 330. Language Proficiency Questionnaire. July 1985.

AR 350-30. Code of Conduct/Survival, Evasion, Resistance and Escape (SERE) Training. 10 December 1985.

AR 380-5. Department of the Army Information Security Program. 25 February 1988.

FM 21-26. Map Reading and Land Navigation. 30 September 1987.

FM 21-31. Topographic Symbols. 19 June 1961.

(C)FM 21-78. Resistance and Escape (U). 15 June 1989.

FM 34-2. Collection Management. 20 October 1990.

FM 34-3. Intelligence Analysis. 15 March 1990.

FM 34-54. Battlefield Technical Intelligence. 5 April 1990.

FM 34-60. Counterintelligence. 5 February 1990.

FM 34-130. Intelligence Preparation of the Battlefield. 23 May 1989.

FM 100-20. Low Intensity Conflict. 5 December 1990.

FM 101-5-1. Operational Terms and Symbols. 21 October 1985.

STP 21-2-SMCT. Soldier's Manual of Common Tasks, Skill Level 1. 1 October 1990.

STP 21-24-SMCT. Soldier's Manual of Common Tasks, Skill Levels 2-4. 10 January 1989.

STP 34-97E1-SM. Soldier's Manual, Skill Level 1, MOS 97E, Interrogator. 27 June 1990.

Documents Needed

These documents must be available to the intended users of this publication.

DA Form 1132-R. Prisoner's Personal Property List-Personal. April 1986.

DA Form 2028. Recommended Changes to Publications and Blank Forms. February 1974.

DA Form 2662-R. United States Army EPW Identification Card. May 1982.

DA Form 4237-R. Prisoner of War Personnel Record. August 1985.

DA Form 5976. Enemy Prisoner of War Capture Tag. January 1991.

DODD 5100.77. Department of Defense Law of War Program.

AR 381-10. US Army Intelligence Activities. 1 July 1984.

AR 12-15. Joint Security Assistance Training (JSAT) Regulation. 28 February 1990.

AR 190-8. Enemy Prisoners of War - Administration, Employment, and Compensation. 1 June 1982.

AR 190-57. Civilian Internees - Administration, Employment, and Compensation. 4 March 1987.

AR 210-174. Accounting Procedures for Prisoners' Personal Property and Funds. 17 September 1986.

AR 500-51. Emergency Employment of Army and Other Resources Support to Civilian Law Enforcement. 1 July 1983.

AR 611-6. Army Linguist Management. 16 October 1985.

FM 19-4. Enemy Prisoners of War, Civilian Internees, and Detained Persons. 23 May 1984.

FM 25-100. Training the Force. 15 November 1988.

FM 25-101. Battle Focused Training. 30 September 1990.

FM 27-10. The Law of Land Warfare. 18 July 1956.

FM 34-1. Intelligence and Electronic Warfare Operations. 2 July 1987.

(S-NF)FM 34-60A. Counterintelligence Operations (U). 6 June 1989.

FM 71-101. Infantry, Airborne, and Air Assault Division Operations. 26 March 1980.

FM 100-5. Operations. 5 May 1986.

(S)TC 34-5. Human Intelligence Operations (U). 3 October 1988.

ARTEP 34-298-10-MTP. Mission Training Plan for Interrogation Platoon Military Intelligence Battalion Light Infantry Division. 8 October 1991.

STP 34-97E24-SM-TG. Soldier's Manual, Skill Levels 2/3/4 and Trainer's Guide, MOS 97E, Interrogator. 27 June 1990.

(S-NF)DIAM 58-13. Defense Human Resources Intelligence Collection Procedures (U). 28 March 1988.

Standardization Agreements (STANAGs)

2033. Interrogation of Prisoners of War. Edition 6.

2044. Procedures for Dealing with Prisoners of War. Edition 5.

2084. Handling and Reporting of Captured Enemy Equipment and Documents, Edition 5.

INDEX

U